XO1451

781

Mary Baker Ed...

MARY BAKER EDDY

The Years of Discovery

Robert Peel

Holt, Rinehart and Winston

New York   Chicago   San Francisco

Acknowledgments

For permission to reprint copyright material, grateful acknowledgment is made to the following:
Trustees under the Will of Mary Baker Eddy for quotations from Mrs. Eddy's published works;
Trustees of The Christian Science Publishing Society
for quotations from works published by them;
The Belknap Press of Harvard University Press
for a passage from Asa Gray in A. Hunter Depree, *Asa Gray;*
Princeton University Press for a passage from Horace Bushnell in
The Shaping of American Religion, eds. James Ward Smith and A. Leland Jamison;
The C. W. Daniel Co., Ltd., for a quotation from Søren Kierkegaard,
Purify Your Hearts, tr. A. S. and W. S. Ferris;
Little, Brown & Co. for two stanzas from *The Poems of Emily Dickinson,*
eds. Martha Dickinson Bianchi and Alfred Leete Hampson,
copyright 1914, 1942, by Martha Dickinson Bianchi;
Doubleday & Co., Inc. for quotations from Loren Eiseley, *Darwin's Century,*
copyright © 1958 by Loren C. Eiseley, and from *Margaret Fuller: American Rebel,*
ed. Perry Miller, copyright © 1963 by Perry Miller;
Alfred A. Knopf, Inc. for a passage by John W. Nevin
in Richard Hofstadter, *Anti-Intellectualism in American Life;*
Harcourt, Brace & World, Inc. for a quotation from Carl Sandburg,
Abraham Lincoln: The Prairie Years;
Bobbs-Merrill Co., Inc. for quotations from
Lyman Beecher Stowe, *Saints, Sinners and Beechers,*
copyright 1934 by Bobbs-Merrill Co., renewed © 1962 by Lyman Beecher Stowe;
Mentor Books for a quotation from
The Nineteenth Century World, eds. S. Métraux and François Crouzet;
The Macmillan Company for a quotation from Perry Miller, *The New England Mind,*
a passage by Paul Tillich from *Reinhold Niebuhr, His Religious, Social and Political Thought,*
eds. Charles W. Kegley and Robert W. Bretall, and part of a letter
by Francis Parkman from Howard Doughty, *Francis Parkman.*
The author also wishes to express gratitude to the
Trustees of the Longyear Foundation, Brookline, Massachusetts,
for permission to quote extensively from the unpublished Baker papers
and other documentary material in their possession.

Published simultaneously in Canada by Holt, Rinehart
and Winston of Canada, Limited.

Library of Congress Catalog Card Number: 66–14855

Published, July, 1966
Third Printing, October, 1966

Designed by William Wondriska
86972–0216
Printed in the United States of America

Contents

Preface

Preface

The emergence of a new religious movement is not often subject to close scientific observation. The great historic religions have sprung from obscure beginnings, clouded with legend and mystery. They are aptly represented by the biblical figure of an angel which, though its face might shine like the sun, came "clothed with a cloud."

Yet even when microscopic analysis has proved impossible, modern science has resolutely attempted to penetrate such phenomena with the telescopic lens of objective historical method. It was the shock of this challenge that caused nineteenth-century Christianity to worry so much about its own beginnings. Could Christians establish scientifically acceptable credentials for the origin of their faith and their Bible, or must both be written off as poetry, superstition, and fraud?

For all the ardor that marked the battles between science and religion in that period, they led only to imagined triumphs and camouflaged withdrawals. Yet almost unnoticed in the din of contention a striking new religious movement emerged, asserting by its name as well as by its claims that Christianity was relevant to an age of science. No child of a remote myth-making past, Christian Science from the start occupied ground in full view of both contending armies.

The founding of a new church would seem a long distance from the discovery of a scientific truth, but the founder of the Church of Christ, Scientist, described herself in her book *Science and Health with Key to the Scriptures* as a discoverer—"the discoverer of Christian Science"—and in the same book she wrote (p. 313): "Jesus of Nazareth was the most scientific man that ever trod the globe. He plunged beneath the material surface of things, and found the spiritual cause."

This bold identification of religion with science, in a meaning new to each of the words, is only one aspect of the system of ideas "discovered" by Mary Baker Eddy. The present book deals with the origin of that system and the manner of its discovery. To do this, it traces the events of Mrs. Eddy's life and the development of her thinking up to the publication of the first edition of *Science and Health* in 1875, with particular attention to the nine germinal years preceding that date. It is not concerned with the founding of the church which was the natural fruit of her discovery, but only with the genesis of Christian Science.

The book has been written as though the story had never been told before—as much of it has not, for it draws on a large quantity of hitherto unused source material. With rare exceptions, discussions of conflicting evidence and of the reliability of sources are to be found in the notes at the back of the book rather than in the narrative. These notes also serve as a bibliography. A chronology of Mrs. Eddy's life during the years under consideration is appended, together with three additional appendices dealing with questions of specialized interest.

The narrative ends before Mary Baker Glover's marriage to Asa Gilbert Eddy, which gave her the name she is now universally known by. The title of the book therefore anticipates events beyond the scope of "the years of discovery," but the narrative confines itself to those years. Some of the problems discussed find their resolution only in the period after 1875, and even the "discovery" went on through Mrs. Eddy's later years. But in a very real sense the subject matter of this book is complete with the first appearance of *Science and Health,* for in that publication Christian Science was effectively "born."

I have resolutely excluded from my treatment any consideration of the subsequent events of Mrs. Eddy's life except where they throw a shaft of necessary light on the earlier period. It seems safe to assume, however, that the reader will be familiar at least with the fact that between 1875 and 1910 Mrs. Eddy devoted her entire time to developing and establishing Christian Science.

When quoting from her later writings I refer to her as Mrs. Eddy or Mary Baker Eddy in order to identify the quotations correctly. At other times she is normally referred to by the maiden or married name she used at a given period of her life. All references to her published writings on Christian Science are to the latest editions unless otherwise indicated.

Her published and unpublished reminiscences have been used sparingly to throw light on otherwise obscure circumstances, but she has not been pressed into service unnecessarily as her own biographer. The notes provide references to relevant passages in her writings, including her autobiography *Retrospection and Introspection,* and these writings may well be considered indispensable for a fuller understanding of the subject in relation to Christian Science. The narrative, however, quotes freely from her letters and poems of each period as well as from other original materials that provide contemporary evidence of her development.

In general, pertinent source material has been quoted in the narrative both for its intrinsic interest and in order to allow the reader to arrive at his own conclusions without necessary reference to the notes. However, certain stories which have become almost canonical among critical biographers but which are clearly disproved by the documentary evidence available are discussed in the notes rather than in the main text in order to eliminate needless side excursions from the narrative

Although I am personally a Christian Scientist, I have endeavored as a conscientious historian to give a straightforward, factual account free from either apologetics or polemics and from *parti pris* interpretations. No writer can pretend to complete objectivity, however hard he may strive for it, but he can identify the grounds on which he has arrived at particular judgments, and this I have done.

As a historian, I owe a debt of gratitude to the Christian Science Board of Directors for allowing me free access to the Archives of The Mother Church and for permitting me to use a great deal of new material from that source. As a Christian Scientist, I am also grateful to them for respecting my intellectual freedom and for not seeking to exercise any guidance or censorship in my use of this material. As a result this is a completely independent book, shaped only by my own sense of scholarly and personal integrity.

The fact that the book is appearing just one hundred years after Mrs. Eddy's discovery serves as a reminder that Christian Science, though properly regarded as a modern religious phenomenon, was not exactly "born yesterday." It has been here long enough to make desirable a longer and closer look at its origin than has thus far been taken. And that, everyone will agree, means first of all turning to the discoverer of Christian Science herself.

ROBERT PEEL
Boston, Massachusetts

Chapter
I

Bow
1821

The Baker homestead on the uplands of Bow looked down on the broad Merrimack valley where the river flowed from just visible mountains through woodland and farmland to the invisible sea. Only two or three generations back the land had been a wilderness, and some of the pioneer rigors remained to give a hard edge to life on the farms. But the tranquil sweep of the landscape and the immense, unbroken arch of sky brought to the scene a sense of spaciousness and airiness not to be found in the narrower valleys of the north, where mountains blocked the sun.

From the hilltop one could pick out an occasional white spire thrusting upward to remind pious Yankees that men might own the land but God owned the men. Though the Church in New Hampshire had been disestablished a few years before, the austere God of Calvinist tradition still laid claim to men's allegiance. Like the winter that descended from the bitter north, Calvinism's unyielding logic would reach down into daily life and strike a chill to the heart of the unregenerate at the same time that it roused the mental and spiritual energies of the elect.

There was still some Puritan iron in the Yankees of the new century. Horace Bushnell has left a revealing account of the little New England church he joined in 1821, and his description might have applied to the congregation of any one of scores of village meetinghouses:

> *The dress of the assembly is mostly homespun. . . . There is no affectation. . . . They think of nothing, in fact, save what meets their intelligence and enters into them by that method. They appear like men who have digestion for strong meat. . . . Nothing is dull that has the matter in it, nothing long that has not exhausted the matter. . . . Under their hard and . . . stolid faces, great thoughts are brewing, and these keep them warm. Free will, fixed fate, foreknowledge absolute, Trinity, redemption, special grace, eternity—give them anything high enough, and the tough muscle of their inward man will be climbing*

sturdily into it; and if they go away having something to think of, they have had a good day.[1]

From all that can be learned today of Mark Baker of Bow, he was just such a man, hard-faced and toughminded, delighting to wage dialectical battle with his friend "Priest" Burnham over fine points of doctrine. Abraham Burnham was pastor of the Congregational church at Pembroke across the river, but the Bakers attended the Bow Meeting House on White Rock Hill, formally known as the Union Church of Christ, as the result of a marriage of convenience between the Congregationalists and the newer evangelicals without a church of their own. Just a few months after the birth of his youngest daughter, Mark Baker was elected clerk of the church, and at the same time it was voted to seek "a coppy of articles of faith and a covenant as a Congregational Church."[2] The new clerk's first entry in the record book was consequently a "Confession of Faith" of impeccable orthodoxy.

"You believe," it enjoined each member, "that there is one living and true GOD, who is an independent unchangeable and eternal Spirit possessing all possible perfections and who has made and governs all things in the natural and moral world." The absolute sovereignty of God in every detail of life was the keystone of Calvinist theology, but it seemed to make God responsible for the deplorable condition announced in one of the subsequent articles of faith; i.e., "that in consequence of Adam's first sin all his natural posterity come into the world personal sinners totally depraved and morally unable to do anything acceptable to GOD until they are renewed by the Holy Spirit."

This was a stern reception for a newborn child: to be greeted as a bundle of total depravity destined for damnation unless God should arbitrarily have chosen it for renewal when and if it lived to an age when penitence and conversion became possible. Fortunately, natural affection could greatly mitigate the logical rigors of such a doctrine in actual practice.

Mark Baker, the evidence shows, had both the theological rigor and the mitigating affection.

He was a moderately successful farmer, with five horses, eight oxen, three cows, nearly two hundred acres of farm, woodlot, and pasture; but even as he strode his land he was conscious of heaven above and hell beneath. Though a poor bargainer in things mundane,[3] he was a hard bargainer in the traffic of salvation. His youngest daughter early in life became familiar with the thunder of theological disputation as she lay awake on her trundle bed at night listening to him debate with Priest Burnham or one of the other local ministers. In later years[4] she remembered the occasion when he argued long into the night with his nephew Aaron Baker, who had fallen under the influence of Hosea Ballou and was entertaining the heretical possibility of universal salvation—a blasphemous doctrine to Mark Baker, who held firmly to the orthodox view that the vast majority of mankind must and would be damned for the glory of God.

Everyone who knew him[5] spoke of his iron will and inflexible sense of righteousness; yet there was generosity and hidden warmth in his nature. The farm boys who were "bound out" to him called him Uncle Mark, and at the end of their lives they spoke of him with respect and even with affection.[6] He exercised discipline, said one of them, but not harshly.[7] His grandson, George W. Baker, who lived with him in later years, wrote: "Although he was as set as the hills on politics and religion he was as kind-hearted a man as ever lived. He never turned anyone from his door hungry. If there wasn't anything handy in the house, he would give them money to get something at the tavern."[8] When his rigid sense of duty brought him into conflict with his high-spirited children, their rebellious respect for him managed to survive the storm, though sometimes scarred by the thunder.[9]

The stereotype of the rock-ribbed Puritan and tight-fisted Yankee is so firmly established in popular thought today that there is value in looking back through the eyes of those who knew the reality at first hand but saw it in perspective. Emerson, who was receiving his bachelor's degree from Harvard about the time Mary Baker was born, wrote later of a religion that was fading from the countryside around Concord, Massachusetts, but was still strong in the countryside around Concord, New Hampshire:

> . . . I acknowledge . . . the debt of myself and my brothers to that old religion which, in those years, still dwelt like a Sabbath peace in the country population of New England, which taught privation, self-denial, and sorrow. A man was born, not for prosperity, but to suffer for the benefit of others, like the noble rock-maple tree which all around the villages bleeds for the service of man. Not praise, not man's acceptance of our doing, but the Spirit's holy errand through us, absorbed the thought.[10]

This was the "errand into the wilderness"[11] which had brought the Puritan fathers to America, and the sense of it still survived in the simpler areas of New England life. Perhaps Puritanism has left no more important heritage than the consciousness of an intense, even terrible sublimity in daily experience, an inner dimension by which the most commonplace earthly duties are related to eternal and inescapable issues. This is the fire that blazes out from the crabbed sermons of early divines; it is the lightning that splits the rock again and again. But a now almost forgotten writer whose girlhood roughly coincided with that of Mary Baker reminds us that there was grace as well as grimness in the life it produced:

> *"Out of the strong came forth sweetness." The Beatitudes are the natural flowing-forth of the Ten Commandments. And the happiness of our lives was rooted in the stern, vigorous virtues of the people we lived among, drawing thence its bloom and song and fragrance. There was granite in their character and beliefs, but it was granite that could smile in the sunshine and clothe itself with flowers.*[12]

If this rather feminine metaphor is inappropriate to Mark Baker, it decidedly applies to his wife, born Abigail Ambrose of Pembroke. Short and plump, golden-haired and blue-eyed, Abigail was the summer to Mark's winter, the New Testament to his Old.[13] A young minister who was a close friend of the Bakers in later years wrote of her as "at all times cheerful and hopeful." She possessed, he said, "a strong intellect, a sympathizing heart, and a placid spirit"; and he went on, in the rather high-flown style of the period, to compare her influence in her home and in the community to that of "the gentle dew and cheerful light."[14]

She represented that strain of New England womanhood which rebelled against the stark absolutes of Calvinism—not the overt rebellion of an Anne Hutchinson, aflame with the Holy Ghost, but the quiet, almost unnoticed rebellion that life itself makes against system.[15] A woman remained silent in church; she was not invited to read the Scripture lesson or offer up the prayer at family devotions. But she thought, she felt, she influenced—like "the gentle dew and cheerful light." In her own subversively simple way she might undermine the curse on Adam's issue.

Mark Baker was like the pastures of his own farm: fixed and bounded, growing boulders. But Abigail Baker seems to have been like one of those almost hidden springs that sends forth a quiet little stream to sparkle through the grass and slip finally into the great river. She can be glimpsed today through a few letters, a few scattered references by others—and through the lifelong outpouring of love and gratitude to her from her youngest daughter.

In a long poem in Popean couplets composed when she was sixteen, Mary Baker was to write about what she called, with the exuberant dolefulness of adolescence, the "withered wastes of earth," but among those wastes was "one stream" which

> Flows gently forth from childhood by my side
> Changeless as pure its ne'er receeding tide
> And oft its fount of goodness bathes from woe
> And in its silv'ry surf and faithful flow
> I see that stream whose fount is purity
> In tranquil course on to eternity
> To mingle with its ocean depths above
> It is a mother's deep undying love.[16]

In her ninetieth year as in her girlhood this was the human relationship which to Mary Baker Eddy would stand out above all others.

2

If seventeenth-century Puritanism still shaped New England theology, the eighteenth century had left its genial legacy of rational enlightenment on education.

Everywhere in the Merrimack valley the white-spired meeting-house was companioned by the little red schoolhouse. While Calvin's God in the one held out grace to a small elect, Jefferson's God in the other promised equal opportunities to all men. Like the music of fife and drum, faith in reason and faith in man made a brisk marching song in the young nation, which had only recently emerged from the War of 1812 with a new spirit of energetic confidence. Optimism took root and flowered even in the stony soil of New England.

In a discourse on the history of education in New Hampshire, the famous Concord preacher Nathaniel Bouton claimed that the Pilgrims had emigrated to America "chiefly to enjoy and propagate their religion, but next . . . *it was to educate their children.*" In the Protestant ethos, literacy was next to godliness as success was kissing-cousin to salvation.

By the early nineteenth century the older respect for learning and the new democratic spirit were in a state of unstable equilibrium. In New England, at least, intellect was cultivated as assiduously as potatoes, and sometimes, perhaps, as crudely. Young John Greenleaf Whittier, a farmer boy turned poet and editor, himself the product of a district country school, spoke for his fellows when he wrote: "We rejoice in New England, as the native home of intellect."[17]

Even the cosmopolitan Tocqueville praised the educational system of New England, while noting that the farther one got away toward the south or west the poorer the instruction became; and the sharp-eyed and sometimes sharp-tongued Harriet Martineau commented: "The Americans, particularly those of New England, look with a just complacency on the apparatus of education furnished to their entire population."

She went on to note that, however widespread, the instruction furnished was not good enough "for the youth of such a country"; that the information provided was both meager and superficial but that it was eagerly received; and that, in the last analysis, the "aristocratic atmosphere of Harvard University" would be "much purified by a few breezes of such democratic inspiration as issue from the school-houses of some of the country districts."[18] Both Harvard and the village schoolhouse might be subsisting at that time on an imported and inevitably diluted English culture, but at least the schoolhouse produced the self-reliance in character that one famous son of Harvard was to preach as the first of virtues.

The district schools in Bow were typical. The year before Mary's birth School District Three had voted to build a schoolhouse "twenty-two feet square according to the plan handed in by Mark Baker."[19] When built, it stood only a mile from the Baker Farm. Here the younger Baker children went to school before they were ready for the academy, and here Albert, the second son, served one term as teacher just before going on to make a brilliant record at Dartmouth College.

Mark himself had never had more than a common-school education, as his homespun though vigorous English showed, but schooling was not the whole story. The unique intellectual position of the New England farmer in that early society has always been a mystery to the inhabitants of other countries. It has never been better captured in words than by Harriet Beecher Stowe in her portrait of one Zebedee Marvyn:

> He owned a large farm . . . which he worked with his own hands and kept under the most careful cultivation. He was a man past the middle of life, with a white head, a keen blue eye, and a face graven deeply with the lines of energy and thought. He was one of those clearly-cut minds which New England forms among her farmers, as she forms quartz crystals in her mountains, by a sort of gradual influence flowing through every pore of her soil and system.
>
> His education, properly so called, had been merely that of those common schools and academies with which the States

are thickly sown, and which are the springs of so much intellectual activity. Here he had learned to think and to inquire—a process which had not ceased with his schooldays. Though toiling daily with his sons and hired man in all the minutiae of a farmer's life, he kept an observant eye on the field of literature. . . . In particular was he a well-read and careful theologian, and all the controversial tracts, sermons, and books with which then, as ever since, New England has abounded . . . lay on his shelves. . . . There was scarce an office of public trust which had not at one time or another been filled by him. He was deacon of the church, chairman of the school committee, justice of the peace . . . and was in permanence a sort of adviser-general in all cases between neighbour and neighbour. Among other acquisitions, he had gained some knowledge of the general forms of law, and his advice was often asked in preference to that of the regular practitioners.[20]

With the absence of a few graces and advantages attributed to this ideal figure, Mark Baker might almost have sat for the portrait.

He would be called on to draw up a will for a neighbor. In a legal dispute between Bow and Loudon he acted as counsel for Bow, argued the case, and won it, though the opposing counsel was a successful young lawyer by the name of Franklin Pierce, who was later to be fourteenth President of the United States. He acted at various times as official agent for Bow in caring for the poor, as surveyor of roads, as coroner for the county of Rockingham, and as sometimes acting chaplain of a regiment in the New Hampshire militia. He served on the school board and as moderator at town meetings, was elected to the office of selectman, and was repeatedly on the committee that settled the annual business of the town. As a result of his general standing in the community, he was sometimes listed as "gentleman" in town records where most of the farmers were described as "yeoman."[21]

Mark's prejudices carried over into his attitude toward education; the dogmas of the seventeenth century overshadowed in him the liberalism of the eighteenth. When his son Albert later began to bring his college books home from Dartmouth for his youngest sister to study, Mark was scandalized at the thought of her being exposed to Bacon, Locke, Voltaire, and Hume, and he issued an absolute interdict against them.[22] There was not going to be any deistic nonsense in the Baker household, let alone any atheism.

Abigail Baker may have been more sympathetic to the young people's widening interests, but again her influence is hidden from view. The friend who wrote her obituary and who was himself president of the New Hampshire Conference Seminary wrote that her "lively sense of the parental obligation" was particularly evident "in regard to the education of her children." Like Mark, she had only a country-school education, and the punctuation, capitalization, spelling, and occasional grammar of her letters bear witness to the fact. But like Mark, she was said to have a "strong intellect," and her commendation of such a book as *Tappan on the Will* to one of her sons gives evidence that she could digest strong intellectual meat.[23]

Nevertheless her influence was probably more in the realm of moral education where seventeenth-, eighteenth-, and nineteenth-century ideals converged. Later she was to write her youngest daughter, "Forget the past, enjoy the present, hope for the future,"[24] but her moral instruction was one of the things from the past which her daughter would not forget. Late in life Mrs. Eddy recalled the Franklinesque maxims her mother had taught her eighty years earlier,[25] and on one occasion she told an anecdote which calls up the very atmosphere of her childhood:

> *When I was a "wee bit" on returning from school I found a pitch pine knot in the woods and carried it home for I liked to see it blaze in the open fire place. Mother asked me where I got it? I said, "In Mr. Gault's woods." She said, "Did you ask him for it?" I replied "No." She said "Carry it right back again, Mary, it is stealing for you to do that and God forbids you to steal." I asked "Must I carry it back now I am tired?" She replied "Would you have God and mother thinking till tomorrow that you have broken His commandment?"[26]*

That sort of morality is rooted in Puritan theology, for all the latter's aversion to moralism; it tinges even Franklin's prudential ethics, for all his anti-Puritanism. Though Calvinism frowned on the heresy of salvation by works, it did not repudiate the need for works as an evidence of salvation. In her copy of Jonathan Edwards' *Treatise on Religious Affections*, Mrs. Eddy in later years underlined these sentences: "Practice is the most decisive proof of the saving *knowledge of God. . . .* It is in vain for us to profess that we know God, if in works we deny him."[27]

It might be true, as Edwards wrote in another passage which Mrs. Eddy also underlined, that "the great business for which man was created" was "the business of religion." But the great business of education was to teach a person to live as a dignified, rational, morally developed, and practically effective member of the human race. American democratic education rested on a faith that the two businesses were not incompatible. With church and state separate, Edwards and Franklin could lead an uneasy coexistence.

Yet we have only to compare Mark Baker's "Confession of Faith" with a rhetorical exercise by his son Albert on "The Perfectibility of Human Nature"[28] to see a yawning ideological chasm open up. Albert, who was elected to Phi Beta Kappa in his third year at Dartmouth, gave the oration at the anniversary ceremony or "literary festival" of that honor society. A few excerpts from this undergraduate production are enough to show how far removed from the Puritan's conviction of man's innate depravity was young America's hope:

> *Wherever [man] turns, oppression and want crowd like spectres before him; he is terrified, and disheartened; and in a fit of despondency, while viewing the accumulated evils to which humanity is subject, is led to distrust that a Providence rules in the affairs of man. But to him whose mind has been inbred with a sound philosophy, whose eye can penetrate the mystery that envelopes nature, who has learned to judge of events, not by their appearance, but by the principle that regulates them, the picture of human life, when surveyed dispassionately, presents nothing which excites in him either horror, or disgust. He views it as the result of necessary laws established in mercy, and with a firm reliance on that Power which formed a universe from chaos, and out of darkness called up light, he looks forward to that day when confusion shall be reduced to order, and man, disenthralled from his passions, shall rise to the destiny that awaits him. . . . We see man crawling into existence, weak and helpless at first, the prey of a thousand calamities inseparable from his condition. Increased in strength by uniting into clans and hordes, driven by a resistless fury, we see him pursuing the endless round of mutual destruction. But when we reflect, that there is nothing like chance in existence, that the whole universe is governed by a Primitive Intelligence, that the events of human life have their laws, as well as the phenomena of matter, and that it is the nature of error, like that of confusion, to destroy itself in the end, we feel the same assurance in the one case, that truth will prevail over error, as in the other, that order has, and will prevail, over confusion. This is the tendency of things, and no power on earth can resist it.*

This billowing flow of words, for all its talk of necessary laws and regulating principles, was clearly a confession of faith rather than a reasoned statement of philosophy. Descended from the Enlightenment and nurtured by the conditions of American life, the new faith was firmly committed to the happy ending. But in the indefinite interim before all error should be self-destroyed and universal order should prevail, evil might weigh no less intolerably on individual human lives. Utopian hopes might dull the pain; they certainly could not heal it.

3

From a Bow hilltop on a summer's day the farms of the Merrimack valley doubtless looked tranquil enough to have come out of the Golden Age, but life on the farms was far from being a rustic idyll.

Always in New England the basic rock was close to the surface. The womenfolk spun and wove and baked and scrubbed, bore children and cared for them, while the men and the bigger boys went off to the fields to dig and hoe and plant and reap in the age-old fashion of the sweating sons of Adam. This is the elementary pattern into which the Bakers fitted, and there is no reason to suppose that their life in its physical essentials differed from that of any other good New Hampshire family.

In addition to Mark and Abigail Baker there were three sons and three daughters and Mark's ancient mother. Their house on the hilltop was of the small salt-box type characteristic of early New England: two stories in front, with a tiny attic and a long roof sloping backward to within a few feet of the ground.[29] Waxing nostalgic over these plain little houses, weathered to "dove-color" by the elements, Oliver Wendell Holmes noted that cottages of this same model could be seen in Lancashire, "always with the same honest, homely look, as if their roofs acknowledged their relationship to the soil out of which they had sprung." A well, a broken millstone at the door, an elm a little to one side, a garden patch with hollyhocks and currant bushes, a barn, and fields stretching away with low stone walls around them—these were the characteristic features of such farms as the Bakers'.

What is puzzling is how nine people could live in so small a space as the house provided. Yet not only did they do so until the sons began to leave home one by one, but surprisingly there also seemed to be room always for guests. Especially ministers and especially cousins. The hills and valleys of New Hampshire were strewn with Baker and Ambrose cousins. Mark was the youngest of ten children, Abigail was one of seven. During Mary Baker's long life, new and unexplained cousins seem constantly to be cropping up, and a surprising number of them appear to have known her as a girl. This must have helped to give her in her earliest years the sense of a settled place in the simple rural society she knew, a society as yet untouched by the huge coming changes of the nineteenth century.

It was still a world where they burned tallow candles at night and used a tinderbox to kindle fire, striking flint and steel on the tinder. Along the river road—the Londonderry Turnpike which ran beneath the rocky ledges on the Baker farm that the children called their "playground"—rolled the splendid Concord stagecoaches and trotted single riders on horseback.

News of great events came into that world as from a vast distance. Napoleon had died just a few weeks before Mary's birth. That was the year Mexico broke loose from Spain and the Greek War of Liberation began. Beethoven had not yet composed his Ninth Symphony; Goethe had not yet written *Wilhelm Meister*. Two years later Byron made his final gesture, and President James Monroe proclaimed the doctrine that told Europe to keep away from the New World— a Europe where names like Castlereagh, Talleyrand, Metternich still reverberated in the air. On a famous July fourth just before Mary's fifth birthday, John Adams and Thomas Jefferson both died.

Within ninety years the world of radium, the airplane, Freud, and Einstein would have emerged; and because Mary Baker Eddy became known to the world only in these latter years, it is easy to forget the simplicity of the world into which she was born. Understandably enough, foreign observers tended to stress the "innocence" of the New World in contrast with the Old. Americans themselves were beginning to form the habit of thinking of their country as a new Eden and of the American as a new and unfallen Adam, a dangerous tendency which the older religion, with its tough-minded insistence on the universal corruption of human nature, deplored. And if Puritanism were not a harsh enough teacher, a child with frail health and a delicate nervous system might soon enough discover a serpent in her Eden.

There is no reliable evidence of the exact form Mary Baker's ill health took during the first fourteen years of her life.[30] Whether it included the acute "spells" that occurred in the later years of her girlhood we do not know. What is certain is that it kept her out of school a good deal of the time and added a weariness of the flesh to the natural liveliness of her spirits, as some of her verse of the period shows.

In the ambitious poem entitled "Shade and Sunshine," which

she wrote at sixteen, with its abundant echoes of Pope, Young, and
Thomson, occur these lines:

> Few were thy pastimes youth! but seldom knew
> I childhood's joyance yet luxuriant grew
> (Or sprang spontaneous from the soil of youth)
> Hopes boundless as delusive. These forsooth
> Cradled in sorrow longings wild and vain
> That held the spirit captive in their train. . . .
> Earth, ocean's wave, night, mountains, moon
> and star
> Had each within my breast its worshipper
> In subtle essence lived that yearning deep
> To mingle with the universe and keep
> Lone vigils, prayer and praise 'neath heaven's
> high dome
> And people earth with visions of my own.

One suspects that this may as easily reflect a passing mood of
romantic, sixteen-year-old melancholy as the childhood it is ostensibly
describing. Another somewhat earlier poem on "My Native Home"
speaks of that spot

> Where halcyon days sped on their flight
> Ne'er haunted by *perspective's* blight
> Or harbingers of wo

and it goes on to announce in Wordsworthian vein that

> Wild rural haunts and running brooks
> Relaxed from studying worn out books
> Were made a loved resort.

There is bound to be an ambivalence of attitude in the child
who loves nature passionately but is kept by ill health from a whole-
hearted, unthinking participation in nature's energies. His cannot be
the experience of the farm child who, like a healthy little animal,
scrambles over stone walls and races barefoot through the fields,
splashing noisily across the brooks, raiding the blackberry patches.[31]

The tradition still lingers in Bow that when the children were
playing together Mary would every now and then slip away and be
found later on top of a great rock, reading. It is not surprising that
her references to the beauties of the natural world so often have a
"literary" quality, as when she speaks of the "singing brooklets" and
"bright berries" of Bow, generalized epithets of the ear and eye
rather than the sharp sensuous immediacy of physical experience.

What added *"perspective's* blight" to nature in those years was probably not just bookishness, although she announced at a precocious age that when she grew up she would "write a book."[32] It may well have been the sense that ill health gives of being a little different, a little alien, in a world which healthy people seem to take for granted. Apparently, even before she could read, Mary had asked strange questions, had had strange thoughts. An anecdote which came down through the grandson of one of her cousins illustrates this rather quaintly.

Clarinda Baker, daughter of Mark's brother Philip who lived just down the road a bit, was one day in her Uncle Mark's house and Mary, then a very small girl, said to her, "Oh, I wish I could cut my thinker off!" Clarinda was so amused by the remark that she delighted to repeat it for the rest of her life.[33] When Mary Baker finally did "write a book," she announced boldly on the first page of the preface, "The time for thinkers has come."

In his report for 1847 the New Hampshire Commissioner of Education said, "It seems to be the destiny of New England, and eminently so of New Hampshire, to produce mind." Certainly New England did produce thinkers and they started their thinking young. One remembers twelve-year-old Harriet Beecher writing her essay "Can the Immortality of the Soul Be Proved by the Light of Nature?" to be read before the literati of Litchfield. Or twelve-year-old Lucy Larcom writing her essay on "Mind" for one of those little papers published, edited, and written by the mill girls of Lowell, and beginning it with the words, "What a noble and beautiful thing is mind!"

Over in Amherst Emily Dickinson wrote:

> The brain is wider than the sky,
> For, put them side by side,
> The one the other will include
> With ease, and you beside.

Here one approaches in a different way what it meant for New England to "produce mind." New England itself has often been called a state of mind, and New Englanders have traditionally tended to translate nature into mind. Surely there has been no region where men have more often found tongues in the trees . . . and good in everything. In the New England mind brute matter has tended to dissolve into thought, and during the very years that Mary Baker was growing up in Bow this tendency was gathering strength among a few young thinkers, to flower at last about 1836 into the Transcendentalist movement.[34]

At the same time the nineteenth century was marshaling its

energies for the tremendous achievements in geology and biology that were to challenge all transcendental interpretations of nature and to plant man squarely in an objective material world, the creature of natural forces that were clearly indifferent to specifically human values.

The very phrase "the struggle for existence" that was later to become a battle cry was used by the great English geologist Charles Lyell in his epochmaking *Principles of Geology,* which began to appear when Mary Baker was nine years old. The phrase occurs in a passage in which Lyell has been speaking of unhealthy plants as the first to be destroyed and choked out by more vigorous individuals. In the world of the new science every organism, child or plant, was sired by chance out of necessity, its destiny shaped by the interplay of physical heredity and social environment, its survival an unequal contest between nature's remarkable adaptive qualities and her ultimate indifference to the individual. Faced by the new scientific world view, the human being who was born weaker than his fellows might well complain that the nature of the geologists and botanists was as arbitrary a despot as the God of Calvin.

This whole vast issue was just stirring in thought as one young girl struck precarious and uncertain roots into the soil of Bow. Consciously or unconsciously countless influences enter into the making of a human life, and the invisible atmosphere of thought may well be part of the development, like the air that is breathed by a growing plant and the light that draws it upward.[35] In a letter written late in his own life the great nineteenth-century Harvard botanist, Asa Gray, declared:

> *When we think of a man's life we are apt to isolate him from his surroundings and consider only his individuality. It is well sometimes to have the fact brought before us that a man's surroundings—what he has seen and known—in the course of it—make up a great part of the man, tho' they do not make the core. But it is well to take into view how much of the natural world, of history, of experience of other minds and of the fruits thereof a man open to it all receives into his own being in the course of eighty years, or less.*[36]

This was the naturalist's view, although a Christian naturalist like Gray could agree that outer circumstances did not make the *core* of the man. The first half of Mary Baker's life was to be a search for that core, for the identity that would give meaning to her experience. She could hardly have imagined how far the quest was to take her from the quiet securities of Bow, from those moments

of Eden-like peace when the sun sifted down through the orchard
trees and the mind mirrored a flawless world—

> Annihilating all that's made
> To a green thought in a green shade.

4

Mary was never much interested in history. Like most Americans,
she looked naturally toward the future. Mark's mother, Mary Ann
Baker, was her link with the past, for this venerable old lady had
grown up during the French and Indian wars and had been thirty-two
years old when the Declaration of Independence was signed. But
what Mary remembered best in after years were her grandmother's
tales of the Scottish Covenanters, reinforced perhaps by her own
later reading of Scott's novels.[37] Her grandmother's mother had been
a McNeil, and it was through her that the stories of the heroic
Covenanters had come down from the family's Scottish past.

Mary's grandfather, Joseph Baker, had died some years before
she was born, but she must often have heard the story of his mother,
Hannah Lovewell Baker. Hannah was the daughter of the famous
Indian fighter, Captain John Lovewell, who was killed while making
New Hampshire safe for settlers and whose exploits caused the
government to bestow on his children a large grant of land in Pembroke. Part of this land Hannah had brought to Captain Joseph
Baker of Boston when she married him, and afterwards they had
settled on it.

The incident for which this young woman is known is told in
the words of the *History of Pembroke:*

> *It is said that Hannah, daughter of the brave Capt. John
> Lovewell, and wife of Joseph Baker, was washing by a spring,
> or stream, when an alarm was given of the presence of Indians
> in the neighborhood, which was signal for all to betake them-
> selves to some garrison-house. [She was urged to go, but refused.]
> Having work on hand, she would not move till she had finished,
> Indian or no Indian. The men, in their hurry to reach the fort,
> left her. Telling there the story, a rescuing party was sent after
> her, and found her leisurely coming to the garrison with her
> basket of clean clothes.*[38]

Other reminders of pioneer heroism were all around. Cousin
Aaron Baker, for instance, whose adjoining farm was on the next
hill to the west, was married to Nancy Dustin, a descendant of the
celebrated Hannah Dustin who was captured by the Indians.

Behind these events lay the history of those earlier pioneers, the Puritan fathers. There was, for instance, Captain Joseph Baker's great-grandfather, Thomas Baker,[39] who was baptized in the Kentish village of Lyminge in the spacious days of Queen Elizabeth; was tried in 1634 for not coming to church and for other acts of independence; removed to New England about 1640; settled in Roxbury, where in due course he owned a tide mill and homestead one mile west of the present site of The First Church of Christ, Scientist, in Boston; and died in 1683, at which time a notation was made in the Roxbury church records: "Old blind godly fathʳ Baker buryed."

Several generations back of Thomas was a John Baker of Lyminge who was tried for failing to pay a church tax and was then condemned "to march before the Procession in church on two Sundays, clad only in ragged shirt and breeches, bearing a lighted candle worth a penny," and he was to do this "with contumely and discredit."[40] It has been supposed from the nature of the punishment and its severity that he may have been a Lollard, one of those followers of Wyclif who risked their necks to take to the people the Word of God in their own English tongue. Lollard or not, he apparently possessed a flash of that stubborn yeoman independence which marked the later Bakers.

But all this was past history, and the evidence suggests that from her earliest years Mary was more interested in shaping than in contemplating history.[41] The pragmatic American spirit has always resisted paying a tax to the past. It would start fresh from the present moment in the spirit of Tom Paine's bold assertion that

> . . . all men are born equal, and with equal natural rights, in the same manner as if posterity had been continued by creation, instead of generation . . . and consequently every child born into the world must be considered as deriving its existence from God. The world is as new to him as it was to the first man that ever existed, and his natural right in it is of the same kind.[42]

This was the faith that rang out in the Declaration of Independence and during Mary's girlhood it was translated into the ebullient democracy of Andrew Jackson. The Bakers were ardent Jacksonian Democrats, critical of Daniel Webster as a Whig representative of "the money power," but venerating Old Hickory as a real folk hero.[43]

It was presumably a great day for eleven-year-old Mary when President Jackson himself came to Concord, attended by Vice-President Van Buren and Secretaries Cass and Woodbury. The cavalcade, with the President on a noble white horse, cantered up the river road past the Baker Farm and was met at Bow by a reception committee and thence escorted into Concord. Ten thousand people descended on Concord that day to see the President. Exactly seventy years from then ten thousand people would pour into the same city to hear a brief greeting from Mary Baker Eddy.

History in the flesh was something different from history in the books. For instance, General Benjamin Pierce, who as an ex-governor of New Hampshire was one of those who greeted Jackson on that exciting day in 1833, was a rough-hewn figure out of the pioneer past, a Revolutionary War hero who still wore the tricornered hat, buckled knee breeches, and high boots; but when he rode over to Bow, as he did sometimes while governor, to visit his friend Mark Baker, he became familiar to the younger Bakers as the genial patron who was to open the way for Albert to enter upon a promising political career.

Another occasional visitor was her grandmother's second cousin, General John McNeil, a giant of a man, the hero of the battle of Chippewa in the War of 1812. General McNeil was married to the daughter of Governor Pierce. His own daughter, Fanny, who was later to act on occasion as hostess for her uncle, Franklin Pierce, when he was in the White House, became a good friend of Mary's, and the girlhood friendship was renewed in 1882 when Mrs. Eddy visited Washington and was escorted by Fanny to the Senate, to the prison cell of President Garfield's assassin, and to the grave of General John McNeil.

This was the simple, fluid society where tag ends of aristocratic pretension and family pride were carried along by the great democratic flood of egalitarianism. In such a society the greatest prizes, spiritual and material, were open to anyone—if not for the asking, then for the striving.

Here in New England the excesses of Jacksonianism were less marked than in some places, and the spiritual roots of the democratic ideal were more evident. Behind the plain-spoken, homespun "heroes" who might ride to high office as they rode to battle was an astringent Puritan ethic that disciplined the heart.

Yet the promise was for all men. If each considered himself as good as the next one and the equal of any king, it was basically because religion had taught the farmer and the mechanic that they approached the gates of heaven and hell on an equal footing with the king. In this respect at least the judgments of the kingdom of God were applicable in the republic of man. Herman Melville, in a burst of visionary eloquence, summed it up in that great passage which began:

> *But this august divinity I treat of, is not the dignity of kings and robes, but that abounding dignity which has no robed investiture. Thou shalt see it shining in the arm that wields a pick or drives a spike; that democratic dignity which, on all hands, radiates without end from God; Himself! The great God absolute! The centre and circumference of all democracy! His omnipresence, our divine equality.*[44]

As Melville, like an American Isaiah, mounted to the climax of his vast apostrophe to "the great democratic God . . . Thou who didst pick up Andrew Jackson from the pebbles; who didst hurl him upon a war-horse; who didst thunder him higher than a throne; Thou who, in all thy mighty, earthly marchings, ever cullest Thy selectest champions from the kingly commons," the American faith reached a new maturity, with undertones of tragedy as well as overtones of triumph.

Yet, in the eyes of a handful of young women scattered through New England and upstate New York, something was lacking still.[45] Did God choose His selectest champions only from the "kingly" commons? Was that august equality, that royal mantle of humanity, withheld from woman by divine decree? Hadn't He once, even among the hierarchal iniquities of the Old World, chosen a peasant girl of Orleans and thundered her higher than the throne of kings? Was woman in America not fit to stand forth with man and speak up for God and humanity?

These were questions that troubled a few earnest women and a few thoughtful men as an obscure little farm girl in New Hampshire wrestled with the larger and older problem of God's judgment on the whole human race.

5

Mrs. Eddy in later years wrote of her father's "relentless theology."[46] To reconcile divine vengeance with human forgiveness was hard enough for a dialectician; it might well be impossible for a child.

In one place[47] she wrote of a small but revealing incident that occurred when she was twelve years old. Her mother had taught her to say, after she had been punished for any naughtiness, "I am sorry and will not do so again." One day, when sorely troubled by doubts, she asked her mother whether she thought that eternal punishment really was true.

Her mother sighed deeply and answered, "Mary, I suppose it *is*."

"What if we repent," said Mary, "and tell God 'we are sorry and will not do so again'—will God punish us? Then He is not as good as my mother and He will find me a hard case."

Certainly Mark Baker found her a hard case. Mark dreaded heresy as he dreaded the plague. He loved his youngest daughter dearly, as all accounts agree, and he feared for her soul when she questioned basic tenets of the children's catechism which she had learned by heart.

We may be sure that Mark's efforts on her behalf were seconded by Priest Burnham. When Mary was eight the Congregational Church in Bow was dissolved, and for the next two years the Bakers went most of the time to the Ambrose Meeting House in Pembroke across the river—named for Abigail's father, Deacon Nathaniel Ambrose. It was here that the Reverend Abraham Burnham preached. Of this doughty figure a later pastor said: "I judge Mr. Burnham was well fitted for the work to which he was called; though some thought that a man of milder and more winning ways would have done better. He was bold and fearless in his preaching, and faithful and laborious as a pastor."[48] From this restrained description one can surmise the fire and brimstone that must have enlivened his sermons.

There is value in reminding ourselves today of the sort of thing that so enraged Horace Mann in 1838 in connection with the Reverend John Abbott's book *The Child at Home*. In this "children's book" a little boy of six who has got into mischief is told:

> *But we must not forget that there is a day of most solemn judgment near at hand. When you die, your body will be wrapped in a shroud, placed in the coffin and buried in the grave. . . . How awful must be the scene when you enter the eternal world! . . . You will see God seated upon that majestic throne. . . . Oh what must be the confusion and shame of the deceitful child. . . . The angels will see your sin and disgrace . . . the Saviour will look upon you in his displeasure. . . . You must hear the awful sentence, "Depart from me into everlasting fire!"*

There were rebels enough against this sort of blasphemy. When the great Lyman Beecher read his second bride Jonathan Edwards' sermon "Sinners in the Hands of an Angry God," she rose with flushed cheeks and said, "Dr. Beecher, I shall not listen to another word of that slander on my Heavenly Father!"[49] Her action led Beecher, who had already modified the extreme orthodoxy of his youth, one step further toward a still remote liberalism, with the result that in 1835 he was tried for heresy, though eventually acquitted.

The next year his daughter Catherine published her heretical letters on the *Difficulties of Religion,* the fruit of her doubts and agonies after the death of her "unsaved" lover. It was those doubts and agonies, felt by so many sensitive souls, that caused her sister, Harriet Beecher Stowe, to write:

> *On some natures theology operates as a subtle poison; and the New England theology in particular, with its intense clearness, its sharp-cut crystalline edges and needles of thought, has had in a peculiar degree the power of lacerating the nerves of the soul, and producing strange states of morbid horror and repulsion. The great unanswerable questions which must perplex every thinking soul that awakes to consciousness in this life are there posed with the severest and most appalling distinctness. These awful questions underlie all religions,—they belong as much to Deism as to the strictest orthodoxy,—in fact, they are a part of human perception and consciousness, since it cannot be denied that Nature in her teaching is a more tremendous and inexorable Calvinist than the Cambridge Platform. . . . But in New England society, where all poetic forms, all the draperies and accessories of religious ritual, have been rigidly and unsparingly retrenched, there was nothing between the soul and these austere and terrible problems; it was constantly and severely brought face to face with their infinite mystery.*[50]

In the light of such comment it is easy to understand the spells of illness that seized Mary after arguments with her father. These arguments have sometimes been presented as simply a clash of wills, but what they may well have involved at the deepest level was the shock of struggle over existential concerns: freedom and destiny, meaning and truth.[51]

The Bible was central in all this. It was to be taken with desperate seriousness. The three cardinal tenets of Calvinism were the absolute sovereignty of God, the total depravity of man, and the inerrant authority of Scripture as the Word of God. The Bible was the bedrock of thinking. As interpreted by Mark Baker, it could be compared to the stone of which Jesus said, "Whosoever shall fall on this stone shall be broken: but on whomsoever it shall fall, it will grind him to powder." Yet to Abigail Baker, according to the later testimony of her daughter,[52] the Word was full of light and comfort and healing: Jesus moving on his compassionate rounds, the Holy Ghost shining in darkened human hearts.

The conflict set up by these two interpretations was as old as the struggle in men's minds between God's wrath and God's love. Even Abigail's natural cheerfulness felt the shadow of the mystery fall across it. In the few letters of hers that have survived from her later years the shadow has lengthened to a sort of troubled resignation, a hovering sense of failure. She stood too far within the thinking of her place and time to be able to break free entirely from her husband's "relentless theology."

Nevertheless, the first step out of Mary's distress was the conviction that God could not be less loving than her mother. In a well-known account,[53] she tells how at the climax of a struggle with her father over predestination, as she lay in a fever, it was her mother's tender counsel to lean on God's love and go to Him in prayer for an answer that brought her sudden healing and release.

Always Abigail was the reconciler. None of her children had yet joined the church or "professed religion," and all of them had certainly rebelled in some degree against the severity of Mark's religious demands on them. But she knew how seriously he took the article of faith he had inscribed in the church records, "You believe that it is the duty of heads of families to train up the children under their care for GOD, by all good precepts and examples and by praying with and for them night and morning."

In a letter to her youngest daughter in 1844 in which she poured out her deep love for her—"sometimes I fear," she wrote, "I worship mary instead of the great jehovah"—she went on to say, "Dear Mary speak and think as kindly of your Father as you can for my sake and pray for him for he has many trials for many has been the prayers he has offered for you he intends to do right he loves you and you are as near and dear to him as any child he has."[54]

Mrs. Eddy's later recollections of her father and mother in connection with the subject of prayer throw light on her own view of the subject. "I have never seen one who had such a gift of audible prayer as my father," she once declared.[55] At morning and evening devotions he read a chapter of the Bible and then launched into one of his long prayers in which, she said, appropriate passages of Scripture "flowed from his lips in boundless measure"; but like any other normal child she sometimes grew restive under these endless exhortations to the Deity. Her references to her mother's prayers are much more subjective and suggest something at a deeper, wordless level.

"Desire is prayer," she was to write in later years,[56] and only the future would be able to reveal what the desires may have been that lay in her twelve-year-old heart. But when she came to have a church of her own, she significantly chose the form of "silent prayer." It was understandable that the daughter of Mark and Abigail Baker should write: "In public prayer we often go beyond our convictions, beyond the honest standpoint of fervent desire. . . . If we cherish the desire honestly and silently and humbly, God will bless it, and we shall incur less risk of overwhelming our real wishes with a torrent of words."[57]

The long sermons she heard every Sunday in church may also have seemed like a torrent of words. Lucy Larcom has given a good child's-eye-view of a typical preacher of the period:

> *Up there in the pulpit he seemed to me so far off—oh! a great deal farther off than God did. His distance made my reverence for him take the form of idolatry. The pulpit was his pedestal. . . . I do not remember anything that the preacher ever said, except some words which I thought sounded well,— such as "dispensations," "decrees," "ordinances," "covenants,"— although I attached no meaning to them. He seemed to be trying to explain the Bible by putting it into long words.*[58]

The entire family attended lengthy forenoon and afternoon services on "the Sabbath." Between services no sort of frivolous relaxation was permitted; they could not go for a walk—"not even to the cemetery," Mrs. Eddy recalled wryly in her last years, and she added, "Father kept the family in the tightest harness I have ever known."[59]

Yet so far as one can judge from her later references, there was much that she loved in these Sabbaths. This would seem to have been particularly the case after the family started to go more to the First Congregational Church in Concord—the Old North Church, as it was called—which Mark and Abigail joined in 1831.

The pastor, Nathaniel Bouton, was a famous preacher, a man of considerable intellectual breadth and character, concerned for the social as well as the spiritual welfare of his fellow citizens. People flocked in from the countryside to hear him, and the large church was always crowded on Sundays. Andrew Jackson worshiped there on his visit to Concord, and Bouton was just the man to preach to the stalwart old warrior.

Writing to Bouton's daughter in 1902, Mrs. Eddy recalled "the long high head, the calm deep eyes, the tall slender form"[60] that she used to see in the pulpit of the Old North. And just the year before, in her annual message to her own church, she paid tribute to all the "grand old divines" she had known in her early years. There was more to these God-fearing shepherds than hell-fire, and the passage sums up her spiritual indebtedness to them:

> *Full of charity and good works, busy about their Master's business, they had no time or desire to defame their fellow-men.*

God seemed to shield the whole world in their hearts, and they were willing to renounce all for Him. When infidels assailed them, however, the courage of their convictions was seen. They were heroes in the strife; they armed quickly, aimed deadly, and spared no denunciation. Their convictions were honest, and they lived them; and the sermons their lives preached caused me to love their doctrines.[61]

The next year, the year she wrote to Bouton's daughter, she returned to the subject in her annual message. Speaking of the changes in America which had led "from stern Protestantism to doubtful liberalism," she added, "I never left the Church, either in heart or in doctrine; I but began where the Church left off."[62]

6

The first clear glimpse of Mary Baker comes through a poem written when she was twelve years old. It is given here in its original form, with all its freshness and with all its faults:

RESOLUTIONS FOR THE MORNING

I'll rise in the morn and drink in the dew,
    From flowers that bloom in the vale—
So mildly dispensing their charms ever new,
    Over hillocks, and flowery dales.

I'll gaze on the orb in yon eastern sky,
    For loftier thoughts 'twill invite!
His beams can enlighten the spiritual eye,
    And inspire my pen as I write.

I'll form resolutions with strength from on high,
    Such physical laws to obey,
As reason with appetite, pleasures deny,
    That *health,* may my efforts repay.

I'll go to the alter of God and pray,
    That the reconciled smiles of His son
May illumine my path through the wearisome day,
    And *cheer* me with *hope,* when 'tis done.

I'll greatful remember the blessings I've shared,
    And make this my daily request:
Increase thou my faith, my vision enlarge,
    Clothe me with the garment of peace.

I'll earnestly seek for deliverance from
  Indulgence in sinful mirth:
From *thoughtlessness,* vanity, all that is wrong,
  With *ambition,* that binds me to earth.

And O, I'll remember my *dear absent* friends,
  Though distance may part us the while,
I'll breathe forth a prayer for their *spiritual* gain,
  That goodness, may sorrow beguile.

To these resolutions should I but prove true
  Through faith, free from spiritual pride,
I'll love to acknowledge my days *must be few*
  For they'll waft me away to my God.[63]

This ingenuous little Puritan ditty, with something both sprightly and otherworldly about it, is revealing. Its twelve-year-old author might use the conventional language of piety and write almost inevitably in the style of Felicia Hemans, whose poetry had taken America by storm eight years before and was now at flood tide, but a very real and original young person comes through the lines.

The year she wrote it revivals were held in the Old North Church in Concord and in Abraham Burnham's church in Pembroke, and the heady revivalistic atmosphere may well have precipitated a religious crisis for her.[64] But the poem shows her suspended in a sense between two worlds: the religious world represented in different ways by her parents and the literary world represented by Albert Baker, then an undergraduate at Dartmouth.

About that time in a paper on "Poetry in the United States," young Baker wrote:

> *Above all our religion is as averse to all true poetry, as the most absolute atheism. No circumstance, perhaps, has exerted so powerful an influence in moulding the character, and directing the genius of the American people, as the peculiar nature of their religion. It contemplates man, not as much to live and enjoy life, but to prepare for an hereafter. Hence whatever is thought, or said, or done, must be in reference to the tremendous issues of eternity. Such a religion is at war with the light, buoyant temper which delights itself in song.*[65]

Here was Mary's problem. Her relish for life and her big-eyed love of learning showed a genuine buoyancy of spirit,[66] but nature proved a very stern Calvinist indeed, threatening to deprive her of these goods at any moment. Poetry she loved fervently, but it never became for her a real escape from the illness that darkened her girlhood. Toward the end of her life she declared, "I thought once that my mission was to write poetry, but my life has had more prose than poetry to it."[67]

If so, her brother Albert helped to shape the prose. To Mary he stood for the great world of scholarship, for reaches of the mind broader than any view from the hills of Bow. It was Albert, she wrote later, who helped her with her lessons and guided her reading when he was home,[68] and through him she caught glimpses of a fascinating new world that she didn't really want to leave at all.

From the beginning Albert had no intention of becoming a farmer, and between seasons of study and farm work he earned the money to go away to college by teaching school. In 1826, when he was sixteen and Mary only five, he taught for a season in School District 18 of Concord, close to home. Three years later he taught a term in Schoolhouse Number Three in Bow, the school Mary attended when she was well enough.

The country schoolhouses of those days were noisy, rough-and-tumble places, scandalously overcrowded, and offering all sorts of hazards to the pupils, as official reports were forever lamenting. A typical report from the School Committee of Bow complains that "the scholars are huddled up together, in the most uncomfortable ways imaginable, and their health and lives often perilled as they sit, day after day, in these contracted school rooms, inhaling the close, poisonous air."[69]

Mary was kept home much of the time, though in some respects she may have made faster progress through her own reading and Albert's help than she would have made in school. The irregularity of her education is seen in the way erudition and youthful faults of expression are found in conjunction. The liveliness of her mind and her love of long and unfamiliar words are apparent in all her early writings. During Albert's vacation times at home in his college years she even picked up what in one place she calls a "smattering"[70] of the ancient tongues and French. She early gained a reputation for unusual learning in her family and among the outlying cousins.[71]

At the same time, the educational limitations of her time and place are also visible. Although Bronson Alcott and others were carrying on Pestalozzian reforms in the schoolroom, the old system of learning by rote still held in most of the country. Thus Mary could memorize Lindley Murray's *Grammar* without its necessarily eliminating from her writings such a rustic expression as "you was," which still enjoyed in the New England countryside the good standing it had had among eighteenth-century gallants in London drawing rooms half a century before.

Spelling was never her strong point. The rural spelling bee and the authority of Noah Webster's new *American Dictionary of the English Language* (1828) had not then standardized "orthography," as it was usually called; moreover, wide reading was not a substitute for classroom drill.[72]

More important for Mary than any other reading except the Bible in those early days were the *Introduction to the English Reader* and *The English Reader* of Lindley Murray. These standard schoolbooks of an older generation were incredibly weighty compilations of English prose and poetry—weighty, that is, in vocabulary, style, moral gravity, philosophical portentousness, and all-pervasive piety. The selections were drawn overwhelmingly from the eighteenth century. With the exception of one or two examples from Wordsworth, there was virtually nothing to represent the great flood of Romantic writing which the nineteenth century had ushered in.

The education of children in a country district like Bow was still eighteenth century in manner and matter, but a child might feel grateful in later years to have had at least such masters to learn from as Addison and Goldsmith, Milton and Pope, Johnson and Gray. The Lindley Murray *Readers* entered into the very bloodstream of Mary's thought and vocabulary.

Some of the things she wrote about her girlhood studies may belong to the immediate years after she left Bow and may be deferred for discussion until that period is reached. The important point to note regarding her education in the Bow years is the bent given to her mind by her admiration for Albert. In his early papers and speeches one frequently comes across phrases that are strikingly close to her own expression of similar thoughts in her published works, written many years later, though the writings of young Baker were never published and were not accessible to her at the time she was writing on metaphysics.[73]

Between Mary and the brother who was eleven years her senior there was apparently a sufficient community of interest and communion of thought to stamp on the young girl's mind some of the very phrases in which that brother expressed his faith in the inevitable victory of truth over error. But where he expressed only the common hope of the Enlightenment, she expressed a conviction that rose like a rocket from her own insurgent heart.

7

Life was not only thought; it was people. Emily Dickinson's elegy on the mortal scene calls up every young girl's world:

> This quiet Dust was Gentlemen and Ladies,
>   And Lads and Girls;
> Was laughter and ability and sighing,
>   And frocks and curls.

In Mary's case it was brothers and sisters, the Gault boys next door, the visiting cousins: a world of people many of whom are only names to us and all of whom became, in time, shadows to her. One by one they were to slip away until only she was left.

In her autobiography *Retrospection and Introspection,* published in 1891, she broke off the narrative suddenly to remark (p. 21): "It is well to know, dear reader, that our material, mortal history is but the record of dreams, not of man's real existence, and the dream has no place in the Science of being. It is 'as a tale that is told,' and 'as the shadow when it declineth.' . . . Mere historic incidents and personal events are frivolous and of no moment, unless they illustrate the ethics of Truth."

Mark Baker would have understood, at least in part, the austerity of that last remark. To a Puritan the frocks and curls of daily experience always stood within the tremendous framework and under the inexorable judgment of eternity. Albert Baker, who believed in reason and science and complained that the education of women led to mere frivolity,[74] might have understood the statement in a different way. To the scientific mind a particular instance is chiefly important as the illustration of a general law. Things and events may come and go in frivolous, dreamlike procession; the law remains, universal and immutable.

It would be of small moment to record the comings and goings of the members of one family on an obscure New Hampshire farm unless there were larger, more universal issues at stake. Yet within the framework of humanity's momentous search for Truth, even the most trivial events may be touched by high significance. If our gaze were sufficiently discerning, there might be no such thing as an insignificant event; the slightest detail of the human "dream" would hint at ultimate realities. Nor would this be to lose the rich particularity and concreteness of existence, the existential "feel" of people and things. Ideally it would redeem them from that ceaseless flow into nothingness which finds its perfect symbol and formula in the second law of thermodynamics.

Mary Baker's poems suggest that even as a girl she felt the force of Job's words: "Man that is born of a woman is of few days, and full of trouble. He cometh forth like a flower, and is cut down: he fleeth also as a shadow, and continueth not." But in those early days human life still had a relatively settled look and the flower was no less entrancing because it was to be cut down.

On January 27, 1835, when Mary was thirteen, her Grandmother Baker died at the age of ninety-one. Her passing broke an important link that bound the family to the old homestead. Mary had written a poem the year before "On the Death of an Aged Friend," so her grandmother's death was not her first encounter with mortality,[75] but it was the first time one of the home circle had disappeared so irretrievably.

Some years earlier the eldest of the brothers, Samuel Dow Baker, had left Bow for Boston and gone into the building business, becoming in time a successful contractor. He never comes to life for us as the rest of the Bakers do, and his chief interest today lies in the impact of his two marriages on his youngest sister.

When Mary was ten he married Eliza Ann Glover of Concord, the sister of a young man who was learning the building trade with him. Mary of course attended the wedding festivities, and there for the first time she met the bride's brother, a dashing young fellow called George Washington Glover. Family tradition has it that he took the pretty little girl on his lap and announced that when she grew up he would come back and marry her—as, indeed, he did. Meanwhile, in the summer of 1835 Samuel and Eliza Ann had a daughter, thus introducing a new generation to replace the one which had passed away with Mary Ann Baker.[76]

The year before, Albert had been graduated with honors from Dartmouth. Immediately afterwards Governor Pierce and his wife had asked him to come and live with them in their handsome mansion in Hillsborough, where he could study law with their son Franklin. Now his brother, George Sullivan Baker, a young man approaching his twenty-third birthday, felt spurred to strike out from home and seek his fortune in the world.

Like all the Baker children George was high-spirited and independent, with no more love of farming than Albert, but, possessing a more happy-go-lucky disposition, he had not disciplined his life toward a particular end. In the summer of 1835 he became involved in some sort of romantic scrape which combined with his restiveness to make him take off suddenly for Connecticut. Change was in the air. Mark Baker himself had decided to sell the Bow farm, but that did not keep George's departure from causing something of an uproar.

The miniature tragedy—Mark outraged at the decision that left him without a son to help him, Albert summoned home from Hillsborough for consultation, the sympathetic mother and sisters arguing that George's "health" required him to live in another climate—soon resolved itself into bucolic peace again. Albert stayed a week to help his father finish the hoeing, then reported to George (or Sullivan, as they often called him) that the old man got over his indignation almost immediately. What Mark intended to do now Albert didn't know, but "he talks of a thousand things."

The letter conveying this news included a brotherly trouncing—"It would puzzle the devil, at least me, to guess or even conceive, what it is, that has benumbed your wits, for a few years past"—but it was full of the liveliness, charm, and affection that mark the Baker letters. It is the earliest of these letters to have been preserved; through it and its successors[77] one gets the picture of a vivid, close-knit family, its members united by warm loyalties but also marked by headstrong opinions.

The youngest and frailest Baker was clearly the favorite. "I loved Mary best of all my brothers and sisters," declared her eldest sister Abigail in later years,[78] and the affectionate concern they all had for her is apparent from the family letters. Mary most certainly must have felt that if there was security anywhere in human life it was in the bosom of her family. But the family was already beginning to break up, and with it the small certitudes of childhood.

Young Abbie was then nineteen. From Hillsborough, where she was living with the Pierces while teaching a term of school,[79] she added a postscript to Albert's letter to George. Although Abbie had more of Mark in her than any of the others, she decidedly did not share Mark's view of the good life. Always socially ambitious and now enjoying her taste of fine living at the Pierces', she expressed satisfaction at her father's selling the old farm—"if he does not get a worse," she added, then commented dryly, "But he cannot very well get a worse one." For George she expressed a vigorous hope that he "would never have to resume hard labour for a sustenance."

As a matter of fact, George now had a reasonably good job teaching textile weaving to prisoners in the Connecticut State Prison. The warden was Amos Pilsbury, a leading penal reformer of the day, who came from Concord. There his less prominent brother, Luther, was deputy warden of the New Hampshire State Prison. A few years later Luther was to marry Martha Baker, Mary's second sister.

Close on the heels of Albert's and Abigail's letter to George were letters from Martha and Mary. They were written on September seventh, just after stirring events had taken place in Concord. The poet Whittier and an English abolitionist had been scheduled to speak at an antislavery rally there but had been prevented by mob violence and pelted with rotten eggs. After taking shelter with a sympathetic friend for the night, they had escaped from Concord about sunrise, galloping in a carriage over the Hooksett Bridge not far from Bow and so defeating the rioters' plan to tar and feather them.

But the two young girls were blissfully unaware of the ominous clatter of those fleeing carriage wheels and their portent of national tragedy to come. They were occupied with far more important things. Martha's letter was full of conspiratorial banter about Sullivan's amorous escapade, in which he had evidently made her his confidante. Mary's letter deserves to be quoted as a whole for its communication of the flavor of a unique young personality just turned fourteen:

Bow Sept 7th 1835

Dear Brother

    As I have an opportunity of sending you a letter by Mr. Cutchins without putting you to that expense which any intelligence that I could communicate would but ill repay I improve it with pleasure. If solitude will make ones thoughts flow on uninterrupted I think I shall have plenty of them this afternoon as Father Mother and Martha (which makes up the family) has gone to attend the funerel of J. L. Cavis and I am left alone to review past events and paint to my imagtion the many hapy sabbaths we have spent together still as you informed us in your letter you enjoyed contentment and health at which I do most sincerely rejoice; and I should were I in your case think the sacrifice at which you obtained it but a mere momentary gratification compared with the enjoyment of health. Yet though in the enjoyment of these blessings you iformed us there was one thing wanting to fill up the measure of your happiness to know that Father was reconciled to your leaving us I think from what we have herd him say in the family and tell others he was sensible as well as all of us the exchange was necessary for your health.

    There is one thing if I have not improved it aright I have lerned from experience to prize more perhaps than ever I did before that is Dear brother *the friendly advice and* council *you was ever giving me and the lively interest you ever manifested in my welfare but now when I sit down to my* lonely *meal I have no brother Sullivan to encourage me as formerly—but there is no philosophy in repining I must extend the thought of benevolence farther than selfishness would permit and only add my health at presant is improveing slowly and I hope by dieting and being careful to sometime regain it. I had entirely forgotten to write you the news I had intended and will only say as Martha has told you all about it that in this Town far kened and* noted *is* your name *and that we are in daly expectation of receiving some of your* poetical *effusions a love dity or something of the kind. This is the news I have to tell respecting your self (and news indeed I sould suppose to you) or of any kind excepting that Mother has been that long contemplated journey to Boston with cousin James B. who was up on a visit at that time and returned with her had an agreeable visit returned in a week from the time she left she wants verry much to see you and wer it not she looks more to your interest than her own personal comfort could scarcely be denyed it she wishes me to geive her love to you and as for Father he will write by Mr. Cutchins if he sees him if not by the Mail and give you the result of his researches at Sanbornton as he is now there with Mother to look of a farm. I have written much more than I intended as sister M. and I have both written and will now close with giving you much thanks for the present you sent me by Mr. C. although I did not receive the tooth pick I shall take the will for the deed and think much of them for coming from you. Write every opportunity excuse all mistakes as this is the second letter I ever wrote and accept the well wishes of your* affectionate sister

Mary M. Baker[80]

The letter speaks of her father's "researches at Sanbornton." Having found a buyer for the farm at Bow, Mark was looking for a new farm.[81] His brother Philip, who lived down the road with his family, had also decided to move and had found property to his liking just outside the promising village of Sanbornton Bridge, eighteen miles the other side of Concord. Mark's "researches" led him to buy a farm close by Philip's, and the winter was filled with preparations for departure.

Shortly before Christmas Albert, having just returned to Hillsborough after several days in Bow, wrote George a letter which gives an appealing picture of Mark as he pulled up his roots in the old farm:

Father is driving about like a thunderstorm. Poor man I pity him. He thinks, because he can get away from Bow, he can get away from trouble, but I fear he will be disappointed. He can manage a farm pretty well, to keep clear of debt, and bring the year round even, but he is the least qualified to make money, of any man that I ever saw of his natural abilities. He knows nothing of the world, and can be duped by the tricks of every knave, that will undertake to practice upon him. For his sake, I am glad he has valor, and purchased where he likes, and if he is contented, it is all I ask; the rest of us can take care of ourselves.

Abigail and Martha could hardly wait to move to new fields of social conquest, though they greatly enjoyed the farewell party given for them at Bow—"not so great as it was good," Martha reported to Sullivan. But to Mary the move seems to have meant sorrow mingled with a somewhat trembling anticipation. It is significant that both she and her mother fell ill when it was time to move, and this delayed the departure a little.

Mary was leaving the only world she had ever known and the friends she had grown up with, including the neighboring Gault boys, Andrew and Matthew. To Andrew, aged eighteen, she addressed a fond farewell in halting verse. Forty years later the Gaults received from her a copy of the first edition of *Science and Health*.[82] It might have come to them from another planet.

Chapter
II

Sanbornton
1836

The new episode started off gaily, with all the charm of a village comedy of manners.

The tone is set in Martha's first letter to her brother George after the family had moved into the new farm. "I cannot tell you how I like," she wrote, "for our acquaintance is yet so limited. . . . The gentleman that teaches the village school is boarding with us—you know we are very partial to that class of people."[1]

Three months later[2] a letter from Abbie (who for a time was calling herself Abba) showed that good progress was being made toward the social conquest of Sanbornton Bridge. Her account of the situation might almost have been lifted out of Jane Austen:

> *We go on finely here, almost as well as we could wish. The people are very kind and hospitable, we find society very agreeable and refined; but we associate with none but the first you may depend. We have been treated, since we came to this place, with every token of respect, by all classes of the people; but we have not showed out much yet, nor do not intend to at present, for we think a gradual rise in the esteem of people, more commendable, than a precipitate ascension. We have some fine young ladies here, brother, I think some of the most refined and accomplished that I ever met with; and they appear very solicitous to render us happy and contented in our new situation. The young gentlemen have not been slow in their attentions. We have had cards and compliments in profusion to attend dancing schools, balls, and parties. Of the latter we have attended a number, and were highly gratified with the proceedings. Balls and dancing schools we have not frequented. Three young gentlemen, of the first rank, called upon us last evening. . . . With all this I am well pleased, and if our buildings and furniture were a little more splendid, and we had a chaise, I think we could appear to much better advantage; but it is extremely mortifying, to my pride, to push off to meeting in a waggon . . . but here is one, that will stay at home, rather than ride in such style.*

The wagon was evidently a great cross for all the girls, and George was urged to write their father and persuade him to buy a chaise in which they could ride up to meeting like young ladies of fashion.[3] Mark remained obdurate to George's championship, but eventually increasing prosperity induced him to buy not merely a chaise but a carriage.

Social life proceeded apace. When young gentlemen callers arrived to visit the girls, Mark would step to the door and say, "Let all conversation and pleasure be in harmony with the will of God,"[4] but after the temporary shock occasioned by this injunction the evening would develop with the proper blend of hilarity and decorum. Martha even succeeded in going to a Fourth of July ball. "A splendid one too," Abbie reported to George, then added, "I suppose she would not have gone if she had asked consent; but she went without leave or license."[5]

All in all, the move to Sanbornton was a great success. In August Albert was able to tell George that Mary's health had permitted her to attend school all summer, while Abigail was teaching in another school, and all "the folks" were well. Of Mark he wrote:

> *Father is as happy as a* clam *and I dont think he will ever want to die, though he were sure of going to Heaven. I am glad it is so, and hope his joy will never end in sorrow. Indeed I see no reason why he may not be satisfied. He lives in the neighborhood of two sanctuaries—a matter of the greatest moment—two academies, a very pleasant village, society agreeable, etc., etc. He has cut a good crop of Hay, though corn and grain are miserable. No matter, he likes it, and that is enough.*[6]

All three girls have been described as strikingly beautiful.[7] In a poem indited to the whole family a cousin saluted the "beauteous seraph sister band,"[8] and the social success of such a trio was only to be expected. The new textile mills in Sanbornton Bridge had introduced into that simple democratic society a stratification which put the Bakers on the side of what in England would have been called the small landed gentry as opposed to the new village proletariat. "Only think," Mary was to write in a letter almost thirty years later, "of Yankee castes in *all* our *country villages.* I thoroughly wish we were understood as a people, the *true American idea.*"[9]

Yet the rustic Yankee simplicities shine through many of these early letters, as when Martha wrote George:

> *Father and Mother have just retired and left Mr. Cutchins and us girls to amuse ourselves; so he and I are writing. Mary is reading and Abbie sits and orders me what to say but I shall not*

regard her. Sullivan they do act so bad it is impossible for me to write and I wish you could make them behave for they keep shaking the table and making me laugh all the time, and now they have brought on a bowl of apple-sauce and a plate of nuts and turnovers and a pitcher of sap beer.[10]

It was, Mr. Cutchins added in a postscript, the most pleasant spot imaginable, a place flowing not with milk and honey but with maple sugar and molasses. On the other hand, a rather serious young man of the neighborhood wrote Mrs. Eddy in his old age that he recalled the times when he would drop in on the Baker ladies "where Shakespeare perchance was the theme of conversation, or checker-playing was the order of the day."[11] Intellect and sobriety flavored the country pleasures. The girls, particularly Mary, were regarded as bluestockings as well as belles, and in this they illustrated Harriet Martineau's observation: "The Americans may be considered secure of good manners generally while intellect is so revered among them as it is, above all other claims to honour. . . . Intellect carries all before it in social intercourse. . . . It is refreshing to witness the village homage paid to the author and the statesman, as to the highest of human beings."[12]

One little girl in another village recalled long afterwards[13] that when Abigail and Mary would drive over to visit a relative of hers who taught philosophy the conversation would be filled with big words so far beyond her fourteen-year-old comprehension that she considered it very dull indeed. In a letter to Mary, Albert wrote:

I have an opportunity of sending a letter by a friend of mine, Mr. Harrison Andrews, who is going to Sanbornton with the intention of attending the academy. I take great pleasure in introducing him to your acquaintance. You will find him a sterling fellow, a little enthusiastick, but none of Sol Wilson about him. What is that poor devil doing? I hope you treat him as he deserves, with entire neglect. Abi will recollect Andrews' sister, a particular friend of hers. He is a very close student, and is as much given to discursive talking as yourself, though he has not quite so much poetry at his command.[14]

Mary's letters to George in 1836–37 reflect the general atmosphere of the home, with a quiet little liveliness of their own. In order to "comply with good *ton,*" she wrote in the earliest of them,[15] "I shall first enquire for your health, spirits, and the like of that." She hoped that after reading the book he had sent she would become "somewhat more civilized," but in her "presant state of ignorance" she found it difficult to express her gratitude adequately.

The civilizing influence of the village school that summer was followed during the next few years, when health permitted, by further study at one at least of the two local academies, and probably at both.[16] Mary, as an aspiring young authoress, was determined to become as learned as she could, but during these years the bluestocking never overwhelmed the belle or caused her to neglect good *ton*.

Throughout her life she was to put great emphasis on polite manners. To some of the poorly educated people with whom she was thrown in her middle years, her carefulness of speech and observance of small points of etiquette seemed like ridiculous affectation. In the Lindley Murray *Readers* she early marked numerous passages having to do with social deportment, including the archetypal niceties of Lord Chesterfield. In later life she wrote, "I insist on the etiquette of Christian Science, as well as its morals and Christianity."[17] It was in part because of her lifelong attention to manners that in her last years, when she was visited by people whose lives had been spent in a sophisticated, cosmopolitan society virtually unknown to her, she impressed so many of them as a great lady as well as a great leader.[18]

There was, however, a difference between Abigail and Mary in this respect. With her social ambition and inflexible will, Abigail succeeded quickly in landing the most eligible young bachelor in town, Alexander Hamilton Tilton, who owned several large woolen mills and amassed a considerable fortune before he died. Eventually Sanbornton Bridge was renamed Tilton after him, and Abigail had the satisfaction of being the first lady of the town. With a deep sense of responsibility and a rigid sense of propriety, she illustrated Harriet Martineau's statement that the "worship of Opinion is, at this day [1836], the established religion of the United States."

As the biologist might view it, her eminence in her own small world was an example of successful adaptation to environment; given her will to succeed within the conventions of her society, her behavior was reasonably predictable. Although in some ways a bold and independent person, Abigail had that fundamental Yankee conservatism or caution which took its chief form, according to Miss Martineau, in "fear of singularity."

Mary, who was outwardly so much more timid than Abigail, was vastly more daring when it came to fundamentals, and her willingness to stand out against the whole world eventually shocked the older sister's sense of propriety and alienated her affections beyond repair. The course of Mary's future could certainly not be plotted by the minor civilities she held in esteem or even by the major ideals of her society. It is a simple fact that she had it in her to shatter existing patterns.

At the same time she clung to family and friends with wistful eagerness. Of the ill health that interfered with the society of friends she wrote to her school friend and close confidante, Augusta Holmes, that "this, Dear Augusta, is the corroding canker of a youthfull and ardent mind."[19] On the eve of Abigail's marriage she wrote George:

> *Abigail is prepareing for the celebration of her nuptials, probably, as soon as June; then there will be another tie severed, she will be lost to us irrevocably,* that *is* certain, *although it may be her gain. How changed in one short year! Dear brother can you realize it with me? if so just take a retrospect view of home, see the remaining family placed round the blazing* ingle *scarcely able to form a semicircle from the loss of its number. But as Burns says, "hope springs exulting on triumphant wings . . ."*[20]

These early letters of Mary Baker contain all the contradictions, the changes of mood, the trivialities as well as the aspirations that one would expect from a normal young girl of talent and sensibility in the 1830's. To be sure, the human comedy was sometimes darkened by pain and weariness and loss, but hope sprang exulting on triumphant wings. And up or down, Mary Baker was always *engaged* with life.

2

In 1876, after the publication of *Science and Health,* Mrs. Eddy received a letter from her cousin D. Russell Ambrose. He recalled to her their friendship forty years earlier when she was "a frail, fair young maiden with transparent skin & brilliant blue eyes, cheerful, hopeful, enthusiastic."[21]

This is the picture of Mary Baker that emerges again and again from the evidence, as distinct from the legend. She is described as "the village beauty," and "the 'belle' of the community, always laughing."[22] Her enormous, deep-set eyes, "overhung by dark lashes," her clear, fresh complexion and chestnut-colored hair, her shapely figure, "slim, alert, and graceful," the *chic* she somehow managed to achieve in her dress even in that rustic community—these were the envy and admiration of Sanbornton Bridge.[23]

She had, said one little girl who knew her a few years later, a "happy disposition" and was "always cheerful."[24] "We miss your good cheer,"[25] her mother wrote her when she was away from home, and a family friend added that they wished she was there "like Samson to make sport."[26] Her brother-in-law in 1848 wrote her: "I am . . . sorry to hear you say that you are not so lighthearted, gay and frolicsome as formerly. Keep up thy joyous spirits, drive care, trouble, and gloomy forebodings from thee, ever keep thy naturally lightsome feelings in the ascendant, and my word for it, you will yet again be the Mary with whom the hours passed pleasantly, smoothly and happily away."[27]

Even when years of struggle had brought a sadness to her eyes which troubled some who knew her, this was not the dominant impression she created. A man who frequently met her socially in 1865–66 described her as "bright and cheerful and very witty,"[28] and one who was closely associated with her during the difficult years of the 1870's wrote, "I should say she was naturally joy-loving and light-hearted."[29] Dozens of people who knew her in her later years have borne witness to the infectious quality of her laughter.

A good deal of laughter rings through her early letters. "Her laugh was very sweet,"[30] remembered one little girl who often heard Mary talking with her mother and laughing. Years later her nephew George W. Baker wrote to her granddaughter: "But she was a beautiful woman, and more beautiful when she laughed. I've read of 'silvery' laughs lots of times, but her's came nearer to the realization of the novelistic description of anything in real life that I ever ran across."[31]

In one of her letters Mrs. Baker spoke of missing her daughter's "prattle,"[32] and what she meant is made clear by the bits and pieces of news and comment scattered through Mary's letters to her brother George:

> *You have perhaps heard Esqr. Pierce is elected senator to congress . . . We attended a party of young Ladies at Miss Hayes last evening she was truly sorry our Brother from Conn. was not there, but she is soon to be married and then the dilemma will close as it is your fortune to have some opposeing obstacle to extricate you. Oh brother I wish I could see you, and I hdly think Abby and I would be as sleepy as we wer the last night you spent with us; but could amuse ourselvs (if not you) by telling you things that would excite laughter if nothing more. . . . I will give you an abridged sketch of a gentleman recently from Boston, now reading medicine with a doctor of this town, a* perfect complet gentleman I met him a number of times at parties last *winter he inviteed me to go to the shakers with him but my superiors thought it would be a profanation of the sabbathe; and I accordingly did not go . . . Father has been speculating of late, although it is an allusion that in a letter might be considered rather abrupt, to tell you he has swaped your favourite horse with Mr. Rogers.*[33]

The ability to rattle on in this cheerful manner made Mary a lively companion as well as correspondent. Inevitably she began to attract suitors, but for the time being she was not interested. "O dear," she wrote to Augusta Holmes when she was seventeen, "how much you have to say about 'Enoch.' As to my being married, I don't begin to think much of that 'decisive step.' "[34]

The nineteenth century put great value on a languishing sentimentality in women, but in Mary's case the tendency was modified not only by her natural enthusiasm but by a certain flavor of wit, sometimes a little quaint but not without pungency. This was to grow with the years, and a psychiatrist who examined her seventy years later in connection with a lawsuit would report, "In her ordinary conversation she is witty, a bit satirical, but with a great deal of gentleness in her demeanor."[35] Even in her ninetieth year, when her secretary, Calvin Frye, gave her an anthology of poetry for a present, one of the few passages she marked in it was the last stanza of Sir John Suckling's "Why so pale and wan, fond lover?" in evident appreciation of its cavalier insouciance.

A poem of her own, undated but clearly written during her young womanhood, illustrates what may be called this daylight phase of her character and at the same time points beyond it:

SONG

Laugh lady laugh
There is a joy in laughing
Tears were never made
To be in beauty's keeping
Tears are of a stream
Where pleasures lie decaying
Smiles like rays of light
O'er sunny waters playing
    Laugh lady laugh

Love lady love
There is a joy in loving
But sigh not when you find
That man is fond of roving
He like the summer bee
Takes wings through beauty's bowers
And knows not which to choose
Among so many flowers
    Love lady love

Weep lady weep
There is a joy in weeping
Christ hath all our tears
Within His own kind keeping

Those He loveth best
He chastens till they love Him
And to his dear breast
He folds the weary lambkin
Weep lady weep.[36]

The poem begins lightly enough, but like Mary's life it moves to an unexpected conclusion. She had entitled her long, earlier, introspective poem "Shade and Sunshine," and to leave out either the sunshine or the shadow would be to falsify the picture. In a letter some years later one of her several suitors wrote her, "I hope and pray you are as lively and gay as you were a part of the time at Hill . . . do you feel as well?"[37] A part of the time was overshadowed by pain.

It is necessary here to distinguish between the genuine suffering that darkened her life in those years and the romantic melancholy she shared as a literary fashion with the age.[38] George Baker, away from family and friends, could feel this no less than Mary, and it is hardly surprising to find him quoting Byron in his notebook and writing: "My book is neglected, not to say forsaken, and my pen laid aside! What are my prospects? Whilst on one hand, a delicate constitution and impair'd health enfeebles, on the other, poverty lays her iron grasp. Behind, in mem'ry's dim perspective, are but joys past and times fled."[39]

But health was for Mary a more serious business than an occasion for romantic melancholy. The Baker letters are full of references to poor health on the part of one member of the family or another, but Mary appears to have been the chief sufferer. In 1837 both she and Martha had long sieges of sickness; in April Martha could write of herself as having been "comfortably ill" through the winter and confined to her room "pretty snugly,"[40] while three months later she wrote of Mary: "In addition to her former diseases her stomach became most shockingly cankered, and an ulcer collected on her lungs, causing the most severe distress you can conceive of; the physician with the family thought her cure impossible, but she has a good deal recovered for two weeks past, and this morning was carried out to ride."[41] After another three months she announced, "Mary's health is gradually advancing on bread and water."[42]

This bleak diet was Mary's lot during a good deal of her young womanhood as a feature of the Graham cure she had adopted. In the circumstances, it is surprising that her "silvery laughter" was heard as often as it was. She could even laugh ruefully about her suffering, as when she wrote Augusta, "Oh, the monotony of *books, books,* with an *agreeable* variety of pain."[43] It is perhaps not surprising that in another anthology which she acquired in her last years she should have marked the lines from Shelley:

Our sincerest laughter
With some pain is fraught.

At this stage her natural cheerfulness and hopefulness appear to have kept her from dwelling overmuch on her own or others' illness. Four months before her uncle Philip Baker died in 1837 she wrote George: "We saw Uncle Baker not long since he is strangely altered and to appearance is wasting verry fast, enough enough of this."[44] A little later she was reporting: "Martha has been very ill since our return from Concord. I should think her in a confirmed consumption, *if I would admit the idea,* but it may not be so, at least I hope not."[45]

This attitude, prophetic of things to come, contrasts with Abbie's "realism" and Albert's anxious solicitude. In a letter in 1837 Abbie wrote: "Mary spent the last week with me and appears quite comfortable, but the poor girl can never enjoy life as most of us can should she live any time, and this is altogether uncertain. It surely is with all of us but it seems to be more so with her, since she retains life only by dieting and brushing, and all such simple expedients."[46]

Albert could never write without urging Mary to take care of her health. "Don't breathe these awful frosts,"[47] he warned, and again: "Be careful that you do not sacrifice too often at the shrine of the muses. Your health is of paramount importance, yet, though you may think yourself partly well."[48] Perhaps the most significant reference to Mary's health occurs in a letter written to her by Albert in 1840: "I received a letter from Mrs. Tilton yesterday, with sad intelligence in relation to your health. I hope she may have exaggerated, that your sufferings are not so severe, as my fears represent them. I wish I were with you. . . . I hope your usual fortitude may not have deserted you."[49]

Mary evidently could bear the ordinary sorts of pain stoically enough. But there were times when something more was involved—when, in her weakened condition the burden of the mortal state became too crushing to be borne. This was when life took on the look of nightmare, overburdened nerves gave way, and she would end in a state of unconsciousness that would sometimes last for hours and send the family into a panic. On such an occasion Lyman Durgin, the Bakers' teen-age chore boy, who adored Mary,[50] would be packed off on a horse for the village doctor; in later years he recalled that on cold winter nights he rode bareback so that the horse might help to keep him warm.[51]

Apparently these attacks were comparatively rare in Mary's youth, since the frequent references to her illnesses in the Baker letters specify colds, fever, backache, lung and liver troubles, and above all dyspepsia as the cause of her family's concern. Yet the occasional torture of nerves could be worse than steady physical pain, and this is suggested by a poem called "Nervousness" which she wrote a few years later:

> O skillful torture! vicegerent of woe
> More to be feared than lover's perjured vow
> Life's little joy shredded and torn by thee
> Floats a mere wreck upon her moonless sea. . . .
>
> Why are poor mortals subject to thy will
> Thou last infirmity of human ill!
> O'er wearied nature at the midnight hour
> Remorseless tyrant! to assert thy power.[52]

The midnight hours were the hours when nature, that great Calvinist, stripped away the puny securities of mortal life and revealed the abyss of nothingness on which the proud dust rears its throne. Mark Baker's religion must take a great share of the responsibility for his daughter's affliction; yet it served also to bring the young girl face to face with ultimate concerns.

When, for instance, she read Young's *Night Thoughts,* it was for her no mere compendium of gloomy splendors and funereal rhetoric; it was a confrontation of the riddle of life and death. That huge philosophical poem, so unreadable to most people today,[53] she read, reread, pondered, and absorbed; it entered her heart, her mind, her imagination; it stayed with her through her life; it echoes and re-echoes through her writings:

> Is Heaven tremendous in its frowns? Most sure;
> And in its favours formidable too;
> Its favours here are trials, not rewards;
> A call to duty, not discharge from care.

On one occasion, when she had one of her spells, she regained consciousness to find Albert sitting beside her with a copy of Young's *Night Thoughts.* Then he read for her comfort a passage which she afterwards copied into her notebook and marked with a notation of the incident:

> Why start at death? where is he? Death arriv'd,
> Is past; not come, or gone; he's never here;
> Ere hope, sensation fails; black-boding man
> Receives, nor suffers, Death's tremendous blow.
> The knell, the shroud, the mattock, and the grave;

These are the bugbears of a winter's eave,
The terrors of the living, not the dead.
Imagination's fool, and error's wretch,
Man makes a death which Nature never made;
Then on the point of his own fancy falls,
And feels a thousand deaths in fearing one.

It would, however, take more than Edward Young and his *Night Thoughts* to banish the king of terrors. It would take long years of battling to the conviction that Life is all.

3

The theme which engaged the Puritan imagination more than any other was that of *Paradise Lost,* of "man's first disobedience" and its fruits. It is not surprising to find among the many passages of poetry which Mary Baker copied into her girlhood notebooks not only selections from Byron, Wordsworth, Shakespeare, and Mrs. Hemans, but also an unusual number of lengthy quotations from that great religious epic which undertook to justify the ways of Milton's God to Adam's seed.

If we may judge by these excerpts, it was the human dilemma, the domestic tragedy, in *Paradise Lost* that interested her more than the cosmic drama. As she copied down the final lines of the poem describing the expulsion of Adam and Eve from Paradise—

They, hand in hand, with wandering steps and slow,
Through Eden took their solitary way—

her sympathy overflowed, and she added in the margin "TOO BAD." Yet the comment applied to more than those two legendary parents of the human race; it applied to the whole human dilemma. There was incipient religious protest as well as spontaneous schoolgirl sentiment in her exclamation. In time Milton's God himself might come to seem too bad to be believed.

Emerson, in his essay on his brilliant Calvinistic aunt, Mary Moody Emerson, wrote, "Nobody can read in her manuscript, or recall the conversation of old-school people, without seeing that Milton and Young had a religious authority in their mind, and nowise the slight, merely entertaining quality of modern bards."

It was all right for Emerson to write of this in the past tense, for in the Boston world which he inhabited a new day had brought radically new religious views and tastes.[54] But in Sanbornton Bridge Milton and Young still had authority for those in the older religious tradition.

To be sure, another sort of religion also had currency and widespread influence there: the religion of the popular revivals, by that time mostly Methodist and Baptist. The important thing about the revivalist movement sweeping the rural United States was that it shifted the ground from hardheaded logic to undisciplined emotion, from doctrine to piety, from an educated ministry to lay preachers and itinerant evangelists who felt themselves moved by "the Sperrit" but who might be all but illiterate.

There was a general feeling that in getting away from the intellectual foundations of the past the revivalists were getting back to the conditions of primitive Christianity and recapturing a religious enthusiasm which their critics did not hesitate to call fanaticism. New England was spared the worst features of frontier revivalism, and the New Englanders' respect for intellect kept them from embracing wholeheartedly the frontier view that piety and book larnin' were natural enemies. Nevertheless the Methodist and Baptist churches in New England did change the religious emphases of that region. Until the time when they themselves grew conservative and intellectually respectable, they illustrated the observation of a German Reformed Church writer of the period: "A genuine sect will not suffer itself to be embarrassed for a moment . . . by the consideration that it has no root in past history. Its ambition is rather to appear in this respect *autochthonic,* aboriginal, self-sprung from the Bible, or through the Bible from the skies."[55]

Mary Baker had connections with Methodism from her earliest years. Father Hinds, Methodist elder at Bow, was a family friend and one of the early spiritual guides to whom she later paid tribute. There was a Methodist church in Sanbornton and periods of revival which swept the town. At one time, possibly during a revival, she wanted to join the Methodist Church but was dissuaded by her father from this dangerous departure from Congregational orthodoxy. It may have been on this occasion, or perhaps during a revival within the Congregational Church itself, that Albert wrote her:

> *Abi informs me that there has lately been a* protracted meeting *at Sanbornton, and that you cherished a hope that you had been brought to embrace the doctrines of that religion, the strange influences of which have thus far puzzled philosophy to solve. I know the anxiety you will feel to know how this intelligence will affect me; and the timidity you will feel to speak of it. But why should you? Though I may differ with you in all these matters of belief, it is far from my wish to discountenance religion. Indeed, in my view, a woman can hardly live without it; and it would be strange philosophy, to*

deny that a place in our affections without which, we seem like strangers in a strange land. You need never fear a repulse or that it will not be received with interest whenever you choose to lay open your feelings to me. One thing do not allow yourself to be suspected of, bigotry or fanaticism. They are as distinct from true religion, as from true philosophy,—its very antipodes.[56]

Along with the danger of fanaticism ran the danger of the rather flashy sort of pietism which many young girls of Mary's age were falling into. A new era was inaugurated in 1837 when eighteen-year-old Victoria, called down from bed to be told she was Queen of England, announced, "I will be good." A number of American young ladies, with rather less regal effect, were proposing to be good in a somewhat self-satisfied or at least self-conscious way.

Very typical of the times is the adjuration by a certain Lydia S. of Claremont in a letter to Mary's close friend Augusta Holmes: "It grieves me to the heart to know of Sally's indifference to salvation. . . . I hope my dear Augusta that you will be faithful & unwearied in your efforts to do her good & by your holy life & pious conversation constrain her to come to the Saviour."[57]

There is little of this sort of thing in Mary's letters. Her religious experience apparently ran at another level. A turning point in that experience may have been the arrival of the Reverend Enoch Corser in September, 1837, to take over the pastorate of the Congregational Church in Sanbornton. A history of the church describes this gentleman with a pleasing vigor:

Then came that strong, blunt, eloquent, and thoroughly devoted man, Rev. Enoch Corser. . . . His sermons were models of method, running through fifthly and sixthly, perhaps not quite to fifteenthly. He was a man of powerful voice and tremendous muscle, which he often used on the desk and Bible in his moments of intense fervor. He used to marshal all his forces of invective against the wrong, and his attacks were nothing short of storm and siege.[58]

Badly underpaid as he was, and with a good classical training, Mr. Corser was forced to teach school as well as preach. He prepared his son Bartlett for the university, but of all his pupils and parishioners Mary Baker appears to have been his favorite. Bartlett wrote many years later, when he himself was leading the life of a retired country gentleman:

As Mrs. Eddy's pastor—and for a time teacher—my father held her in the highest esteem; in fact he considered her, even at an early age, superior both intellectually and spiritually to any other woman in Tilton [then Sanbornton Bridge], and greatly enjoyed talking with her. It was in 1837 when, if I remember rightly, Mrs. Eddy was about 15 [actually 16], that I first knew her, she being several years younger than myself. I well remember her gift of expression which was very marked, as girls of that time were not usually possessed of so large a vocabulary. She and my father used to converse on deep subjects frequently (as I recall to mind, from remarks made by my father) too deep for me. . . .

If he were living today I am sure his recommendation of her would be unqualified. She stands out in my mind distinctly as his brightest pupil, and I also remember her great admiration for him. . . . I never heard a lisp against the good name of Miss Baker, but always praise for her superior abilities and scholarship, her depth and independence of thought, and not least, spiritual-mindedness.[59]

Mark and Abigail Baker united with the Congregational Church at Sanbornton on June 17, 1838, and on July 26 of the same year their youngest daughter was received into membership, the only one of the six Baker children to have joined the church up till then. In an interview which Mrs. Eddy gave in 1903, not long after Bartlett Corser had written the letter quoted above, she spoke of his father as the clergyman "who would not let me enter into the church unless I believed in foreordination, and I told him I would not be saved and my brothers and sisters have no chance. I was made sick by it, because I could not believe in it, and I stood out and would not join the church and the old man gave in and took me in."[60]

The bare statement tells us little of the urgent spiritual and intellectual wrestlings involved. Foreordination may seem no more than an academic question now, but for a Congregationalist in 1838 it went right to the heart of man's relation to God. The Methodists and most of the Baptists had dropped or softened this doctrine, that God predestines all but a chosen few to damnation, substituting for it a looser concept which made hell the punishment for particular sins committed by the individual of his own free will. But if they thereby lost a little of the ferocity of Calvin's God,[61] they also lost the fierce logic of his theology.

The struggle between Mary and her pastor must have been severe, given the character of the two, but it ended with the young girl's being admitted to membership—"and my protest along with me," as she later wrote. In her published account of the experience she tells of one other incident which occurred at the time she was being examined for membership:

> *The minister then wished me to tell him when I had experienced a change of heart; but tearfully I had to respond that I could not designate any precise time. Nevertheless he persisted in the assertion that I had been truly regenerated, and asked me to say how I felt when the new light dawned within me. I replied that I could only answer him in the words of the Psalmist: "Search me, O God, and know my heart; try me, and know my thoughts: and see if there be any wicked way in me, and lead me in the way everlasting."*[62]

Corser relented, she went on to tell, and this second obstacle was successfully vanquished, too. There is more than meets the eye in such a victory. " 'Tis a tyranny," wrote old Cotton Mather, "to impose upon every man a record of the precise time and way of their conversion to God. Few that have been restrained by a religious education can give such an one." The theory behind the requirement was that by nature one was wholly alienated from God, naturally and entirely wicked, and that the first movement of divine grace upon one's soul must therefore have been apparent as something completely distinct from ordinary experience. But if a person had been conscious of divine grace in his daily life as far back as he could remember, it might well be difficult or impossible to settle on any one spiritual experience as decisive. In standing out against this requirement, Mary Baker was in effect standing out against the doctrine of natural and total depravity.

Yet her rebellion at this time was only partial. She was orthodox enough when she wrote in "Shade and Sunshine":

> The moral power to will in Adam died
> Till mercy whispered from her blest abode
> Who died in Adam lives through Christ in God.

When a person writes about the natural depravity of human nature it is not always possible to tell whether he is writing merely out of low spirits and unhappy circumstances or out of some more basic insight into the mortal state. The former is illustrated in an entry made by George Sullivan Baker in his notebook when he was working with the inmates of the Connecticut State Prison:

> *Here, my own heart is my only associate, my only comparison. . . . I have abandon'd reading novels and am reading Shakespeare! Not as good as Waverly or Bulwer, the moralist would say, but it takes me, so I am taken with it! For a knowl-*

51

edge of human nature (the great study of my life) I think him preferable to any author. He shows it in all its naked deformity, as I daily see it practic'd with scarely one redeeming quality![63]

The Puritan has always been trained to see not only a naked deformity in others but bottomless sinfulness in himself. A passage in a letter to Augusta which may have been written by Mary Baker illustrates this attitude:

Dear A—, would that I could give you advice with regard to the religious state of your mind. But I feel that I wander far, very far from the path of duty, therefore I cannot say as much as I would to others. O, the sinfulness of my own heart! When I look within, and see the vileness existing there, and how exceedingly prone I am to wander from the Source of all good, I can but wonder at the forbearance and long-suffering of God towards me. Pray for me dearest Augusta, and be assured you are remembered by me.[64]

If this passage was in fact written by Mary, it shows her momentarily reflecting the religious atmosphere of her time and place, with its morbid excitement of the sense of guilt. It is an attitude not to be found in any of her other letters, but it seems reasonable to believe that she may have passed through some such phases and that they may well have sharpened her insight into the psychology of religious experience. Fifty-four years later she would write:

The baptism of repentance is indeed a stricken state of human consciousness, wherein mortals gain severe views of themselves; a state of mind which rends the veil that hides mental deformity. Tears flood the eyes, agony struggles, pride rebels, and a mortal seems a monster, a dark, impenetrable cloud of error; and falling on the bended knee of prayer, humble before God, he cries, "Save, or I perish." Thus Truth, searching the heart, neutralizes and destroys error.[65]

Again, in her copy of the *Imitation of Christ* by Thomas à Kempis Mrs. Eddy marked the sentence: "The more spiritual a man desires to be, the more bitter does this present life become to him; because he sees more clearly and perceives more sensibly the defects of human corruption." In comment on this intensely realistic judgment, she laconically wrote one word: "Spirituality."[66]

Sin, in biblical terms, brought death, and human corruption involved not only perverted will but inevitable death. At every turn one was confronted with mortality. A heaven beyond the grave, where all the saved would meet again, was the traditional consolation of

52

religion; but it was coupled inevitably with the threat of hell, and little assurance that all one's family and friends would go to the more blessed place. The promise of heaven and the threat of hell seemed as inexorably yoked as Abigail and Mark Baker. Although Mary might opt for her mother's God of love rather than her father's God of wrath, human life appeared to justify and even necessitate both views.

It has often been wondered whether she was acquainted with the theology of the Shakers who lived in the nearby village of Canterbury[67] and who were familiar figures in Sanbornton as they peddled the austerely beautiful products of their expert craftsmanship.[68] Her reference in 1837 to an invitation to visit the Shakers suggests that it was a usual thing for the young people to do, even though she could not go on that occasion.[69] In any case she may well have heard something of their beliefs.

What attracted most people's attention were their four leading principles of virgin purity, Christian communism, confession of sin, and separation from the world. Less well-known but no less striking was their concept of God as Mother as well as Father, reconciling the maternal attribute of love with the paternal attribute of terrible and unlimited power.[70] The reconciliation, however, was only verbal; there was nothing here to resolve the paradox of a loving God and a world abounding in evil. When Mrs. Eddy later presented the concept of God as Father-Mother, she related it to a concept of creation which revolutionized the meaning of both terms.[71]

More pertinent to her development was the conviction of God's love that came to her through her own mother. Yet such is the complexity of human life that even her mother's religion was overcast by her father's theology. When Mary was about to leave home at the time of her marriage, her mother asked her to read every night a poem which began:

> What have I done for him who died
> To save my guilty soul . . . ?[72]

The inherited guilt of the human race was never to be forgotten.

There is no record of what Mary taught her Sunday School class at the Congregational Church, including the little girl who thought that "with her curls she was just lovely."[73] A little more is known about her instruction of Lyman Durgin, the lonely, teen-age country lad who lived with the Bakers and helped with the chores. Distressed over his illiteracy and his lack of religious training, she undertook to teach him to read the New Testament, and her patience and interest won his ardent devotion. To the end of his life he cherished the New Testament she gave him. After she had married and moved away from Sanbornton, Martha wrote her: "Lyman loves you dearly and wishes me to say so for him."[74]

From this it is reasonable to assume that, whatever she taught him, she did not leave Lyman feeling that he was a miserable sinner, a worm in God's sight. It was, after all, the story of Christ's redemption rather than of Adam's fall that she had used in teaching him to read.

4

In the year the Bakers moved to Sanbornton, Mount Holyoke Female Seminary was founded by Mary Lyon in Massachusetts, a defiant assertion that women had minds. The following year four girls were admitted to Oberlin College in Ohio as candidates for the Bachelor of Arts degree. But to most Americans of that time the higher education of women would have seemed as unthinkable as it was unnecessary.[75]

In cultivated urban society there were girls who received a private education fully as rich, broad, and thorough as did their brothers at the university, and even at the popular level women flocked to lyceum lectures for intellectual stimulation and instruction. But the highest formal education to which a girl in a village like Sanbornton might aspire was the academy, that select, private predecessor of the public high school or junior college of later years. Of the comparatively small number of girls who went on from the district school to one or another of the local academies, the majority would be content to take the course provided for young ladies who fancied a little literature and languages along with their embroidery.

Yet there was hardier fare for those who wanted it. The academies of those days offered, in addition to the classical course, an introduction to the natural sciences and philosophy, as well as to modern languages and literature. In her autobiography Mrs. Eddy mentioned as her favorite girlhood studies natural philosophy (i.e., natural science), logic, and moral science (i.e., ethics), and elsewhere she spoke of chemistry, astronomy, and rhetoric as among those studies.[76]

The academies were not free, as the common schools were, so Mary's and Martha's attendance was conditioned by finances as well as health. Evidence indicates that Mary may have attended Holmes Academy at Plymouth in 1838 and certainly attended Sanbornton Academy in 1842.[77] Very probably she attended other terms in between, possibly at a third institution known confusingly as the Woodman Sanbornton Academy.[78] Dyer H. Sanborn, author of a popular grammar of the day, was principal of this latter institution but later transferred to Sanbornton Academy. For a time Martha Baker was his assistant and then advanced to being "preceptress."[79]

One of Mary's school friends, Julia Sargent, who afterwards served as a bridesmaid at her wedding, stated in later life that Sanborn would often speak of "the high grade of scholarship attained by Mary Baker and the brilliant future in store for her."[80] While this reminiscence may be colored by what transpired later, it seems evident that, however irregular her schooling may have been, Mary stood out from the other girls in the village as a lively thinker with a knack for learning.

It has been pointed out already that the secular education she received came straight out of the Age of Reason—or that part of the Age of Reason which stayed on good terms with Christian piety. She was taught that truth must submit to the test of reason, that revelation and reason must be reconciled, that the universe was run on a system of invariable and ascertainable laws, and that science was the great glory of modern man. Some lines in her notebook asked:

> Does gravitation change its given law
> The rivers from the rocks their waters draw?
> Do thorns yield grapes, the barren thistle figs,
> Oaks become acorns, mighty forests twigs?
> Shall reason bold the law of God assail
> In that the beam-filled eye can e'er avail
> Itself of good in undisputed right
> And change its darkness to meridean light. . . .[81]

In a college paper ironically entitled "The Heresy of Reason," Albert Baker had asked rhetorically whether one must be considered a "heretick" because one relied on reason as a guide to truth. His answer has relevance to his sister's later thinking:

> *The Being whom we adore, and a knowledge of whom we would fain attain, combining in himself all that is holy and perfect, the nearer we approach him and the more intimate our acquaintance, the purer will be our love and the stronger our attachment. . . . But how shall we obtain this knowledge? By the aid of reason. What! exclaims the Zealot, subject the inscrutable ways of Providence, the Infinite God, to blind, erring, deceitful reason? . . . But, we would ask, will that steady and bright torch, which of old guided its followers to the very throne of virtue fail him who lights it for religion and in an eternal cause? . . . "God," says Plato "is truth." . . . If truth exists it can be separated from error. . . . If . . . there exists throughout nature an invariable and uniform consistency, is Nature's great Author inconsistency? And if his essence be truth, and truth be*

attainable by reason, will not reason in her slow but unerring progress attain to a knowledge of it? What? exclaims the Zealot, attempt to pattern infinity? . . . But while we would concede the infinitude of the Divine Mind, we would maintain the ability in man of an infinite increase of knowledge; and though he can never reach perfection, he may forever approximate. . . .

Baker was expressing here the common faith of the Enlightenment; intellectual young America grew up in the conviction that truth must be reasonable and that God operates with perfect and unvarying consistency through universal laws. But the curious fact was that most people did not really believe this when it came to Christianity. They might reject the idea of an inscrutable Providence when they were dealing with everyday affairs, but in effect they believed that God had set aside His own laws in the case of the Christian revelation. Something more than unaided reason was necessary to resolve this anomaly.

Mary Baker never appears to have shared her brother's faith that reason alone was a sufficient guide to truth.[82] That immediate perception of truth which in theology is termed revelation and in philosophy intuition must furnish the starting point for reason; logic, after all, was a process, not a position. She could find this implied in one of her favorite textbooks, Whately's *Elements of Logic*,[83] for the author's religious orthodoxy saved him from Albert Baker's extreme espousal of eighteenth-century rationalism. But Whately, like most of the authors whom Mary studied in school, asserted that reason confirmed the Christian revelation, without ever really coming to grips with the problem.

Another of the books that influenced Mary in her early years[84] was *Watts on the Mind*, or, to give it its proper title, *The Improvement of the Mind* by Isaac Watts, D.D. "Deeply possess your mind," wrote that worthy Lockeian, "with the vast importance of a good judgment, and the rich and inestimable advantage of right reasoning." What gave an attractive *élan* to his otherwise grave disquisition was his sense of new possibilities ahead for the rational mind:

Let the hope of new discoveries, as well as the satisfaction and pleasure of known truths, animate your daily industry. . . . The present age, by the blessing of God on the ingenuity and diligence of man, has brought to light, such truths in natural philosophy, and such discoveries in the heavens and the earth, as seemed to be beyond the reach of man. But may there not be Sir Isaac Newtons in every science? . . . Think with yourself, with how much ease the God of spirits can cast into your mind, some useful suggestion . . . whence you may derive unspeakable light and satisfaction in a matter, that has long puzzled and entangled you.

But Watts insisted on the need for both revelation and reason. It was a fault to try to determine any question by natural reason alone when help might be derived from revelation. On the other hand, it was a "culpable partiality" to examine some doubtful or pretended revelation without the use of reason. Although the Christian gospel might safely be taken as a divine, infallible, and proven revelation, it would be well to remember that "we are but fallible interpreters" and we may well discover "a fairer light cast over the same scriptures, and see reason to alter our sentiments even in some point of moment."

Here was an open invitation to make new discoveries in the Christian revelation,[85] although Mary Baker was not yet ready to accept the invitation. While her mind was rational and inquiring, it was not speculative. As a woman and as an American, she was eminently practical, and it would be practical need and circumstance that would call forth her own discoveries. Whately, Watts, and the other writers she was studying were providing her with useful tools of thought, but she was not drawn to the study of philosophy as such. Though familiar with Locke, she apparently knew nothing of Berkeley.[86] When she finally came to a conviction of the unreality of matter, it was by a quite different route from that of the good bishop, who crowned his philosophical achievements with a panegyric on the salubrious properties of tar water.[87]

For all its empirical background, English philosophical idealism remained as theoretical as did the later German varieties. Even French positivism was concerned with systems more than with facts. Tocqueville at this time was observing that in Europe men confined themselves to "the arrogant and sterile researches of abstract truths, whilst the social conditions and institutions of democracy prepare them to seek immediate and practical results of the sciences." Time would amply disclose the danger that lay in both extremes, but the English utilitarian influence and its essential American outcome in pragmatism at least opened the way for philosophy to relate itself more directly to practical life.

There was little in Mary Baker's education that would ordinarily be thought of as practical, but there was little in her character that would allow ideas to remain abstract and unrelated to daily life. She might well have agreed with Keats, "Axioms in philosophy are not axioms until they are proved upon our pulses." The very word "demonstration," in Christian Science, was to signify a practical proof rather than a logical argument.

Yet reason and logic were important, immensely important, to one who was to think of Christianity as Science, to see all evil as error, and to relate practical results to metaphysical premises on the basis of Jesus' words: "Ye shall know the truth, and the truth shall make you free."

<h1 style="text-align:center">5</h1>

The practical, workaday world lay all around, and beyond it lay the great world of public affairs. Albert Baker was for Mary the link between the two, together with the *New Hampshire Patriot and State Gazette.*

This fiercely Democratic weekly newspaper, edited for many years by the powerful Isaac Hill, was read religiously by the entire Baker family. Isaac Hill, known as the Democratic dictator of New Hampshire, was a member of Jackson's "Kitchen Cabinet," and the *Patriot* was therefore thought to give an inside slant on Jackson's policies. In 1836 Hill resigned from the United States Senate to become governor of the state.

That same year was the beginning of a severe economic depression which was to last for some four years and greatly exacerbate political passions during the Van Buren administration. This was also the year that Albert Baker, because of ill health, came back from the Pierces to spend most of the summer with his family. Like so many other young men feeling the financial pinch, he decided at that time to go west. A college friend, James W. Grimes,[88] who had established himself in the booming town of Burlington in the Iowa district of what was then Wisconsin Territory, urged him to come out and join him there.

At the last moment Albert's plans were changed and he went instead to Boston, where he spent the winter of 1836–37 reading law in the firm of Richard Fletcher. During this time he lived with the family of General John McNeil (whose wife was Franklin Pierce's sister) and tutored young Benjamin McNeil to earn his keep. In a letter to George Sullivan Baker in October he announced that he and General McNeil would go out to Wisconsin in spring or early summer when navigation opened up, and then in a burst of typical Baker high spirits he wrote:

> *I suppose the query will occur to you—The Devil, where do you get your money, to meet all these freaks of yours? Where get it? By the great Gods, I am as rich as a prince. I have sold my . . . classicks for the round sum of* ten dollars, *and when that is gone, I shall sell my* shoes. *What a glorious thing, this*

idea of borrowing money, and dying insolvent. That is doing something the world will remember you for. Isn't it, my darling?[89]

In April, 1837, he was admitted to the Massachusetts bar, but at the same time his health broke down; he was sent to the hospital, barely escaped with his life, and returned for convalescence to Sanbornton, where he wrote George moodily that he would probably spend the rest of his life hoeing potatoes. The three or four months he actually spent there were Mary's intellectual gain, but by September he was back in Hillsborough, where Franklin Pierce, now a senator, turned his law practice over to him before hurrying off to a special session of Congress summoned to meet the financial crisis.

The pattern of Albert Baker's life for the few short years that remained was now established. Old Governor Pierce and his wife, both practically helpless, were put into his care by the young senator, who henceforth had to divide his time between Washington and Concord. The governor wrote Mark in 1838: "Sir your son the lawyer I think is doing well nothing is wanting but health . . . he is a young man of . . . correct habbits and gentlemanly deportment a strict attendant of public worship when his health will admit."[90]

But Albert Baker was more than that. His law practice increased rapidly, his name soon became known throughout the state as a young man of uncommon promise as well as correct "habbits," and before long he was in the thick of politics. In March, 1839, he was elected to the state legislature and soon afterwards was on the Democratic State Committee.

It was now that he came into conflict with Isaac Hill, who had split with Jackson and was growing steadily more conservative. Class lines were drawing tighter under the impact of the depression and Van Buren's stand on the banks. In a Fourth of July oration Albert Baker inveighed against money, privilege, oligarchy, bankers, monopoly, and corporations. He belonged to the Locofoco or "Radical" wing of the party, but in New Hampshire politics "Radical" meant something more like Populist—a radical determination to support the farmer's rights.[91] It was the farmers at Bow rather than the mill operatives at Sanbornton who had formed Baker's picture of a class discriminated against by oligarchic legislation.

Earlier, on June 27, 1835, the day the Boston and Lowell Railroad opened, a corporation backed by Isaac Hill obtained a charter to build a railroad to Concord. As plans proceeded, Baker and his friends entered on a crusade to protect the rights of the farmers through whose land the railroad would pass. Hill, who by this time had sold the *Patriot,* now started a rival paper known as *Hill's Patriot* to fight the Radicals on behalf of the railroads. The bitterness of the ensuing factional struggle was reflected in the villainous invective and slander which accompanied it.[92] When Hill attacked young Baker with intemperate animosity, Mary Baker had an early lesson in the ways and means of character defamation.

Of course, Hill finally won. The day of the railroads had come, and despite a last-minute attempt by Baker to repeal all laws granting to corporations the right to take land without the owners' consent, the line was completed and the first passenger train rolled into Concord on September 6, 1842, one year after Albert Baker's death.

Before that untimely event, however, the young man had rolled up a creditable legislative record and had become a leading figure in Democratic state politics. On at least one issue he was highly conservative, and that was the question of slavery, which was coming increasingly and painfully to the fore.

Back in 1820, the year of the Missouri Compromise, the New Hampshire Legislature almost unanimously passed a resolution that the "existence of slavery within the United States is a great moral as well as political evil, the toleration of which can be justified by necessity alone, and the further extension ought to be prevented." But since then various factors, including Nat Turner's slave revolt in Virginia in 1831, the firebrand tactics of the northern abolitionists, and commercial self-interest, had turned the tide of feeling toward a more sympathetic view of the white South. Both Mark and Albert Baker looked on the abolitionists as disrupters of the Union, and in this respect at least they found themselves in league with the conservative interests of both North and South.

In 1840–41 the younger Baker had some correspondence with the great John C. Calhoun himself regarding a dispute between Maine and Georgia over the return of fugitive slaves, and Calhoun wrote him expressing cordial admiration of the report he drew up on the subject. Moreover, as chairman of a special committee on slavery in the legislature, Baker succeeded in having resolutions passed which all but reversed the antislavery statement of 1820. So far as her family was concerned, Mary Baker heard nothing but the case against the abolitionists;[93] slavery itself was regarded by them as a lesser evil than national disunion.

Mary remained at the edge of all these affairs, but the stir and bustle of politics entered into her view of life and she never lost her interest in them even though she later lost her partisanship.[94] There were letters and visits from Albert, reports of his speeches and discussions of his views in the *Patriot*, exciting glimpses of a world where big issues were at stake. Nor did Albert neglect his family. His letters to the temperamental George show brotherly concern:

I am sorry to find your mind in such a state of excitement. Is it possible that you can converse daily with the shades of such sages as Shakespeare and Cobbet and Stewart, and not learn philosophy? . . . One would think from the style of your letter, that all the furies were at work within you. My rule at all times, is, to do the best I can, and whatever happens, if it cannot be avoided, to submit cheerfully. Is not this true philosophy?[95]

Yet for all his philosophy, Albert himself was driven by a passionate energy, as were most of the Bakers, and this lends some poignancy to a letter he wrote early in 1840 to Mary and Martha.[96] In it he told them that he was to give an address before the Bay State Association in Boston—"I shall give them *Radicalism* in all its horrors. No doubt I shall be abused for it, but no matter"—and that he was to go to Baltimore the first of May as a delegate to the Democratic National Convention; but of chief interest is one passage:

If you knew how much satisfaction I take in reading your letters, you would write oftener—though I never wrote. If there is a brother in this world, who is happy in the love of his sisters, it is I. Indeed, it is to me the oasis *in the desert of life—the only spot upon which I rest with* entire *safety. I know there is* honesty *and* sincerity *in a sister's love. But my joy was saddened, upon reading in your postscript, that Mary's health is again in danger.*

The day before Christmas in that same year he wrote Mary a letter which showed that he was being fairly consumed by his own energies:

I think I have never answered your good and kind letter written while at Concord, in which were those lines acknowledging far more than I ever deserved. But it speaks the goodness of your heart, and was worth more to me than money. *I think they excel anything I have seen of yours. . . . I set out for Boston this morning. I am almost worn out. I have scarcely slept two hours for the last two days.*

Before ten months were over he had died.[97] All over the state, as might be expected, eulogies appeared. The one in the *Patriot*, having told how he was graduated from Dartmouth "with the reputation of being one of the most talented, close and thorough scholars, that the institution has ever produced" went on to say:

Of an ardent and enthusiastic temperament, he applied himself soul and body, with a zeal and a perseverance, which never flagged till his physical strength became utterly prostrate, to the improvement of his mind and the acquisition of knowledge. . . .

Mr. Baker was a man of strongly marked character. What he did, he did with all his might. If he pushed things to extremes, it must be attributed to his warm and ardent feelings.[98]

But the strength of factional politics was such that five months later *Hill's Patriot* saw fit to launch an attack on Baker which caused the *Patriot* to reply:

The fiendish malignity with which the lamented Baker has been pursued, even beyond the sacred confines of the tomb, by men who should have defended his memory as a brother in the glorious cause of Equal Rights, will not be lost upon the democracy of New Hampshire. That "young man" defended their principles with honesty and ability to the day of his death.[99]

A few months later the attack was renewed, causing a new burst of eloquence in defense of Baker's memory. Sometime during these months Mary wrote a poem entitled "Lines on reading an attack upon the political career of the late Albert Baker Esqr." The death of Albert was hard enough in itself; now she was learning that character assassination could persist beyond a person's lifetime. If she had only known, she was catching a glimpse of her own future.

6

Albert's death brought her face to face with mortality. The brother and sister had both known the precariousness of human life from their earliest years. But here was the thing itself, so intimately bound up with her hopes for the future that she seemed at first to have lost a piece of her own life.

A month later in a poem which began "O! health, for thee I languish,"[100] she foresaw an early death for herself and wondered whether she would be forgotten. It was not a very good poem, but it showed her baffled by the pain and mystery of finiteness. Back in 1840 Albert had written her:

I hope . . . that amidst the depth of your sufferings, you may receive the satisfaction, to feel, that however great may be your afflictions, it is for your good—that the chastisement is inflicted by that Hand which is never laid upon us but in mercy, though it may appear in anger.

I hope you may yet enjoy health, but whatever may be your lot, I pray you to reflect upon it, with calmness and resignation. The ways of Providence are inscrutable, but however far above us, I rely, with entire confidence in the justice of God; and whatever may happen to me, for good or for evil, I see the same hand in it all—and seeing it, I can say no less, than that God rules, let the earth submit.[101]

This was a far cry from the skeptical Albert of earlier years, but it was also a far cry from his spirited sister. Her poems and letters show her effort to bring herself to a complete acceptance of that "Christian resignation" which the age held out as a prime virtue, but one senses in them a stubborn conviction that life was *meant* for love and joy. It was all very well to submit to God's will, but *was death God's will?*[102]

For many years Mary Baker would pay lip service, and perhaps something more than lip service, to the traditional concept of death as the gateway to heaven, but the eagerness with which she clung to life was in effect a denial of the doctrine. Even when in moments of near despair she would express a longing to join those she loved in a heavenly beyond, one feels beneath the words that resilient love of life which kept her determined to find heaven in the here and now. She was always one who felt that things *mattered* as they happened.

And they did happen, at least to other people. Martha married Luther Pilsbury a year later and moved to Concord. Augusta Holmes shortly before had married Samuel Swasey, a young Democratic politician who was a close friend of Albert's and speaker of the New Hampshire Legislature, and they had settled farther north in Haverhill.

Fortunately George Sullivan Baker had returned to Sanbornton in 1838 to go into partnership with Abigail's husband, Alexander Tilton, in the manufacture of cassimeres and tweeds. He was a warmhearted, popular young man of whom old Governor Pierce had written Mark at the time of his return: "I Sir have had the pleasure of the company of your son Sullivan for two days I think him a young gentleman of fine tallants well informed and of much promise."[103] It was George who had the task of settling Albert's affairs after his death, auctioning off his law library, and incidentally saving his private papers for future biographers of his sister Mary.

There were several young men in Mary's life at this time. John Bartlett of Hill, a student at Sanbornton Academy, was an admirer and would reappear in her life a few years later in a more important role. Then there was her cousin Hildreth Smith, who "discussed philosophy" and "recited poetry"[104] with her and then fell deeply in love with her. Because consanguinity seemed to him an insuperable obstacle to his proposing marriage, he parted from her and went to the South, where in time he became a well-known educator and scholar.[105] In 1906 when Mrs. Eddy was under public attack, he issued a statement worded with old-school gentility:

> I have known the Rev. Mary Baker Eddy from childhood . . .
> She was always a beloved visitor in our home. We corresponded

for several years while I was in college; the correspondence ended with my regret. I have always admired my cousin's sincerity and devotion to good works. Her brother Albert was one of the ablest lawyers of New Hampshire; but Mary was deemed the most scholarly member of her family. She has always held a sacred place in my heart. It gives me great pleasure to find that God is always protecting her.[106]

In 1841 Mary's former teacher, Sarah Jane Bodwell, had married one Charles Lane, who published a local weekly called the *Belknap Gazette*. Miss Bodwell had encouraged Mary's poetic efforts, and now her husband began to publish some of them in his paper. Before long, poems signed by Mary M. Baker began to appear also in the *New Hampshire Patriot and State Gazette*. In a modest way her career as an author had been launched.[107]

Early in 1843 she wrote Augusta, now Mrs. Swasey, a letter in which the normal trifles, jokes, and pieties of the village scene all tumbled out in a heap:

> *Two weeks after you left, I had taken my pen for a long "tete a tete" with dear Augusta; and had not sooner commenced, than all of a sudden a ride was proposed to Concord. . . . Found Martha like yourself believing a lost paradise restored in "the green bower of home" while I unlike his "Satanic Majesty," gaze only to admire and approve. . . . I again sought my materials for a conversation with you; when who should present themselves as the sure precursorer of my letter's fate, but the* marvelous *James Smith! Your* crazy *correspondent* was correct, *so far as pretensions warrant: he professes to have religion, and so far succeeded in* exhausting *that interesting and exalted subject, I grew weary and retired. The next morning (Sabbath) a long series of meetings commenced at the Methodist Church, and continued five weeks held alternately at both societies. . . . But dear Augusta, the meetings were so very interesting, and every day brought with it some extra labor (the constant arival of friends or connexions). . . . Almost all of your acquaintances are now rejoicing in the hope set before them of higher aims and nobler joys. The sceptic's scoff, and the ribaldry of the multitude is scarely left among us.*[108]

Among the converts were her sister Abigail and "Mr. *Bartlett*." Although she feared for some, she rejoiced with many "whom I doubt not possess the 'pearl' which is priceless." A brief "Hymeneal" was added as a postscript: "J. Tilton married—S. Bartlett is soon to be married to Electa Curry (second choice)."

In July, 1843, she took a week's trip to the White Mountains with her brother George. Always a lover of mountain scenery, she entered her rhapsodies in a journal and also wrote a poem, "The Old Man of the Mountain," which was to become one of her most popular verses. At Littleton she parted from George and took the stagecoach to Haverhill to visit Augusta. Two days later she reported in a letter to her brother that she had been the only passenger in the stagecoach "and such a *sky-rocket* adventure I never had; some times I really thought I was at least *midway* between heaven and earth, till the driver's shrill whistle, or a more tolerable road would restore my senses; Mr. Hale is the very most polite good natured driver in the *whole world* (as *I have seen it all*) and was very kind to me on your account I suppose."[109]

The Swaseys wanted her to stay at Haverhill "until commencement," but she found so much to excite her and such a "teazing etiquette" in the village that "it is not best for my health," and she left after a couple of days. Before leaving she took a walk to an Indian encampment "with Mrs. Redding sister to the political demagogue (I. Hill) and a Mrs. Horatio Hill; the latter is from New York and a consummate fool." Mrs. R., on the other hand, "is a sanguine politician, purely radical, and I should think possessing a stored and discriminating mind." The Indians were "healthy and happy, a very good hint from nature." And as a final touch: "Had a very fine game at 'Nine pins.' "[110]

But the journey home brought a night of unexplained anguish in the stagecoach and a determination never again to travel alone at night. Arrived at the inn at Lebanon on the way back to Sanbornton, she threw herself on the bed in utter exhaustion. There seemed to be a heavy price to pay for every pleasure; the jolly Pickwickian stagecoach ride of two days before could be transformed into the nightmare horror of De Quincey's fleeing mail coach.[111]

Trivial in themselves, these incidents suggest something much deeper. On the other side of the world about this time, Søren Kierkegaard was exploring in *Fear and Trembling* and *The Concept of Dread* the immeasurable solitude and subjectivity of human existence. A young girl full of lively hopes but alone and terrified in a stagecoach clattering through the unknown night might serve as the very symbol of the individual predicament as Kierkegaard saw it. A few years later in *The Sickness unto Death* he wrote:

> *Even that which, humanly speaking, is the most beautiful and lovable thing of all, a feminine youthfulness which is sheer peace and harmony and joy—even that is despair. For . . . in the hidden recesses of happiness, there dwells also the anxious*

dread which is despair; it would be only too glad to be allowed to remain therein, for the dearest and most attractive dwelling-place of despair is in the very heart of immediate happiness. All immediacy, in spite of its illusory peace and tranquility, is dread, and hence, quite consistently, it is dread of nothing.[112]

Mary Baker herself would more than once in later years use the gothic image of the death's-head at the feast. Her silvery laughter could never quite drown out the rattle of mirthless bones in the plunging coach at midnight. She had, in a sense, known all her life that mortal existence stood poised on nothingness. While it was fashionable for young ladies to read and write melancholy poems about death, the lines she copied into her notebook at this time seem to have something of the genuine shiver of mortality within their conventional words—perhaps simply because of the eager love of life out of which they were written. Arrived back in Sanbornton from her mountain trip, she copied a poem of Barry Cornwall's which ended:

> We toil through *pain* and *wrong*,
> We *fight* and *fly*,
> We love, and then ere long
> Stone dead we lie.
> Oh! life, is all thy song
> *Endure,* and *die?*

There seems to be more than rhetoric in the words she wrote in the margin: "O God, *is it all?*"

Yet at this very time she had just become engaged to be married. George Washington Glover, who had taken her on his knee at Samuel Baker's wedding twelve years before and said that he would come back to marry her, had come back. A successful builder now in Charleston, South Carolina, he had returned to New Hampshire on occasional visits and on one or two of these occasions had seen the little girl who had so taken his fancy transformed into an attractive young woman, frail in health but with an undeniable radiance that marked her off from the languishing maidens who were very much the fashion just then.

It is not really surprising that a heightened dread of mortality should have accompanied her heightened anticipation. The future opened as boundless possibility—and as unpredictable mystery. It would probably be a mistake to suppose that the foreboding poems she wrote and copied at this time represented her constant or even usual mood. Much of her time was undoubtedly given to excited preparations for departure, to all the normal delights and passing worries of a bride-to-be. And in at least one hour she and her mother

shared an inspiration so unforgettable that it became something
sacred to them.[113]

Yet the premonition of mortality remained. Her family noted
and shared the troubled doubts that accompanied her hopes. At
Thanksgiving George Baker handed her a poem expressing his
concern:

> Say Sister,
> > Why that tear o'er youth's fair cheek
> To scald its hope flushed glow
> Why shrinks that heart in sadness deep
> Which joys of youth should only know
> Thy bark though frail the bark of life
> May safely mount the swelling tide
> Whilst sterling worth and pious aim
> Anchor and helm—with thee abide.[114]

As December closed in with its leaden skies and the day of the
wedding drew near, Mary paid a farewell visit to Albert's grave
and afterwards wrote a poem in which triumph and foreboding were
once more joined, though in a rather bouncing rhythm. Albert's
struggle was ended now, and she wrote:

> "Tis finished" the Saviour triumphantly cried
> "Tis finished" the tears of Gethsemane dried
> And divinity stooped to humanity's tomb
> With the light of his love to encompass its gloom.[115]

But as her thoughts turned back to herself, the shadow fell again,
and she reminded herself:

> Thou too may soon follow the spirit that's fled
> When far from thy kindred and place of the dead.

A few days later, on Sunday, December 10, 1843, she and George
Washington Glover were married at her home in Sanbornton. Following the wedding they left for Concord and during their short
time there took a quick drive to Bow. Later they went on to Boston,
and there, on Christmas Day, 1843, they embarked by ship for that
lovely and tragic South which was everything New England was not.

7

And who, exactly, was George Washington Glover? Mary might
almost have put the question to herself as they settled down for the
stormy sea trip that would take them first to Wilmington, North
Carolina, then on to Charleston.

She had seen little enough of this handsome, successful young man, eleven years her senior,[116] who was so at ease in a world she could scarcely imagine. Yet she had traded her own loved world for him, and now the promise and the problem of the future merged into one.

"Wash" Glover, as his friends called him, Major Glover as he was more formally known by reason of his appointment on the staff of the governor of the state,[117] had gone to Charleston in 1839. There he had quickly become a successful builder in partnership with George W. Logan, member of a prominent Charleston family. Logan was married to Anne D'Oyley Glover of that city, and it may be that the Charleston and Concord Glovers were related. In any case, by 1841 George Glover was "in the heighth of prosperity," as he wrote his friend George Baker.[118] Of seven builders in the city he was doing half the business, and a single Saturday's payroll for his workmen was $1,267, a considerable sum in those days.

His office was just off exclusive Wentworth Street, where the Logans lived. He made casual mention in his letters of dining at the Alhambra, a fashionable coffee house. He was prominent in Masonic affairs, a Royal Arch Mason, an officer of St. Andrew's Lodge. His letters were filled with a genial sort of swagger—if Abbie would name her first son after him ("as I am a Bacheldor") he would give the lad a Negro servant worth a thousand dollars. His spelling rivaled Andrew Jackson's for picturesque phonetic approximations. "I received more solled cumfut in N H in Apral those 3 Dayes than I have receved for the Last 5 years before," he wrote George ("Frend Baker") in 1841.[119]

Such intellectual niceties as spelling were no prerequisite to being accepted as a gentleman in those days in the South, and George was a naturally friendly and popular person. The phrenologist was probably right who said that he was ambitious to excel and liked to be commended "if done genteely."[120] There is in his letters, however, no sign of the sort of sensitivity one might have expected would appeal to Mary, none of the intellectual sensibility that had marked Albert.[121] It may have been the very fact that he was a normal, healthy, well-adjusted young man which attracted Mary— the appeal the ordinary has for the extraordinary.[122]

That George Glover had the power of inspiring both admiration and devotion in his friends is indicated by a letter sent to him in May, 1844, by a French friend on leaving America:

> *Je pars mais mon seul regret est de m'éloigner de vous! Que j'admire cette sincérité! cette franchise! qui font l'ornement de votre âme! oui! je me trouve heureux d'avoir eu un ami, un frère tel que vous; mais malheureux mille fois encore de me*

trouver dans la nécessité de vous abandonner! car le devoir d'un
père de famille m'appelle; et je vous quitte avec le coeur rempli
d'amertume![123]

Mary's own letters home appear to have reassured her family
that beneath George's extrovert cheerfulness there was a tender concern for her welfare. As she lay "hopelessly sea-sick"[124] in their cabin
during the trip south, he opened and read the poem Mrs. Baker
had given them to read midway on their journey—"The Mother's
Injunction" by Lydia Sigourney—and Mary saw "the tears wet on
his cheek" as he read the sentimental yet apposite lines.

The stay in Charleston cannot have been more than a month
at most. It has usually been assumed that Glover had a house and
servants waiting for his bride, but this is questionable.[125] From the
beginning her family spoke of her as bound for Wilmington, to
which the young couple returned very quickly, and from there they
expected to go to Haiti, where George had business. They may
very well have stopped at a hotel or in temporary lodgings for the
short stay in Charleston.

If this be so, it is unlikely that Glover had any house slaves
at the time, although, being a young man of some means and ambition, he may well have had a body servant for himself and a personal
maid for his wife.[126] He may have had the intention of building
a house for himself when the Haiti business had been brought to
a financially successful conclusion or of taking over a fine house on
Hassell Street which he partly owned and was probably renting to
a tenant at the time.[127]

However this may be, almost nothing is known today of the
weeks at Charleston. Here was a vivid scene, crowded for Mary with
new sights and impressions, and all that is known of her response
is the fact that her health was still not good.[128] It might almost be
doubted that she had been there at all, were it not that she was
part of a new literary enterprise being planned at the time. Before
the end of the year *Heriot's Magazine,* subtitled *The Floral Wreath &
Ladies Monthly Magazine,* made its appearance and was advertised
in the Charleston papers. Edited by one Edwin Heriot of Charleston,
it was advertised as containing "besides original contributions, a
variety of selections in prose and verse from the most popular
American female writers, and distinguished writers of this city."
High on the list of contributors was Mary M. Glover, and her name
continued to appear both in the magazine and in the advertisements for it. Here is one tangible link with Charleston.

With the move to Wilmington at the beginning of February
or earlier, the scene becomes concrete again. The Glovers probably

moved straight into the Hanover House, a large boardinghouse or quasi hotel which had just been opened. Glover had been to Wilmington the year before on various construction projects, since a great deal of building was going on there following a devastating fire in 1843. He was consequently already well-known and well-liked, active as in Charleston in Masonic affairs and apparently also in the Oddfellows.[129]

The young couple made an immediate hit, and the months in Wilmington were happy ones for Mary. Among their friends was Thomas W. Brown, a prominent Mason, master of St. John's Lodge. Many years later his daughter Harriet said of Mary: "She was extremely beautiful, one of the prettiest young women I have ever seen. I imagine that she was always great for writing verses, for she had no sooner come to Wilmington than she began contributing rhymes to the local paper. . . . Her enthusiasm about the local scenery amused us."[130]

Her enthusiasm for almost everything there was unbounded. Two blocks north of their hotel was a beautiful old theater where Jenny Lind later sang, and perhaps for the first time in her life Mary was able to go to the theater. Her contributions to the local papers include an ecstatic review of *The Death of Rolla* as performed there.[131]

Also, there were trips—one in particular up the Cape Fear River to Fayetteville with a Mrs. Cook.[132] A Fayetteville friend of Mrs. Cook's, a Mrs. Charles Smith, gave a dinner party for her, and years later a venerable old lady who had been invited to the party to meet her recalled her as "a very beautiful woman, brilliant in conversation, and most gracious in her manner."[133]

In Wilmington the Glovers attended the Episcopal Church. In later years Mrs. Eddy told of how she had missed the simple New England services of her youth and how, in an effort to find that simplicity, she persuaded her husband to take her to a Negro church one Sunday. But the emotionalism she found there was as strange to her as the ritualism of the Episcopalians.[134]

Everywhere, of course, she was confronted with the fact of slavery. Among the marked passages in her Lindley Murray *Reader* are the lines of Cowper:

> [Man] finds his fellow guilty of a skin
> Not colour'd like his own; and having pow'r
> T' inforce the wrong, for such a worthy cause
> Dooms and devotes him as his lawful prey. . . .
> I would not have a slave to till my ground,
> To carry me, to fan me while I sleep,

And tremble when I wake, for all the wealth
That sinews bought and sold have ever earned.

During her stay in the South, Mrs. Glover was probably shielded from the uglier aspects of slavery and saw only the cheerful domestic face it turned to the visitor; yet she can hardly have helped being deeply shaken by the *fact* of slavery. In later years she told of sending pseudonymous antislavery articles to the local papers while she was there, but almost certainly they were never published.[135] In those heated times, if her antislavery views were known at all they may easily have caused her to be labeled an "abolitionist," even though she was not an abolitionist in the political sense for some years to come.

The Jacksonian Democrats detested the abolitionist agitation because it alienated the white South, whose support was vitally necessary to carry through the economic reforms to which they were dedicated. Intensely loyal to the political faith in which she had been brought up, Mrs. Glover found herself involved in contradictions—as, in fact, the whole country was.

Thus when the political campaign of 1844 got under way, she entered the lists not on the side of the abolitionist candidate, James Birney, or even of Henry Clay and the Whig governor of North Carolina, John Morehead, who was as antislavery as a southern governor could be. Instead, she went all out for the Democrats, including Morehead's opponent, Michael Hoke. It is an interesting sidelight that her cousin Hildreth Smith, frustrated in his desire to marry her, was later to wed a relative of Hoke's and that their son, Hoke Smith, would one day be governor of Georgia.

When Clay campaigned through the South in April, Governor Morehead and a delegation of Whigs went to Charleston to escort him to Wilmington. Mrs. Glover seized the occasion to send an anti-Clay jingle to the newspapers. Two months later she was asked by Hoke to write two toasts for a Democratic dinner, one denouncing Whiggery, the other praising Democracy.

Meanwhile, all was not going well with Glover's business. He had put practically all his money into building supplies for a prospective cathedral in Haiti, undoubtedly the largest contract he had yet received, but there were delays that kept him in Wilmington. Moreover, he could not have been very happy about the prospect of taking his bride to such a troubled spot. By 1844 the revolution of the preceding year had been succeeded by new revolts and the island was in a ferment. The Wilmington newspapers of 1843–44 were full of alarming tales of Haitian massacre and terror.

It was reassuring to read on June 12 that "Captain Wescott of the Brig Elizabeth . . . reports that when he sailed May 22nd, the island was gradually recovering its tranquility."[136] But there must still have been misgivings, and a poem by Mrs. Glover entitled "Written in Wilmington N.C. when expecting to leave for the West Indies" shows that now she felt she was *really* leaving her family and the "Home of my heart New England's shore."

Suddenly two calamities fell. The building supplies in which George had invested his money were lost by fire or theft,[137] and Glover himself came down with yellow fever.[138] Stunned with horror, Mrs. Glover sat by his side day after day, praying earnestly and no doubt desperately. His brother Masons did what they could. The records of St. John's Lodge contain an entry on June 25: "Bro. G. W. Glover being represented as very sick and in indigent circumstances, his case was referred to the committee of charities." But nothing was any use. In two more days it was all over.

The next day the City of Wilmington issued and distributed a black-bordered announcement which read: "The citizens of Wilmington are respectfully invited to attend the funeral of Maj Geo W Glover, dec'd, at 6 o'clock P.M. from the Hanover House, to the usual place of interment. June 28th, 1844." The members of St. John's Lodge convened and moved in procession to the Hanover House and thence to the Episcopal Burying Ground, where the Reverend Dr. A. P. Repiton conducted the service.[139]

Of Mrs. Glover's feelings at this time the most significant expression may be a poem she entitled "Thoughts at a Grave":

> Spread o'er the turf
> The spirit's fetterless
> And free to range the golden streets of Heaven
> A higher boon than earth to it was given
> Tenant of loathsome clay
> From sin how blest to be away . . .
> Ye stricken ones who sorrow o'er the sod
> No love of thine outweighs the love of God.
> It is for thee
> Meek at this mystery
> Of Heaven's dark fiat calmly to submit . . .
> Linger not here . . .
> Go forth and to thy duty once again . . .
> Say unto youth say to the hoary head:
> Prove faithful to the living as the dead.

The Puritan ideal had never been merely a passive resignation to God's inscrutable will. There was a commitment to an active faith in life.

Chapter III

Return
1844

Mary Baker Eddy would later write of God as having been "graciously preparing" her during the first half of her life for the discovery of Christian Science. The grace might be visible in retrospect; it was far from evident at the time. In many ways her life now seemed to be a progress from frustration to frustration rather than a triumphal march toward greatness. Yet the final pattern disclosed that delicate interlocking of events which makes a great life seem inevitable when it rounds to its unpredictable end.

To go forward toward her destiny the widowed Mrs. Glover had first to go back toward her beginnings. There was neither reason nor means for her to stay in Wilmington. Glover's money had all been sunk in the lost building materials. Whatever slaves he had— probably not more than one or two at this time[1]—she allowed to go free.[2] The only legacy of importance she would carry back from her brief marriage was Glover's unborn child. The only place for her to go was "home."

Even in the midst of her earlier happiness, home had been reaching out to draw her back. For one thing, there had been family letters, filled with love and anxiety about her health. Mark had written with obvious misgivings, gravely exhorting the young couple: "Give your hearts to God and consult duty and if it should be to quit that unhealthy clime and come to a better it would be pleasing to me."[3] Abigail Baker's letters also gave counsel, though in a gentler fashion: "Dear child receive instruction and in return impart some to your dear George and be happy." "Dear Child be faithful to yourself and you will gain a rich reward."[4]

Unfortunately Abigail found it hard to think of her youngest daughter as other than a little girl. She was glad to hear, she had written in February, that George, like a mother, "tries to make you a good little girl." In the increasingly stifling atmosphere of the mid-nineteenth century there was little recognition of the emotional hazards of such an attitude, and for all that she owed to her mother's love, Mrs. Glover was to have a struggle to escape the thralldom that came from this well-meant but excessive protectiveness.

In May Abigail had written, with a touch of quaint irony, that her "ever dear Child" would undoubtedly be glad "to hear again from your aged mother in her own Ancient style of communication," and then she had poured out the loneliness she felt at being separated from Mary:

> *Dear Child your memory is dearer to* me *than gold every thing reminds me of you language cannot express my feelings my sight is almost failed with weeping & when shall I see you & Dear George I think not very soon but I rejoice to hear from you so often don't write too much for fear it hurts you how is your health and how is your back can you lie down and rise again without a groan? . . . do you remember our Twilight meeting? it is a precious time to me for there I feel like meeting with you and sometimes I fear I worship mary instead of the great jehovah.*[5]

Mrs. Glover's feelings had been expressed in a poem entitled "To my Mother, after a long separation," written during these months and published later in *Heriot's Magazine*,[6] and the lines she wrote when expecting to leave for Haiti were also full of her love for the scenes of her youth. These were normal enough expressions of sentiment from a young bride thoroughly delighted by her new life but looking back a little nostalgically to the one she had left. It is reasonable to assume that if it had not been for Glover's early death she would have grown into her new life with increasing absorption.

For three weeks after that unhappy event, she remained in Wilmington, settling Glover's affairs and gaining strength for the ordeal of the journey to New England. The Wilmington Masons arranged for one of their number to accompany her North; in fact, their kindness to the young widow was something she would remember with gratitude for the rest of her days.[7] When she finally left on July 19, they all came to see her off, including Dr. Repiton, the chaplain of the lodge.[8]

In the poem which she inevitably wrote to commemorate the occasion, she addressed the friends who "crowd in throngs around me" and with a sense of real regret at the parting announced, "I am now alone in soul." The poem ended by turning back in thought to "childhood's home" and asking whether "a *Mother's* fondest welcome" could fail to dry her tears.[9]

Before she could receive the ambivalent comfort of her mother's welcome she and her Masonic escort had to make a long, slow journey in midsummer heat and painful discomfort; first, by rail to Weldon,

North Carolina; thence "through the dismal swamp" to Portsmouth, Virginia; from there by steamboat to Baltimore and then by another steamboat to Frenchton, where they changed to railroad again and crossed Delaware to New Castle; there another steamboat took them to Philadelphia and still another to Bristol, Pennsylvania; from there the railroad carried them to Jersey City and the ferry to New York.[10]

After one night's rest in the American Hotel in that city—from whose overpowering heat Edgar Allen Poe had just rescued his child-wife by finding her a cottage outside the city—the travelers proceeded by boat to Stonington, Connecticut, thence by rail to Boston, where they changed cars once again for Concord, finally arriving by stage or carriage at Sanbornton Bridge, having traveled about fourteen hundred miles in four days and nights, according to Mrs. Glover's calculations in her notebook. It was a grim enough journey for anyone; it may well have been a nightmare to the exhausted young widow in her advanced state of pregnancy.

At the end of the journey was "home." In one way it was comfort and safety, a return to the well-loved nest, to the brooding wings of the mother bird. In another sense it was failure and defeat, a return to dependency, to the tyranny of the customary and the outgrown. The independence she had begun to savor as a socially successful young matron must now be surrendered. The adventure was over.

As always, she tried to make the best of adversity. In a poem entitled "The Widow's Prayer," which was published along with Glover's obituary in the *Freemasons' Monthly Magazine*,[11] she wrote:

> For trials past I would not grieve,
>> But count my mercies o'er;
> And teach the heart Thou hast bereaved
>> Thy goodness to adore.
> Thou gavest me friends, in my distress,
>> Like manna from above;
> Thy mercy ever I'll confess,
>> And own a Father's love.

Yet a bright hope lay extinguished in George Glover's grave: the promise of romantic escape to freedom and fulfillment. There had scarcely been time for the young couple's love to grow deep roots, but her grief was probably no less sharp for that. A special poignancy attaches to the eager hope that is cut down before it has had a chance to measure itself against life.

Something of this is suggested in another poem Mrs. Glover wrote a little later, called "Wind of the South."[12] Carried back in thought by that "gay restless essence," the south wind, the author confronts George Glover's grave in an image whose sudden, flawed beauty has just a touch of the dark lyricism of the Jacobean poets:

> Oh say do worms dare revel round
> The *casket* where no gems can rust?
> Hath loveliness a level found
> Beneath the cold and common dust?

It was her farewell to the more romantic dreams of youth.

2

When George Glover's son was born on September 12, 1844, he wailed in protest long beyond the time that is held proper for babies to cry.[13] He was born into a house of gloom, to a mother who remained deathly ill. It has been frequently stated, although the evidence for this is not clear,[14] that Mrs. Glover received a serious injury during the birth of her child. In any case, the trials preceding if not during the birth, coming on top of her chronic ill health, made her an almost total invalid for several months.

During this time the baby was nursed by a Mrs. Morrison, who had recently had twins and then lost one of them. Mrs. Glover meanwhile was cared for by Mahala Sanborn, the blacksmith's daughter, who was a cross between "hired girl" and family friend in the Baker household.

A letter from Mahala to "Dear Dear Mary," written while Mrs. Glover was still living happily in Wilmington, shows the warmth of this simple countrywoman's feeling for her "Dear and old friend M" and also gives an indication why she was chosen first to care for Mrs. Glover and then for Mrs. Glover's son during the periods when illness prevented his mother from looking after him:

> *Mrs. Ack is vary sick indeed they fear she is in a consumption she apears vary well reconcild indeed I am not certain whether she is aware of her situation or not but should rather think she was: what a lost those Dear little children will meet with to be left orphans so young my heart akes for them when I think of their being left in a cold hearted world alone without Father or Mother to protect them from the cold looks and words of this unfeeling uncharitable world Mary I know how to pity them you know vary well. . . .*[15]

As soon as Mrs. Glover was well enough, little George Washington Glover[16] was given back into her care; but the presence in the same household of Abigail Baker, constantly watchful to see that she did not take on too much responsibility, and of Mahala Sanborn, whose maternal instinct quickly attached itself to the baby, did not make the young mother's task any easier.

That she felt a deep hunger for children throughout her life is suggested by the way she spontaneously reached out to them whenever possible, delighted in their society, formed close attachments to them, and in return was adored by them.[17] Yet in her relationship to her son George she was constantly balked by circumstance— "circumstance, that unspiritual god," to use the phrase she copied into her notebook and quoted in her writing. Later she might see in this same circumstance the indirect working of providence, weaning her affections away from a limited purpose to a limitless concern; but at the time it looked only like frustration.

In her later relationship to the church she founded she sometimes used the metaphor of a mother and child. The ideal of motherhood set forth in such a passage as the following one contrasts with the role forced on her by ill health in relation to her own son:

> *The true mother never willingly neglects her children in their early and sacred hours, consigning them to the care of nurse or stranger. Who can feel and comprehend the needs of her babe like the ardent mother? What other heart yearns with her solicitude, endures with her patience, waits with her hope, and labors with her love, to promote the welfare and happiness of her children? Thus must the Mother in Israel give all her hours to those first sacred tasks, till her children can walk steadfastly in wisdom's ways.*[18]

In her last years, with a worldwide movement to care for, she would frequently recount to members of her household incidents of George's babyhood or childhood, the sort of anecdote treasured by mothers even in the age of Freud and Spock. But the first picture to emerge from these anecdotes is that of a baby who howled lustily and refused to be comforted. Mrs. Baker at one point asked her daughter if there was anything she had longed for during her pregnancy in the South, and Mrs. Glover like a true daughter of New England answered that she had longed for Boston baked beans. The liquid from the beans was thereupon tried on the baby, who gulped it down with relish but continued to howl.[19]

More effective than this old wives' treatment was the psychology of a young man who was a friend of the family—possibly John Bartlett of Hill. Visiting them one day, he found the baby screaming in his mother's arms. With her permission he took the child into the next room, where she could hear him addressing it: "I know what you want; you want a father, you want your Papa. I am going to be your father, little man, I'll be your Papa." The baby quieted down and never again screamed in the same inconsolable fashion.[20] The incident gave Mrs. Glover something to think about, but it did not give the baby a permanent father.

As George grew, he developed into a boisterous, headstrong child who seemed to have inherited all his father's bouncing energies and none of his mother's sensitiveness. In temperament he might almost have been the child of Mahala, who was good-hearted and coarse-grained, not particular about niceties of behavior and totally without "nerves." Mrs. Glover simply lacked the health and independence to bring up George in accordance with her own ideas.

It is doubtful that in any case she would have conformed to the Victorian ideal of a penniless widow with a child. In Catherine Sedgwick's novel *Home,* which Harriet Martineau had praised for its high moral tone, the author told of a pastor's daughter who "married a merchant, lived prosperously in a city for two or three years, and then returned a widow, penniless, and with an only son, to her father's house"—a New England farm, as it happened. "She bore her reverses meekly," wrote Miss Sedgwick, "and directed all her energies to one subject,—the *sine qua non* of a New England mother,—a good education for her son."[21]

Mrs. Glover was certainly concerned about the education of her son.[22] Even in *Science and Health* she would take occasion to remind the reader: "A mother is the strongest educator, either for or against crime,"[23] and in a poem addressed to George while he was still a small child she wrote:

> O heaven-born task, to watch thy dawning mind,
> Each day's development of ripening thought—
> To sit and see almost the twig inclined,
> The pliant sapling form the sturdy oak.[24]

But her "meekness" did not follow the pattern of her day, which so often meant cloaking a psychologically unhealthy possessiveness in the garments of self-sacrificing devotion. She was not prepared to make her son a substitute for further creative living of her own, an emotional surrogate for the fulfillment of her still undiscovered capacities.

The genteel ideal of womanhood is typically stated by one writer of the period: "The peculiar province of a Woman is to tend with patient assiduity around the bed of sickness; to watch the feeble steps of infancy; to communicate to the young the elements of knowledge, and bless with their smiles those of their friends who are declining in the vale of tears."[25] This sort of watery self-effacement was not the path that led to the discovery of Christian Science.

Seldom in the history of the sexes has there been an age when women suffered more than in the nineteenth century from the false ideals imposed on them by the prevailing culture. Words like "home" and "mother" were debased to a level of sentimentality so extravagant that the twentieth century still winces away from them. Few women escaped entirely the insipidity of language and the pretentious falsity of sentiment that were part of the phenomenon; but common sense and spiritual honesty broke through again and again, as they will in any age, to let in the fresh air.

So far as can be judged from the available evidence, and so far as her health allowed, Mrs. Glover exercised the normal responsibilities of motherhood and experienced its normal joys and worries.

Both her sisters had had children about the same time as she. Martha Pilsbury had given birth to a daughter, Ellen, several months before, and Abigail Tilton to a son, Albert, several months after. When George was three, Mrs. Glover wrote Martha: "Oh! Mat, to see the three *beautiful* children meet and gather in wonder. . . . Little Geo. is very good and very *naughty,* not subject to any judicious discipline. He loves you and Nell most dearly . . . he identifies Nell with every little girl he sees; kiss her a thousand times for us both."[26]

It was her love of children which suggested to Mrs. Glover a possible way of supporting herself and George. About the time of his birth the old Sanbornton Academy was succeeded by another institution, the New Hampshire Conference Seminary, under the auspices of the New Hampshire Conference of the Methodist Episcopal Church. The new principal was a young Methodist minister, the Reverend Richard S. Rust, who soon became very friendly with the Baker family. At his suggestion, Mrs. Glover in 1846 opened an "infant school" which has been described by a later principal of the seminary[27] as one of the first kindergartens in New England, although Mrs. Glover clearly knew nothing of the theories of Pestalozzi and Froebel.[28]

The most vivid memory which the children in the school appear to have retained of it in later years was of marching around the room and singing,

> We will go to Mrs. Glover
> And tell her we love her—

an adaptation of a popular song of the period. However, two of them, half a century or more later, added rather more illuminating recollections or comments.

Sarah Clement Kimball, who as a little girl all but idolized Mrs. Glover, recalled the one occasion on which she was afraid of her:

> *I was an "enfant terrible" at times and one day [Mrs. Glover] said she would have to whip me so to go out and choose a stick. I went out in fear and trembling and brought in a little twig, the smallest I could find. When I took it to her, she looked at it and then at me and then she smiled—and I don't have to go way back to remember her smile because no one who has ever seen it would be likely to forget it, for she had the most beautiful smile. She told me to go and take my seat and that ended the incident.[29]*

Thomas F. Page wrote in more philosophical vein, "Looking backward now to those days I can see in her that which I could not then because of my age and inexperience." There seems to be in some people, he went on, a genius "wholly unknown to any but they of the Spirit." Such individuals "find hard contact with the masses, and, wherein they excel, such excellence is counted at a discount, they are reckoned as not quite up to the human standard by those who are not strong in spirit."[30]

As this reminiscence suggests, Mrs. Glover's experiment was not accounted a success in Sanbornton Bridge. This is not altogether surprising when one remembers the way in which the earlier innovations of an inspired teacher like Bronson Alcott caused him to be ridiculed and driven out of a similar country community. However, for several years afterwards the seminary conducted a primary department, a fact which a present-day educator in Tilton (as Sanbornton Bridge was renamed in 1869) takes as evidence of the essential effectiveness of Mrs. Glover's effort.[31] That she herself was not asked to conduct the department may have been due either to renewed ill health or to village opposition.

In any case, the young principal of the seminary, Dr. Rust, retained what in 1902 he described as his "high appreciation of [Mrs. Glover's] character and ability."[32] He employed her as a substitute teacher in the seminary at one period[33] but was unable to offer a regular position which would allow her to maintain herself and George independently. The care of the child, her own recurring poor health, and the fact that despite her intellectual liveliness her schooling had been far from regular or systematic, these were all obstacles to her making a career of teaching. In 1848 she wrote Martha:

> *I feel as if I must begin something this summer, if my health is sufficient. I am weary working my way through life*

from the middle *to the* end. *I want to learn to play on a piano so that I can go south and teach. Tis all I shall ever be* able *to do, and this* once *accomplished and I am independent. . . . O, how I wish I had a* Father *that had been* ever *willing to let me know something. . . .* [34]

The sense of frustration she felt was shared by a good many women of her time. It is not surprising that she read with delight the novels of Charlotte Brontë[35] as they appeared; she may well have felt a kinship with those spirited young heroines, outwardly so decorous and inwardly so rebellious. Even while she wrote a sentimental poem "To a Wild Rose" for the Young Ladies' Literary Society[36] at the seminary or a gushingly feminine tribute to "Odd Fellowship" in *The I.O.O.F. Covenant*,[37] she was in a state of far deeper protest against women's lot than she yet knew how to express.[38]

She was not, however, a part of the feminist movement which was then forming. In 1845 Margaret Fuller's *Woman in the Nineteenth Century* had been published, with its passionate statement of woman's special genius. All soul is the same, wrote the great Margaret, but "in so far as it is modified in her as Woman, it flows, it breathes, it sings, rather than deposits soil or finishes work; and that which is especially feminine flushes in blossom the face of the earth, and pervades like air and water all this solid seeming globe." Women of genius, she wrote, even more than men, "are likely to be enslaved by an impassioned sensibility. The world repels them more rudely, and they are of weaker bodily frame. . . . Sickness is the frequent result of this overcharged existence." She herself knew this wearisome disability, and it was in vain that she wrote a friend, "I intend to get perfectly well, if possible, for Mr. Carlyle says 'it is wicked to be sick.' "[39]

Other women, less sibylline than Miss Fuller, were taking up the more prosaic but vitally necessary task of battling for women's rights in the civil sphere. Under the leadership of Lucretia Mott and Elizabeth Cady Stanton, the Seneca Falls Convention of 1848 launched a Declaration of Sentiments which was in effect a Declaration of Independence for women.

There is no evidence that Mrs. Glover was aware of this development, nor did she ever become a militant member of the crusade to which it led. In her chapter on "Marriage" in *Science and Health* she would later write:

> *Our laws are not impartial, to say the least, in their discrimination as to the person, property, and parental status of the two sexes. If the elective franchise for women will remedy*

the evil without encouraging difficulties of greater magnitude, let us hope it will be granted. A feasible as well as rational means of improvement at present is the elevation of society in general and the achievement of a nobler race for legislation,— a race having higher aims and motives.[40]

Even more basic than her concern with women's lot was her concern with the human lot. Legislation might help to correct social inequities and implement women's natural rights, but a "nobler race" would demand a new concept of both man and woman.

During the years of her widowhood in Sanbornton Bridge, Mrs. Glover's concern with her own immediate predicament outweighed any interest she may have had in questions of abstract social justice. At least on the surface, she appeared to be a talented but untrained young mother seeking some means of supporting herself and her son. The occasional teaching and writing she did was far from adequate for the purpose. She may have looked forward to a distant future when young George Glover would climb to eminence in the world of men and champion the right, but meanwhile she had a life to live, a purpose of her own to find.

3

When Andrew Jackson died in 1845, a glowing elegy entitled "Death of Jackson" by Mary M. Glover appeared in the *Patriot* soon after.[41]

It has been remarked ironically that Mrs. Glover was probably the only writer in America to refer to the tough old warrior as "sainted," and the epithet is certainly remarkable even if put into the context of the religiously moving accounts of the scene at his deathbed. In a degree it was the tribute of a young woman sheltered from the rough-and-tumble conflicts of a man's world, but it was also an index of Mrs. Glover's genuine love and admiration for a real fighter.

In her study of nineteenth-century woman, Margaret Fuller had just written: "Male and female represent the two sides of the great radical dualism. But in fact they are perpetually passing into one another. Fluid hardens to solid, solid rushes to fluid. There is no wholly masculine man, no purely feminine woman."

Intensely feminine though she was, Mrs. Glover yet possessed qualities which in time would cause Mark Twain to refer to her as "the most daring and masculine and masterful woman that has appeared on the earth in centuries."[42] A hint of these qualities appears in her attitude to the Mexican War.

These were stirring times. A sense of limitless possibilities contended with a sense of intolerable injustices. It was Texas that focused the moral issues for many Americans when at the end of 1845 that great territory was annexed to the Union. A few months later Mexican and American soldiers clashed. The common man, South and North, rushed to recruit. But when war was actually declared in May, public opinion was split down the center.

Henry Thoreau went to jail (for a day) rather than pay a tax to a government which he considered to be waging an iniquitous war for the extension of slavery. James Russell Lowell and John Greenleaf Whittier launched powerful attacks against it in their poetry on the same grounds. The abolitionists opposed the war almost to a man.

On the other hand, most of the old Jacksonians hailed it enthusiastically. It was manifest destiny, an inevitable struggle waged for the extension of American democracy, however marred that democracy might at present be by the exploitation of black slave and, for that matter, white wage earner. Walter Whitman, the Brooklyn editor who had not yet become the bardic Walt of later years, urged that it was for "the interest of mankind" that the power and territory of the United States should be extended—"the farther the better."

Mrs. Glover had no doubts. In a poem written at the start of the war she declaimed:

> Rouse free men from the lethargy
> Of peace—ye long have slept
> Rouse if your country's honor calls
> To victory or death . . .
>
> Save from dishonor save from crime
> And guard each priceless pearl
> Unfold a second Washington
> To an admiring world.[43]

Actually the war unfolded only General Zachary Taylor,[44] but Mrs. Glover's enthusiasm remained undiminished to the end. In the last months of the war the *Patriot* published four poems by her on the same theme: "Lines on the Death of Colonel Ransom," "The Grave of [Major Samuel] Ringgold," "Our Country," "American Heroes' Festival."[45] For all their marks of being hastily composed journalistic verse, they show a certain verve and energy, while here and there a line or phrase leaps out with sudden power.[46]

It is worth noting that these verses were written in the very year that a Connecticut Yankee, Elihu Burritt, initiated the first world peace congress at Brussels. In her last years Mary Baker Eddy was to give warm support to the peace movement, but in 1848 she was caught up in the romantic heroism of war, although it was obviously the courage rather than the carnage that she admired.

The historian Francis Parkman, on board a British troopship a few years earlier, gave the soldier's case with a sort of truculent male energy. Describing a Church of England service on shipboard, with "rough soldiers and sailors" making the responses in the litany, he wrote:

> *A becoming horror of dissenters, especially Unitarians, prevails everywhere. No one cants here of temperance reform, or of systems of diet—eat, drink, and be merry is the motto everywhere, and a stronger and hardier race of men . . . never laughed at the doctors. Above all there is no canting of peace. A wholesome system of coercion is manifest in all directions—thirty-two pounders looking over the bows—piles of balls on deck—muskets and cutlasses hung up below—the red jackets of marines—and the honest prayer that success should crown all these warlike preparations, yesterday responded to by fifty voices. There was none of the new-fangled suspicion that such belligerent petitions might be averse to the spirit of a religion that inculcates peace as its foundation. And I firmly believe that there was as much hearty faith and worship in many of those men as in any feeble consumptive wretch at home, who when smitten on one cheek literally turns the other likewise—instead of manfully kicking the offender into the gutter.*[47]

Mrs. Glover may have admired the courage and energy of those who were ready to do battle for their convictions, but her concept of manfulness led her to a far different conclusion from Parkman's. Through the logic of her own Christian convictions she was eventually to arrive at the point where she would give her chief admiration to the spiritual hero who has sufficiently conquered himself to turn the other cheek.

Later in the century Gerard Manley Hopkins, with a vigor equal to Parkman's but with a good deal more perceptiveness, wrote of the Christ who "knows war, served this soldiering through," and explained the soldier as spiritual metaphor.[48] It was as metaphor that the fighting man, and especially the heroic leader, appealed to Mrs. Glover. Her verses celebrate majors, colonels, and—above all—generals, and one catches in these symbolic figures the hint of her own coming generalship. Margaret Fuller had seen no reason why a woman should not be a sea captain if she wished, and one might say that Mary Baker was born to lead an army.

Yet in 1848 all this was undeveloped, prophesied only in an occasional flash of poetry. That was the year Elizabeth Blackwell won the degree of M.D. and thus became the first woman physician of modern times, but Mrs. Glover still thought of becoming a piano teacher.

That was also the year of the *Communist Manifesto* and Thoreau's *Civil Disobedience,* of the Chartist movement in England and the Free Soil movement in America, of the California Gold Rush and the tide of Irish immigration. Moved by the desperate plight of the Irish peasant in the potato famine, Mrs. Glover had written in the September, 1847, issue of *The Covenant* an article called, surprisingly enough, "Erin, the Smile and the Tear in thine Eyes," which bears witness to her wider interests:

> *When Burke and Berkeley are forgotten; when the name of Emmett shall cease to be spoken; when the last thunder-tones of O'Connell shall have died along the shore of the sweet isle of the ocean, then may Ireland be accused of want of intellect. . . . It is not that the Irish are naturally indolent, that their condition is thus wretched; and in proof thereof we have only to look at the rail-roads and canals that checker our country, wrought by Irishmen, who were driven cruelly from their native land, by abject poverty. Compelled to pay rent for that which is his own by right, taxed for the support of a government which does little else but multiply his wrongs, tithed for the support of a ministry he cannot hear preach,—he is kept like the drowning man who inhales the fresh draught, but to struggle, and sink, and rise and sink again.*

Now, in 1848, it seemed as though all tyranny were to be overthrown. Revolution swept through Europe. Bourbons tumbled and Hapsburgs trembled as names like Kossuth and Mazzini were caught up into the electric atmosphere. Soon enough it was all over: reaction triumphant, disillusionment rampant, liberalism driven to exile in America. In a poem "To General Cass" in the *Patriot* Mrs. Glover wrote:

> From o'er the wave a wail of woe
> Booms like the midnight gun;
> And shall our free-born souls forego
> Scorn for the Austrian crown,
> In purple gore of martyrs dyed?
> Life, liberty down-trod!
> Brave Hungary, thy tears be dried,
> Stretch forth thine arm to God![49]

If we seem to catch here a prophetic glimpse of the founder of *The Christian Science Monitor,* it is only in the most general sort of way. Mrs. Glover was interested in the world around her but she was not yet ready to give herself to any cause.

There were causes enough to choose from. The great nineteenth-century wave of reform was daily gathering volume. A characteristic reformer of the day was Dorothea Dix, who in 1845 completed a ten-thousand-mile journey around the land, visiting jails, almshouses, state prisons, and other institutions to examine and expose the intolerably callous treatment of the insane. There was the temperance movement, in which Albert Baker had been active, and which succeeded in having prohibition voted in New Hampshire in 1848 by state referendum, although it was not implemented by law till 1855. There was the plight of the mill operatives, including the "ladies of the loom" at Lowell, hard pressed by cheap immigrant labor; and although New Hampshire legislated a ten-hour working day in 1847 ostensibly to protect these girls, the mill owners (probably including Abigail's husband, Alexander Hamilton Tilton) had taken steps to circumvent the law and procure the signatures of their employees to contracts permitting them to work as many hours as the employers saw fit.

Above all, there was the crusade against slavery. Three days before Jackson died the issue flared up in New Hampshire in a famous debate in the Old North Church in Concord, Nathaniel Bouton's church. The debate was between Franklin Pierce and John P. Hale, the first abolitionist member of the United States Senate. Mrs. Glover's sympathies were inevitably divided between her anti-slavery sentiments and her personal loyalty to Pierce, the loyalty persisting right down to the presidential election of 1852. In that year her crusading zeal went into the election campaign for Pierce,[50] clear evidence that she was still not an abolitionist in the political sense despite the passage of the Fugitive Slave Law two years before.[51]

To some extent she may even have resisted an emotional involvement which, ill and dependent as she was, could have exhausted her energies in a harrowing struggle she was simply not equipped to carry on at that time. This is suggested by her response to *Uncle Tom's Cabin* when it flamed across the world and shook the nation's conscience as nothing else had. She had read the book, she mentioned in a letter, but didn't think much of it.[52]

Chattel slavery was evil enough, in all conscience, but it was not the form of enslavement that was to call forth her own astounding generalship. That was still a long way off, and meanwhile she struggled with personal circumstance. Later she would become convinced that if one went deep enough one might find in the most private circumstance the common source of every form of slavery.[53]

In a famous passage in *Uncle Tom's Cabin*,[54] Harriet Beecher Stowe put into the mouth of St. Clare, the idealistic Louisiana slaveholder, a pronouncement which throws much light on the times:

> *One thing is certain,—that there is a mustering among the masses, the world over; and there is a* dies irae *coming on, sooner or later. The same thing is working in Europe, in England, and in this country. My mother used to tell me of a millennium that was coming, when Christ should reign, and all men should be free and happy. And she taught me, when I was a boy, to pray, "Thy kingdom come." Sometimes I think all this sighing, and groaning, and striving among the dry bones foretells what she used to tell me was coming. But who can abide the day of His appearing?*

It was a question that occurred to many as the shadow of apocalypse wavered across the complacent materialism of the age.

4

Today human life is frequently interpreted as a search for identity. The existential questions which so often lie beneath the surface of thought have been brought up for intense and troubled examination. Who am I? Why am I? Is it possible to live authentically in a world that exists on the edge of nothingness? Is there an "I" separable from the accidents of heredity, the limitations of environment, the common doom of mortality?

In the years of her young widowhood Mrs. Glover appears to have been groping for a valid answer to these questions. Torn between being a daughter and a mother, a girl with an unfulfilled craving for happiness and a general without an army, a commission, or even a cause, she seemed in a sense adrift in the human scene. This is reflected in several letters she wrote in the early months of 1848.

In one to her brother George, who had been away from home for some months and was at that time ill, she wrote:

> *Oh! if I could be near you when you suffer, I might prove by acts what it is no use to talk about; but this has never been and perhaps never will be my chance yet Geo. my heart has its own secrets, and sometimes they are unfriendly to my eyes in solitude. But what is the use for me to weep? . . . Fate has always denied me an opportunity to fulfill my nature, and never but in one instance did I enjoy the luxury of sorrow relieved by effort;*

and that was when day and night I watched alone by the couch of death—and Oh! when I think thereon I love to weep . . . but enough—forgive me![55]

Later on, in the same letter, she rallied her naturally cheerful spirits to tell of an evening when William Sleeper, the young principal of the Woodman Sanbornton Academy, and one Luther Bean had come around with her friend Martha Rand, who eighteen months later would marry George, to get a Christmas box ready for him. As she describes the scene, we see the country schoolgirl of ten years before, still a dependent daughter in a Puritan home:

> *I was placed in peculiar circumstances Sleeper . . . would get off his jokes about a ledge and Martha would blush! well I didn't know just how to manage that but I tried to make the evening as pleasant as I could to all but we got pretty loud once a laughing and the door opened and Mother came in. Father was a bed and I supposed she was. Well she governs her own house so she sat till they left. I tried to keep up the sport with her. . . . Do forgive this horrid writing Geo is at my elbow and I have been but a short minute writing it Little Geo often speaks of you and asks me when he is in the parlor to lift him up to kiss uncle Geo. [i.e., his picture] and I have done it.*[56]

A letter to her sister Martha shows the same vacillation of mood. Looking forward to the time when she and little George would be able to greet Martha and her Nell "with a torrent of screams resembling some semi-savages," she went on to lament the fact that her life seemed to have no direction, and then she continued with a rapid alternation of melancholy and high spirits:

> *My heart aches for you and Luther both, to be separated as you have been; besides* I know how *to sympathise with all the sons and daughters of poverty or distress! and then I know what it is to be sick and alone from home; and last tho not least, what it is to feel completely unhappy at home But I hope to be able to take care of myself again sometime at least by the help of friends. . . . There has been some sleigh riding—and because of the license of Leap Year I and Miss Lane the Sem. teacher and Miss Rand invited our Driver and took a ride to Concord! after driving, returned to Loudon; supped, then came home, had a real spree with ourselves no Gents. Made the driver (Sleeper) foot the bill and laugh at the joke. What do you think of this. Wasn't it genteel?*[57]

A third letter, this time to Martha Rand, shows a certain listlessness behind a good deal of "literary" melancholy and indicates the young widow's feeling of planlessness: "I have almost relinquished the hope of being at Concord this Summer to take lessons on the Piano; and shall wait at home for some breeze or billow to stir my future course. Oh, Mathy, how I wish we could be together this ensuing summer, get a school together or in some way manage it."[58]

It was inevitable that Mrs. Glover should regard the village life that flowed around her—even before the Bakers in 1849 moved from their farm into the village itself—in an equivocal fashion.

In her copy of *The Scarlet Letter* (an 1883 edition) she later marked several passages of Hawthorne's introductory essay on the Salem Custom House. These passages were of no intrinsic significance but were evidently of interest to her because of the parallels she could draw with her own feelings about Sanbornton Bridge. In one of the scored passages Hawthorne remarked that although he had dwelt much away from his native town, it "possesses, or did possess, a hold on my affections, the force of which I have never realized during my seasons of actual residence here." On the other hand he was weary of "the old wooden houses, the mud and dust, the dead level of site and sentiment, the chill east wind, and the chillest of social atmospheres."

The Sanbornton atmosphere had its own chill. Mrs. Glover, as widow and mother, was still an extremely attractive young woman, and this inevitably caused a certain amount of small-town gossip. Sarah Clement, the niece of her girlhood friend Augusta Holmes Swazey, sixty years later described her as she was at this time:

> Tall, slender, and exceedingly graceful, she was altogether one of the most beautiful women I have ever seen. Her hair was wonderful, soft, silky, of a reddish brown tint, and very curly, the sort that is dark in the shadow, but has a gold or reddish tint in the sunlight. Both she and Mrs. Tilton wore it looped up in ringlets, parted in the middle of the forehead, and drawn toward the back of the head where it formed a cascade of curls. . . . She had beautiful eyes, bluish gray I should say . . . her teeth even, white, and very lovely. . . . My uncle, who died only a few years ago, said that as a boy he used to sit in church without thinking of the service, his thoughts being busy contemplating Mrs. Glover's beauty.[59]

This same witness also spoke of "gossip" and "silly stories" about Mrs. Glover which had wide circulation in the town—criticism, for instance, of the many visits to the Baker house by Dr. Rust, the young Methodist minister who was president of the seminary: "Mother said that no one who knew [Mrs. Glover] would dream of commenting upon [these visits], but the factory hands, a low lot themselves, made a great deal of it." Mark Baker had been a trustee of the old San-bornton Academy for eight years, his home was one where books were read, and it was natural enough that Rust should find it congenial. If he was in love with anyone, it was with the whole Baker family, as his published tribute to Mrs. Baker after her death makes clear.[60]

However, there were actual suitors to set tongues wagging. Particularly there was John H. Bartlett, formerly a student at the San-bornton Academy and now at the Harvard Law School. From the early occasion in 1837 when he was groomsman and Mary Baker bridesmaid at a local wedding, he reappears from time to time on the scene. At one point he gave her the inevitable autograph album, and in succeeding years he made her gifts of James Thomson's *The Seasons* and Martin Tupper's *Proverbial Philosophy*.

In the spring of 1847 she paid a visit to his home at Hill, but in 1848 she disclaimed any intention of marrying him. To Martha Pilsbury she wrote, "I *shall not marry* anyone I know at present—the future however may do better by me in this respect."[61] To Martha Rand she wrote that Bartlett had been visiting her home (not her personally), that he intended to go to Wisconsin after his graduation in August, and that she hoped people would then mind their business about the two of them "for I am getting a little *mad* at their lies."[62]

Despite this protest, the two evidently drew nearer an engagement, for Mrs. Baker wrote George Sullivan in September of the same year that "Mary . . . went to Cambridge and attended Commencement saw Mr. Bartlett take his degree I think her mind is fully established."[63] Apparently a secret engagement followed at some point, the secrecy perhaps reflecting Mrs. Glover's continued uncertainty. The impelling motive for considering marriage may well have been to get a home and a father for young George, but Bartlett could not yet offer that sort of security. In 1847 he had written her, "Shall I despair and repine because *poverty gazes* at *me* with *eyes* as *big* as full *moons?*"[64] In 1849, after a short period of law practice, he headed for Sacramento, at that time booming with opportunities of every sort as the Gold Rush mounted to fever pitch. Presumably Mrs. Glover was to follow him there when he made good.

This was an age when a healthy realism between the sexes was hard to achieve. Artificiality, sentimentality, prudery—the nineteenth-century convention of "the lady"—affected not only manners, clothes, household furnishings, and literary style but almost every aspect of human relations. When Sarah Josepha Hale opened the door for women to enter journalism by her long, commercially successful editorship of *Godey's Lady's Book,* she achieved her success by catering to just this cosseted-and-corseted, blushing-and-fainting feminine ideal.

Many of Mrs. Glover's journalistic contributions in these years reflect the taste of the period—like the sentimental potboiler she called "Emma Clinton, or A Tale of the Frontiers."[65] Such writings suggest her general uncertainty of direction as well as her desire to earn a measure of independence for herself and George. Like the fashions of the day which she followed in her dress, they relate her to her age without giving any hint of the free, forward movement of which she was capable.

Griswold's *Female Poets of America*, first published in 1847, illustrates all too generously what readers wanted.[66] A year or two before in a series of articles on "The Literati" written for *Godey's Lady's Book*, Poe had praised "the starry sisterhood" which was producing verse of this genre, though Hawthorne was later to complain that the whole literary scene was given over "to a damned mob of scribbling women." The queen of all the women poets was Felicia Hemans; and the 1847 edition of her *Poetical Works* which Mrs. Glover owned is well marked and underlined. In one place the ardent reader wrote the word "Glorious" opposite a passage on romantic love which started out, "Oh love, love, strong as death!"

Mrs. Glover's own verses returned again and again to the theme of death as the other pole of romantic love; and although many of these poems fall within the category of the sentimental graveyard verse so popular then, her concern with the theme suggests more than morbid aesthetic fancy. The precariousness of the human condition was driven home to her by the insecurity of her own existence, and there were times when she could almost say with Keats, "I have been half in love with easeful death."

It was death which in 1849 once again ripped apart the dailiness of Sanbornton life. For some time the burden of existence had been growing heavier in Abigail Baker's heart. A year earlier she had written her son George: "I may have my health again but Dear George I feel as though my glass was almost run. . . . I must say that every line from you is a luxury except when you begin about *Fate* that's a great word and it distresses me for I know too well how to sympathize with you."[67]

In August, 1849, she wrote him: "I reflect and remember the days when our Family Circle were compos'd of six Children with tallents (pardon me) and voices sufficient to raise a Mothers heart to Heaven . . . but O how have we all perverted our tallents." The common guilt of Adam's race lay heavily on her natural goodness.

Two or three months later, after selling his farm,[68] Mark Baker prepared to move with his wife, his daughter, and his grandson to a house in Sanbornton Bridge, a change which may have been designed to make things easier for Abigail but which came too late. On November 4, George Baker and Martha Rand were married in the old farmhouse, leaving at once for Baltimore where George had a new position. On November 21, a short time before the date set for moving, Abigail died at the age of sixty-five and after more than forty years of married life. More revealing than Rust's fervent obituary in the *Patriot* was the simple statement of one of her sisters in a letter some years later, "I loved most tenderly all my brothers and sisters, but she was a Benjamin."[69]

What she meant and what her passing meant to her youngest daughter is more easily read in the latter's life than in her words. A brief, choked letter to George the next day told the news. "I have prayed for support to write this letter," she added, "but I find it impossible to tell you particulars at this time." Then she burst out: "Oh! George, what is left of earth to *me!* But oh, my Mother! She has *suffered long with me;* let me then be willing she should *rejoice,* and I bear on till I follow her."[70]

In a poem "To my Mother in Heaven," published in the *Patriot* on December 20, Mrs. Glover's feelings broke through the literary conventions of the period with a certain simple directness.[71] George Baker, down in Baltimore, seemed to be as stirred by his sister's plight as by his mother's death. He himself was moved to write a poem imagining the deathbed scene as the daughter sat beside her mother in "meek dispair":[72]

> No agonising jesture, wild
> With frantick raving, marks her grief;
> But as a chasten'd, lovely child,
> She prays that Heaven would grant relief.

This he followed up with still another poem, written for the *Republican and Argus,* in reply to her lines in the *Patriot.* Assuring her that their mother heard her "sinless prayer of deep lament," he went on to write of the joys of heaven which made all sorrow impossible, and held out hope that the daughter might there rejoin her mother before too long:

> Then patience, Mary, a few years,
> Or months, or weeks,—perhaps e'en days;
> Endure each pain, subdue each fear,
> The blessing's yours—"Who Christ obeys."

While this doleful cheer was held out to her, Mrs. Glover had new cause for grief. Three weeks after Abigail Baker's death, John Bartlett died in Sacramento. It may not have been a deep personal sorrow to her as the earlier loss had been, but at the very least it was the loss of a way out, at a moment when loneliness made her particularly vulnerable. Now she would have to search for another way, and the urgency of the need increased with every year.

5

Through all these years Mrs. Glover had struggled unsuccessfully against ill health. At the end of 1847 her mother had written George, "Mary has not been able to make her Bed since you [left] though she is able to sit and work." In the summer of 1849 she spent two months in Warner, New Hampshire, under the treatment of Dr. Parsons Whidden, and her mother at that time expressed an anxious hope that "she may be reliev'd from her distresses the Dr. sayes she could not live long as she was."[73]

Her regular physician was Dr. Nathaniel Ladd. Disentangled from the fantasies spun by later legend,[74] his diagnosis appears to have been that the dyspepsia which constituted her chief suffering was caused by a disease of the spinal nerves, there being "a connection between stomach and spine."[75] Such a theory was typical of the medical impressionism which flourished between the decline of the old "heroic" school of medicine, with its humoral theories, its bleeding and purging, and the rise of the new clinical school with its headquarters in France.

It is hardly surprising that Dr. Ladd's treatment was of no avail. Psychosomatic medicine was not to appear on the scene for almost another century, and even then doctors would be little inclined to pay attention to the possible *theological* causes of nervous disease. Ladd may well have been baffled by the distressing course of his patient's multiple ailments, and his bafflement may sometimes have taken the form of exasperation with the nervous paroxysms which seized her when she was in a state of extreme physical debility; but an incident which she reported in a letter to her brother in 1848 throws light on Ladd's opinion of her.[76]

She had been to a lecture on phrenology, that fashionable pseudoscience which was to the middle nineteenth century what psychoanalysis has been to the twentieth. The lecturer "called for a lady's head," and Ladd, Hamilton Tilton, and the ubiquitous William Sleeper all urged her to go forward. She did, and the phrenologist spoke "of my attachment to friends—said I would stick with a friend through evil report or good report, yes, he added this lady would die for a friend! he said there were three marked points in my character—

what do you suppose these were dear Geo?—*Philosophy*—truth combined with conscience—and affection."

Afterwards the phrenologist asked whether someone present who knew the lady would be "good enough to say if he told right—*whereupon* Dr. Ladd answered, 'You have in no point exaggerated!' only hear this Geo. from *him*. Oh! this deceiving world." Her last comment indicates that the relations between Ladd and herself were not always smooth; but, as she wrote George in another connection, "My temper is hasty but not sullen,"[77] and Ladd evidently recognized beneath the ups and downs of her volatile temperament the fundamental seriousness of her character.

A further strain was soon to be put on that character. To live alone with her father, young George, and a hired girl was not in itself easy. Then Luther Pilsbury suddenly died of cholera on a Mississippi steamboat, and the household was augmented by Martha and her two children—for Ellen now had a baby sister, called Mary after her aunt. There was a melancholy pleasure in having the grief-stricken Martha with her, but this was only the prelude to a much more drastic change.

Thanksgiving Day, 1850, was a sad affair. Mrs. Baker had died less than a year before, Pilsbury less than a month. Mrs. Glover wrote George: "This anniversary has indeed passed—but the absent and the *dead*—where were they? Not with us as we gathered slowly and silently about the table and at evening with deeper memories separated!" Although the three sisters were once again together, she felt "the most solemn impression" that before another Thanksgiving they might again be at a distance from each other or among "the quiet dead."[78]

From this melancholy she is roused to more spirited comment by the next piece of news:

> *Father is to be married to Mrs. Duncan of Candia N. H. next Thurs week; her best carpets and goods have arrived. Last year a little later than this I went into that cold damp house with Father, helped cleanse and set it in order and lived alone with a little girl and him all winter; in the spring he told me if George was not sent away he would send him to the* Poor House (*after abusing him as he did through the winter.*) Now *he comes to me to help arrange the things of his bride; but I will see them in the bottomless pit before doing it. Everything of our departed Mother's has to give place to them and Father is as happy as a school boy.*[79]

Mrs. Glover appears not to have realized at first how greatly this change would affect her own life. On December 2, three days before Mark Baker married Mrs. Elizabeth Patterson Duncan at Candia, she wrote a friend cheerfully:

> *Next week is the time I have anticipated to visit my Uncle*
> *and cousins at Boscawen and the latter part of it go to Fisherville.*
> *I have little confidence in the scheme of visits when the weather*
> *is so cold and changeful. Yet this seems the first opportunity I*
> *have had for a year to leave home and if my health remains*
> *sufficient I cannot well deny myself the pleasure. I expect to be*
> *very busy this winter compiling my stray sketches and think it*
> *will at least amuse me and all (who may chance to read them*
> *doubtless).*[80]

But there was really no "home" for her to return to after the
"scheme of visits" had served its purpose. Though the new Mrs. Baker
was kindly enough, her coming inevitably gave Mrs. Glover an uncomfortable visitor status. Moreover, Mark made it clear that he had
no intention of letting six-year-old George Glover stay on in the
household.

Abigail Tilton now opened her more spacious home to her sister,
but the hospitality was not extended to George. Abigail's son Albert
was a weak, spoiled boy, a year younger than his boisterous cousin, and
this may have been reason enough for not wanting George in the
house. Helpless to provide for him in any other way, Mrs. Glover was
forced to make temporary provision by sending him off on his own
round of visits.

It was probably Abigail who came up with the final solution.
Mahala Sanborn, who had been like a second mother to George, had
married one Russell Cheney, and the two were going to the village
of North Groton to live, forty miles away in the foothills of the White
Mountains. George was to go with them. It would certainly have been
presented as a temporary arrangement at first, but the strong-minded
Mrs. Tilton was doubtless convinced that her ailing sister would be
better off if she were relieved of all further responsibility for the boy.
Mahala was delighted to have George, and Cheney was willing. All
that anyone left out of account was Mrs. Glover's own feelings—and
possibly George's.

A letter to her brother-in-law, Andrew J. Glover, and his wife
on April 22, 1851, gives a quick glimpse of the situation. George was
staying with his uncle and aunt at Concord when Mrs. Glover wrote
them:

> *My dear Bro and Sis,*
>
> *Mrs. Cheney came here last Thurs. and will return next week*
> *on Saturday. You can send my dear child when you please the*
> *latter part of the week, as she is very anxious to have him when*
> *she goes home. She is very fond of children and Georgy in par-*
> *ticular, but her health is very poor, this I regret. She told me*

their school (which is about one quarter of a mile distant) will commence in a few weeks and I am anxious to have him attend. But Oh! how I miss him *already! There seems nothing left me now to enjoy. . . . Won't you send me a line by him or come yourselves? I want very much to know how you have succeeded with him and if he has been a good boy (some naughty things of course). There is no child whom we expect mature in every respect, but take Georgy with the aggregate, is he not a pretty good and very dear boy? You can speak to the conductor to take care of him and his little baggage and Mr. Tilton is always at the depot so he will see to him there. Will dear little Sully be sorry to have him leave? . . . Kiss the little one for me and tell him aunty remembers those roguish eyes.*

> *In much haste yours—*
> *Affectionately,*
> *Mary*[81]

In her notebook is a poem "Written on the 9th day of May on parting with my babe," which gives us another glimpse into her feelings:

> Go little voyager, o'er life's rough sea—
> Born in a tempest! choose thy pilot God.
> The Bible, let thy chart forever be—
> Anchor and helm its promises afford. . . .
>
> A Father's love! my heart, be still or break,
> Not to thy infant hours in joy made known,
> And thou mayest live to learn thy hapless fate,
> Reft of thy parent stock, frail, sick, and lone.
>
> Then wilt thou share thy Mother's voiceless woe
> Too keen for utterance, too deep for tears!
> Yet God forbid, thy guileless heart should know
> The early blight of unprotected years. . . .[82]

The first result of George's removal appears to have been a marked decline in Mrs. Glover's health. By August Martha Pilsbury was reporting in a letter that "dear Mary" was in a much worse state of health and they feared she would never be well again.[83] A few months later the same writer described the still more critical situation in a letter to Martha Rand Baker:

> *Found her very sick, from one of her most severe attacks of dispepsia, liver-complaint and nervous disease. It would be impossible to point out the changes, or trace the progress of*

disease down to the present time, or describe the hopes and fears, doubts and expectations that have affected us respecting the result, during this long period of continued suffering, having been all the time confined to the room and bed, except when possibly able to be helped into a carriage to ride. And what can I say of her now? How tell you, that after so long and inconceivable suffering, though still living, and perhaps doomed to yet longer and greater affliction by an all-wise but inscrutable Providence, yet, there is scarcely a ray of hope left us of her recovery. Her strength gradually fails, and all the powers of life seem yielding to the force of disease. O, Martha! it would move the sternest soul, and make mortality shrink, to witness the agony she often endures, while it pierces a sister's heart, with a pang that only affection can feel, or can endure. . . . May [my own health] continue that I may contribute to dear Mary's comfort while she may live, if she cannot recover.[84]

It is evident that the family considered her increased sufferings a justification for keeping her separated from George, rather than a result of the separation. But they did everything possible for her comfort. There was on the porch a swing in which she liked to rock, and the swinging seemed to ease her pain. For bad weather and times when she was too ill to lie outside, a sofa was fitted with rockers, and on occasion a neighboring boy, Will Lang, would be hired to rock it for hours at a time, so that "swinging Mrs. Glover" became a neighborhood phrase.[85]

While she had still been living with her parents, Mark Baker would sometimes take her in his arms and rock her like a child when she was suffering, and he would have the road strewn with straw and tanbark to lessen the noise of passing cartwheels.[86] In desperation he had even tried such new-fangled systems as mesmerism and homeopathy, to see if they could help her. Dr. Ladd had developed a little interest in the former; and Dr. Alpheus Morrill, who had married a cousin, Hannah Baker, opened an office in Concord in 1847 as the pioneer homeopathist in New Hampshire. But each of these systems brought only temporary relief.[87]

In her autobiography Mrs. Eddy wrote, "During twenty years prior to my discovery [1866] I had been trying to trace all physical effects to a mental cause,"[88] and in *The Christian Science Journal* she wrote, "As long ago as 1844, I was convinced that mortal mind produced all disease, and that the various medical theories were in no proper sense scientific."[89] The phrase "mortal mind" belongs to a later period, but young Mrs. Glover had every reason to doubt the adequacy of the prevalent medical theories to explain the real cause of disease.

Moreover, her early education had tended to fix before her gaze the great problem of the relation of matter to mind, as the eighteenth century had raised it for the nineteenth. A single quotation from Young's *Night Thoughts* may do duty for the many passages in her early reading which could have set her questioning whether cause was to be looked for in matter or in mind:

> Who bid brute matter's restive lump assume
> Such various forms, and gave it wings to fly?
> Has matter innate motion? Then each atom,
> Asserting its indisputable right
> To dance, would form a universe of dust:
> Has matter none? Then whence these glorious forms,
> And boundless flights, from shapeless and repos'd?
> Has matter more than motion? has it thought,
> Judgment, and genius? is it deeply learn'd
> In mathematics? has it fram'd such laws,
> Which, but to guess, a Newton made immortal?—
> If so, how each sage atom laughs at me,
> Who think a clod inferior to a man!

It was in 1844 that the great Michael Faraday himself, the discoverer of electromagnetic induction, in a paper published in the *Philosophical Magazine* avowed his belief in the immateriality of physical objects. And in a newspaper article "On Protoplasm" which Mrs. Glover pasted into her scrapbook some years later occurs this passage: "But who can say what 'matter' and 'spirit' are, except as names for the unknown and supposed substrata of our conscious states? As Professor Huxley says, 'Matter may be regarded as a form of thought, or form may be regarded as a property of matter.'"

These speculative, philosophical questions were reinforced in her case both by religion and practical experience.

Her own explanation of the religious motivation is found in *Retrospection and Introspection:* "From my very childhood I was impelled, by a hunger and thirst after divine things,—a desire for something higher and better than matter, and apart from it,—to seek diligently for the knowledge of God as the one great and ever-present relief from human woe."[90]

Experience early drove home to her the conviction she expressed in a girlhood poem: "This life is a shadow, and hastens away."[91] The sentiment was a traditional Christian one, but a more rigorous schoolmaster than the church catechism taught her the fleeting and insubstantial nature of values rooted in matter.

Even in the teeming, bustling America of that day a doubt sometimes slid across men's minds as to whether it might not all be an illusion. Such a doubt found expression, for instance, in an 1847 essay on "Shadows" by the successful New York banker and *Knickerbocker* writer Henry Carey ("John Waters"), but that may have been no more than the expression of a momentary weariness with the passing show. A deeper note sounds in an incomparably greater New Yorker, Herman Melville, whose outcast Ishmael arrived at his doubts and convictions from something other than fashionable epicureanism:

> *Methinks that what they call my shadow here on earth is my true substance. Methinks that in looking at things spiritual, we are too much like oysters observing the sun through the water, and thinking that thick water the thinnest of air. Methinks my body is but the lees of my better being. In fact take my body who will, take it I say, it is not me.*[92]

On the basis of her experience Mrs. Glover may well have suspected that life in matter is but a play of shadows. Yet from all she wrote in these years it is evident that she never doubted the existence of a world of absolute, indestructible values, usually envisioned in orthodox terms of a heavenly hereafter but undoubtedly sensed at times as the spiritual dimension of present experience.

In the same year as Carey's article, *The Covenant* announced in April that its next issue would contain an article entitled "The Immortality of the Soul" by Mrs. M. Glover "written in the pure and chaste style so characteristic of her writing."[93] When the article appeared in May it included the following paragraphs:

> *Who does not sometimes conjecture what will be his condition and employment in eternity? Will the mind be continually augmenting its stock of knowledge, and advancing toward complete perfection? It cannot be otherwise.*

> *We shall there apprehend fully the relations and dependencies incomprehensible to understandings encircled by clay. The boundless ocean of truth will be fathomed and investigated by those, whom, like Newton, a residence here scarcely acquainted with a few pebbles on its trackless shore. The result of all experiments will then be satisfactory, since they will accord with the deductions of enlarged and enlightened reason.*

> *Most authors have but dimly shadowed forth their own imaginings, and much of what they intended is involved in obscurity. This makes an approach to the regions of science and literature so extremely difficult; there this obstacle will be removed. No veil will hide from our observation the beauties,*

lovely, inimitable, of wisdom and philosophy; all their charms will there be displayed.

The imperfection of language will be no hindrance to the acquisition of ideas, as it will no longer be necessary as a medium of thought and communication. Intelligence, refined, etherealized, will converse directly with material objects, if, indeed, matter be existent. All will be accessible, permanent, eternal!

Almost casually she raised the question that has racked philosophy since its earliest beginnings: "if, indeed, matter be existent." The doubt might relate to whether matter exists in a future heaven or whether it has actual existence anywhere at any time. In either case, the statement evidences a suspicion that matter was no part of ultimate reality. At some point she revised two lines of an early girlhood poem to read:

> But hope, as the eaglet that spurneth the sod,
> May soar above matter to fasten on God.[94]

6

The English historian H. A. L. Fisher has written of the discoverer of Christian Science:

Prayer, meditation, eager and puzzled interrogation of the Bible, had claimed from childhood much of her energy, so that those who met her in later times were conscious of a certain quiet exaltation, such as may come to a woman nursing a secret spiritual advantage. . . . The great ideas of God, of immortality, of the soul, of a life penetrated by Christianity, were never far from her mind.[95]

The evidence of the troubled years of her widowhood bears this out. In a poem entitled "Prayer" she wrote:

> What is the Christian's balm for grief,
> When pain and wo invade?
> A holy calm, a sweet relief,
> In prayer to God.[96]

A revealing phrase occurs in a poem entitled "The Mother at the Loss of her Drowned Son Whose Body Was Not Recovered," written two years before George was taken from her:

> Grant me submission to the God who gave me
> A well-spring of deep gladness to my heart.[97]

The submissiveness did not always come easily, but her later experience shows that when she rebelled the rebellion came from that same deep wellspring—the perpetually renewed conviction of God's goodness—to which she appealed against the evidence of God's wrath. Like a more youthful Job, she may be said to have wrestled with God for the glory of God.

In a poem written in 1846 she had expressed an unquestioning faith that was to be shaken harshly in the years to come but never really dislodged. Entitled "The Bible," it ran:

> Word of God! What condescension,
>   Infinite with finite mind,
> To commune, sublime conception.
>   Canst thou fathom love divine?
> Oracle of God-like wonder,
>   Frame-work of His mighty plan,
> Chart and compass for the wanderer,
>   Safe obeying thy command.
>
> By Omniscience veiled in glory,
>   'Neath the Omnipresent eye—
> Kingdoms, empires, bow before thee,
>   Sceptic, truth immortal see!
> Spare O then the querist's cavil,
>   Search in faith—obey, adore!
> Ponder, pause, believe and "marvel
>   Not, I say," forevermore.[98]

In the later poem addressed to her son at the time he was taken from her she urged the small "voyager" to look to the Bible for "anchor and helm" in his problematical voyagings. It was unthinkable to her that one should face life's challenges without it. She was seriously distressed because young Sarah Clement, whose Unitarian family took religion rather casually, had not read the New Testament, and she urged her to read a chapter a day until she had finished the four gospels, promising her a present as a reward.

Actually Sarah soon tired of her bargain and stopped reading. When Mrs. Glover learned this, she charitably commended the child for reading as much as she had, then gave her the present anyway. It was a heart with a cardboard cover which opened "and you pulled out texts from the Bible and little verses or leaflets." Sarah's comment years later was: "I liked the verses better than the texts, and the painted flowers which encircled them best of all, but taking it all in all, the present was something of a disappointment."[99]

Whatever Mrs. Glover's own disappointment may have been over the formal shortcomings of Sarah's religious education, she unfailingly responded to that quality in childhood which a post-Freudian age may be permitted to call its frank and fresh innocence.[100] Like the child, she felt that boundless good should be possible. Always there was something like astonishment at the successive blows struck by fate. She wrote the words "Oh how true" opposite these lines from Mrs. Hemans:

> . . . Manhood rears
> A haughty brow, and Age has done with tears,
> But youth bows down to misery, in amaze
> At the dark cloud o'ermantling its fresh days;
> And thus it was with her.

In a letter to a friend in 1850 she enclosed a poem which started off:

> Why does pain come,
> Marring each pleasure;
> Why does want come;
> Spoiling each treasure;
> Making us doubtful, and gloomy, and sad?
> Why does wo dim
> Eyes full of brightness,
> Why does time rob
> Steps of their lightness,
> Bowing the proud form with beauty once clad?[101]

These questions were more than subjects for idle verse. They lurked in the subterranean corridors of consciousness. They gnawed in the dark at liver and spine and nerves. At times they dragged at one's limbs and weighed on one's heart like iron. Was an unquestioning resignation man's only recourse in the face of fate, even though body and mind rebelled at the injustice?

"*Fate*," she wrote in 1848, "has always denied me an opportunity to fulfill my *nature*."[102] Abigail Baker had shrunk from the implications of the word *fate*,[103] and her daughter would quote and requote the gloomy lines:

> And circumstance, that unspiritual God
> And miscreator, makes and helps along
> Our coming evils with a crutch-like rod,
> Whose touch turns hope to dust—the dust we all have trod.

Here circumstance or fate plays the part of Satan, marring God's creation, frustrating God's will. How, then, could it be equated with

God's will and accepted with meek resignation? Mark Baker's theology did make the equation, and there was logic in this if God was omnipotent and circumstance was bound by an iron chain of causality. In that case Satan became God's hired assassin, allowed to do His dirty work for some ineffable and inscrutable purpose of His own.

But if God's goodness was to be saved in any terms that would make sense to suffering humanity, He must somehow be absolved from complicity in the evil of the world. Increasingly the nineteenth century was seeking to so absolve Him. In 1851 Lyman Beecher's son Edward brought out his own radical revision of Calvinist doctrine, *The Conflict of Ages*, which demolished original sin, total depravity, and a literal hell. He explained the inborn tendency to do wrong by a pre-existent state in which the soul was free to do right but chose wrong. His sister Catherine thereupon wrote him:

> *I reply how do you get this? If you say by a Revelation from God, I say before I can confide in his teachings I must have* proof *that all this horrible misery and wrong resulting from the wrong construction or nature of mind is not attributable to the Creator of All Things. His mere word is nothing from the Author of a system which is all ruined and worse than good for nothing. He must clear his character before he can offer me a Revelation.*[104]

One is reminded by this of twelve-year-old Mary Baker's comment to her mother regarding a God who would inflict eternal punishment on corrigible men: "Then he is not as good as my mother, and he will find me a hard case." This sort of refractory, feminine common sense ran wholly counter to the ideal of submissive piety which was held to be appropriate for Christian ladies. It refused to accept the traditional wisdom of men as an adequate substitute for a clear revelation of God's will.

Oddly enough, Mrs. Glover found support for refusing to call evil good in an unexpected place. Martin Tupper's *Proverbial Philosophy*, which Bartlett had given her, is usually looked on as the *ne plus ultra* of Victorian platitude. Nevertheless, among all Tupper's bourgeois moralizings there is a certain amount of vigorous common sense.[105] Mrs. Glover marked numerous passages, including one which attacks the sort of "meekness" ordinarily enjoined on the fair sex:

> Wherefore let the evil triumph, when the
>   just and the right are on thy side?
> Such humility is abject, it lacketh the
>   life of sensibility,
> And that resignation is but mock, where

the burden is not felt.
Suspect thyself and thy meekness: thou art
   mean and indifferent to sin;
And the heart that should grieve and forgive,
   is case-hardened and forgetteth. . . .
And cheat not thyself of the reverence which
   is owing to thy reasonable being. . . .
Better is an obstinate disputant, that
   yieldeth inch by inch,
Than the shallow traitor to himself, who
   surrendereth to half an argument.

Doubtless many of Mrs. Glover's arguments were with herself as she attempted to reconcile the deep assurance of God's love which she drew from the Scriptures with the evidence of cosmic disarray which she drew from experience. In this period of her life we can catch only hints and flashes of what was happening in her thinking—through the poems she wrote, the books she read—although there is good reason to believe that her deepest nourishment and her deepest questions were drawn always from the Bible. Nothing could answer more directly to her inmost needs than the Psalmist's eloquent range from simple trust to anguished questioning; nothing could hold out more promise of an ultimate answer than the life which reached from the Sermon on the Mount to the Passion on the Cross.

These were years when throughout the western world a greater agony of questioning over God, faith, and the problem of evil was going on than in any other period of modern history—the years when, according to Nietzsche, God died. It was not just the theologians who wrestled, but the poets and men of science. There was the year, for instance, when in the hills of neighboring Massachusetts Hawthorne and Melville met and looked together into the dark, Hawthorne with sad austerity, Melville with passionate rebellion. The problem of evil hangs over *The Scarlet Letter* and *Moby Dick* like the thunderclouds over Mount Greylock. Mrs. Glover may not have known the works of either of them at the time, but the same thunderclouds hung over Sanbornton Bridge.

Harriet Beecher Stowe reduced the problem to the simplest terms in *Uncle Tom's Cabin*. Under the lash of Simon Legree, Uncle Tom is confronted with the question, "Is God Here?"

> *Oh, how is it possible for the untaught heart to keep its faith, unswerving, in the face of dire misrule, and palpable, unrebuked injustice? In that simple heart waged a fierce conflict: the crushing sense of wrong, the foreshadowing of a whole*

life of future misery, the wreck of all past hopes . . . Oh, was it easy here to believe and hold fast the great password of Christian faith, that "GOD IS, and is the REWARDER of them that diligently seek Him"?

Mrs. Stowe's answer was the conventional one of reward in a future heaven. In a curious way the same answer turned up in the new science blowing from across the Atlantic. The "development" theory, as evolution was then called, was itself developing toward Darwin. The anonymous *Vestiges of the Natural History of Creation* was more than a seven-days' wonder in England and America.[106] Cosmic fantasy rather than sober science, it yet made brilliant guesses and popularized useful concepts, rousing the ire of theologian and scientist alike—the work of a nineteenth-century Velikovsky who happened to be looking in the right direction.

A copy of the book quickly found its way into George Baker's library.[107] The problem involved in its new cosmology—the same that darkened the old theology—was made explicit by the author in a preface to the tenth American edition, which appeared in 1853:

> *[The] system of nature assures us that benevolence is a leading principle in the Divine Mind. But this system is at the same time deficient in a means of making this benevolence of invariable operation. To reconcile this to the character of the Deity, it is necessary to suppose that the present system is but a part of the whole, a stage in a Great Progress, and that the Redress is in reserve.*

Always perfection lay ahead—in a promised heaven or an evolved earthly paradise. But would even that hypothetical redress justify the cruelty and waste of the present, all the needless suffering inflicted on those whose only guilt was to have been born? One had need of a deep wellspring of gladness in the heart to face such questions.

7

Three related problems hung over the two years that Mrs. Glover lived with Abigail Tilton: her separation from her son, her increasingly severe attacks of illness, the difficulty of being a proud dependent in a still prouder home. Yet she apparently put as cheerful a face on the matter as she could and at least to outside eyes appeared tranquil enough.[108]

It was during these years that young Sarah Clement lived across the street from the Tiltons and saw Mrs. Glover almost daily.[109] "I have never seen her when she was the least depressed," she declared later. Mrs. Glover read a great deal, she added, and used to borrow books from the Clement library; she would stand talking with Sarah's mother, and her laughter would ring out. Toward night Sarah would see her working in the garden: "She always wore gloves with the finger tips cut off. I used to run across the road and hang over the gate and discuss things." Mrs. Glover was always willing to talk, though she worked assiduously over her herbarium and the flowers were pressed, tabulated, dated, and pasted in an album.

The warm affection felt by the little girl for Mrs. Glover did not extend to Mrs. Tilton, who was also a handsome woman, she stated in her recollections, "but extremely determined and very fiery when angry." Her "domineering nature" and "strong prejudices" made themselves keenly felt in her home and in the community. "Politics ran high at the time, and the Tilton home was the center among the well-educated folk of the day who gathered there to discuss the political situation and other current topics."[110] In such an atmosphere it was inevitable that there should be clashes of conviction between the two sisters, as apparently there was over the issue of slavery.

Young Albert Tilton, who was not turning out too well, now had a sister, Evelyn, a sickly child. In March, 1853, Martha Rand Baker gave birth to a son, called George after his father, who was to play an equivocal role in Mrs. Glover's later life.[111] But it was her sister Martha Pilsbury's second daughter—the little namesake, Mary—who really engaged her affections.[112] This diminutive Mary would come and sit at the edge of her bed when she was ill, and Mrs. Glover would draw from her laughing little presence the comfort she always seems to have found in the ingenuousness of children.

There was occasional literary activity through these years: poems in support of Franklin Pierce's candidacy in the *Patriot,* a poem "Woman's Rights" in *Gleasons's Pictorial Drawing-Room Companion* in February, 1853, and in the same month a poem "Lake Winnipiseogee" in *Godey's Lady's Book.* Earlier verse was also receiving modest recognition. Her lines "To my Mother in Heaven" were reprinted in *The Sunday-Book,* an anthology published in New York for the "moral improvement" of children, and two earlier poems were picked up in *Gems For You,* an anthology of prose and poetry by New Hampshire authors.[113]

But a wry little verse which she wrote sometime before New Year's Day, 1853, marks the beginning of an entirely new phase of her life. It was about something as trivial, and as exasperating, as a toothache. Melville had marked in *Much Ado About Nothing* Leonato's observation to the effect that "there was never yet philosopher/ That could endure the toothache patiently," and he later wrote Hawthorne that a raging toothache was enough to demonstrate the nonsense of Goethe's transcendental dictum, "Live in the all." Mrs. Glover managed to be sufficiently philosophical about her toothache to make a joke of it and of the unfortunate fact that, once a tooth is drawn,

> [Then] treacherous joy reveals the worthy crime
> And gaping gums betray the tooth of time.

The important thing about this little sally is that it was enclosed in a letter she wrote her dentist, Dr. Daniel Patterson. Dr. Patterson had only lately come to live in Franklin, three miles from Sanbornton Bridge. He was a relative of Mark Baker's second wife, and was thus acquainted with the Bakers socially as well as professionally. A letter Mrs. Glover wrote him in December, 1852, refers only to his professional services, but by the following New Year's Day a sufficient friendliness had developed for her to send the poem, along with a book "selected from my little library," when she again wrote about the dental work he was doing for her.

Patterson was a handsome, genial man, tall, dark, bearded, a bit of a rural dandy. He is reported to have dressed always in broadcloth and fine linen, kid gloves and boots, frock coat and top hat. Starting as a farm boy in Maine, he had achieved a precarious success as a dentist, riding on his horse through the countryside to do business with the farmers when there was not sufficient dental work to keep him busy in the small communities where he located at various times. A certain progressiveness is evident in the fact that he was very quick to make use of the new discovery of anesthesia in his work.

With all this, there was an underlying simplicity in the man which probably appealed to Mrs. Glover. He, on his part, was evidently captivated at once by what one critic has called her "valiantly gay bearing."[114] She must by this time have decided that desperate measures were necessary if she was ever to have a home of her own where she could once again have George with her. Patterson, full of confidence and good intentions, held out just this promise to her.

By March the two were engaged, but apparently not without some misgivings on her part. There was the matter of religion, for one thing. Patterson was a Baptist. After a sleepless night she wrote him, "I have a fixed feeling that to yield my *religion* to yours I *could not,* other things compared to this, are but a grain to the universe," and then she added somewhat ominously, "Last night I conversed anew with my dear Father."[115] Mark would certainly have been adamant against her embracing the Baptist heresy. Her letter ended: "One thing

I beg you to remember that we will be *friends. . . . Farewell.* May God bless and protect you."

A speedy reply from Patterson[116] expressed the "shock which waked me from my dreams of happiness" and went on to say:

> *I then thought your Father had pronounced the religious test, I will not call it Bigotry, which has caused more blood and tears than any other cause in the world, if your Father did counsel in that matter as you decided I wish simply that you would just ask him, who would have yealded if there had been the same point of difference between him and his wife.*

A few days later new objections arose from Mrs. Glover's family. Patterson wrote her, "You say they have heard 'Dark Things.' " He protested the slander which had apparently been at work defaming his character, and offered to take Mark Baker to every place where he had ever lived so that Mark might enquire of the best citizens as to his life and reputation. Instead of sending this letter, however, he wrote another the next day:

> *It seems that I have lost you at last—That you have made your final decision against me—and refuse to see me again, and there is nothing left for me to do but submit to your decree—*
>
> *I thought I would at first vindicate my Moral character, and prepared a letter for your Father's perusal—but on more mature deliberation, and knowing that you had become dissatisfied with my Disposition and wished—yes had already irrevocably dismissed me, I concluded to withhold all I had written.*[117]

This was not the end, however. For one thing, he was still working on her teeth occasionally, and this gave him an opportunity at the same time to mend his fences. Before the end of April their differences were smoothed over, and the engagement was again in force. Some lingering doubts on Mrs. Glover's part may have contributed to the condition about which she wrote him on April 29:

> *I am sick—Wed. afternoon my illness increased . . . Neuralgia in the spine and stomach seems to be the cause, producing a state of nervous inflamation. My sufferings are at times extreme I do want to see you. I know not what this attack may result in, but one thing I pray, that it may be the divine will that I am not to languish out months on a sick bed; nevertheless, "not my will but Thine be done."*[118]

A few days later, after sending him a note in the morning, she wrote him at greater length in the afternoon or evening:

I regret this morning having written you I was sick. I am vastly better, and fear you are still anxious and perhaps will make quite a sacrifice in coming to see me. But this I told you not to do. I hope you will have more caution than I had, and wait till you receive this. Still, if I were as sick now as when I wrote you, I should think such, a very cool proceeding.[119]

In the letter she had written him a few days earlier she had mentioned that she had no physician except "a call from cousin Willie Chamberlain who is at home now to see his Mother," but she had little confidence in him as he was a mere boy. Abigail Tilton had a violent prejudice against Dr. Ladd, whom she accused of neglecting her mother during her last illness,[120] and this may explain his not being called in.

In the same letter Mrs. Glover mentioned that she had had to take morphine, "which I so much disapprove," as the only relief from her pain. The doctors of the day prescribed this drug freely without a thought of the possible consequences. Evidently Mrs. Glover's reluctance to use it caused her to abandon it almost immediately.[121] By the time she wrote Patterson a few days later the medical picture had changed completely. Another cousin, Dr. Alpheus Morrill, the homeopathist, had entered the scene:

I have not called a Physician but received counsel of Dr. Morrill; the practice has been all my own, and considering the severe attack, my previous debility, and chronic complaints, I think we managed a little wisely for me to be on the list of recovery today. Cold water and homeopathic remedies have been the Hygeine only. . . . Yea, hope and despondency are the twin sisters of earth, and the smile and tear follow each other in quick succession.[122]

Patterson, too, had his moods. Looking on Mrs. Glover as a superior being far beyond his deserving, he strained to reach an intellectual and aesthetic level which he thought would be pleasing to her and, exhausted by the effort, fell back on a simple frankness which was undoubtedly more winning than all his gaudy rhetoric:

I had to go out and get this paper to write you this un-readable matter on, and returned in a heavy Thunder Shower, I then sat down by the window, (not a window) to see the terrible God hurl his formidable Shafts of Lightning through the humid atmosphere, with such terrible velocity, as made even the dark-ness turn pale, and shrink away, in a vain attempt to hide itself behind the "Rocks and Mountains" from the august presence of Deity when he came forth to tread on the clouds as a pave-

ment for his feet. . . . "The Thunder of his power" who can withstand, and my Soul said O! God how great, and terrible thou art! ! !

There was one time in my ride in this place, when I said to myself—"now I wish Mary was with me"—it was on attaining the summit of a hill, the first view of the Lake burst on my vision with its smooth face scarified, and lacerated by numerous Islets, and points, and yet it was beautiful; then I really wished you by my side. . . .

But Mary Dear, I have scrawled my sheet nearly all over, and have not written a sentence that will please you, I have only wasted the time. . . .

It is proper that you should know me thoroughly so that when we are married . . . you may not look for either a philosophic, or a Poetical letter from your husband . . . and say O! that I had only had sense enough to have married a man of genius, an intellectual, literary man, who could write me something readable, that I would be proud to show my friends, or at least not ashamed to, but my Dear you will never find me better in this respect than I have exhibited myself. I probably never wrote any better letters in my life than those I have to you.[123]

One thing the letters do show: there was genuine affection in this marriage. In her autobiography Mrs. Eddy wrote that her dominant thought in marrying again was to get back her child, but it is to her credit that she did not use Patterson simply as a convenience toward this end. He was hardly all she could have hoped for, but she took him seriously as a man, a husband, and a possible father to her son. That he would fail in all three respects was almost inevitable in the circumstances.

Chapter
IV

Wilderness
1853

Wilderness: 1853

These were the years of the great westward movement. Adventure, hope, need were driving increasing numbers into the wilderness to face the unknown, to subdue or be subdued by it. A new Children of Israel pushed across new deserts to a new Promised Land. America's most remarkable religious phenomenon of the first half of the century —the great Mormon migration to Illinois, to Utah—had been part of the westward surge.

It was all manifest destiny, people said—what in an earlier generation had been called America's errand into the wilderness. And many a man or woman was swallowed up in the loneliness of the continent and never heard of again.

Yet there were lonely and dangerous wilds closer to home for those who stayed in New England. Henry Thoreau, who had traveled widely in Concord, knew them. So did Emily Dickinson, who wrote that to make a prairie it takes only one clover and a bee and revery, and who found that revery alone could lead one into a silent, trackless, terrifying land.

Mary Baker Patterson stood on the verge of such a wilderness. For two or three years we almost lose sight of her—a slight figure disappearing among the darkening trees. We know that she and Dr. Patterson moved to Franklin and, after a few months in a boarding-house, lived on the first floor of a small house on the side of the Pemigewasset River, which joins with Tilton's Winnepesaukee River to form the Merrimack. But we know little of their life.

Daniel Webster had been born in Franklin, and the local monument to him stands today across the road from the Pattersons' unpretentious house, the upper floor of which they rented for a tailor shop. Nearby is the Christian Church which they attended, perhaps a compromise between their respectively Congregational and Baptist inclinations. The minister was a Reverend Mr. Moses, whose son George was later to become a friend of Mrs. Patterson's when he was a politically prominent Concord editor and she was Mary Baker Eddy, leader of a worldwide religious movement.

The most vivid glimpse we catch of her during her two years at Franklin is through the eyes of a twelve-year-old girl, Lucy Clark, who came to Patterson for some dental work. While he worked on her teeth, Mrs. Patterson sat in the window and read Ossian aloud to her. That wild, windy rhetoric, so alien to the taste of our own day, filled the little girl with a sort of spiritual exaltation, so much so that when she later went to Mount Holyoke College she started eagerly to read Ossian, then gave it up in dismay. This time there was no spiritual illumination.

Years later she heard Ossian read at Jackson, Michigan, with the same disappointing result. Still later in life she read *Science and Health,* completely unaware that the author was the Mrs. Patterson she had known, and instantly the illumination and exaltation she recalled from childhood were there again. When she later identified the author with her childhood friend, she wrote Mrs. Eddy telling her of the deep impression the long past incident had made on her, and even today it strikes a small match-flame in the darkness of the Franklin years.[1]

Legend, busily supplying the deficiency of fact, has associated Mrs. Patterson with one "Boston John" Clarke who lived in Franklin. Clarke was both a brilliant (though untaught) hydraulic engineer and a locally notable mesmerist. Earlier in the Sanbornton days, when mesmerism was a novelty of unknown possibilities, Mrs. Patterson apparently met him on one occasion at Sarah Clement's house and allowed him to experiment on her for the purpose of locating the body of a drowned student; but several respected Franklin citizens who knew them both denied that they had any acquaintance with each other during the years she lived in Franklin.[2]

The most important fact of these years was Dr. Patterson's refusal to allow George Glover to be brought back to live with them. Evidently he was convinced that the boy would be too great a burden on Mrs. Patterson's health, and this attitude in turn may have contributed to the deterioration of her health. The year after their marriage, Patterson sold his horse and bought a cow, which meant that he was giving up his periodic dental jaunts through the countryside and settling down to greater domesticity; but there was still no home with them for George.

The urgency of her pleas to be reunited with the boy can be measured by the fact that in March, 1855, they moved to North Groton to be near him. This lonely village in the foothills of the White Mountains was a far from ideal spot for Patterson to carry on his dental practice. A niece of Mahala and Russell Cheney, Mrs.

Sarah C. Turner, who described George as having been placed in the care of her uncle and aunt by Mark Baker, went on to say, "In making the effort to be with her boy by coming to Groton, Mrs. Patterson ultimately sacrificed her husband's profession for a time at least, there not being enough support for a dentist in that little place."[3]

However, he managed to acquire a timber lot of one hundred acres on the mountain two miles away and, nearer the village, the four acres on which his house and a small sawmill stood, augmented later by two acres more. A heavy mortgage on the property was held by Martha Pilsbury; but with two cows (later reduced to one), the sawmill, and his dental work, Patterson succeeded in eking out some sort of living for two or three years. Eventually the one cow was replaced by a horse—evidence that the dental trips had begun again.

To Mrs. Patterson the move was one more bitter disappointment. George was "wayward and headstrong," in Sarah Turner's words, and was not much liked in the village. Patterson not only took an aversion to the boy but was more than ever sure that it would upset the mother to have him with her. As a result, he did everything possible to keep the lad away.

George, now eleven years old, showed such a conspicuous lack of schooling and such a disinclination to learn that his presence may indeed have disturbed his mother almost as much as his absence grieved her. At a later date she wrote that she considered being deprived of his early education her severest calamity, then crossed out the words, perhaps remembering others more severe.[4]

The upshot of the affair is well described by Elmira (Myra) Smith Wilson, the blind girl who served the Pattersons as a maid for a year or two:

> *Mrs. Patterson came there [North Groton] with the Dr, to be near her child, and so that she could teach him, but this she was not permitted to do as the Dr did not like children and would not allow him to come to the house. The boy was not liked by the other children at school and the Cheneys did not make him go. My Brother was working for Mr Cheney and while there he and the boy slept together. My Brother did not like him because he was rough and would not mind anyone. Mrs. Patterson grieved and worried, because she could not see her child and told the Dr that she had given up her folks and had come off up there with him and that she must see her boy and teach him, but Patterson would not let him come near, and without her knowing it one day the Cheneys moved away, out west and took the boy with him [sic] and before they left my*

Father had a hard fight to get the money from him, that he
owed to him for my Brothers years work.[5]

To Mrs. Patterson this was the end. When the Cheneys moved
out to Enterprise, Minnesota, in April, 1856, first paying a farewell
visit to Sanbornton Bridge, they vanished out of her life completely,
and George with them. They might have been swallowed up by the
wilderness, for all she was able to discover. Some years later George
got in touch with her again by letter,[6] and almost a quarter of a
century later he came back east to visit her; but practically he was
lost to her from this time on—in a raw, vigorous western movement
which in time would carry him prospecting into the Black Hills and
into the stridently materialistic Deadwood of Wild Bill Hickok and
Calamity Jane.

Mrs. Patterson's physical inability to do anything about the
situation was compounded by the legal helplessness of the women of
her day in the face of such happenings. Only a year or two before,
Elizabeth Cady Stanton had appalled the legislature at Albany, New
York, with her detailed bill of particulars: a mother legally unable
to save a son from being apprenticed to a gambler or a daughter from
being forced into prostitution, women forcibly separated from their
children through the arbitrary and despotic action of a husband.

In her later years Mrs. Eddy wrote of the Cheneys' move to
the west as a plot to deprive her of her son; and indeed Abigail
Tilton may well have furnished Mahala and her husband financial
help for their migration. Evidently the family agreed that it was best
not to let Mrs. Patterson know anything about the move until it was
completed and then to close off all correspondence.

In the history of Christian Science the event has crucial importance. It is at this point in her autobiography that the discoverer
of Christian Science breaks off to say:

> *It is well to know, dear reader, that our material, mortal*
> *history is but the record of dreams, not of man's real existence,*
> *and the dream has no place in the Science of being. It is "as a*
> *tale that is told," and "as the shadow when it declineth." The*
> *heavenly intent of earth's shadows is to chasten the affections, to*
> *rebuke human consciousness and turn it gladly from a material,*
> *false sense of life and happiness, to spiritual joy and true*
> *estimate of being.*[7]

As George Glover vanished with Mahala Cheney into the west,
he might almost have been that young Ishmael, the son of the bond-
woman, who was carried into the wilderness in order to make way

for the true son of promise. That, at least, was the way it would look to some in the future who accepted the promise.

2

The immediate effect of George's removal was to plunge Mrs. Patterson into almost total invalidism. Family letters report this change for the worse and also the fact that Patterson was now having to give virtually all his time to looking after his bedridden wife.

As a result he was unable to pay Martha Pilsbury the interest on the mortgage, and this in turn caused his sister-in-law grave financial difficulties. "What shall I do," she wrote George Baker, "foreclose at once? I suppose I can do this as he has broken his obligation by not paying annual interest." But she pitied him. Mary was sick, he was unable to work, and "I expect they are brought to *absolute want!*"[8]

Martha had a new loss of her own to mourn in the death of her daughter Mary, which occurred just about the time that young George moved west. For Mrs. Patterson, too, the death of this enchanting little niece to whom she had felt so close must have been one more cause for grief. In her scrapbook, opposite several items which spoke of immeasurable woe, she simply wrote "1856."

A year after George's departure she entered in her scrapbook a poem "Consolations" by Park Benjamin and wrote opposite it: "Mine, April 5th 1857." It read in part:

> My childhood knew misfortune of a strange and weary kind,
> And I have always worn a chain, though not upon my mind,
> And I render thanks to thee, oh God! from my prison, that I live
> Unshorn of that best privilege which thou alone canst give!
> I mean a soul to apprehend the beauty that is spread
> Above me and around me and beneath my feeble tread . . .
> And though bereft of freedom in the body, I can fly
> As high as Heaven on wings of thought, like an eagle to the sky.[9]

A month later another entry showed deeper discouragement:

> *I slept very little last night in consequence of* memory *and wounded feelings. My spine is so weak and inflammatory that the least mental emotion gives me suffering that language cannot depict. Then the debility which follows seems nearly as distressing. Oh! how long must I bear this burden life? . . .*

After still another month Martha Pilsbury wrote to George Baker's wife, Martha Rand Baker, who was now living again in New Hampshire:

What dreadful news you gave me of Sam O, Martha I some-times feel that a fearful doom rests on our family—And yet tis so wicked to question the designs of Providence or seek there an excuse for our misfortunes.

But why in every condition in life we must meet with dis-appointment and failure is to me a mystery. . . . Abi's visit to Mary has been constantly before my mind. I long to hear the particulars in a letter from her. I hope it will not make dear Abi worse, though such a picture of suffering and misery is enough to break a sister's heart. But Mary! poor child—Alas what words can express her condition Everything is nought compared to that. One year and a half confined to her bed, and perhaps now there is not even a hope that she will ever be able to rise again, though how long life may last, God alone knows.[10]

These were years that were extremely difficult on Patterson, improvident husband that he was. A sort of tough affection held to-gether the two rather battered warriors in life's struggle. There were sometimes quarrels between them, when his irresponsibilities and her nerves met and clashed; yet somehow love persisted. Shortly before George was taken out west, she wrote a poem "To my absent husband" with the refrain, "I think of thee! I think of thee!"[11] After expressing her longing for the absent one, the poem ended:

> Since first we met—through weal and wo
> It hath been thus and must be so
> Till bursting bonds our spirits part
> And love *divine* shall fill this heart.

He, on his part, wrote her a letter from Sanbornton Bridge in either 1857 or 1859,[12] which shows very clearly his own feeling. Addressing her as "Very Dear Wife," he retailed to her various bits of family news interspersed with anxious expressions of concern for her:

Your brother Samuel came up last Saturday . . . he is greatly changed in his appearance for the better, has left Mr. Parker's Meeting and attends regularly the Baptist Church on Park St. has resolved, to persue a new course of life—has left all of his profanity and other disagreeable practices—and in fact has the appearance of a Christian We attended Mr. Curtice's Meeting last sunday and he preached two of his searching practical ser-mons and Samuel expressed great interest in them, thinks as you and I do that Mr. Curtice is one of the best of men Saml seems pleased to talk on religion . . . with a very different feeling manifested from what I have ever seen in him before. . . . All that rough almost rudeness in his manners has given place to a sober gentlemanly turn which makes him the dignified brother which you and I so much admire and there is nothing in him apparent that we could wish changed unless it be the removal of a shade of melancholy. . . .

I have been out ransacking the village to try to find something for you and in the box you will find the plunder. I hope it will find your poor sick appetite and shake it hard till it wakes it up and sets it going in good earnest so that when I get home I may find you a good "Freemonter" . . . .

George's wife has been in just gone out she says she made arrangements last fall to go up and stay with you a while— but George S. did not go away as she expected and consequently she could not go to you seems very unhappy about her situation, says she will go to keeping house on her own hook soon if nothing new takes place—but I have written a murderously long letter and will close with a long embrace imaginary it is true but still I think I feel it with the warm kiss of unwavering love.

Husband

D. Patterson

Some of her neighbors felt less sympathetic toward Mrs. Patterson's physical struggles. In North Groton, as elsewhere during most of her life, she was a controversial figure. In the first place, people complained that she held herself aloof. In Franklin, too, her extreme "reserve" had been noted by one or two prominent citizens who nevertheless expressed high regard for her.[13] Sarah Turner of North Groton, who thought her "a very spiritual woman," went on to say: "There was much dignity in her manner. Some folks thought she assumed an air of superiority which made them feel inferior and consequently disliked her for it."[14]

A more serious cause of misunderstanding may have been the nature of her disease. In the rough and ready life of a remote New Hampshire village at that time there is not likely to have been much comprehension of the tortures of an obscure complaint which left her in a complete state of nervous collapse at one moment and mysteriously recovered at another. "Her invalidism," Sarah Turner explained, "combined with her extreme nervousness, sometimes repelled the young people of that day and caused her to be misunderstood by many of the younger set."

One of these told of the time Mrs. Patterson seemed to be dying and he was sent through the bitter night over snow-piled roads to a distant village to get Dr. Patterson. When the two of them returned the next day, exhausted and all but frozen, they found her sitting up, cheerful and quite unmindful of the urgent errand she had sent him on. To a simple, healthy young countryman this seemed like nothing but a piece of outrageous play acting to get Patterson home, and that was the way the story was told in the village.

This attitude is reflected in an item which appeared in the *Plymouth Record* in 1904 at the time of the dedication of the Christian Science Church in Concord.[15] A North Groton correspondent wrote that the dedication had recalled the thoughts of some of the older inhabitants to the time half a century before when Mary Baker Eddy was the wife of Daniel Patterson and lived there. He went on:

> *These people remember the woman at that time as one who carried herself above her fellows. With no stretch of the imagination they remember her ungovernable temper and hysterical ways, and particularly well do they remember the night ride of one of the citizens who went for her husband to calm her in one of her unreasonable moods. The Mrs. Eddy of today is not the Mrs. Patterson of then, for this is a sort of Mr. Hyde and Dr. Jekyll case, and the woman is now credited with many charitable and kindly acts.*

She was, however, credited with charitable and kindly acts by some who knew and loved her while she was at North Groton, especially by those who were children at the time. The truly simple-hearted did not seem to find her uppity. She was, wrote Elias F. Bailey in 1911, "a lover of children and in return all children loved her."[16] One of his wife's cousins was named Mark Baker Kidder as a token of respect, and the "whole familey were verrey fond of her."

The reminiscence of Mrs. Sarah G. Chard is typical of the anecdotes told by those who saw her as a kind and loving friend:

> *She was very fond of children. My little sister, Nettie, and I used to go and play in her house and Mother used to leave us with Mrs. Patterson for half a day sometimes when she went to the village. . . . Days when Mrs. Patterson was not up around she used to lay on a couch which had a head board that could be raised or lowered. When she was laying down she used to tell us to take the string and pull her up. The string would fall back. Then she would lie and laugh at us and tell us to try it again. . . . Days when she was able to sit up she would take my sister on her lap and I would stand beside her and she would talk to us. I don't remember what she told us but I guess it must have been good. We always wanted to come back.[17]*

Of special interest is the concern she took in the education and welfare of young Daniel Kidder, who lived on the nearest farm and was in his middle teens. She spent many hours tutoring him, and as late as 1921 his eyes filled with tears when, along with two other old men who had known and loved her, he talked of her to Elbert S. Barlow. Earlier he had written:

> *She was a fine looking woman. Intellectual and stately in appearance. She kept her house in the most perfect order. She wrote for the magazines of the day, mostly poetry. This was a source of much interest and pleasure to me. Mrs. Patterson took a great interest in the education of the young then living near her. She was a great help to me in my studies at that time. I remember her as a sincere friend.*[18]

The "stateliness" suggests again the reserve that kept some people at a distance from her. But breaking through it is the evident desire to help a young boy face the world successfully—a young boy she may have reached out to with special warmth because her own son, unlettered and unready for life, had been taken out of her hands and thrown into a wilderness where she was powerless to help him.

3

In a moment of social indignation Emerson wrote:

> The God who made New Hampshire
> Taunted the lofty land
> With little men;—
> Small bat and wren
> House in the oak.

The trouble was by no means confined to the hills of New Hampshire. Emerson's friend Margaret Fuller, writing in the *New York Tribune,* drew on her experience in the Massachusetts village of Groton:

> *It is a current superstition that country people are more pure and healthy in mind and body than those who live in cities. . . . We have lived in a beautiful village, where, more favorably placed than any other person in it . . . we heard inevitably, from domestics, work-people, and school-children, more ill of human nature than we could possibly sift were we to elect such a task from all the newspapers of this city in the same space of time.*[19]

In her remote village, stripped of the one vital reason that had brought her there, Mrs. Patterson must have felt trapped in smallness.

With only the laughter of other people's children for her music, village gossip offered her little sustenance. Triviality and narrow-minded provincialism lay all around, and, worse than that, no visible escape lightened the future.

To one with the sense of greatness in her it was a dead end. The Brontë sisters had burned their hearts out at Haworth with less cause.

The life expectancy of a girl child born in 1821 was only thirty-seven years, and Mrs. Patterson passed this age while she lived at North Groton. She had entered what was then considered middle age, and there was little reason to believe that she would get far into it. And what if she did? What if she lingered on for a score more painful years? If she died in this obscure corner of the world, what would she leave behind her? A handful of verses in yellowing newspapers.

Yet she held on to her rooted conviction that life held more than this, that life *was* more than this. In her scrapbook she pasted a verse entitled "The Young Poet" by a Mrs. Abby. Significantly she marked these undistinguished but highly relevant lines:

> The poet sadly sighed,
> "Expect no song of pride,
> Lady, from me, no glad and bright revelings. . . .
>
> "I occupy alone,
> An intellectual throne.
> My shrinking subjects will not let me love them:
>
> "Even my kindred, learn
> In trembling awe to turn
> From the kind gaze of him who towers above them. . . ."

She must have known by this time that she would never be a great poet; yet some inner fountain of conviction, some unquenchable inspiration, assured her that she was in touch with realities that set her apart from her village friends and even from her family.

There is a hard realism in the dreams of a Joseph who sees his brother's sheaves bow down before his. This is not egotism; it is facing a simple qualitative fact, intolerable though the fact may seem to the workaday brothers.[20] Nothing that could ever have happened would have made Abigail Tilton, for instance, the founder of a new world religion.

All this was well below the surface of the Groton years. Meanwhile, Mrs. Patterson kept up appearances. Despite her invalidism, her home was always immaculate and furnished attractively. "I thought it was one of the most beautiful houses in the world," remembered one old lady who had often been in it as a ten-year-old child.[21] Mrs. Patterson was "fond of society" and always "polite and entertaining to her numerous callers," wrote a woman who worked for her through part of this time.[22] "She was a very handsome woman," said Sarah Turner. "Her grace of manner, together with the invariable neatness and good quality of her dress, made her a fascinating personage."

F. B. Eastman, who lived in Rumney, told of how his sister went to North Groton to have some dental work done by Patterson. "She met Mrs. Patterson," he stated, "and her impression of her was that she was the most beautiful woman she had ever become acquainted with, the most beautiful disposition."[23] Part of this attractiveness probably lay in the fact, which was commented on by someone who knew her back in the happy Wilmington days, that she was "sincerely interested in other people—the people around her."[24] But where these people were so far her mental inferiors and her own physical energy was so limited, the cost of social life was very high.[25]

Something of this is suggested in the reminiscences of Myra Smith, the blind girl who was her maid for a year or two.[26]

Sympathetic though she was to the sufferings of her mistress, and appreciative of her kindness, she did not find it an easy household to live in. She told of disagreeable scenes between the Pattersons and of sharp words and quick reactions from Mrs. Patterson. In the perspective of time Myra was able to see that "this was not her usual self but was the breaking of overwrought nerves." Still she had little understanding of just what that meant and her own feelings toward her mistress remained as changeable as Mrs. Patterson herself, who, after becoming violently impatient with her, would go up to her, put her arms around her lovingly, and say that she was sorry.

No reservations clouded the love of Myra's little sister, who helped with the housework twice a week. In later years she wrote of Mrs. Patterson, "I thought her a lovely Lady almost an Angel and have always cherished her as a dear friend in memory."[27]

Myra commented on the fact that her mistress spent much of her time reading, especially the Bible. Although there was a small library in Groton, she seems to have been shut off from the great books that were pouring out: Emerson's essays, *Walden, Leaves of Grass, Barchester Towers, Madame Bovary*, Mill's *Essay on Liberty*, Browning's *Men and Women*, and a rich profusion of others which might have watered the thirsty desert of her days.[28] When, in her seventies, she read a book of selections from Carlyle, she wrote opposite his name the wondering exclamation, "O immortal," and one cannot help thinking what it would have meant to her in the Groton days to hear the thunder-tone of his Everlasting Yea . . . or the clear, peaceful fluting of an Emerson.

In the pattern of her whole life this can be seen to have been a necessary deprivation. Denied the cultural solace which might have made the desert tolerable, she was driven to ask the one question which none of these others had asked.

When Susan B. Anthony, doughty fighter for women's rights, retired for a brief season of rest to Seth Rogers Hydropathic Institute in 1855, she read Carlyle's *Sartor Resartus,* George Sand's *Consuelo,* Madame de Staël's *Corinne,* Frances Wright's *A Few Days in Athens,* and Mrs. Gaskell's *Life of Charlotte Brontë,* making notes in her diary of passages she particularly liked, and all these books enriched and energized her life purpose. But Mrs. Patterson had a different task— and a different necessity.

Instead of the notebooks into which she had once copied passages from Milton and Pope and Wordsworth, she now had a scrapbook into which she pasted an astounding miscellany of items—hardly solid nourishment, but bits and scraps gathered for the most part from the newspapers of the day.

One might find a recipe for potato yeast or a cure for hydrophobia next to a minor poem by Whittier, Longfellow, Bryant, or Poe. A phrenological description of Mrs. Lydia H. Sigourney shared honors with "A Mother's Evening Thoughts" by that lady. Columns of moral maxims entitled "Gems of Truth" and "Dewdrops of Wisdom" yielded such thoughts as, "Philosophy, like medicine, has abundance of drugs, few good remedies, and scarcely any specifics." There were clippings on "Russia, her Extent and Resources" and on a successful new "vegetable anaesthetic." Above all, there were masses of graveyard poems, moralistic tear-jerkers on the evils of gambling and drinking, sentimental poems on home and motherhood—the sort of thing with which the midcentury newspapers were filled. There were even one or two indifferent translations of poems by Goethe and Schiller and, for good measure, "Hints to Young Men" by Henry Ward Beecher.

This was thin fare for an eager mind, not unlike the bare subsistence diet she endured in her efforts to fight the torments of dyspepsia. She extracted from this reading what nourishment she could, pondering and marking many of the "Dewdrops" and "Gems." An intense and pure gaze, a gaze not merely of the intellect but of the whole man, can find even in a platitude values that elude the casual or scornful glance. Mrs. Patterson related these fugitive pieces to her own experience, and phrases from them turned up in her later writings loaded with new significance. But it seems clear that the secret springs nourishing her during this period lay deeper than the level of her scrapbook.

One of the aphorisms she marked referred to the Bible as "the learned man's Masterpiece . . . the ignorant man's Dictionary . . . the wise man's Directory." The epithets crept into her own writing later; but, far more important, the fact to which they pointed was already imbedded in her life. The Bible was always there to keep hope alive, to keep her importunate. She might weary of life, but perpetual renewal was to be found in the Bible promises. "All my springs are in thee," the Psalmist had cried in a similarly sparse and thirsty land.

F. B. Eastman recalled a Baptist meeting at which someone asked Patterson why his wife had not come and he replied, "O, she is at home reading her Bible."[29] All her life the Bible seems to have formed another dimension of reality for her.[30] At that time it was apparently the dimension of promise rather than of revelation, but her later writings make abundantly clear how directly and concretely the promise spoke to her.

In the 54th chapter of Isaiah, for instance, she found not merely high poetry, comforting and inspiring in a general sort of way, but an intense vision of the means of grace by which the heart is prepared for God's transfiguring purpose:

> Sing, O barren, thou that didst not bear; break forth into singing, and cry aloud, thou that didst not travail with child: for more are the children of the desolate than the children of the married wife, saith the Lord. . . . Fear not; for thou shalt not be ashamed: neither be thou confounded; for thou shalt not be put to shame: for thou shalt forget the shame of thy youth, and shalt not remember the reproach of thy widowhood any more. For thy Maker is thine husband; the Lord of hosts is his name; and thy Redeemer the Holy One of Israel; The God of the whole earth shall he be called. For the Lord hath called thee as a woman forsaken and grieved in spirit, and a wife of youth, when thou wast refused, saith thy God. For a small moment have I forsaken thee; but with great mercies will I gather thee. In a little wrath I hid my face from thee for a moment; but with everlasting kindness will I have mercy on thee, saith the Lord thy Redeemer. . . . For the mountains shall depart, and the hills be removed; but my kindness shall not depart from thee, neither shall the covenant of my peace be removed, saith the Lord that hath mercy on thee. O thou afflicted, tossed with tempest, and not comforted, behold, I will lay thy stones with fair colours, and lay thy foundations with sapphires. . . . And all thy children shall be taught of the Lord; and great shall be the peace of thy children. In righteousness shalt thou be established: thou shalt be far from oppression; for thus shalt not fear: and from terror; for it shall not come near thee. . . . No weapon

that is formed against thee shall prosper; and every tongue that shall rise against thee in judgment thou shalt condemn. This is the heritage of the servants of the Lord, and their righteousness is of me, saith the Lord.[31]

We do not know how clearly the sense of destiny may have been with Mary Baker Patterson in these years. But, conscious or unconscious, it would have made doubly agonizing the "little wrath" that hid God's face. Many years later she would write, "The very circumstance, which your suffering sense deems wrathful and afflictive, Love can make an angel entertained unawares." But she would also write, "Physical torture affords but a slight illustration of the pangs which come to one upon whom the world of sense falls with its leaden weight in the endeavor to crush out of a career its divine destiny."[32]

4

The Patterson house today stands in a little wilderness. High in the hills, it is almost hidden from the narrow, seldom traveled road that winds past it to North Groton. Through part of the year the roar of a brook fills the tiny hollow in which it stands. Trees and wild shrubs crowd around the patch of grass on its northern side, and the light falls greenly and secretly on the empty house. The windows on the south look straight down to the plunging brook, like windows in a fortress high above a moat, and across to the steep, wooded wall of the ravine.

It is a small, remote, self-enclosed world, with something lost and forgotten about it—though visitors come to it every year from faraway places, from England and Africa and Japan, to gaze at the lonely beauty which imprisoned a great religious leader for five years. It is like coming to the end of the world, to a place shut off from the forward movement of life, where only the flash of a goldfinch and the chipmunk's scramble and chatter seem to belong. This is high country, but the Patterson house lies cupped in obscurity.

On either side the wilderness stretches away, with a tumbledown barn where the Kidder farm once stood. Of course, it was not like this when the Pattersons lived here. There were other farms then, cornfields and pastures, a flourishing little village, a good deal more traffic on the road—enough to make Patterson take sawdust from his mill and put it on the bridge across the ravine to deaden the sound of wagon wheels which so disturbed his wife. But even then the wilderness was all around, shuffling forward to reclaim the land, nudging down stone walls and edging into the pastures with poplar and birch. Even then it was like the end of nowhere.

There were hours and days of utter solitude for Mrs. Patterson—and even nights when her husband was away and the only sound was that of the brook and the whippoorwills and perhaps the distant barking of a dog or the angry oratorio of the bullfrogs. Worst of all, there were the long snowbound winters turning the whole world into a crystal chaos, a formless, frozen emptiness where the wind went howling crazy through the hills. Always, after these years, Mrs. Patterson would see the giant snowstorms which piled obstruction everywhere as the enemy of order, a negation of life.[33]

From earliest girlhood she had loved the natural world; but just as she was denied the solace of escape through culture, so she was denied the solace of escape through nature. No Wordsworthian pantheism, no mystical identification with natural forces was possible to one who felt in her own body the jarring dissonances of nature. The myth of the American Adam, or Eve, was not for her.

Down through the nineteenth century, the American wilderness was often celebrated as lost Eden. The wild was the good; the natural man was the man of spiritual health. No Pauline dichotomy between natural and spiritual troubled this faith, which reached its highest expression in the loose-limbed paganism of Whitman:

> Me imperturbe, standing at ease in Nature,
> Master of all or mistress of all, aplomb in the midst
>   of irrational things,
> Imbued as they, passive, receptive, silent as they . . .
> Me wherever my life is lived, O to be self-balanced
>   for contingencies,
> To confront night, storms, hunger, solitude, accidents,
>   rebuffs, as the trees and animals do.

Central to this faith was mother earth, the goodness of her energies, her brutal innocence. Even sky-minded Emerson sang her praises, though Margaret Fuller complained that his head was too far in the clouds: "We doubt this friend raised himself too early to the perpendicular and did not lie along the ground long enough to hear the secret whispers of our parent life. We could wish he might be thrown by conflicts on the lap of mother earth, to see if he would not rise again with added power."

Yet all these eloquent tributes to nature presupposed physical health. Emerson himself wrote: ". . . I dilate and conspire with the morning wind. How does Nature deify us with a few and cheap elements! Give me health and a day, and I will make the pomp of emperors ridiculous." But suppose the health were not given. After all, nature maimed and withheld and destroyed as much as she gave. Did the wounded lark sing hymns at heaven's gates?

Mrs. Patterson's heart might mount and sing on a morning when the sun flashed through the twinkling leaves and all was dappled and fresh and dancing, but her weary limbs might even then tell her that wherever there was matter there was death. Through the dew-wet grass of Eden, blazing like emerald fire, slid the inevitable serpent, and the shudder of mortality passed across the scene.

Neither then nor later did she become indifferent to natural beauty. The Park Benjamin poem, already quoted, expressed gratitude for the "last privilege" that remained after all else was gone—the capacity to apprehend the beauty spread above and around and beneath her. And after her discovery of Christian Science she wrote:

> *To take all earth's beauty into one gulp of vacuity and label beauty nothing, is ignorantly to caricature God's creation, which is unjust to human sense and to the divine realism. In our immature sense of spiritual things, let us say of the beauties of the sensuous universe: "I love your promise; and shall know, some time, the spiritual reality and substance of form, light, and color, of what I now through you discern dimly; and knowing this, I shall be satisfied. . . ."*[34]

But before she could reach the point of discrimination represented by that statement, she had to see deeply into the wild and savage, even the demonic,[35] in physical nature. And here her own body served her as well as an untamed continent would have done. Even in a quiet corner of New Hampshire, battles fought with obscure and malevolent forces might be linked to cosmic issues.

Sibyl Wilbur writes of talking with an old lady at North Groton who, on one occasion in younger days, heard the tinkling of the little bell which Mrs. Patterson kept at her bedside. Going to her aid, the woman found that she had fallen unconscious, with foam on her lips, and only slowly was she brought back to consciousness.[36] Her lonely battles were sometimes fought in total solitude, and although she was thrown to the lap of mother earth, as Margaret Fuller recommended, she did not rise with added strength.

Nor if she looked up to where the stars wheeled calmly through the night sky did she find an answer there. This might be the army of unalterable law, as Meredith said, but a young German scientist called Rudolf Clausius had just defined a law which in time would lead to the conclusion that the universe must end as a cold, dark, blind, inert chaos. Mrs. Patterson could not have known of this second law of thermodynamics, but she knew in her bones that destruction and chaos were written into the universe of matter as surely as she felt in her heart that life and order were the mandate of God.

Through all of nature there was a thrust toward life, something moving in opposition to the drag of entropy. Yet the animal energies which seemed to push life along were themselves sucked back into the great whirlpool of physical energy, into ultimate nothingness. Only ideas endured, and the forms of nature remained as ideas when particular instances had passed away.

Mrs. Patterson at this time or later read what Louis Agassiz was saying about some of these things. "A species is a thought of the creator," he wrote, and again, "Natural History must, in good time, become the analysis of the thoughts of the Creator. . . ." The capacity of the human intellect to comprehend the facts of creation was, he thought, "the most conclusive proof of our affinity with the Divine Mind."[37] But Agassiz, who was captivating Boston audiences with his transcendental interpretations of nature, was soon to be rendered obsolete by Darwin, and, in any case, brute nature transcendentalized left one with a beautiful but brutal pageant of thoughts in the mind of a creator who seemed largely indifferent to the particular individual.

It was in 1859, while the Pattersons were at North Groton, that *The Origin of Species* made its stunning impact on the world. All order and design seemed to slip out of the universe, although many of Darwin's champions refused to admit this. Darwin himself was more tough-minded. A species, like anything else in the physical world, was the chance product of blind material forces, without permanence or logical necessity; and if this was true of the lower species, then it was true of man as the physical senses knew him.

An English Darwinian two decades later would write, "That man is an animal is the great and special discovery of natural science in our generation." It would take a still later generation to reduce the human animal to a collocation of electrical impulses, but he was well on the way. Already Thomas Huxley was considering thought as a mere by-product of material force, like the heat thrown off by the passage of an electric current through a wire.

Yet thought had its own universe, a realm where design, purpose, meaning, and values all had place. Even Huxley had to acknowledge this realm as a reality in acknowledging the value of truth. It was a universe that seemed to be constantly striving to break through all the waste and violence of the long evolutionary struggle, as though the first pre-Cambrian sandworm had been trying to be man and the first brutish cave dweller to be the son of God.

Regarded as an effort of the material universe to lift itself by its own bootstraps to the condition of pure mind or spirit, the whole process was foredoomed to failure; but there might be other ways of looking at it, without falling into the religious sentimentalism of those who merely glossed over the cruelty and waste inherent in the trial-and-error process of natural selection.

Kierkegaard had given a hint in his *Purity of Heart:* "The temporal as we know it cannot . . . be the clear radiance of eternity; so far as it has reality at all it is through the eternal that strives to master it. The more the eternal stirs within its witness, the mightier is the struggle. . . ."[38] *So far as it has reality at all.* This could mean that the struggle has meaning only to the degree that the eternally real breaks through into temporal experience. The ceaseless struggle of animate nature would then belong with the blind dance of the atoms except as it let through a larger measure of spirit.

"The whole creation groaneth and travaileth in pain together until now," waiting for "the manifestation of the sons of God," Paul had written. Yet once in history a total breakthrough had occurred and a new and wonderful reality, a new kind of man, had appeared. Orthodoxy had relegated that event to the realm of special miracle, but both the orthodox believer and the unorthodox seeker knew that here if anywhere was the answer to life's riddle.

Mary Baker Patterson would pass through many years of development before she could write:

> When we admit that matter (*heart, blood, brain, acting through the five physical senses*) *constitutes man, we fail to see how anatomy can distinguish between humanity and the brute, or determine when man is really* man *and has progressed farther than his animal progenitors. . . .*
>
> *As a material, theoretical life-basis is found to be a misapprehension of existence, the spiritual and divine Principle of man dawns upon human thought, and leads it to "where the young child was,"—even to the birth of a new-old idea, to the spiritual sense of being and of what Life includes.*[39]

But if the dawn of that idea still lay some years ahead, Mrs. Patterson at least turned puzzled eyes toward the supreme Teacher who had demonstrated a new order of nature in which Spirit had dominion over all.

5

It has been said that one way of escaping the tedium of conventional American life in the nineteenth century was to go west, the other way was to go "beyond." The great wave of spiritualism which swept through the United States after the Fox sisters in 1848 began hearing mysterious rappings bore witness to the lure of the beyond.

Soon the busy tapping of telegraph keys, which had brought new lines of communication to the West, was matched by the busy tipping of tables the length and breadth of the republic. But whereas the first message sent over the first telegraph wire was, "What hath God wrought!" the messages tapped and rapped and tipped out on the tables were remarkable for their sheer banality and lack of any real religious significance. The ghostly small-talk of departed spirits seemed to promise a beyond which reproduced most of the drearier features of the here.

Back in Sanbornton Bridge Mrs. Patterson, then Mrs. Glover, had shared in the general interest in the new phenomenon. Apparently her natural curiosity was soon satisfied, for during the Franklin and North Groton years she was indifferent to the subject and indeed argued with her credulous Groton neighbor, Mrs. Kidder, against it.[40] Had she been seeking to win personal attention, as her enemies claimed, this would have been a rich field for her to exploit; but it was not, she evidently felt, the way of true spirituality.

From her earliest years, according to her own later account, certain unexplained phenomena had marked her experience. As a small child, she had repeatedly heard a mysterious "voice" calling her. Her mother, persuaded at last of the reality of the occurrence, had read to her the story of the prophetic call which came to the child Samuel. Subsequently she had had instances of what today would be called extrasensory perception and precognition, experiences not uncommon to one who is extremely sensitive to the atmosphere of thought. But she kept these things to herself when they occurred, and pondered their meaning. No record of them exists apart from the reminiscences of a few intimates to whom she recounted them in her later years.[41]

Then and since, spiritualists have been eager to claim her as one of their own. Many who knew her were convinced that she could be a great sensitive. After she became famous, newspaper reports would periodically quote stray individuals who "knew" her as a practicing medium (or sometimes it was a fortuneteller) in Boston or St. Louis— oddly enough during the very years that she was lying in a state of helpless invalidism in North Groton. Investigation has shown that a Mrs. Eddy and a Mrs. Glover, wholly unconnected with Mrs. Patterson, did apparently operate in one or another of those cities in the 'fifties and 'sixties, but most of the reports did not have even that much shadow of substance to rest on.[42]

Very early Mrs. Patterson seems to have drawn a distinction between the psychic and the spiritual, as T. S. Eliot did when, referring to the psychic interests which W. B. Yeats introduced into his poetry, he complained that Yeats was concerned with the *wrong* supernatural world. If Mrs. Patterson retained her faith in an orthodox heaven where she would be reunited with those she had loved and lost, this was a supernaturalism which at least ruled out occult gossip with departed spirits in some psychic half-world, earth-bound and dream-burdened.

In her scrapbook is an entry, "Written in bed April 24th 1857," which reads: "Mother waits for me in the far beyond! and through the discipline, the darkness and the trials of life, I am walking unto her. She has walked the still road that leads from the sepulchre to the seraphim . . ." with more of the same. This is the language of orthodox Christian yearning, not of spiritism. The communication with her mother for which she evidently longed was to be found through a spiritually disciplined life leading to a brighter hereafter rather than through the interposition of a medium, a spirit control, and all the rest.

With her active mind it was inevitable that she should give some thought to what lay behind these spiritistic phenomena, but she would not find a rational answer that would completely explain them—or such part of them as could not be written off as fraud—until she discovered Christian Science. Then she would devote a full chapter of *Science and Health* to the subject, a chapter first entitled "Imposition and Demonstration" and later "Christian Science versus Spiritualism."

It is useful to remember the thorough grounding she had had in the teaching that any pretended revelation must be subject to testing by reason. Locke and Watts, not to mention Albert Baker, had armed her against undue credulity. One of the schoolbooks which had influenced her most was Whately's *Elements of Logic*,[43] and Whately had made some thought-provoking distinctions in his chapter "On the Discovery of Truth":

> There . . . are two kinds of "New Truth" and of "Discovery."
> . . . First, such truths as were, before they were discovered, ab-
> solutely *unknown*. . . . Such are all matters of fact *strictly so
> called*, when first made known to one who had not any such
> previous knowledge, as would enable him to ascertain them a
> priori. . . . The communication of this kind of knowledge is
> most usually, and most strictly called information. We gain it
> from observation, and from testimony. . . . The other class of
> Discoveries is of a very different nature. That which may be
> elicited by Reasoning, and consequently is implied in that which

we already know, we assent to on that ground, and not from observation or testimony. . . . To all practical purposes, indeed, a Truth of this description may be as completely unknown to a man as the other; but as soon as it is set before him, and the argument by which it is connected with his previous notions is made clear to him, he recognizes it as something conformable to, and contained in, his former belief.

Mrs. Patterson had time both to observe new facts and to reason on them. Among the questions which loomed large in her life at this time none was more pressing than the problem of health, and the particular field of her investigation and reasoning was homeopathy. This system of medicine had been growing tremendously in favor during the past decade or two, and her own favorable results with it in 1853 had started her off on a long series of experiments, and had also led Daniel Patterson to practice homeopathy as a sideline to his dentistry.

In her possession was a copy of Jahr's *New Manual of Homeopathic Practice,* edited by A. Gerald Hull and popularly known as Hull's *Jahr.* Myra Smith told of Mrs. Patterson's devotion to this huge volume which, next to the Bible, probably constituted her chief reading matter at that time. The blind girl also told how some of the neighbors would come to Mrs. Patterson for medicine: and her own later accounts of her experiences with these rustic patients show the immense importance homeopathy had in the development of her thought.

The feature of it which appealed to her especially was not its basic medical theory that "like cures like" but its emphasis on the attenuation of drugs to the point where they all but disappeared from the remedy.

The midcentury was marked by a healthy scientific skepticism of drugs, particularly of the all-service calomel which, together with the lancet, had been the badge of the old "heroic" practitioners. The Massachusetts Medical Society announced that a prize would be offered in 1857 on the theme, "We would regard every approach toward the rational and successful prevention and management of a disease, without the necessity of drugs, to be an advance in favor of humanity and scientific medicine," a theme which a distinguished Harvard clinician a century later thought might profitably be revived by his generation.[44]

The founder of homeopathy, Hahnemann, himself had held that diseases were the immaterial alterations of an impalpable vital principle and must be combatted by forces of the same kind—by what one commentator on his system called the spiritual essences and virtues of medicine.[45] That vigorous English homeopathist and Sweden-borgian, J. J. Garth Wilkinson, in a book which he dedicated to his good friend, the elder Henry James, stated that the efficacy of drugs rested in part on "the smallness of the doses, or we would rather say the use of the spirit and not the body of the drugs." Drugs so attenuated, he added, "are more like ideas than material bodies," and "we are obliged to desert the hypothesis of their material action, and to presume that they take rank as dynamical things."[46]

Mrs. Patterson's homeopathic experiments carried her further toward a mental theory of disease. In *Science and Health*[47] is an account of a sick woman who came to her at North Groton, a woman in a dropsical condition who "looked like a barrel" and for whom she prescribed "the fourth attenuation of *Argentum nitratum* with occasional doses of a high attenuation of *Sulphuris*." The woman improved, but Mrs. Patterson was anxious to get her to drop the medicine and decided to try unmedicated sugar pellets, without telling her what they were. The improvement continued, except when the pellets were withheld for a day or two. The woman finally recovered.

This was obviously an experiment in the use of what today would be called placebos, but in Mrs. Eddy's words in 1907 it "was a falling apple to me—it made plain to me that mind governed the whole question of her recovery."[48] On another occasion when she was successfully treating a sick woman with a highly attenuated remedy, she sent a specimen of it to Dr. Charles T. Jackson, a prominent chemist of Boston, for analysis. He found that she had so diluted it that he could not discover a trace of the "drug," which was nothing more than common table salt to begin with.[49] This experience was probably behind her statement in her autobiography, "One drop of the thirtieth attenuation of *Natrum muriaticum,* in a tumbler-full of water, and one teaspoonful of the water mixed with the faith of ages, would cure patients not affected by a larger dose."[50]

But these discoveries were also disillusioning. The hocus-pocus of attenuating the drug, shaking the new solution vigorously each time, might serve to focus thought on the process and, in a sense, substitute thought for the drug, but it reduced the whole thing to a sort of magic in which the patient's faith was the decisive factor. With the progress of her experiments, Mrs. Patterson's own faith in homeopathy decreased. Sometime in 1859 or 1860, when Myra Smith was with her, the girl was making up her bed one day and accidentally knocked onto the floor and broke the little bottle of pellets which she kept under her pillow, but she quickly told Myra "not to mind as they were no good anyway."[51]

It was something to have discovered that faith, an attitude of mind, was behind cures attributed to drugs. But faith in what? The age was prolific in systems appealing to men's credulity. There was the Graham system of diet, which Mrs. Patterson herself followed with indifferent results. There were the "botanics" and the "eclectics," the hydropathists and the hygienists, and a score of others earnestly following out their theories and sometimes even contributing a minor element to the development of orthodox medicine.

In addition, there were the endless varieties of patent medicines and quack nostrums sold by an endless variety of scoundrels. The one virtue all the remedies had was that they might conceivably enlist the patient's faith to the point where he would recover. But it was a desperately hit-or-miss proposition, fraught with perils.

The classic picture of all this activity at its lower extremes is to be found in Melville's *The Confidence-Man,* with its subtle array of "the most extraordinary metaphysical scamps." The confidence man, in various guises, argues that confidence, or faith, is all. A sick philosopher, says this rogue, is incurable because he has no confidence: "Because either he spurns his powder, or, if he take it, it proves a blank cartridge, though the same given to a rustic in like extremity, would act like a charm. I am no materialist; but the mind so acts upon the body, that if the one have no confidence, neither has the other."

Mrs. Patterson could have agreed ruefully that she had no confidence in the pellets that worked wonders with a sick neighbor; she was indeed a sick philosopher. Melville's confidence man, on his Mississippi steamboat, took issue further with "science"—those "chemical practitioners, who have sought out so many inventions"—on the ground that they showed "that kind and degree of pride in human skill, which seems scarce compatible with reverential dependence upon the power above." But then followed a passage which gave the game away. Hearing of a book entitled *Nature in Disease,* the confidence man continues:

> "*A title I cannot approve; it is suspiciously scientific.* Nature in Disease? *As if nature, divine nature, were aught but health; as if through nature disease is decreed! But did I not before hint of the tendency of science, that forbidden tree? Sir, if despondency is yours from recalling that title, dismiss it. Trust me, nature is health; for health is good, and nature cannot work ill. As little can she work error. Get nature, and you get well.*"

To this expression of faith in physical nature, which might be termed the basic fallacy of nineteenth-century American optimism, Mrs. Patterson might have replied with the skeptical Missourian a few chapters later: "Look you, nature! I don't deny that your clover is sweet, and your dandelions don't roar; but whose hailstones smashed my windows?"[52]

Confidence had to reach higher than nature, and for Mrs. Patterson there was only one real place where it could anchor: God. Throughout her life, faith in God had brought healing to her—on one or two occasions physical healing and on many more occasions healing of grief and despair.[53] In later years she told of healing the diseased eyes of a baby at this time through prayer alone, through turning with her whole heart to the love of God.[54] She also told of making a vow one day that if she herself were healed she would devote the rest of her life to helping other people.[55]

This was the decade when Florence Nightingale's work in the Crimean War was winning the admiration of the world, and it may well have stirred Mrs. Patterson's imagination.[56] The discoverer of Christian Science would later write with great respect of the founder of modern nursing, who, in turn, came to place more and more emphasis on the mental and spiritual elements in health. But whereas Florence Nightingale took final refuge in mysticism, Mrs. Patterson felt the answer must be found in science—not the science of the "chemical practitioners" but the spiritual science of the Healer by Gennesaret.

How clearly this was formulated in her mind at this time we do not know; it may have been no more than an inarticulate sense of what ought to be. But with her desperate search for health and the unquestioning authority she gave the Bible it would be surprising if she had not pondered the New Testament records and promises of healing. "He that believeth on me, the works that I do shall he do also," Jesus had said, but was this a matter of blind belief only? "Ye shall know the truth, and the truth shall make you free," he had also said.

Science, as the word was used in the textbooks which had helped to mold her thought, was just that—knowledge or understanding of truth; the tried, tested, systematic, and liberating knowledge of objective fact. While one could *believe* anything, one could *know* only what was rationally and experimentally verifiable, and that must necessarily be coherent with all other proven knowledge, or science. Since science compelled the admission that behind every phenomenon was a law, must there not be a still undiscovered law behind the healings of Jesus?[57]

A Christianity which taught that God may send sickness as a punishment but that man is entitled to use medicine to get rid of the punishment divinely intended for him was at least anomalous.

Such an attitude put religion and science in opposition to each other and both in opposition to logic. What God universally willed for man through law must logically be in accord with the purpose and method of New Testament healing.

There was an interesting new phrase that was cropping up here and there. As early as 1834 a circular advertising Oberlin College announced, "Where this Institution is beginning to diffuse the cheering beams of Christian Science, less than one year since was the darkness of a deep Ohio forest without inhabitant." In 1847 *The Youth's Magazine, or Evangelical Miscellany,* published in London, quoted the verse from Philippians, "Yea doubtless, and I count all things but lost [sic] for the excellency of the knowledge of Christ Jesus my Lord," and added, "The sentiment of the text is,—*The transcendency of Christian Science. . . .*" The following year a volume of poems by Sarah Josepha Hale contained the lines:

'Tis Christian Science makes our day,
And Freedom lends her gladdening ray.[58]

In 1850 a volume entitled *The Elements of Christian Science, A Treatise upon Moral Philosophy and Practice* by William Adams was published in Philadelphia. It was a high-minded but commonplace discussion of Christian ethics, specifically disclaiming any metaphysical interest; and indeed all these early uses of the phrase Christian Science were imprecise and without deep significance. The same thing is true of the article "Three Graces of Christian Science" which appeared in Charles Dickens' weekly journal *Household Words* (Vol. VIII, No. 14) in 1854.

There undoubtedly were other examples of similar usage,[59] and Mrs. Patterson may or may not have run across one or more of them. The important point is that the phrase, the idea, was in the air. Christianity *ought* to be a Science.

6

The great financial panic of 1857 was followed by several years of economic depression. By September, 1859, Martha Pilsbury felt that she could no longer hold back from foreclosing the mortgage on the North Groton house where the Pattersons lived. An entry in the diary of Cyrus Blood, a neighbor, on September 20, states laconically, "Dr. Patterson has had an auction today."[60] An entry in Mrs. Patterson's notebook for the same date reads, "On this day my sister sells our homestead."

Beneath these words she wrote:

Father didst not thou the dark wave treading,
Lift from despair the struggler with the sea?
And seest thou not the scalding tears I'm shedding,
And knowest Thou not my pain and agony? . . .
For my sick soul is darkened unto death,
With Stygian shadows from this world of wo;
The strong foundations of my early faith
Shrink from beneath me, whither shall I flee?
Hide me O, rock of ages! hide in thee.

This seemed like the absolute end. All her life a home of her own was a matter of deepest importance to Mrs. Eddy, and one of her greatest hardships was the fact that so much of her existence had to be lived in other people's houses. In *Science and Health* she would write, "Home is the dearest spot on earth, and it should be the centre, though not the boundary, of the affections."[61]

Now this last refuge was to be taken from her. Her most cherished possessions had to go in auction. It is not clear exactly what happened, for she and Patterson managed to stay on in the house for almost six months more, but their days there were clearly numbered. On October 26 Cyrus Blood noted in his diary, "Dr. Patterson sold out today," but this may have had reference to the sawmill or his timber holdings. Through another season of snow and ice and darkness they lingered on in the house, and towards the end of February a strange scene took place, a scene described three weeks later in the *Nashua Gazette* of March 15:

FEMALE BRAVERY—*A North Groton (N H) correspondent of the Concord Patriot writes that on the 20th ult. Dr. Patterson, a dentist in that place, while employed in splitting wood before his door, was assaulted by two men, father and son, named Wheat. The elder Wheat rushed upon him with a shovel, which the Doctor knocked from his hands with his axe, at the same time losing hold of the axe.*

The elder assailant then attempted to get him by his throat, but the Doctor knocked him down; when young Wheat rushed upon the Doctor with the axe, striking him upon the head, stunned and felled him to the ground. The father then seized him by the neck, and called upon his son to strike. The son was about to comply with the murderous request, when the wife of Dr Patterson, almost helpless by long disease, rushed from her bed to the rescue of her husband, and, throwing herself before their intended victim, seized, with unwonted strength, the son who held the axe and prevented him from dealing the intended blow. Help soon came, the assailants fled, and the feeble but brave wife was carried back to her bed. . . .

It has often been supposed that Patterson, weary of the difficulties and responsibilities of his life at home, was engaging in flirtations on his dental jaunts, and perhaps nearer at home, and that the murderous attack by the Wheets, *père et fils,* was caused by their discovery of impropriety between him and the elder Wheet's wife. This sounds plausible enough; but Myra Smith, who was there at the time, declared in her reminiscences that the dispute was over a load of wood purchased by Patterson from Joseph Wheet but not paid for by him.

Cyrus Blood's diary for February 29 states, without further explanation, "The Wheets were tried today." But ironically enough, it was they who took possession of the house about a month later. Sometime in March Abigail Tilton drove up to North Groton, collected her sister in her carriage, and drove her out of the village, as Joseph Wheet and his son tolled the bell of the village church in triumph. Patterson rather typically was away at the time. Myra Smith chose to stumble along behind rather than ride in the carriage and hear Mrs. Patterson's sobs. The five years in North Groton had ended in total desolation and defeat.

Yet actually it marked the faint beginning of an upturn.[62]

Abigail Tilton drove her to the boardinghouse of Mrs. Lydia Herbert at Rumney Station, only six miles away, where Patterson had engaged quarters. After getting her settled, Mrs. Tilton, who was probably paying for the accommodation, left. The two newcomers were watched with avid interest by the other boarders, and gossip and speculation abounded as to Mrs. Patterson's strange indisposition, the "spinal inflammation" which was said to be responsible for her sufferings. It was noted that she sometimes seemed more helpless when Daniel Patterson was there to carry her upstairs and down, and the knowing ones drew their thin-lipped conclusions as to *that.*[63]

She must have thought a good deal about the remarkable strength she was able to muster when she went to Patterson's rescue in North Groton. Here was confirmation that a mental state could overcome a physical difficulty. On one occasion after her arrival at Rumney Station she expressed a desire to see the village assembly hall, but the good ladies of the boardinghouse assured her that "they could not carry her and there were no men in."[64] Thereupon she announced that she would go anyway, rose up, and walked there—to the consternation of all, but strengthening the conviction of those who said sharply that her illness was a pretense. Yet the illness did not vanish then and there, and afterwards she found herself as helpless as ever. The sudden access of strength that had come to her in the North Groton emergency was not to be regained and retained by an act of will.

After a few months, by some means or other, Patterson managed to acquire a new house. It was in Rumney village a mile back in the hills, and it stood a little above the village, opposite the schoolhouse, with a wide view toward the mountains. It was a beautiful spot, with a lovely sweep to the landscape, and it seemed to match the rise in Mrs. Patterson's spirits.

Not that she was much better physically. But she had touched bottom, she had survived the ordeal, and she found that life was still good. One letter of hers which probably belongs to this period was written to her "Dear Hubby" while she was on a visit to Sanbornton Bridge.[65] The letter is very affectionate and gives a revealing glimpse of her situation:

> I have had one good ride with D. Lang and Barns. He took us over to Franklin. . . . I paid, 50 cts—and I can't go again for lack of money. I felt better for the ride; 'twas yesterday and the air did so brace me, and O! 'twas so delightful to see so much of beauty on this earth.

While at Rumney she began to write again, and two of the poems in her notebook hint at the inner development that had gone on during the Groton years. One of them is called "The Heart's Unrest" and ends:

> Yet through the rough billows and pitiless storms
> The Pilot acquires his art
> And thus our dear Savior by conflict forms
> The meek and enduring heart
> These, these are the teachings of wisdom and love
> So lean on thy Fathers breast
> Tis the fold for the lambkin the cote of the dove
> Where the love of thy heart *can rest.*

Beneath the known "facts" of even the most carefully recorded life invisible currents run, to be guessed at only from hints and indirections and from the sudden surprises of later years, for even a commonplace and almost predictable life never loses entirely the capacity to surprise us. This must be vastly more so in the case of one in whom an unseen spiritual purpose is slowly and perhaps unconsciously forming. Where the known outward facts are few we doubly value the sudden revealing glimpse of hidden movement that an upturned fragment of evidence may offer. Such a fragment is a passage in the "Ode to Adversity" which Mrs. Patterson entered in her notebook at this time:

Am I to conflicts new to be innured?
No! I have long the utmost wrongs indured
And drawn fresh energies from sharpest blows
Thus from rude hammer strokes or burning heat
With each successive change refined complete
The gold is purged of dross and brightly glows.

7

The trumpets of war were sounding, and the martial mood blended with the vigor of Mrs. Patterson's renewed determination to break through to *life*.

The thunderous events of recent years had shaken her loose from the old Jacksonian ties and had put her squarely behind the new party of Fremont and Lincoln. The poignantly dramatic return of the fugitive slave, Anthony Burns, from Boston to slavery; the brutal caning of Charles Sumner in the Senate; the Dred Scott decision; the Old Testament tragedy of John Brown striding toward doom in the smoky light of Harper's Ferry—here was a crescendo of moral challenges that came to its climax when Old Abe Lincoln came out of the wilderness to his appointed task.

In the anxious months between Lincoln's election and his inauguration, as the nation waited and watched the suspended drama at Fort Sumter, Mrs. Patterson wrote a poem charged with astonishing if uneven energy and directed to the commander of the beleaguered fort. Written on February 6, 1861, and entitled "Maj. Anderson and our Country," it read in part:

Brave Anderson, thou patriot-soul sublime
Thou morning Star of errors' darkest time!
Prince of the lion-hearted Jackson mould,
Thy valor mocks the rebel at his hold. . . .

O! thou Supreme, who reign'st o'er human power,
God of our fathers, still avert the hour
When sins' repentance shall be sealed in blood,
To stain this nation blessed o'er field and flood.

The hour was not averted, war came in mid July, and the defeat at Manassas plunged the North into despair. A month later Mrs. Patterson addressed a letter to General Benjamin F. Butler of Massachusetts, called forth by his July 30 letter to Secretary of War Cameron.[66] Though an unscrupulous politician and an iron-fisted general, Butler argued with both moral eloquence and legal persuasiveness against returning to the southern lines the slaves who fled to the northern army for protection. Mrs. Patterson, with an oversimplified estimate of Butler but an earnest regard for man, wrote him:

> . . . *You, as we all, hold freedom to be the normal condition of those made in God's image. . . . The red strife between right and wrong can only be fierce, it cannot be long, and victory on the side of immutable justice will be well worth its cost. Give us in the field or forum a brave Ben Butler and our Country is saved.*

Once again the "general" was coming out in her, as she responded to the demand of the times. Before the end of the year she had written a "Sonnet to Maj. Gen. John C. Fremont," and some of its vigorous lines suggest anything rather than a sequestered invalid as its author:

> What other beams O! Patriot, shine
> In that commanding glance of thine,
> No shade of doubt or weak despair
> Blends with indignant sorrow there.

Meanwhile the war had an unexpected effect on her life.[67] Following the death of Mahala Cheney, George Glover, not yet seventeen, ran away from home and joined the Eighteenth Wisconsin Infantry Regiment, giving his age as a year older than it was. There he became acquainted with one David Hall of Iowa, who wrote letters home for many of the soldiers who were illiterate or not gifted with the pen. Through Hall's inquiries Mrs. Patterson's whereabouts were discovered,[68] and the result was that on October 10 she received a letter from George, Hall acting as amanuensis. Cyrus Blood, who happened to be present when she received it, noted the date in his diary and afterwards told of the tears of joy she shed at hearing from her son at last. Until Glover was wounded a year later, Hall saw to it that he wrote more or less regularly to his mother.

Early in 1862 Patterson himself became strangely involved in the war. Entrusted by the governor of New Hampshire with a commission to take funds raised in New Hampshire to help northern sympathizers in the South, he journeyed down to Washington to carry out his assignment. While there he went out sightseeing to the battlefield at Bull Run, but venturing too near the southern lines, he was captured and carried off to prison. On April 2 he wrote from Richmond:

> *You will be amazed to learn that I am in prison. . . . But*
> *God alone can tell what will become of my poor sick wife with*
> *none to care for her "but God who tempers the wind to the*
> *shorn lamb" will care for you. . . . My anxiety for you is intense*
> *but be of as good cheer as possible and trust in God.*[69]

Mrs. Patterson at once rallied to the emergency and began sending letters to anyone, including Franklin Pierce, who might prod the War Department to greater efforts to have him released through an exchange of prisoners.

On May 12 she wrote Patterson's brother James in Saco, Maine, enclosing "the last intelligence from my poor husband," telling him of the fruitlessness of her efforts to date, and signing herself, "Your desolate sister, Mary M. Patterson."[70] A week later Patterson wrote her that he had been transferred to the appalling prison at Salisbury, North Carolina, and expressed a hope that George Glover might be discharged before long and come to her rescue, "as I can do nothing for you or even myself."[71]

Obviously something had to be done for her, since her health had taken a turn for the worse. For some time she had been hesitating between two new modes of treatment which she had not yet tried. One of these was hydropathy or the water cure. Back on December 12, 1861, while Patterson was still with her, she had written a letter to a Mr. and Mrs. Taylor of Hill, New Hampshire, where the Vail Hydropathic Institute was located:

> *If I should go in to Dr. Vail's establishment . . . could you*
> *take me? . . . I am rather better than when I applied to you*
> *for board last Autumn. . . . I want to board near a Water Cure,*
> *so if necessary I could call for aid. My husband I believe knows*
> *Mr. Taylor and thinks your quiet family just the thing for*
> *me. . . . My food is of the simplest sort. I take nothing for break-*
> *fast but Graham bread (Wheat meal bread) and a little thickened*
> *milk cold, in the shape of toast gravy. Eat but two meals a day*
> *no meat or butter I do want to come and board with you very*
> *much and let dear husband attend to his profession which calls*
> *him away.*[72]

Now that Patterson was away so irremediably, she decided definitely to go to the Hydropathic Institute, and there she accordingly moved sometime in June.

Dr. William T. Vail, founder of the institute, was a buoyant, sensible, open-minded man, gentle and kindly. He has been described by his friend Dr. John A. Tenney, who was an orthodox practitioner, in these words:

He relied much upon mental influences in his treatment. The first rule posted in the rooms was to the effect that patients should never talk to each other about their ailments. In one of his consultations with his physicians he said there were a number of patients under his care that could be cured simply by talking to them. He balanced their minds by helping them to get rid of their fears.[73]

In addition there were baths, rest, a simple diet, fresh air, and plenty of water inside and out. Yet none of these was able to counter the decline in Mrs. Patterson's health which had started again with her husband's capture. More and more she felt that she should have tried the alternative mode of treatment which she had weighed against hydropathy. This was the system of a Dr. Phineas P. Quimby, who was reputed to be performing marvelous cures in Portland, Maine.

Patterson had written to Quimby in October of the preceding year, just four days after his wife had first heard from her son.[74] He explained that she was an invalid and "we wish to have the benefit of your wonderful power in her case," if it were possible for them to get to him.

Evidently the obstacles seemed too great and the idea was dropped at the time, but shortly before leaving Rumney for Dr. Vail's, Mrs. Patterson herself wrote Quimby. She explained that she had "been sick 6 years with spinal inflamation, and its train of sufferings—gastric and bilious." Although she had been getting better, a relapse had been brought on by the shock of her husband's imprisonment. "I want to see you above all others," she wrote. "I have entire confidence in your philosophy as read in the circular sent my husband Dr. Patterson. *Can* you, *will* you visit me at once?"[75]

Quimby could not or would not, and once again the idea was dropped. But when a former patient at Dr. Vail's, who had gone off to Quimby and been wonderfully helped by him, returned to the institute singing the Portland doctor's praises, Mrs. Patterson wrote him once more. She had made a mistake in coming here, she declared, and was considerably worse than when she arrived. In her state of discouragement she felt she would have to choose between going to Portland to be healed and going home to Sanbornton Bridge to die among her friends.[76]

Eventually it was arranged that she should go to Portland. She was accompanied by her brother Samuel—evidence of the new sense of responsibility he had taken on with his second marriage—and his wife. This good lady, Mary Ann Cook Baker, had formerly been a missionary to the Indians and was the author of a biography of the respected missionary Judsons. She appears to have won the affection of all who knew her; and, on her side, she gave unstinted admiration and love to the sister-in-law whose ideas were to depart so radically from her own. For the rest of their long lives the two remained warm friends.[77]

Forty years later Mrs. Baker recalled how, as they prepared to go to Portland, she had to dress her sister-in-law "one article of dress at a time and allowing her to rest, before proceeding further, so feeble did she feel."[78] It appears from her somewhat ambiguous account that Mrs. Patterson may first have gone to Samuel's house at Boston to stay and thence by sea to Portland. She wrote of the invalid's being helped into a carriage by Samuel and the driver, then driven "to the wharf for the night boat."[79] On board, the stewardess helped Mrs. Baker look after her sister-in-law, and the latter's high expectations of a coming cure doubtless helped to lighten the rigors of the voyage.

They arrived on October 10 in Longfellow's

> beautiful town
> That is seated by the sea

where quiet, tree-lined streets looked down on "the beauty and mystery of the ships." The copper and gold of the trees, the blue of "the tranquil bay," the "black wharves," the "sailors with bearded lips"[80]—here was a fresh scene to one long imprisoned in the lonely hills; and the strong, unaccustomed sea air may well have seemed to Mrs. Patterson like the breath of a new promise as her carriage rolled along to the International Hotel where Quimby lived and carried on his work.

Quimby's daughter Augusta, looking out the window, saw her lifted from the carriage and carried upstairs to her room.[81] Shortly afterwards the new arrival made her appearance in the waiting room where Quimby's patients gathered. Young George Quimby, who had recently returned from the West to act as his father's secretary, noted her as being tall and "of consumptive appearance" and judged her age to be about thirty-five instead of the forty-one it actually was.[82] But Mrs. Patterson's interest was wholly absorbed by one person, the "doctor" himself, a little man with shrewd, piercing eyes, a genial manner, and a confidence that emanated from him like an electric current.

Chapter
V

Portland
1862

The road that led from Franklin's lightning rod to the age of electronics was the brilliantly lit highway of scientific reason and research. There was nothing occult about the discovery of electromagnetism by Faraday in 1831. The great physical contributions of Maxwell, Hertz, Thomson, and a host of others could take place only in that atmosphere of mathematical clarity inherited from the Enlightenment and indeed from the Greeks themselves.

Yet there was a dark, somewhat disreputable path which ran beside the highway, sometimes close to it, at other times losing itself in tangled woods and swamps. Along this path Mesmer had moved, and behind him more shadowy figures: Van Helmont, Paracelsus, alchemists and astrologers, Egyptian and Assyrian priests, prehistoric shamans. Here went on that exploration of the unconscious, of the vast, unknown forces of the mind, which has been left so often to charlatans and cranks.

This was the path of animal magnetism, as it was still generally called in the 1860's, although many preferred the term mesmerism. Its practitioners for the most part assumed the existence of a magnetic fluid by which one living organism could influence or control another. A classic statement is to be found in the book *Practical Instruction in Animal Magnetism* by J. P. F. Deleuze, who in 1828, three years after the book appeared, was appointed librarian of the Museum of Natural History in Paris. Deleuze postulated "a substance [which] emanates from him who magnetizes, and is conveyed to the person magnetized, in the direction given by the will." He explained that although the magnetic fluid escaped from all the body and the will sufficed to give it direction, "the external organs, by which we act, are the most proper to throw it off," and therefore "we make use of our hands and eyes to magnetize."

The work of Deleuze was translated by a Rhode Islander, Thomas C. Hartshorn, in 1837, and in that same year appeared another significant book by a Frenchman, Charles Poyen, called *Progress of Animal Magnetism in New England*. Poyen claimed that when he had begun lecturing on the subject nineteen months earlier it was virtually unknown in New England but that it was now the subject of popular discussion and experiment everywhere. The *New Hampshire Patriot,* which the Baker household at Sanbornton read so sedulously, bore witness to the mounting tide of public interest in the subject during those years. A book published in 1843 stated that there were by then "two or three hundred skilful magnetizers in Boston," as well as "some twenty or thirty lecturers in New England."[1]

At this very time in England James Braid was approaching hypnotism, as he called it, in a more soberly scientific spirit, but the researches of Charcôt and Bernheim still lay a generation ahead, and the public exhibitions of New England lecturers were untouched by the methodology or conscience of the psychological laboratory. Nevertheless the rudiments of scientific curiosity were to be found among some of these popular magnetizers, and the gross deficiencies of the prevailing systems of medicine gave impetus to their crude explorations in the field of psychotherapy.

Notable among these early experimenters was Phineas Parkhurst Quimby, who was first drawn to the subject in 1838 by attending a lecture and exhibition by a popular mesmerist.

Quimby was at that time a 36-year-old clockmaker in Belfast, Maine. Though a man of little education, he had a lively mind and a knack for mechanical invention. On becoming interested in the new "science," he discovered that he himself possessed great mesmeric power. Before long he had found a young man by the name of Lucius Burkmar, who proved to be the perfect subject for his experiments. Together they traveled through Maine and New Brunswick giving exhibitions of Quimby's magnetic power and of Burkmar's clairvoyant skill while in the magnetized state—or, in more modern phrase, under deep hypnosis.

It was common for such traveling pairs to perform feats of mind reading, with the result that in many cases the magnetizer's "subject" or "somnambulist" came to be referred to as the "clairvoyant." A particularly popular practice was to have the magnetized subject diagnose diseases and in some cases prescribe remedies. Quimby and Burkmar did this until gradually it was borne in on Quimby that Burkmar was simply describing what the patient or Quimby himself *believed* was wrong. At the same time he began to realize that any medicine would cure if Burkmar ordered it. "This led me," Quimby wrote in later years, "to . . . arrive at the stand I now take: that the cure is not in the medicine, but in the confidence of the doctor or medium."[2]

The next development in Quimby's thought is best described in his own words:

I then became a medium myself, but not like my subject. I retained my own consciousness and at the same time took the feelings of my patient. Thus I was able to unlock the secret which has been a mystery for ages to mankind. I found that I had the power of not only feeling their aches and pains, but the state of their mind. I discovered that ideas took form and the patient was affected just according to the impression contained in the idea. For example, if a person lost a friend at sea the shock upon their nervous system would disturb the fluids of their body and create around them a vapor, and in that are all their ideas, right or wrong. This vapor or fluid contains the identity of the person.[3]

Here is stated the principle that was to govern his thinking to the end of his days, though he would describe it in different terms at different times. Mind, he explained in an early letter, is the name of "the fluids of the body," by which he apparently meant the magnetic or "electro-nervous" fluids which are so prominent in the literature of animal magnetism, and he added, "Disease is the name of the disturbance of these fluids or mind."[4] Later he came more and more to speak of mind as "spiritual matter" and to describe the mental atmosphere in which disease was formed as a "spiritual" identity, but his idea of spirit remained largely that of the materialist Hobbes who wrote that "a spirit is a physical body refined enough to escape the senses." As late as 1861 Quimby wrote: "My foundation is animal matter, or life. This, set in action by Wisdom, produces thought."[5]

Quimby's development was probably influenced by a much-discussed book entitled *The Philosophy of Electrical Psychology* by John Bovee Dods which was published in 1850 with an endorsement by Henry Clay, Daniel Webster, and other prominent figures.[6] Dods had written an earlier book, *Lectures on the Philosophy of Animal Magnetism,* and for a time he lured Lucius Burkmar away from Quimby to become his own mesmeric subject, although Burkmar later returned to Quimby until the latter finally dispensed with him altogether.

Even in his earlier book Dods had written: "Animal Magnetism is a very inappropriate name. . . . As it is a science of mind and its powers, so it is the highest and most sublime science in the whole realm of nature, and so far transcends matter." In the development which he called "electrical psychology" he came to see "Infinite Mind" as producing all form through "electrical action," but he denied the immateriality of mind and spirit. "Electricity is matter," he wrote, "and matter is the medium of God." In one of many striking parallels Quimby was later to write: "Matter is the medium of God. Mind is spiritual matter."[7]

Dods' doctrine of disease also had a strong influence on Quimby. The following passage by Dods anticipates Quimby's later writings:

> ... I have ... proved that the mind by shrinking back on itself in fear, melancholy, and grief, in the day of adversity ... can disturb the electro-nervous fluid, and allow it to concentrate itself upon any organ of the body and engender disease. If, then, the mind can disturb the equilibrium of the nervo-electric force and call it to some organ so as to produce disease, then the mind can also disperse it, equalize the circulation, and restore health. ... Medicine produces a physical impression on the system, but never heals a disease.[8]

In all Quimby's ideas, as they developed, there were confused echoes and variations of the ideas to be found in the vast literature of animal magnetism in his day. His theories have been seriously misinterpreted by writers ignorant of this literature. The same thing is true of his practice. Even after he decided that all disease was caused and could be cured "mentally," he continued to rely on magnetism to change the patient's "mind," i.e., the electro-nervous fluids. Eventually he discovered that it was not necessary to cause the mesmeric trance in order to get control of the patient's mind; simple suggestion was enough. Sometime in the 1850's he moved out of the stage of overt or recognizable mesmerism and cut down on his use of the word; but he continued to accompany his verbal suggestions with bodily manipulations and to follow stock magnetic practices. So long as he remained in Belfast he was known as a "magnetic doctor."[9]

In his last year there, 1857, he healed his brother-in-law, E. C. Hilton, of typhoid fever, and many years later Hilton described the incident in an affidavit:

> His first treatment consisted of passing his hands over my chest and stomach which seemed to relieve me. A few days later he took a basin filled with water, sprinkled me with the water and made passes with his hands before my face. He then told me to lift the end of a sofa which I did. Then he requested me to put my arms around him and lift him from the floor, but I refused to do this.[10]

After describing another healing in which Quimby manipulated his lame knee, Hilton concluded, "I always considered his healing to be through animal magnetism."

Another witness, Judge Charles K. Miller, of Camden, Maine,

told in an affidavit of being taken to Quimby about this same time to be healed of the effects of a severe case of rheumatic fever. Quimby was called to the hotel where the then thirteen-year-old boy had been carried on arriving in Belfast.

> *He rubbed me and then they put me in a chair. He then looked me straight in the eye, and such eyes I never beheld before, told me to get up and walk. I told him I couldn't. He said you can. He took hold of me and pulled me on my feet and I walked two or three steps and fell, but he caught me and I was then put to bed again. The next day I went back home again and was able to ride on the seat with my parents. . . . I was not treated mentally, but by rubbing and through mesmerism.*[11]

Quimby's fellow townsmen continued to look on him as a practitioner of mesmerism even though he no longer sent them into a mesmeric trance. As the *History of Belfast* by Joseph Williamson (1877) put it: "Having become deeply interested in the art or science of mesmerism, then in its comparative infancy in this country, he devoted the last twenty years of his life to the development of its principles, especially with reference to the healing art."

Again a tribute to him in the *Belfast Republican Journal* on May 5, 1887, included a tell-tale phrase: "The good that he accomplished, the suffering that he averted, crippled forms that were restored under his kind magnetic hand, cannot be told in this simple tribute to his pleasant memory." The "kind magnetic hand" was what most people remembered, not the strange theories with which he attempted to "explain" their disease to them. This is equally true of the years after he left Belfast, as a number of affidavits and written reminiscences make plain.[12]

Many of his patients remembered particularly the burning sensation which seemed to come from his hands as he manipulated them. When questioned about it, he habitually answered that he thought it was electricity passing from him to them. The phenomenon was a common one, according to the manuals of animal magnetism then current—and also according to the reports given today by many who experience the "laying on of hands." Following the usual practice of that time, Quimby dipped his hands frequently in water. As the Reverend Jacob Baker wrote in *Human Magnetism* (1843), quoting Deleuze, "If the magnetizer perceives a burning sensation in his hands, he can from time to time moisten them in acidulated water."

Water played a very important role with the magnetizers. Deleuze wrote: "Magnetized water is one of the most powerful and salutary agents that can be employed. . . . It carries the magnetic fluid directly into the stomach, and thence into all the organs." Quimby used it in his practice internally as well as externally. If Dr. Vail of the Hill Water Cure sometimes healed patients just by talking with them, Quimby accompanied his therapeutic conversations with a veritable flood of water. One patient in 1862 wrote: "He gives no medicine. The whole scope of his *Materia Medica* would comprehend water, and a pitcher to hold it. The application consists, if the case demands, in an imbibition of this fluid that would put the votaries of Lager to blush."[13]

Quimby's letters to patients frequently tell them to take a tumbler of water and sip it while they read his letter or while he (mentally) rubs the back of their head or the roots of their nose or some other affected part. On occasion he would write them to hold a tumbler of water in one hand and his letter in the other, a request which suggests that he wanted them to think of the letter itself as magnetized. It was a common belief that a letter could be magnetized, rather as an amulet is "blessed." A knowledge of this superstition is evidenced in a school friend's laughing remark in a letter to Augusta Holmes back in 1843, "I will magnetize a letter with 'sap-sugar' and send you."[14]

Quimby may not have taken this particular superstition much more seriously than the schoolgirl, but he did not despise anything that would help to concentrate his patient's attention on him. Such concentration was in itself a form of "magnetism" and it was, he felt, highly desirable. As he frequently wrote, in his sort of healing by suggestion the confidence of the patient in the healer was all-important; hence his repeated verbal and written admonitions to patients to fasten their thoughts on him at the time of treatment and to think of nothing else.

Toward the end of 1857 Quimby moved to the neighboring town of Bangor, where he took rooms at the Hatch House. The *Bangor Jeffersonian* greeted him as "a disciple of 'mesmerism,' a faith and belief which he now scrupulously adheres to," but added that he refrained from the usual mesmeric manipulations and "gets control of the patient's mind . . . with no other appliance but the power of his speech."[15]

The description is inexact in several particulars, as is shown by the reminiscences of patients who went to him during the two years he practiced in Bangor. The most important of these is a long account by Charles A. Quincy Norton, who was a young medical student there at the time and who accompanied his mother in 1859 when she visited Quimby to have her facial neuralgia treated:

We found about thirty patients in waiting [in the dining room of the Hatch House, which Quimby used as an office between meals]. The patients arranged themselves about the long room, Mr. Quimby directing where each one should sit, and in giving his treatments he passed from one to another. He asked but few questions, but in a loud voice demanded that each patient look him straight in the eye. An assistant followed him about the room holding a large dish of water. In most cases not a question was asked, in some, however, Mr. Quimby would say: "Where is your pain," in others he would say: "What ails you." In some cases he would hold the patients hands for a moment. In others he would put his hands on the head. In some, as in my mothers case, he would wet both hands in the water and gently press or stroke the face, neck or head of the person being treated. In a number of incidences [sic] he would say, in a quick, sharp voice: "Get up, walk away! you can walk, walk!," the patient almost always doing as bid. To one suffering with rheumatism he said: "The pain is going, it is gone!" With a number he arranged for private treatments. . . . All paid an assistant $1.00, as a fee as they passed out of the door.[16]

Norton's mother later arranged for private treatments, and Norton himself made notes of the conversations which he and his father had with Quimby when the latter came to their house to treat his patient.[17]

Water, he explained to them, was "a good conductor of vital energy, and when the hands are wet the current flows better from the treater to the patient." But he stressed the importance of the "utmost purity of thought" in the former, and when the senior Norton asked him how he could charge himself with vital energy, he replied that the first thing was "a pure life," then pure food and drink. He also discussed the more advanced views which he was developing at that time, and young Norton concluded that his "confusion of thought and lack of ability to formulate a precise theory" was owing to his lack of training and his materialistic background.

But the young man was fascinated by Quimby and admired him. He later described him as "a man of a most kindly nature" and as an "honest, honorable man, always fearlessly speaking the truth as he understood it." He was a man "of a deeply religious nature without being pious," though Norton felt that his nature was basically intellectual rather than spiritual. Had he been trained or educated he "would have, without doubt, reached a commanding place among able thinkers."

The dangers of his treatment were obvious. Mrs. Norton's neuralgia improved so long as she had his personal attention, but when he moved to Portland toward the end of 1859 a relapse occurred. She made several visits to Portland to receive treatment, and each time was helped, but afterwards was worse than ever. A more dramatic example was recorded by her son:

> *A young lady was brought into his rooms one day, while he was at Bangor, in a wheel chair. Before she had been placed with the other patients who were waiting for treatments Mr. Quimby turned quickly, and in a loud, stern voice said, addressing the young lady: "Get out of that cart; git up and walk." Her father who attended her said: "Doctor, she can not walk, she has not put her foot on the floor for over a year." Mr. Quimby again said, and in a more commanding tone than before: "I said get out of that cart. Put your feet on the floor and walk, walk out of this room, and do it quick." The young lady did not take her eyes from Mr. Quimby, nor did she speak a word. Slowly, and trembling like a leaf, she put first one foot then the other on the floor. Then Mr. Quimby again said: "Now walk, you can and must walk, walk out of this room." Slowly and tottering she moved towards the door. Again he commanded: "Walk." She then passed out of the room and walked slowly to her own [room] near the end of the long hall. When she reached her door she gave a low, startled moan and dropped to the floor. She was laid on her bed and soon developed a strong fit of wild hysteria. . . . The next day she declined to see Mr. Quimby, and that day left the hotel.*

Quimby lacked completely the modern understanding that systematic suggestion even without throwing the patient into the sleep or trance state of deep hypnosis is still hypnoidal in character. In his own estimate he had left mesmerism behind him. But an instance such as the one just cited shows how close he remained, in practice if not in theory, to the animal magnetism described by Charles Poyen in his 1837 book. Poyen had written:

> *So thoroughly am I convinced in regard to the effects of will upon my patients, that if the science were called the* power *of will, instead of Animal Magnetism, it would convey to my mind a much clearer idea of what it really is. . . . We cannot better define it, than by calling it the influence which the will of one human being exerts, through the nervous system, upon the will and all the bodily functions of another . . . who, for the time, is to a greater or less extent the mere creature of our will.*

Here was the background of Quimby's later practice, a background from which he could never quite break free. An austere moral commentary on that background is to be found in the writings of Nathaniel Hawthorne, who in 1841 had written his *fiancée* when she proposed trying mesmerism as a cure for her headaches:

> *. . . my spirit is moved to talk to thee to day about these magnetic miracles, and to beseech thee to take no part in them. I am unwilling that a power should be exercised on thee, of which we know neither the origin nor the consequence, and the phenomena of which seem rather calculated to bewilder us, than to teach us any truths about the present or future state of being. If I possessed such a power over thee, I should not dare to exercise it; nor can I consent to its being exercised by another. Supposing that this power arises from the transfusion of one spirit into another, it seems to me that the sacredness of an individual is violated by it; there would be an intrusion into thy holy of holies. . . .*[18]

The words "electric" and "magnetic" echo almost malevolently through *The House of the Seven Gables* and *The Blithdale Romance*. In the earlier book Hawthorne grants that psychology may "endeavor to reduce these alleged necromancies within a system, instead of rejecting them as altogether fabulous," but his attitude through both books is summed up in a passage in *The Blithdale Romance* where a stranger tells of the wonders of animal magnetism:

> *He cited instances of the miraculous power of one human being over the will and passions of another; insomuch that settled grief was but a shadow beneath the influence of a man possessing this potency, and the strong love of years melted away like a vapor. . . . Human character was but soft wax in his hands; and guilt, or virtue, only the forms into which he should see fit to mould it. . . . It is unutterable, the horror and disgust with which I listened, and saw that, if these things were to be believed, the individual soul was virtually annihilated, and all that is sweet and pure in our present life debased. . . .*

Quimby might strain toward the clear gray light of Hawthorne's moral vision, but his power remained rooted in something closer to the strange, nocturnal, pseudoscientific world of Edgar Allan Poe.

2

When Daniel Patterson in 1861 first wrote Quimby about his wife's ailments, he had received one of the Portland healer's circulars. It started off by announcing where Quimby could be consulted, then went on to say:

. . . he gives no medicines and makes no outward applications, but simply sits down by the patients, tells them their feelings and what they think is their disease. If the patients admit that he tells them their feelings, etc., then his explanation is the cure; and, if he succeeds in correcting their error, he changes the fluids of the system and establishes the truth, or health. The Truth is the Cure.[19]

There was nothing in the circular to show Quimby's background of animal magnetism, but much to arrest the attention of a searcher for health—and for truth—whose thinking had been gradually leading her toward a mental theory of disease. Mrs. Patterson already had a thoroughgoing skepticism of medicines and of "outward applications" —the salves, plasters, and poultices which were the stock in trade of nineteenth-century doctors. And with her biblical background the final sentence in the quoted passage can hardly have failed to strike a responsive note.

That being the case, it is not surprising that in May, 1862, she wrote Quimby, "I have entire confidence in your philosophy as read in the circular sent my husband." His philosophy was to offer her a greater challenge than any she had yet encountered. Quimby himself usually referred to it as his "theory" or simply as "the truth,"[20] but in order to understand what he meant by the latter term it is necessary to turn once again to developments before 1862.

Among the early practitioners of animal magnetism were those who thought it should be a purely scientific study and those who gave it all sorts of religious and mystical interpretations. Theorists who sought religious sanction for it were apt to cite the second chapter of Genesis, in which Jehovah cast Adam into a "deep sleep," as the first recorded instance of magnetism. Especially was it popular to identify magnetic healings with the healings of Jesus, and every biblical instance of the "laying on of hands" was hailed as an example of mesmerism.

Of those who attempted to make it both a science and a religion, none attracted more attention than Andrew Jackson Davis. In 1843 in the village of Poughkeepsie, New York, seventeen-year-old Davis had his first experience of the mesmeric trance state. In subsequent experiences he was guided by the "spirits" of Galen and Swedenborg into a strange amalgam of mesmerism, spiritualism, Swedenborgianism, pantheism, and deism which profoundly impressed large numbers of his contemporaries.

In 1845–46, in New York City, he gave a singular series of lectures on "The Principles of Nature, Her Divine Revelations, and a Voice to Mankind" while in the trance state. The next year they were published in book form with the same title and had a wide influence on many—including, apparently, Quimby.[21]

At the outset the book declared, "Fear not, for Error is mortal and can not live, and Truth is immortal and can not die!" It went on to explain with oracular authority, *"Truth is a positive principle:* Error is a *negative* principle; and as truth is positive and eternal, it must subdue error, which is only temporal and artificial." This was the eighteenth-century faith which had found expression in the dissertations of Albert Baker. But truth and error have meant many things to many men, and to Davis they were linked with strange cosmological speculations:

> *In the beginning, the Univercoelum was one boundless undefinable, and unimaginable ocean of Liquid Fire! . . . It was without bounds—inconceivable—and with qualities and essences incomprehensible. This was the original condition of Matter. It was without forms; for it was but one Form. It had no motions, but it was an eternity of Motion. It was without parts; for it was a Whole. Particles did not exist; but the Whole was one Particle. There were not Suns, but it was one Eternal Sun. . . .*

> *Matter and Power were existing as a Whole, inseparable. The* Matter *contained the substance to produce all suns, all worlds, and systems of worlds, throughout the immensity of space. It contained the qualities to produce all things that are existing upon each of these worlds. The* Power *contained Wisdom and Goodness,—Justice, Mercy, and Truth. It contained the original and essential Principle that is displayed throughout immensity of space, controlling worlds and systems of worlds, and producing Motion, Life, Sensation, and Intelligence. . . .*[22]

This is typical of those bold, ignorant, imaginative ventures into what might be called scientific mythology in which the nineteenth century abounded. Poe was to do the same sort of thing in his *Eureka* the next year.[23] And just as Poe wrote of electricity as the "strictly spiritual principle" to which all vitality, consciousness, and thought must be attributed, so Davis used the language of idealism to express a basic materialism. His two co-eternal principles—mind and matter, or Father-God and Mother-Nature as he was later to call them— really gave matter the primacy even when he seemed to deny it.

He could write in the vein of Agassiz:

> *The* Thoughts *of the infinite Mind . . . constitute the laws of Nature. . . . Nature . . . is merely a* Thought *of the divine*

Mind, as forms are the thoughts of Nature. . . . It is perfectly clear that nothing is, *and nothing* can be, *but the Divine Mind, which is the* Cause, *and the Universe, which is the* Effect.

But elsewhere he explained, "All ultimates, to me, are still *matter;* but to you they are spirit." And again, "It is a law of *Matter* to produce its ultimate, *Mind.*"

Here is the probable source of Quimby's description of mind as "spiritual matter." Logical consistency is not to be looked for in any of these backwoods thinkers, and a curious blend of idealism and materialism is to be found in most of them; but when they use the words "spirit" and "spiritual" it is usually with a far from Christian meaning. The fruits of the spirit are more likely to be regarded as electricity and magnetism than those qualities of heart and mind enumerated by Paul.

Despite his elaborate and arresting biblical interpretations, Davis has generally been considered to be an essentially irreligious man. In Quimby's case opinion has differed.[24] His son George, writing in 1901 regarding his father's formulation of "a theory whereby he claimed to cure disease through the mind," added that "there was no religion connected with it."[25] Yet he was certainly not without religious feeling, though highly critical of the Christian churches and prone to use the word "Christian" as a term of opprobrium. While in Belfast he frequently attended the Unitarian church, in Bangor the Universalist, and either in Portland or earlier became "interested in Swedenborg's ideas."[26]

Back in the days when he was giving mesmeric exhibitions Quimby had made an important discovery: "I found that my own opinion could have but little effect upon the mind of the audience. Their religious opinions would govern in most all cases."[27] So with his healing practice he found it necessary on occasion to relate his philosophy of mind-cure to the Bible in order to reach the minds of his devout, Bible-reading patients.

Gradually he developed some pungent, highly original interpretations of the Scriptures to support his own views, as Davis had done before him, the chief difference being that Davis's interests were metaphysical and cosmological while Quimby's were primarily psychological. The influence of Swedenborg, with his spiritual interpretation of the "inner" meaning of the Scriptures, doubtless accentuated this tendency. A Portland patient wrote to her sister in 1860, "I delight to have him talk Bible [which] he interprets after a medical Swedenborg as I tell him."[28] It may be significant that Swedenborgianism was closely connected with both spiritualism and mesmerism, particularly through the person of Davis, the connection having been spelled out in detail in 1847 by a New York professor, George Bush, in his book *Mesmer and Swedenborg.*[29]

Quimby had been accustomed to speak of his developing theory of healing by mental suggestion as his "wisdom," which combatted the patient's "opinions" as to the material basis of his disease. In Swedenborg he found God designated as Wisdom, as well as Love, and gradually he began to give the word the meaning of God. Thus, semantically speaking, he deified his own theory. His "wisdom" became his God.

A related development occurred in his use of the word "Christ."

Like many of the animal magnetizers he had become accustomed to speaking of his method of cure as that which was used by Jesus in healing the sick. "It is clear," Davis had written in *The Great Harmonia* (1850), ". . . that Christ cast out diseases, satans, or devils, by the exercise of that spiritual power, which, in our century, has unfortunately been termed 'Animal Magnetism.' "[30] Davis himself preferred to speak of an *"infinite, divine principle"* by which all material elements could be brought into harmony, and he sometimes referred to this as "the Christ-principle," which was by no means confined to the historical Jesus.[31]

Davis was not the first to have made this distinction, which has recurred in one form or another throughout the history of Christianity, but he was the first to have related it to animal magnetism. Quimby, who doubtless took the idea from him, related it particularly to the principle of clairvoyance on which he based his healing.[32]

He wrote, for instance, in 1859, "This eternal life was in Jesus, and was Christ," and even to an orthodox ear the sentence taken by itself sounds reasonably Christian. But the preceding sentence defines this eternal life of Christ as an understanding of the clairvoyant principle; and, just before that, clairvoyance is described as a "higher state entirely disconnected with the natural man, but [which] can communicate information through him while in a dreamy or mesmeric state."[33] Elsewhere he wrote, "As Jesus became clairvoyant He became the son of God."[34]

In various places he described the clairvoyant faculty as the ability to perceive directly the aura, odor, or spiritual identity of an individual.[35] It also included the ability to condense one's spiritual identity so that it would be visible to others. Quimby would write his absent patients to think of him at a certain hour when he would give them a treatment and would perhaps mentally rub their heads— and at the appointed hour they would sometimes see him appear before them like a visible bodily presence. While most people would take this as an illustration of the power of suggestion, Quimby related it to his theory of the Christ:

*I cannot tell how much I can condense my identity to the
sick [who are absent], but I know I can touch them so they can
feel the sensation. . . . When you read this I will show you myself and also the number of persons in the room where I am
writing this. Let me know the impression you may have of the
number. This is the Christ that Jesus spoke of.*[36]

When he sat down beside a patient for a private treatment, the
first thing he did was to enter into the clairvoyant state in which
he felt the patient's pains and woes. "As it is necessary that he [the
patient] should feel that I know more than he does," he wrote in the
Portland Daily Advertiser, "I tell his feelings."[37] Having thus astonished the patient and won his confidence, he proceeded to "explain"
the disease as the result of mental causes—usually false medical beliefs
implanted by the doctors or false theological beliefs implanted by the
clergy.

The patient might understand little of what he said but would
feel his energy and confidence. As Quimby wrote in another connection: "The [medical] doctor can produce a chemical change by his
talk. It makes no difference what he says. A phenomenon will follow
to which he can give a name to suit his convenience."[38] The name
which suited his convenience for the clairvoyant faculty and its attendant phenomena was the Christ.

The term was not used in the circular which Mrs. Patterson had
seen. There it simply mentioned that Quimby felt the patient's pain,
described it, "and in the explanation lies the cure." Of the hundreds
of patients who streamed through his office every year only a small
proportion received any explanation of his *theory.* Most of them
remembered only that he seemed to understand their sufferings and
that he manipulated them. Typical statements by those who visited
him in the Portland years were: "He never told me how he healed,
but employed rubbing in my case." "He told me to look at him, and
he looked me straight in the eyes for five or ten minutes, still holding
my hands. After this process he dipped his hands in water and vigorously rubbed my head." "Mr. Quimby told me that I must have
explicit faith in him and believe that I had no pain at all. The treatment was entirely by manipulation. I never, in the different times that
I visited him, heard him mention God in any way."[39]

One man stated that Quimby talked politics while rubbing the
head; a woman remembered that "society talk" accompanied the treatment; and a patient who knew him well wrote: "While manipulating
his patients, Dr. Quimby invariably entertained them by telling stories

or carrying on a conversation in a light vein. He was of a happy disposition, jovial and honest and I had great respect for him."

One of his leading champions in later years explained that "very often after a sitting with a patient the patient would say, 'O doctor, tell me how you cure?' Usually he would say, 'Oh, I don't know myself,' simply to get rid of the patient."[40] This is corroborated by the reminiscences of many patients, and a particularly interesting instance is given in an affidavit by Mrs. Emma A. Thompson, then Emma Morgan.[41] Quimby was called to her home outside Portland in 1862 to treat her for severe neuralgic pains. He came late in the afternoon, stayed overnight, and left the next morning.

> *His treatment consisted in placing bands on his wrists, plunging his hands in cold water, manipulating the head and making passes down the body. He asked me to concentrate my mind on him, and to think of nothing and nobody but him. He requested the members of the family to leave the room as he said he could not control my mind with any one else present. As the relief came to me, he suffered greatly himself saying that he took on my pain. I learned afterwards that his pain was so intense that it became necessary for my father to assist him to bed. . . . When he left that morning I told him that I would have another attack at eleven o'clock, as the attacks came periodically, and asked what I should do. He left instructions for me to think of him and to drink water until relief came. The following day I was taken to his office in a carriage for further treatment. . . . After following his directions for about four years, I experienced only temporary relief. . . . He never spoke of God to me, or referred to any other power or person but himself. . . . I distinctly recall that before he left our home that morning, my father offered him a check for One thousand Dollars if he would impart to him or any member of his family his method of treating disease, to which the Doctor replied, "I cannot. I don't understand it myself."*

To some, however, he was willing to go into explanations. F. L. Town, an army surgeon from Louisville, Kentucky, wrote in the *Portland Daily Advertiser* on March 6, 1862:

> *He will explain to you his way of practice—give you the benefit of his treatment, entertain you with stereoscopic views of his theory or belief, and end off perhaps by explaining a few passages of scripture. . . . Considering the means employed, and the diversity of cases, Dr. Quimby's success is remarkable—*

whether it depends more upon the man, or he acts upon the first principles of that, which when better understood shall be recognized as a new remedial agency.

Two weeks later the same paper ran an extended account of his theory, the most rational to appear in print during his lifetime. (See Appendix B.) This probably represents the effort of a better educated mind than his to bring order into the confusion of his system, and it anticipates the later efforts of New Thought writers to make his theories more conventionally respectable. But for primitive vigor and chaotic eloquence, for a certain crude power of mind and will and imagination, those writings which are certainly—or almost certainly[42] —Quimby's own surpass anything in New Thought. A characteristic example, from a letter to a patient in 1861, shows him in full torrent:

To make you understand I must come to you in some way in the form of a belief. So I will tell you a story of some one who died of bronchitis. You listen or eat this belief or wisdom as you would eat your meals. It sets rather hard upon your stomach; this disturbs the error or your body, and a cloud appears in the sky. You cannot see the storm but you can see it looks dark. In this cloud or belief you prophesy rain or a storm. So in your belief you foresee evils. The elements of the body of your belief are shaken, the earth is lit up by the fire of your error, the heat rises, the heaven or mind grows dark; the heat moves like the roaring of thunder, the lightning of hot flashes shoot to all parts of the solar system of your belief. At last the winds or chills strike the earth or surface of the body, a cold clammy sensation passes over you. This changes the heat into a sort of watery substance, which works its way to the channels, and pours to the head and stomach.

Now listen and you will hear a voice in the clouds of error saying, The truth hath prevailed to open the pores and let nature rid itself of the evil I loaded you down with in a belief. This is the way God or Wisdom takes to get rid of a false belief: the belief is made in the heavens or your mind, it then becomes more and more condensed till it takes the form of matter. Then Wisdom dissolves it and it passes through the pores, and the effort of coughing is one of Truth's servants, not error's. . . . So hoping that you may soon rid yourself of all worldly opinions and stand firm in the Truth that will set you free, I remain your friend and protector till the storm is over and the waters of your belief are still.[43]

The recipient of such a letter might well feel that an electric storm had burst about his ears, and in the general excitement he might even get well!

3

In later life Mrs. Eddy recalled that when she found herself in Quimby's office she felt remarkably improved in health even before he gave her a treatment, so great was her faith in him.[44] The improvement continued with a rapidity that seemed like a miracle. A week later she was able to climb the one hundred and eighty-two steps that led to the dome of the City Hall, and every day she gained in strength and freedom.[45]

For the moment it looked as though Mary Baker Patterson had emerged at last from the endless, weary years of suffering.

A flood of gratitude to Quimby swept away all doubt, all caution. "I was never luke-warm but always fervid," she explained years later,[46] and in her unbounded fervor she wrote to the *Portland Evening Courier* a month after her first meeting with Quimby: "As he speaks as never man before spake, and heals as never man healed since Christ, is he not identified with truth? And is not this the Christ which is in him?"[47]

Mrs. Patterson stood at a crucial point in her career. She was only a little more than three years away from the event that would bring her whole life into focus. From that new perspective the years of suffering and searching would seem only the necessary discipline for her real life task.

The period of her life between October, 1862, and February, 1866, was one of tremendous stimulus and tremendous hazard. Quimby's insistence that disease was both caused and cured by the mind confirmed the position she had long been groping toward, but beyond that lay the crucial question as to what mind was. Mrs. Patterson was familiar enough with the Pauline admonition to "let this mind be in you which was also in Christ Jesus," but to have this mind defined as spiritual matter was to be launched into an area of thought both startling and bewildering.

On one occasion a little later she was to write Quimby asking him to include a certain trouble in his treatment "when you send the subtle fluid of mind, or *spirit,* to conquer matter."[48] The phrase sits oddly in the context of the Christianity to which she was committed by training and temperament. There would inevitably be a violence to Christian convictions involved in any serious attempt to reconcile the "subtle fluid" emanating from Portland with the transcendent power implied in Jesus' words: "It is the spirit that quickeneth; the flesh profiteth nothing: the words that I speak unto you, they are spirit, and they are life."

The words that Quimby spoke to her had an almost electrifying effect, but they left her groping for a meaning that eluded her. He insisted emphatically that intelligence was not in matter and then placed it in a "mind" which he described at various times as a sort of odor, vapor, or mist arising from matter. So far as can be judged today, Mrs. Patterson swept aside this part of his theory and tried for a time to give his terms a genuine Christian content. Seen in retrospect it was an impossible task, but so long as the warm, humanitarian figure of Quimby was present the contradictions might be swallowed up in his own intense convictions.

The next few years were to test her ability to separate her search for truth from the magnetism of a powerful personality. The problem is illustrated by her earliest letter to the *Courier,* published on November 7, 1862. When this letter was publicly resurrected twenty-five years later, Mrs. Eddy commented that she had been at that time "as ignorant of mesmerism as Eve, before she was taught by the serpent," and that her head had been "so turned by Animal Magnetism and will-power" under Quimby's treatment "that I might have written something as hopelessly incorrect" as the letter in question.[49]

After recounting her dramatic healing—and time was to prove mistaken her hopeful assumption that this was a permanent cure—the letter went on to deny that Quimby's power was spiritualistic. Quimby was indeed opposed to that popular faith, although his theory of the ability of the spiritual man to condense himself so that he could be seen physically was closer to spiritualism than to orthodox animal magnetism. Then followed a paragraph that expressed all the ardor of her new hopes:

> *Again, is it by animal magnetism that he heals the sick? Let us examine. I have employed electro-magnetism and animal magnetism, and for a brief interval have felt relief, from the equilibrium which I fancied was restored to an exhausted system or by a diffusion of concentrated action. But in no instance did I get rid of a return of all my ailments, because I had not been helped out of the error in which opinions involved us. My operator believed in disease independent of the mind; hence, I could not be wiser than my teacher. But now I can see dimly at first, and only as trees walking, the great principle which underlies Dr. Quimby's faith and works; and just in proportion*

to my right perception of truth is my recovery. This truth which he opposes to the error of giving intelligence to matter and placing pain where it never placed itself, if received understandingly, changes the currents of the system to their normal action; and the mechanism of the body goes on undisturbed. That this is a science capable of demonstration becomes clear to the minds of those patients who reason upon the process of their cure. The truth which he establishes in the patient cures him (although he may be wholly unconscious thereof); and the body, which is full of light, is no longer in disease. At present I am too much in error to elucidate the truth, and can touch only the key-note for the master hand to wake the harmony. May it be in essays instead of notes! say I. After all, this is a very spiritual doctrine; but the eternal years of God are with it, and it must stand firm as the rock of ages. And to many a poor sufferer may it be found, as by me, "the shadow of a great rock in a weary land."[50]

Mrs. Patterson had glimpsed—or perhaps it would be more accurate to say, had sensed—her goal afar off, but around it the mist swirled thickly. For one thing, she had accepted unquestioningly Quimby's view that since he did not produce the mesmeric sleep there was nothing of animal magnetism in his practice. His linking of his theory with the Christ had aroused in her an elated expectation of spiritual insights which his earnest but earthbound speculations would inevitably fail to satisfy. When finally she penetrated the opacities and ambiguities of his language, she was to find that the "rock" on which her future life would rest stood starkly apart from the basic assumptions of his psychology.[51]

A hint of this is conveyed by an incident that occurred about this time. Mrs. Patterson was boarding in Portland with a Mrs. Martha Hunter, who had known and loved Quimby from childhood. Almost forty years later, long after Mrs. Hunter had remarried and moved to the State of Washington, she became a Christian Scientist without once suspecting that Mary Baker Eddy was the Mrs. Patterson she had known in Portland. Eventually she learned that this was so and wrote out her memories of the earlier period.[52] One of these memories concerned an evening she had spent with Mrs. Patterson at the home of a friend, a homeopathic doctor by the name of Burr.

The conversation had inevitably turned on the subject of healing. As they were leaving, Mrs. Patterson had remarked that "if all diseases are unreal and not good, God who is good and real should be our only healer, and I believe that if we only knew how to ask Him we should need no other."

The remark, casual as it is, indicates that even then she was having difficulty in identifying Quimby's deified "wisdom" with the God of Hebrew-Christian tradition. Theism has always insisted on the transcendence of God, and in this respect Mrs. Eddy the Christian Scientist would be as thoroughgoing a theist as Mary Baker the Congregationalist. The majesty of a God who made and ruled the universe was not to be translated into the mere energy of human mind and will; the creator was infinitely greater than the individual to whom He revealed Himself as the source of all being.

In the New Thought writers who went back to Quimby for inspiration the one common element is an emphasis on the "God within" or the "Christ within," whereas Mrs. Eddy's writings constantly insist that God is not *in* man.[53] "Is not our comforter always from outside and above ourselves?" she would ask,[54] and in her theology God necessarily transcends every expression of His own being.

In Quimby's writings, on the other hand, God is absorbed into man as a principle to be *used* by the individual, almost as a technique to be learned, in order to bring about healing. Although Quimby gives passing mention to God as First Cause, his "theology" is almost wholly subjective and empirical. God, Christ, "scientific man," and science are used as synonyms, and they all refer essentially to the higher processes of the human mind rather than to the "Wholly Other" of Christian encounter. It is not surprising that, dazzled though Mrs. Patterson was by Quimby the healer, he still seemed to block for her a fuller reliance on the God to whom she had prayed from childhood for healing.

Quimby's son George, who wrote in 1908 that he believed Mrs. Eddy had "finally landed in *prayer cure,* pure and simple," declared proudly of his father's system: "There were no prayers, there was no asking assistance from God or any other divinity. He [Quimby] cured by his wisdom."[55] What is involved here is the distinction traditionally made between religion and magic, or theism and theurgy. This distinction effectively separates the prophet who waits for God's commands from the magus who commands God to act or arrogates divine power to himself.

Mrs. Hunter, although she remained firm in her praise of Quimby's sincerity, expressed astonishment in her reminiscences—as did various others of the Portland healer's patients who later became Christian Scientists—that anyone should think there was anything basically in common between the two systems.[56] Yet the distinction between Christianity and Quimbyism was far from plain to Mrs.

Patterson in 1862 or for some years afterwards. For Christianity uses the language of immanence as well as of transcendence to describe its God, and the line between theological immanence and psychological subjectivity was not at first clear to her. In Christianity the immanence of God necessarily grows out of His transcendence, as the New Testament grows out of the Old and the Son proceeds from the Father; but when Quimby borrowed the terms of Christian immanentism to give theological force to his psychotherapy, they had no root in the vision of a God utterly transcending the natural world and the forces of the human personality.

Many years later Mrs. Eddy would still remember with gratitude Quimby's "rare humanity and sympathy,"[57] but there was no place in his system for God's grace. Put in more metaphysical terms, there was nothing comparable to the distinction she later made between the divine Mind, or God, and what she would call mortal mind, or the mind of mortals.

It is evident that very soon after her first acquaintance with Quimby Mrs. Patterson began to try to sort out her ideas in writing, and this inevitably meant some effort to see Quimby's ideas in the light of her own biblical religion. A couple of months after returning home she wrote a Portland friend, a Mrs. Williams, "I will try to send my Philosophy by Mrs. Tilton when she accompanies her son [to Portland]."[58] In the final preface to *Science and Health* (p. viii) she would write, "As early as 1862 she [the author] began to write down and give to friends the results of her Scriptural study, for the Bible was her sole teacher." Even in 1862 the Bible was fighting for ascendancy over Quimby's influence. On the surface she was still engaged in an enthusiastic attempt to reconcile the two, but a deeper struggle was going on—perhaps at a largely unconscious level.

Something of this may be reflected in the rapid decline of her health again. Although she wrote Quimby after leaving him, "I am to all who once knew me, a living wonder, and a living monument of your power,"[59] she soon found her old ills returning, as did so many of his patients when away from his magnetic presence. In one letter she announced that his "angel visit" had removed her gastric pains; in the next she reported their return and added, "Please come to me and remove this pain and tell me your fee."[60]

This was an appeal not for a personal visit but for another treatment, though Quimby usually described such treatments as a projection of his spirit form to the patient's side at a given hour. This accounts for her request in another letter when, after giving a catalogue of old ills which had returned and were causing her much suffering, she wrote: "I would like to have you in your *Omnipresence* visit me at 8 o'clock this eve if convenient. But consult your own time, only come once a day until I am better."[61]

The ills and the appeals both continued. One year after the "healing" she had so fervently announced in the *Portland Courier* she wrote her brother-in-law: "I hope soon to be better; the Dr.'s patients tell me all difficult cases are worse after a time some with divers maladies. I have lost no faith even if I am worse."[62] But she was not soon better. The same story continued through another two years up until Quimby's death.

On several occasions in the last two decades of her life Mrs. Eddy made careful evaluations of the part the Quimby episode played in her development. She told of asking him one day why he kept wetting his hands when he rubbed her head and of his answering to the effect that "friction evolved electricity and water was a good medium for conveying this electricity throughout the system."[63] This manipulation constituted what Mrs. Eddy later called his *practice,* or method, as distinct from his theory, and she elsewhere indicated that this was the only explanation he gave her of this practice.[64]

But his theory was another matter. Even in her last years she referred to him as "a deep thinker" and "an advanced thinker" whose ideas were compounded of truth and error.[65] In one place she wrote that as homeopathy was the intermediate step from allopathy and matter to mind, so Quimbyism was the intermediate step from animal magnetism and matter to mind. But homeopathy, she added, was inconsistent in believing that a drug cured while diluting the drug till it sometimes disappeared entirely; and Quimby, she pointed out, "used to repeat, 'There is no intelligence in matter,' while at the same time he used water and manipulation to heal his patients."[66]

In another place she wrote of Quimbyism as the next step beyond homeopathy; yet "here I found not Christianity." Nevertheless she "lauded his courage in believing that mind made disease and that mind healed disease," and expressed her gratitude "with my native superfluity of praise." Yet, she went on to say, she still lacked "the one thing needed," and her health again declined.[67]

In *Science and Health* (pp. 185 f.) she would later write:

> *Erroneous mental practice may seem for a time to benefit the sick, but the recovery is not permanent. . . .*

> *A patient under the influence of mortal mind is healed only by removing the influence on him of this mind, by emptying his thought of the false stimulus and reaction of will-power and filling it with the divine energies of Truth.*

This might well stand as her own final reading of the extraordinary stimulus and reaction that marked her experience during the Quimby years.

4

While this inner drama went on, the outward events of Mrs. Patterson's life moved forward. After her apparent recovery in October, 1862, she lingered in Portland for almost three months. Her brother and sister-in-law, who had accompanied her there, returned home quickly, glad that she was better but far from convinced that Quimby was not a quack.[68]

At Mrs. Hunter's boardinghouse at that time were Julius Dresser, a newspaperman,[69] and Annetta Seabury, whom he was to marry a year later. Both were patients of Quimby's and leading members of the small circle of permanent devotees gathered around him. To them, as to the other members of the circle, Mrs. Patterson's vivid advent may have been somewhat startling, for it was soon clear that she had made as great an impression on Quimby as he had made on her. She was a threat, in a way they may have sensed vaguely, to the preeminence of their idol.

Then there were the Misses Emma and Sarah Ware, daughters of Judge Ashur Ware of the United States Supreme Court, who devoted their whole time to serving Quimby and to copying out his scribbled writings.[70] In a letter twenty years later Emma Ware recalled Mrs. Patterson as "a bright, clever lady, who took an interest in his 'theory.' "[71] Everyone seemed struck by the brightness. Mrs. Hunter later recalled her "sprightly ways and quickness of wit,"[72] and Quimby himself is alleged to have referred to her as "a devilish bright woman."[73]

George Quimby, who acted as his father's secretary, in later life remembered her as being "very intelligent and smart," and added, "She seemed to take a great interest in his ideas and could see into them, and father talked with her a good deal."[74] Twenty-year-old George himself "took no interest whatever in his ideas," and although it was Quimby's "devout wish that I might be his successor, still I would not take hold of it, not having a turn that way." But he enjoyed running the business side of his father's flourishing practice and he greatly admired him as a man.

Quimby had a good deal of publicity in the Portland papers in 1862. Soon Mrs. Patterson's name also began to appear from time to time. In addition to her published letters on Quimby and the editorial comment they called forth, a revised version of her already published poem "Woman's Rights" was printed in its new form in the *Portland Advertiser*. Dresser referred to her in his diary as "Mrs. Patterson, the authoress." Before long she delivered a successful public lecture, which may conceivably have been on Quimbyism but was much more probably on her experiences in the South.

For the Civil War was still dominating public thought. George Glover had been severely wounded in the neck at Corinth a week before his mother arrived in Portland, although she was not to learn of that for some time yet. And Patterson, who had been thrown for seven days into the Black Hole in his Salisbury prison because of his refusal to pledge himself not to escape, had implemented his refusal by actually escaping on September 20. Then followed what were later described by the bellicose press as "incredible hardships, and many narrow escapes in his journey of 400 miles through the domain of wild beasts, venomous reptiles, and rebels," until he arrived almost two months later in Washington, "worn down and destitute."[75]

By that time Mrs. Patterson had learned of his escape, but during her first weeks in Portland she was ignorant of it. On being restored to health, her first thought had been that now she would be able to go to Washington to plead for her husband's release through an exchange of prisoners. She borrowed money for this purpose from Patterson's brother John, who lived not far from Portland in Saco, Maine.[76] She appealed to the governor of New Hampshire and received from him a written statement on October 23 certifying her entitlement to sympathetic help on her journey;[77] but the journey was never made, for she then learned of Patterson's escape.

Sometime in December he rejoined her in Portland, having gone first of all to Sanbornton Bridge. The serious privations he had suffered seem to have damaged his health, weakened his will, and increased his restlessness—ironically enough at the very time his wife's energies were gathering toward that concentrated purpose that would emerge a few years later. From this time on they were moving in different directions.

The contrast was made all too clear when Patterson decided that he too would give a public lecture and turn his recent adventures into cash. The lecture was announced with some fanfare in the press; but on December 20, the day after it was to be given, the *Eastern Argus* announced: "For the benefit of our readers who may be asking 'what became of the squirrel' we would say that Dr. Patterson's lecture, unlike that of his wife, proved a failure. According to the records he had only a small handful in attendance and abandoned the lecture."

Before long they had both abandoned Portland; for on January

13, 1863, we find Mrs. Patterson writing Quimby from Sanbornton Bridge, where they were stopping with the Tiltons, "I eat, drink, and am merry; have no laws to fetter my spirit now, though I am quite as much of an escaped prisoner as my dear husband was." Patterson, she added, yearned to take up arms to serve his country, "and I shall try to acquiesce."[78]

Then it was that the unhealed past rose up again, and old ills began to return. Patterson could not bring himself either to enlist or to settle down to earning a living and providing a home for his wife. While he drifted around New England giving none too successful lectures on his prison experiences, Mrs. Patterson was again thrown on Abigail Tilton's charity. In that difficult situation she lacked the tranquility to help herself, she wrote Quimby,[79] and so began the series of appeals to him.

She persuaded Abigail to take her son Albert to Portland for treatment for smoking and drinking. The young man responded quickly to Quimby's treatment, but as soon as he returned to Sanbornton the habits began to reassert themselves. Mrs. Patterson tried to help him by Quimby's method, but all she succeeded in doing was to feel his cravings in the same way as Quimby felt his patients' sufferings. Again she had to appeal to Quimby to rid her of this unpleasant phenomenon as well as of "old habits, pain in the back and stomach, a cold just now, and bilious."[80]

The worsening state of her health drew her back to Portland in the summer of 1863. Because of the need to earn money she "essayed . . . to take notes for the Press . . . but was too ill for the enterprise," as she later explained.[81]

Nevertheless an extract from her July journal was printed in the *Portland Daily Press* in October.[82] Though obviously written as a potboiler, there is a sort of summer lightness about it that recalls the letters in which Mary Baker as a girl rattled along cheerfully with bits of neighborhood news:

> *July 20th. Rose at an early hour to look out upon the mist enveloping the slumbering city. . . . A little later and the fog dispersed—the spires detached themselves from the mist, and Eastern Promenade sweeping round Munjoy's Hill, lay, a glorious view, before me. The far-reaching silvery sheen of waters—with its emerald isles laughing in sunlight—called Casco Bay, the ocean and rocky shores of the Cape, the sheltering headlands of Falmouth and Cumberland, were bathed in glory.*
>
> *Ascending the Observatory on the summit of this Hill, 225 feet above tide water, we saw from the lookout a view which our*

limited space could portray but poorly. . . . A look at the inner harbor takes in the shipping, the spires, and shade trees of the embowered city. . . .

In the Natural History Room Science has a rich store-house and garniture of research. Collections of minerals, shells, birds, insects, reptiles, fossils, &c. . . . Some fine minerals in Calcite Malachite and marble, of the latter there were 50 varieties. The shells reminded us that "those who do business in great waters see the works of the Lord and His wonders in the deep." Some beautiful specimens of Madrepores, Harpa Ventricasa, Camea and the delicate transparent Nautilus pretty as Peri's dream, Univalves and Bivalves in perfect formations. . . . The birds were various and rare, numberless parrots of brilliant plumage. . . . The Taxidermist, Mr. Batchelder, did the civilities of the occasion with an old school politeness. . . . In the catechetical round of office we thought he exhibited in himself one of the rarest specimens of the museum, viz.: amiability in the genus homo.

Called at the sculptor's room. Found his Newsboy the chief attraction. . . . Defining his ideal seemed the chief excellence or truth; we cannot say beauty, believing this term indefinite, not self-defining, but dependent for a standard on different tastes. As Shakespeare has it, the lover frantic sees Helen's beauty in a brow of Egypt.

Later in the autumn Mrs. Patterson began writing regularly for the Portland papers, both prose and verse. After a while a column by her entitled "Way-side Thoughts" began to appear in the *Daily Press* at irregular intervals, discussing matters of private sentiment and public moment. She might write of slander as "a midnight robber, the red-tongued assassin of radical worth," or express the hope that "our faithful Abraham will continue to blend justice with victory, that the rebellious States may be saved for a few just and loyal ones who may be found in them." Poems addressed to personal friends alternated with ones "Written on Reading the Call of the Governor of New Hampshire for Soldiers" or in praise of "The Women of Tennessee."[83]

At times she found refuge in the home of one or the other of Patterson's brothers at Saco, Maine, conveniently near to Portland. To James Patterson she wrote in November, 1863:

When I get able to go I want to return at once to N. H. My son started by slow travelling a fortnight ago to come North this

makes me very anxious to return, he may have reached Sanborn-
ton. . . . I cannot live here as sick as I am. . . . I am homesick—
almost. O! I want to see my Daniel so much. I cry half the time.[84]

The report about George Glover turned out to be untrue, one
more in a series of disappointments. Instead of returning East after
being discharged from an army hospital, he re-enlisted.[85]

When Christmas Day came, Mrs. Patterson wrote a poem in which
the words "Merry Christmas" echoed with a sort of wistful irony.
Remembering the "blank despair" or "trembling joy" to be found at
"bier or banquet," she broke out suddenly: "What is thine, my
soldier boy?"[86] All the loss and failure of the past seemed to haunt her:

> How these sad eyes dim with weeping
> Long to gaze upon my son;
> Gazing back upon his childhood,
> Wishing more I could have done.

Quimby's "wisdom" had no comfort for an ache like this. It was
to Christianity she turned for the deep and abiding solace that had
nourished her darkest hours. In one of her articles in the *Daily Press*
she wrote:

> *Paul was my Christian hero, when he looked down into the*
> *stillness of a great soul and said, "all these things cannot move*
> *me"; and yet I can almost see the thoughts which accompanied*
> *that saying, falling down into that deep well, splash the water up*
> *into his eyes.*
>
> *Wisdom lives near the bottom of human life that with*
> *humility it may ascend to the gate of heaven. . . . All things*
> *shall work together for good to those who love Him. Engrave*
> *this upon your banner, you tried and tempted, life-tossed hero.*[87]

There were depths in traditional Christianity open only to
experience, not to theory.[88]

5

In the year 1864 it was still considered a scandalous thing that a
woman should give a speech in public. In that very year Charles
Sumner, veteran warrior for the black man's rights, uttered a shocked
protest at the suggestion that Julia Ward Howe should give "readings"
before a group of the élite in the parlor of her Washington friend,
Mrs. Sprague.

Yet on January 10 Mrs. Patterson again took her courage in her hands and gave her second public address in Portland, this time before the Spiritual Association in Mechanics Hall. Her talk "drew together a very respectable audience," according to one newspaper account, which then continued:

> This lady is not in the habit of public speaking, at least we should judge so from the tone of her voice which was too feminine to fill the hall. She possesses a symmetrical and graceful form, and her manners were modest and unassuming. Her intellectual culture appears to be good, and her spirit touched to very fine issues, but she spins an exceedingly fine, silken thread, and her thoughts run closely on the borders of refined and highly sub-limated transcendentalism which ordinary thinkers fail to com-prehend. . . . Having been cured of a disease by Dr. Quimby, she alluded in the course of her remarks to the nature of the ills flesh is heir to, and endeavored to explain the cause of such diseases upon metaphysical, physiological and philosophical prin-ciples, but she reasoned so high above the ordinary plane upon which we stood that we failed to comprehend her meaning. We understood her, however, to say that in most cures "disease is an error of the spirit, and it only needs Truth to combat it."[89]

Mrs. Patterson was exploring her way forward with a mixture of confidence and uncertainty. The historian who attempts to follow her progress through this ambiguous period has the advantage of drawing on the known facts of her future development for retrospective in-sights. Without these he might well lose himself and his subject in the inconclusive and frequently contradictory evidence of the period itself.

The preceding two decades of American life had been marked by a blind pushing and striving toward the great philosophical issues. A sort of frontier democracy of the mind encouraged all who would to tackle the age-old riddles. With utmost confidence but with obvious ignorance of the problems involved in what he was saying, an Andrew Jackson Davis could write:

> God is positive, all else is negative. If there exists an Evil principle, would not that principle be an integral element in the constitution of the Divine Mind? If there exists any where, in the realms of infinitude, an empire of sin, misery, and endless wretchedness—"a lake of fire prepared for the Devil and his angels"—would not God be also there? God is all-in-all;—would he not, therefore, be in the evil principle? God is omni-present;—would he not, therefore, be as much in Hell as in the regions of the sinless and blessed? There is no principle, antago-

nistic to God; no empire at war with Heaven! It can not be said that God "permits" sin and wretchedness; because he has eternally fixed habits or laws of right.[90]

Quimby did not go in for such broad metaphysical considerations; his concern was more practical and psychological. His God was a wisdom to be used to correct the mental mechanism which governed the body. In one sense Quimby remained to the end of his days a clockmaker with a flair for mechanical invention. Yet he obviously yearned to raise his system into a more spiritual dimension. This was shown by the religious terminology he so often used when writing or talking about his theory, though not as a rule in his practice.

Although he had no fixed name for his philosophy,[91] Quimby began at some point to think of it as a science and to relate it to the Christ. An even more audacious idea may have come to him through Davis, who had described the laws by which the universe is governed as constituting the Holy Ghost.[92] Quimby, too, used this theological term to describe his "science." Thus a theory which had risen from the swamps of mesmerism was identified with God's promised revelation of Himself to the human heart.

Yet spiritually presumptuous as the claim may be, behind it was a groping conviction that God must reveal Himself to a scientific age through law, as principle. And if this was so, then the saving knowledge of His holy laws must come as an eternal science.

This is the conviction that Mrs. Patterson appears to have reached early in her association with Quimby.

From the outset he had been impressed by her spirituality. One of his theories was that man tended toward the animal, woman toward the spiritual:

> *Man, like the earth, is throwing off a vapor, and that contains his knowledge. Out of this vapor comes a more perfect identity of living matter. . . . The spiritual rib that rises from man is more perfect matter or soil, called woman. . . . I do not mean that woman means every female. Nor do I pretend to say that man means everything of the animal. But that the mind of the female contains more of that superior substance required to receive the higher development of God's wisdom. For this element is pure love. . . . It separates her from matter and brings her into that spiritual state that rises from all animal life [i.e., like a vapor]. . . . Then she becomes a teacher of that Science which puts man in possession of a wisdom that can subject all animal life to his own control . . . and man stands to woman as a servant to his Lord. . . .*[93]

Back in October, 1862, Quimby one day had introduced Mrs. Patterson to young Emma Morgan in his office with the words, "This is a very wonderful woman, and in comparison I am the man but Mary is the Christ."[94] Mrs. Eddy herself in later years wrote that she would never forget an occasion on which they were talking and he startled her by saying, "I see now what you mean, and I see that I am John, and that you are Jesus." She was shocked at the time, she said, but afterwards concluded that he did not mean it personally but referred "to the *coming* anew of Truth, which we both desired."[95]

A passage in the Quimby manuscripts refers to this coming in similar terms:

> *I will not go back further than John the Baptist. John saw that the time was very near when his truth or Christ was to become a science, therefore he says, "As the truth is laid at the root or foundation of their theories, every tree or supposed science that cannot stand the test of true science must be hewn down." Therefore his belief was like water that could wash away some of their errors, but when the Truth or Holy Ghost should come then it would be reduced to a science. At this time Jesus had not received the Holy Ghost so as to explain it. Therefore He went with others to John to be baptized or hear John's ideas, and when Jesus asked John to explain to Him, John modestly replied, "I have need to be baptized or taught of you." Jesus declined explaining, so John then went on to tell his ideas or belief. Jesus entered into his water or belief, and understood it, and when He came out of the water, the Heavens were opened to Him alone, and the Holy Ghost descended like a dove and lit on Jesus and a voice said to Him alone, "This is my beloved Son (or Science), in whom I am well pleased."*[96]

The passage suggests interesting possibilities, if John and Jesus are taken as representing two different orders of *thinking* and not merely two persons in a particular historical situation. Further reflections on the ambiguities of the master-disciple relation are suggested by a passage from Ernest Renan's sensationally successful *Life of Jesus* which was published in 1863:

> *On the whole, the influence of John had been more hurtful than useful to Jesus. It checked his development; for everything leads us to believe that he had, when he descended toward the Jordan, ideas superior to those of John, and that it was by a sort of concession that he inclined for a time toward baptism. . . . It seems also that his sojourn with John had, not so much by the influence of the Baptist, as by the natural progress of his own*

*thought, considerably ripened his ideas on "the kingdom of
heaven." His watchword, henceforth, is the "good tidings," the
announcement that the kingdom of God is at hand.*[97]

The interesting suggestion here is that the temporary discipleship
of a superior mind to an inferior may have both a retarding and a
ripening effect, but that what counts essentially is the natural progress
of a man's own spiritual genius.

During the winter months of 1863–64 Mrs. Patterson spent hours
with Quimby almost every afternoon, observing his cases, talking with
him, discussing the notes he jotted down on his cases. Mrs. Sarah G.
Crosby, a Quimby patient who roomed in the same boardinghouse
with her, told later how Mrs. Patterson would come home at the end
of the afternoon and sit up until late at night writing.[98] As she had
been stimulated by her first acquaintance with Quimby a year earlier
to put down "my Philosophy," so she was now moved to pour out in
writing the thoughts that were stirring in her.

What she wrote during those long night hours has never come
to light. She herself spoke later of leaving certain manuscripts with
Quimby. Annetta Dresser wrote in 1895, "Those interested would in
turn write articles about his 'theory' or 'the Truth,' as he called it,
and bring them to him for criticism,"[99] but there is no record of anyone's actually doing this but Mrs. Patterson. George Quimby wrote of
the latter as "sitting in his room, talking with him, reading his Mss.,
copying some of them, writing some herself and reading them to him
for his criticism."[100] Perhaps only George Quimby knew what
eventually became of the writings she read to his father.

Mrs. Eddy also spoke later of "correcting" for Quimby some of the
manuscripts which he lent her.[101] When she first visited him in 1862
she noted that he withdrew from time to time to write at a desk in
the next room. She asked to see his writings, but what he showed her
at that time were merely notes on the individual cases he was treating,
including her own.[102] Soon afterwards, when she wrote the *Portland
Courier,* she expressed a hope that the master hand would elucidate
his theory more fully, and added, "May it be in essays instead of
notes, say I!"[103]

It is a curious fact that in none of the many newspaper articles
about Quimby which appeared from the beginning of his career till
his death is there mention of any manuscripts by him, except for this
passing reference by Mrs. Patterson and another one in her second
letter to the *Courier* a few days afterwards. In this she offered to
furnish "some quotations from P. P. Quimby's theory of Christ (not

Jesus); if he is willing and you will publish it." The newspaper was evidently not interested, and the quotations were not published.

Actually no excerpts were made public until 1887 when some were included in a lecture by Julius Dresser entitled "The True History of Mental Science."[104] These were all from articles said to have been written in 1863, after Mrs. Patterson had met Quimby. An article in the *Mental Science Magazine* in 1888, written by A. J. Swartz after he had examined the manuscripts in George Quimby's possession, stated: "His [P. P. Quimby's] views were often written by those associated with him, and then submitted to him for approval or correction. These writings by himself, and by those in his employ for years who wrote for him, constitute the [Quimby] manuscripts."[105]

The possibility cannot be ruled out that some of Mrs. Patterson's writings, perhaps emended by Quimby, or some of her emended versions of his own writings may be mixed in with what are now known as the Quimby manuscripts.[106] This is the view taken by an English historian who for the most part is highly critical of Mrs. Eddy. Largely on the basis of his study of the manuscripts, H. A. L. Fisher concluded that part of their confusion came from their representing an amalgam of "Quimby's own processes and convictions" and "the very opposite religious preconceptions" held by Mrs. Patterson.[107]

It is undeniable that the bulk of the Quimby manuscripts in their present form seems clearly to be the work of one vigorous though untrained mentality. Nevertheless there are recurrent elements of spiritual idealism which contradict the author's basic position. If these do not represent an intermixture of Mrs. Patterson's own writings, then they may represent the influence of her thinking on him.

When the Quimby manuscripts were finally made available to the public in 1934 by Quimby's heirs, it was discovered that very few of them were in his own handwriting. Most were copies, or copies of copies, by his widow and son and by the Misses Ware. In the vast majority of cases the originals had been destroyed after the copies were made, so that it is now impossible to know whether any of the originals were in Mrs. Patterson's handwriting.

It is also impossible to trace with assurance the "progress" of Quimby's thought, under whatever influence, because of the manifestly questionable accuracy of the dates attached to them. There are not only obvious anachronisms, such as assigning to early 1863 a group of writings which contain two articles on "President Lincoln's Death" and "Assassination of Lincoln"—hardly to be explained as examples of precognition—but there is also the more significant fact that the articles showing elements of greater spiritual maturity are assigned for the most part to the years 1859–1861, while those allegedly of later date are often cruder, more incoherent, and with more obvious traces of the early mesmeric period.[108]

In an article on "Aristocracy and Democracy," said to have been written in 1863, the term "Christian Science," already used by half a dozen other writers, turns up. Actually the article may have been written in 1865, since it belongs to the group of writings that included the two on Lincoln's assassination. The term itself runs counter to Quimby's generally derogatory use of the word "Christian"—as distinct from the word "Christ,"—and it may consequently reflect Mrs. Patterson's Christian convictions. Yet in its context it is rather casual and vague, as in its earlier usage by other writers, and has no more than a slight prophetic significance.

What is more important is that during the early months of 1864 there was evidently growing in Mrs. Patterson's mind a strong conviction that there must be such a thing as a real Science of Christianity—so much so that for some years afterwards she looked on this year as crucial in her development. But the figure of Quimby still dominated her own intuitions. Years later she wrote:

> . . . I tried him, as a healer, and because he seemed to help me for the time, and had a higher ideal than I had heard of up to that time, I praised him to the skies, wrote him letters,—they talk of my letters to Quimby, as if they were something secret, they were not, I was enthusiastic, and couldn't say too much in praise of him; I actually loved him, I mean his high and noble character, and was literally unstinted in my praise of him, but when I found that Quimbyism was too short, and would not answer the cry of the human heart for succor, for real aid, I went, being driven thence by my extremity, to the Bible, and there I discovered Christian Science.[109]

But in the early months of 1864 that event lay two years ahead.

6

Late in March Mrs. Patterson left Portland to visit Mary Ann Jarvis, an ailing spinster of Warren, Maine, who had been to Quimby for help earlier. From Warren she sent him a series of letters full of her characteristic liveliness, her yearnings and tribulations, her tentative steps forward and her persistent looks backward.[110]

With some zest she described her journey there, how at Wiscasset she "got into a villainous old vehicle and felt a sensation of being in a hencoop on the top of a churn-dash for about 6 hours! when the symptoms began to subside, and so did the old cart." On the journey she had met a Methodist lecturer who thought Quimby was "a defunct spiritualist," but she had set him right in short order.

At Warren, too, she found that people thought her a spiritualist because they had heard that Quimby was one; so in order to disabuse them of that misconception she gave one or two lectures in the village on "P. P. Quimby's spiritual Science healing disease—as opposed to Deism or Rochester-Rapping Spiritualism." The first, she reported, was thinly attended, but the precious few "were those whom a lady present (the manufacturer's wife) said were the uppertendam," and she went on to describe it with a certain lightheartedness:

> I began like this—ladies and gentlemen, ahem! To correct any misconceived ideas on the subject we would first say—that a belief in spiritualism, as defined by rappings, trances or any agency in healing the sick, coming from the dead, we wholly disclaim. I had no poetry at the close, 'twas all truth.

The second lecture she changed to meet what seemed to her "a spiritual need of the people," and she added, "I like much the hearts of Warren folks, i.e., better than their heads."

Repeatedly her loneliness shows through. "I do not want to return to Portland to stop if I can avoid it," she wrote. "If I could have my husband with me and be at home, I would like it there; but! but! but!" And again: "I am a little bit lonesome, doing and suffering. Am wishing I was around the home-hearth with my child and husband amid the joys of liberty."

A distrust of her own capacities at that point is also evident. She had received a letter from the editor of *The Independent* asking her to write for his widely read journal: "But I am not strong enough to step out upon the waves yet. I fear at least wetting my feet. . . . I long, long to be strong." And again:

> I have a strange feeling of late that I ought to be perfect after the command of science, in order to know and do the right. So much as I need to attain before that, makes the job look difficult, but I shall try. When men and above all women, revile me, to forgive and pity. . . . I can love only a good, honorable and brave career; no other can suit me.

The most important part of her two months in Warren was her experience in helping Miss Jarvis get over her ailments. In this task her own reliance on God was still weighted down by the Quimby theory of transference, by which the healer took on his patient's sufferings.[111] "My dear friend does all in her power to make me enjoy my stay here," she wrote, "but you know her body of belief 'is full of wounds and bruises' which in geting her out of I stumble," and she asked Quimby to treat her for two symptoms "that Miss Jarvis has just got rid of and saddled on to me."

Even when she experienced what later seemed to her a real spiritual breakthrough and healed Miss Jarvis of one of her major troubles[112] without any transference of symptoms, she immediately gave the credit to Quimby. Her lack of assurance at that time is apparent in her letters. In the middle of a passage pungently expressing her own views, she broke off suddenly to exclaim, "Jesus taught as *man* does *not;* who then is wise, but you!" Again: "I am up and about today, i.e., by the help of the Lord (Quimby)." She even experienced the phenomenon so familiar to many of his patients: his phantom form suddenly appeared in the room one day, complete in hat and dress coat, at a time when he was directing his thought to her from Portland.

By the end of her stay in Warren Mrs. Patterson was in worse health, lower spirits, and a greater state of dependence on Quimby than when she arrived—although she had gained some valuable experience while there and had felt at least one small breakthrough of spiritual power. Miss Jarvis fell ill with divers complaints every time her guest spoke of leaving, but eventually the latter felt she must go. At the urgent plea of her erstwhile Portland companion, Sarah Crosby, she had planned to move on to Mrs. Crosby's home at Albion, Maine, but her intentions were changed by an unexpected development.

The chronically restless Patterson had settled down to work. For a brief period the preceding year he had practiced dentistry in Lynn, Massachusetts. Now he returned there and opened an office in the Spinney Building, advertising in the Lynn papers regularly for the next six months. Mrs. Patterson quickly joined him there, but she was not to find the home she had hoped for.

In July of 1864 she wrote Quimby that her husband was suffering from erysipelas, and added, "He only laughs at *me* when I talk the truth to him."[113] More disturbing was the fact that his tendency to flirt with women patients had increased and his whole nature coarsened. It was probably her discovery of the first of several instances of his unfaithfulness at that time that drove Mrs. Patterson later in the summer to go to Mrs. Crosby's at Albion and remain there several months, or it may simply have been that Patterson was unable to provide for her.[114]

Sarah Crosby was a vivid, decided, mentally alert but emotionally unstable young widow who had been greatly attracted to Mrs. Patterson when they met in Portland early in the year. Mrs. Patterson, on her part, described her to Quimby as "one of the precious *few* affinities with whom I meet."[115] Though their later relations were stormy, Mrs. Crosby in 1903 wrote a letter to Mrs. Eddy recalling the days of her 1864 visit:

> *. . . in fancy I often go back to the old farmhouse in Albion as it was forty years ago with grandma Crosby the presiding spirit, ruling as with a rod, the rather too yielding* nominal *mistress of the household, the brood of noisy children frolicing from cellar to garret, the "hired girls" and "hired men" forming a little colony by themselves.*

> *These form the background of a picture in which the central figures are two* lone *women. The one, fired with the prescience of a great mission, even in the depths of poverty, looking forth upon the world conscious of coming power;—the other, peering wistfully into a future that* seemed *full of shadows, yet with the aspirations of a young goddess.*

> *Days and nights they sat in the little chamber of the* one, *or the nursery of the* other, *in such communion of soul as is seldom experienced by mortals; so full of tender love and sympathy for each other.*

> *And then when the separation came, what loving letters came and went;—they would fill a volume, and I do not much wonder that Dr. Patterson declared it a pity that such epithets of affection should be wasted between* women.[116]

The "loving letters" have never come to light, and Mrs. Crosby undoubtedly exaggerated the degree of affinity, for in 1907 she wrote Lyman Powell, "One of the trying things to her, was my utter indifference upon the subject which was so vital with her."[117] Actually she inclined more toward spiritualism than toward Quimby, and this must evidently have distressed the friend who only a few months before had lectured against "Rochester-rapping spiritualism."

In an episode that has been variously interpreted, Mrs. Patterson simulated a trance and wrote "spirit letters" to Mrs. Crosby purporting to come from Albert Baker. The most reasonable explanation, in view of her known opposition to spiritualism and of the admonition in these letters to "lean on no material or spiritual medium,"[118] is that she used this rather drastic method to show Mrs. Crosby how easy it was to produce such sham "manifestations." Mrs. Crosby, on the other hand, refused to believe they were not genuine.

The episode indicates, if nothing else, the overheated mental atmosphere of that period. On the one hand the "psychic" and on the other the "magnetic" laid claim to the word "spiritual." The over-credulous or self-willed person was likely to find either one of these more attractive than the path of rational and spiritual self-discipline to which a serious explorer of ideas was necessarily committed, whatever his temporary bafflements and expedients.[119]

Nevertheless, the advice in the "letters" to Mrs. Crosby was not all wasted. Later she wrote: "I am sure my experience with Mrs. Eddy gave me a clearer understanding of my own capabilities as well as a better knowledge of the world."[120] Not long after the visit Sarah Crosby studied stenography, became a court stenographer, and pushed ahead in a keen if rather hard way.

During the stay at Albion Mrs. Patterson gave a lecture at Water-ville, Maine, on "The South and the North." It was reported in the *Waterville Mail* of September 9 by a Dr. Sheldon, pastor of the Unitarian Church and for many years president of Maxwell College, who also introduced her.[121] The attendance was small, but the chivalrous Sheldon reported that the subject was presented "with a sharpness of logic and a beauty, purity and force of language rare in the most finished orators."

Later in the autumn Patterson apparently came to Albion, perhaps in penitence or with the assurance that he could now provide a real home for his wife, and she returned to Lynn with him. The sincerity of his protestations may be judged from the aftermath.

On December 14 Mrs. Crosby wrote her friend that she had received an amorous letter from the dentist, urging her to visit them in Lynn. Quoting various broad insinuations from his letter, she broke out, "Now Mary dear what . . . did *he* mean by saying 'Mortal natures tend downward,' was that *me,* he meant, O Mary I *am* alone,"—with more of the same. The letter showed a curious insensitiveness to Mrs. Patterson's own feelings, and Mrs. Crosby's protestations of injured innocence are not altogether convincing.[122]

Still Mrs. Patterson struggled to keep things going. She wrote potboilers for the Lynn papers, which helped to augment her husband's irregular income. As in earlier days when they had been together she tried to help him with his practice by coming to the aid and encouragement of fearful patients, especially children. One young girl accompanied a school friend to Patterson's office one day. As she sat in the waiting room she heard her friend in the dentist's chair suddenly exclaim, "Doctor, *I can't.*" Immediately a door on the opposite side of the waiting room opened, and "a little woman" flew across the room and disappeared into the dental office to comfort the frightened friend. Another woman in a letter to Mrs. Eddy in 1906 told her of a visit she had paid to Patterson's office as a little girl and added, "You were in the office and showed your love for children by your kindness to me."[123]

Although Patterson was by this time a social embarrassment, his wife soon after settling in Lynn had many friends. She was especially intimate with two Quaker families, the Phillipses and the Winslows, and the friendship meant a good deal to her. She and Patterson also joined the Linwood Lodge of Good Templars, a temperance society which mingled moral earnestness and social conviviality. Before long she was elected Exalted Mistress of the Legion of Honor, the women's auxiliary of the Good Templars, and her experience as presiding officer of the organization gave her a familiarity with parliamentary procedure that was useful in her later career.

Edwin J. Thompson, who in 1865 was head of the Linwood Lodge, was a dentist like Patterson. In 1907 he wrote:

> I remember Mrs. Patterson was a woman who had the welfare of humanity at heart and seemed to be imbued with an earnest desire to do good. She was active in the Lodge work . . . used to speak often at the meetings, saying sensible and helpful things . . . an attractive woman both in looks and manner . . . bright and cheerful and very witty . . . a good woman, and I never knew her to do any wrong or to wrong any one.[124]

An account by Mrs. Patterson in the *Lynn Weekly Reporter* of an excursion to Marblehead by the Good Templars calls up an atmosphere of hearty provincial jollity—"After dinner, the continued bits of mirth-provoking wit and humor became well nigh uproarious"[125] —but the more somber evidence of the period suggests that such interludes were rare. Bright and cheerful she may have been, but the precarious foundations of her domestic life were rapidly giving way.

At the moment, too, there was something larger than personal tragedy to shake the heart. The surrender at Appomattox brought jubilation and a sense of relief to the North, but quick on its heels came the stunning news of Lincoln's assassination.[126] Mrs. Patterson may well have felt that promise and reversal were the order of the day.

7

The year 1865 was the last of Quimby's life. Mrs. Patterson visited him again in the early part of April and once more received temporary relief.[127] A month later he retired from Portland to his home in Belfast to carry on a less active practice and probably with the hope of getting his chaotic notes into some sort of form for publication.

A writer in the *Portland Daily Press* on May 17 lauded his twenty-year search for the origin and nature of disease, and for the first time in public[128] referred to his theory explicitly as a science:

> *By a method entirely novel, and at first sight quite unintelligible, he has been slowly developing what he calls the science of health; that is, as he defines it, a science founded on principles that can be taught and practiced like that of mathematics, and not on opinion or experiments of any kind whatsoever.*

Behind his retirement lay not only a particular illness but also a growing weariness. Not surprisingly, the energetic little man who had poured so much of his energy into his patients was feeling the limits of his power—and perhaps an added frustration. Theoretically, those patients of his who had talked with him at length and studied his notes should be able to practice as he did. Yet not one of them—with the exception of Mrs. Patterson, whom he apparently recognized as acting from some spiritual position beyond his own[129]—seemed able to heal by his method.

Emma Ware wrote in 1882, "I devoted myself exclusively to his instruction as long as he lived—but I never learned the art of healing,"[130] and the same thing was true of her sister, who suffered from extreme ill health all her life. Julius and Annetta Dresser began healing only in 1882 after they had emerged from obscurity to take a course of instruction with one of Mrs. Eddy's students, Edward J. Arens, and even then they were never really successful healers. Their son Horatio, Quimby's most persistent propagandist, wrote in 1910, "One searches his manuscripts in vain for a clear explanation of his method of silent cure."[131]

The reason is indirectly made clear by a Methodist minister turned Swedenborgian, Warren Felt Evans, who had visited Quimby in 1863. Evans had been practicing healing for several years before that. In an interview published twenty-five years later,[132] he stated that he had called twice briefly on the Portland doctor and satisfied himself that Quimby's methods were "like those he [Evans] had employed for some years, which was a mental process of changing the patient's thinking about disease." The interviewer, A. J. Swartz, added that his own inquiries in Portland confirmed the fact that modern mind cure had "originated with these two men, and that it is difficult to say which practiced it first."

In the next twenty-five years Evans wrote several highly successful books on mental healing. Commenting on these Horatio Dresser declared:

> *In all his writings one finds a well-reasoned account of what Mr. Quimby meant to say, what he would have said had he possessed all the data as well as a trained mind. For there was remarkable affinity between the two men. To one who has read Mr. Quimby's manuscripts it is a constant satisfaction to note the constant harmony of thought and unity of purpose in their writings. Although Mr. Evans only once refers to Mr. Quimby, there is nothing he wrote in [his books about healing] that does not directly relate to the Quimby teachings.*[133]

Evans, however, repeatedly and explicitly identified his method of healing with animal magnetism.[134] Where Quimby had repudiated the term, Evans recognized frankly that his method was that of suggestion directed toward a patient in "the conscious impressible condition," which he described as a magnetized state not involving sleep. It took the more sophisticated realism of Evans—not to mention the later religious analysis of Mrs. Eddy—to bring to the surface the real source of Quimby's power. Because the latter's theory (at least in part) was in advance of his practice, a semimetaphysical smoke screen of words hid its basically hypnoidal character.

Mrs. Patterson's fears may have been causing her unconsciously to avoid this recognition. As one human reliance after another was taken away from her, she clung to Quimby as almost her last human hope.

Toward the end of June, the *Lynn Weekly Reporter* announced that business of importance made it necessary for Patterson to be absent from his office for a few weeks. On first leaving, he agreed to send his wife four dollars a week and did so for four weeks; then the remittances stopped.[135] The important business again appears to have been of an amorous nature.

On July 29 Mrs. Patterson wrote Quimby a distraught and anguished letter. She had just received word that George Glover was dying of consumption of the bowels in Enterprise, Minnesota. Though sick herself and without means or knowledge of how to reach the boy, she would start out next Monday to go to him, but almost incoherently she implored Quimby to save him by his power.[136]

The report she had received may have been false or exaggerated and she may have learned this in time. At any rate, Glover did not die and she did not leave for Minnesota.

The next we know of her she was in Quimby's home town, Belfast, writing on September 7 to her sister Martha Pilsbury.[137] In a deeply exasperated letter she returned ten dollars which Martha had sent to help her in her "want" and spiritedly reproached her for an unspecified indignity to which she felt her sister had just put her. It is apparent that there was already a widening rift between Mrs. Patterson and her family.

A month later, on October 6, Mark Baker died at Sanbornton. The stern, rather lonely old man, who had loomed over her childhood like a granite peak, left to each of his three daughters the sum of one dollar. The bulk of his not inconsiderable estate went to George Sullivan Baker, who had given him a grandson to carry on the Baker name. The daughter whom he had anxiously rocked in his arms was thus left to the dubious mercies of a Calvinist Deity whose favors were as unpredictable and arbitrary as Mark's own.

Nine days later the *Lynn Weekly Reporter* announced that "Dr. D. Patterson has returned to Lynn, and will be happy to greet his friends and patrons at his office." Wearily Mrs. Patterson took up the shattered remnants of her marriage and attempted to put them together again. The two were now living at 23 Paradise Court in the fishing village of Swampscott, adjoining Lynn. Though their second-floor apartment was attractive enough and the house had a charming garden in which Mrs. Patterson spent hours on fine days, reading and writing, the location may have been deliberately chosen by the dentist to keep his wife farther away from his office and his affairs, professional and otherwise.

Within three weeks of reopening his office he was engaged in the columns of the *Weekly Reporter* in an unseemly altercation with another dentist who accused him of dunning patients unfairly. It must have seemed to his wife, as the discreditable episodes mounted, that life was taking on the character of the "ghastly farce" she later described material existence as being.

Yet in a poem entitled "Our National Thanksgiving Hymn," published in the same paper on December 30, she praised the God

> Who giveth joy and tears, conflict and rest,
> Teaching us thus of Thee,
> Who knoweth best!

Somewhere, behind the dingy veil of appearances, the unalterable goodness of God persisted. And in another poem "To the Old Year— 1865" she asked

> One word, receding year,
> Ere thou grow tremulous with shadowy night!
> Say, will the young year dawn with wisdom's light
> To brighten o'er thy bier?

The first thing the New Year brought was the death of Quimby. What Mrs. Patterson called the shadowy night had been gathering about him for some time. An internal tumor, which he is said to have kept under control by his active will for several years, grew worse as his will weakened. Taking on the suffering of a patient who visited him the preceding October, according to one account, he found himself unable to throw off the pain as he had always done previously.[138] Toward the end he yielded to the entreaties of his family and received medical treatment, but without avail. The end came on January 16, 1866.

To Mrs. Patterson it seemed that she was now entirely alone. All the generosity of her feeling for Quimby, all the spiritual ideals with which she had endowed his questing, prophetic little figure, welled up in a poem which she wrote on January 22 and called "Lines on the Death of Dr. P. P. Quimby, who healed with the truth that Christ taught, in contradistinction to all isms." Ask her not, she said,

> To mourn him less: to mourn him more were just,
> > If to his memory 'twere a tribute given
> For every solemn, sacred, earnest truth
> > Delivered to us ere he rose to heaven.
> Heaven but the happiness of that calm soul,
> > Growing in stature to the throne of God:
> Rest should reward him who hath made us whole,
> > Seeking, though tremblers, where his footsteps trod.[139]

In the perspective of time there is a strange irony in the lines. For all the sincerity of her grief, the writer could not know that within a fortnight her own footsteps, very literally "trembling," would lead her into a world utterly beyond the clairvoyant gaze and inquiring mind of Phineas Parkhurst Quimby.

Chapter
VI

Discovery
1866

On Saturday, February 3, 1866, the *Lynn Reporter* carried a short item:

> *Mrs. Mary M. Patterson, of Swampscott, fell upon the ice near the corner of Market and Oxford Streets, on Thursday evening, and was severely injured. She was taken up in an insensible condition and carried to the residence of S. M. Bubier, Esq., near by, where she was kindly cared for during the night. Dr. Cushing, who was called, found her injuries to be internal, and of a very serious nature, inducing spasms and intense suffering. She was removed to her home in Swampscott yesterday afternoon, though in a very critical condition.*

The accident had occurred when Mrs. Patterson, together with a group of friends, was on her way to a meeting of the Good Templars. As soon as it was realized that she was badly injured she was carried into the nearest house. Dr. Alvin M. Cushing, a popular homeopathic physician and surgeon, was immediately called. He found her, according to his account almost forty years later, "partially unconscious, semi-hysterical, complaining by word and action of severe pain in the back of her head and neck."[1] After examining her he gave strict orders that she should not be moved. Two or three friends offered to stay with her through the night.[2]

Cushing paid two visits that evening.[3] When he returned the next morning the women who had been watching with her told him that she had been unconscious all night, and she was still not able to speak.[4] An effort had been made to find Patterson, who was away on one of his jaunts; he was finally reached in New Hampshire by telegram in the morning and hurried back that same day.[5]

Meanwhile Mrs. Patterson regained consciousness sufficiently to insist, against Cushing's advice and to her friends' alarm, that she be moved to her home at Paradise Court. In order to lessen the pain of the move the doctor gave her one-eighth of a grain of morphine and this plunged her into a deep sleep which lasted for several hours. The move by sleigh was made under his superintendence; he stayed until she recovered consciousness; and later that day (Friday) he visited her again.[6]

During the day George Newhall, a milkman, called to deliver the milk. He found two members of Mrs. Patterson's church, Mrs. Carrie Millet and Mrs. Mary Wheeler, in charge. They told him that she "had met with an accident by falling on the ice and had broken her spine and would never be able to take another step alone." Mrs. Millet asked him "to go down to Marblehead line and inform the Minister, the Rev. Jonas B. Clark, of the accident." Years later he recalled the ride "with the mercury below zero and a slow horse and business pung." He arrived back "so near finished with cold I could not speak for some time."[7]

The "broken spine" to which he referred was probably Mrs. Millet's version of Cushing's diagnosis of the injury as concussion and possible spinal dislocation.[8] Although Cushing later stated that he was called on the case by Mrs. Patterson's friends as a surgeon rather than as a homeopathist,[9] the remedy he prescribed for her was a homeopathic one. In 1907 he recalled it as having been "the third decimal attenuation of arnica diluted in a glass of water,"[10] though in 1894 when telling a patient in Springfield, Massachusetts, about the incident he remarked, "I have never been able to remember just the medicine I used, for I never have been able to heal any one else with what I thought I gave her."[11] Mrs. Eddy's own accounts of the episode all state that after the move home she did not take any of the medicine which the doctor left for her, since she had no faith in it.[12]

On Saturday there was no improvement and Cushing felt there was nothing further he could do for her.[13] Friends hovered round her all day, and on Sunday morning the clergyman, "Father" Clark, called in to see her on his way to church. He felt it necessary to prepare her for the worst, prayed with her, and agreed to return following the afternoon service.[14] It was perhaps the gloomy theological comfort he offered that roused her to more strenuous spiritual effort. At any rate when her friend, Mrs. Ira P. Brown, who had driven over to see her about noon, was taking her leave, Mrs. Patterson astonished her by saying: "When you come down the next time, I will be sitting up in the next room. I am going to walk in."[15]

Nine-year-old Arietta Brown was with her mother, and in later years she recalled Mrs. Brown's exclamation, "Mary, what on earth are you talking about!" But when they returned in the evening, Mrs. Patterson was indeed "sitting up in the next room." She had got up, dressed, and walked in unaided. The clergyman, calling back, had been met by her at the door, and was so startled that for a moment he thought he was seeing an apparition.[16]

At this late date it is impossible to know the exact nature of the injuries from which Mrs. Patterson recovered, but her recovery seemed to those about her a miracle. Christian Scientists, disbelieving in the miraculous in the ordinary sense of the word, have held that whatever happened on that occasion was natural—the natural working of God's law. The miracle lay primarily in what happened to her thinking. Other people had had remarkable recoveries through prayer, but other people did not find in the experience something on which to found a new church.

At some point during that Sunday afternoon when she lay helpless in bed, Mrs. Patterson had asked to be given her Bible and to be left alone. Turning to one of the healings of Jesus, she began to read. In later years she found it difficult to remember the exact passage,[17] but as she read it the words of Jesus flooded into her thought, "I am the way, the truth, and the life: no man cometh unto the Father, but by me,"[18] and quite suddenly she was filled with the conviction that her life was in God—that God was the only Life, the only I AM. At that moment she was healed.

Writing of the incident in later years she declared, "That short experience included a glimpse of the great fact that I have since tried to make plain to others, namely, Life in and of Spirit; this Life being the sole reality of existence."[19] It was as simple as that. In a moment of vision she saw all being as spiritual, divine, immortal, wholly good. There was no room for fear or pain or death, no room for the limits that men define as matter.

It was apparently a moment of indescribable wonder and joy. Half a lifetime later, when Mrs. Eddy's companion Laura Sargent asked her what it was that she *saw* at the instant of healing, Mrs. Eddy did not answer, but the far-off gaze that came into her eyes and the light that filled her face caused Mrs. Sargent to draw back in sudden awe.[20] At the end of her life Mrs. Eddy's last written words were, "God is my life," and that perhaps sums up the whole experience.

Its immediate fruit was healing; but more than that, it was the beginning of a new life.

The next day Mrs. Patterson sent for Dr. Cushing to show him that she was healed. His alarm at her being up and about caught her unaware. Always intensely responsive to the mental atmosphere about her, she felt his fears and doubts overshadow her buoyancy, and to her dismay she sank back in sudden weakness again. But after he left, the vision returned "with such a light and such a presence," as she put it later, that she rose feeling she could never be conquered again.[21]

At that time she was unable to explain to Cushing or to anyone else how the healing had taken place, nor did she recognize at once that she was embarked on a new course. There had been healings before in moments of faith and exaltation, as when she had cured Miss Jarvis. There is an obvious continuity between her earliest and her latest religious experiences as they are reflected in her writing, and she herself felt that in one sense she was only seeing more deeply now into the Christian faith she had had since girlhood.[22] Yet in the perspective of years she identified this healing as the decisive moment of discovery in which the allness of God, or Spirit, began to give every detail of experience a radically new dimension.

But all around her lay the stubborn, cloddish world of material appearances, waiting to claim her back. While some of her friends accepted her healing with delight, others expressed dark forebodings that she would suffer a relapse. The ruins of her marriage, the uncertainties of the future, the magnetic hold of the past—all these challenged her momentary glimpse of Life and Love unbounded. She was, in her own later words, but "a trembling explorer in the great realm of mental causation."[23]

Describing this period in 1883 (when she habitually used the editorial "we" in public statements) she wrote, "One individual with strong intellectual power, and little spirituality, even gave us some momentary fear of our ability to hold on to this wonderful discovery." It was at such a moment of fear, she went on, that she sent an appeal to Julius Dresser, Quimby's erstwhile disciple.[24]

Some years were to elapse after her discovery before she would realize that her trembling explorations had already led her far beyond Quimby's mental world. It is a human tendency to try to fit the new into the old, and Mrs. Patterson had still to discover the impossibility of reconciling her new vision of reality with his attempted science of suggestion. In the sudden reaction that can follow the birth of a revolutionary idea, she wrote to Dresser for help. The backwash of past attitudes was evident in every word, even to the recrudescence of Quimby's emphasis on will, as the vision seemed temporarily to be obscured.

The letter was dated February 15 and read in part:

> *I am constantly wishing that* you *would step forward into the place he has vacated. I believe you would do a vast amount of good, and are more capable of occupying his place than any other I know of.*
>
> *Two weeks ago I fell on the sidewalk, and struck my back on the ice, and was taken up for dead, came to consciousness amid a storm of vapors from cologne, chloroform, ether, camphor, etc., but to find myself the helpless cripple I was before I saw Dr. Quimby.*

The physician attending said I had taken the last step I ever should, but in two days I got out of bed alone and will walk; but yet I confess I am frightened, and out of that nervous heat my friends are forming, spite of me, the terrible spinal affection from which I have suffered so long and hopelessly. . . . Now can't you help me? I believe you can. I write this with this feeling: I think that I could help another in my condition if they had not placed their intelligence in matter. This I have not done, and yet I am slowly failing. Won't you write me if you will undertake for me if I can get to you?[25]

Dresser's reply came three weeks later from Yarmouth, Maine, where he was working as a newspaperman:

I am sorry to hear of your misfortune, and hope that with courage and patience neither the prediction of the Dr. nor your own fear will prove true. . . . As to turning Dr. myself, and undertaking to fill Dr. Q's place and carry on his work, it is not to be thought of for a minute. Can an infant do a strong man's work? Nor would I if I could. Dr. Q. gave himself away to his patients. To be sure he did a great work, but what will it avail in fifty years from now if his theory does not come out. . . ? He did work some change in the minds of the people, which will grow with the development and progress of the world. . . . So with Jesus. He had an effect which was lasting and still exists. But his great aim was a failure. He did not succeed, nor has Dr. Q. succeeded in establishing the Science he aimed to do. The true way to establish it is, as I look at it, to lecture, and by a paper make that the means, rather more than the curing, to introduce the truth. . . .

No, I would not cure if I could, not to make a practice of it, as Dr. Q. did, yet, Mrs. Patterson, I would be glad to help you in your trouble, but I am not able to do it. My attention has not been given that way, and my occupation . . . is of a nature such as to keep my mind from even the theory, much more the practice of it. I do not even help my wife out of her trouble, if she has serious ones, and of all in the world I could help her quickest and easiest, owing to the greater interchange of mind. My wife has lately given birth to a son . . . and I have a good opportunity to know whether I could easily become a Dr. or not. But I am not even Dr. for them. How then could I cure those to whose minds I have little or comparatively no access at all?[26]

It was clear that Quimby was irretrievably gone. There was no *person* to whom Mrs. Patterson could turn. She might cling for a while to some of the things she had learned from Quimby; but if she was going to heal herself or others, she would have to trust to the truth she had glimpsed that Sunday afternoon. There was only one place she could go to understand it better. That was the Bible, and to the Bible she turned.

Events, however, did not allow her at once to give herself wholly to the study and thought which now seemed all-important. The next six months or so were a transitional period in which inspiration and mental distress were juxtaposed in startling chiaroscuro.

The Armenius Newhalls, who owned 23 Paradise Court and lived on the first floor beneath the Pattersons, wanted to sell their house. Mrs. Patterson was glad to help them by writing a lyrical article on Swampscott for the *Lynn Reporter,* ending it with a frank puff for the Newhall residence. "The skies of Swampscott," she wrote, "are unvailed. We can see them! and O! they are spiritually bright, beautifully blue, and wondrous in their change."[27] But the change in residence which she and Patterson were forced to make late in March because of the Newhalls' plans was anything but wondrous.

They moved into an unfurnished room in the house of the Reverend Philemon R. Russell at the corner of Pearl and High Streets, Lynn. Russell, who is said to have been known chiefly for his intolerant hatred of the abolitionists, was a former Baptist minister of the narrowest, most dogmatic variety. His son and daughter-in-law occupied half the house, and the daughter-in-law was at first deeply attracted by Mrs. Patterson and her challenging new religious ideas; but the elder Russell soon had the whole household lined up against the newcomer. A sister, Mrs. Julia Russell Walcott, became in time a mine of sensational stories about Mrs. Patterson.[28]

According to the Russells, Patterson came to the final parting with his wife after they had been living in this forbidding stronghold of bigotry for a month or two. There is reason to doubt the accuracy of their statement, as subsequent events show, but the dentist apparently did indulge in one of his periodic disappearances, leaving Mrs. Patterson destitute for the time being. As a result, she was unable to pay the weekly rent of $1.50 for lodging, and after a few more weeks Russell had her evicted.

It was at this time that, desperately in need of money and probably at the urging of anxious friends, Mrs. Patterson presented a petition to the city of Lynn. She must have been for the moment in one of the darkest valleys of discouragement, suffering again from the old symptoms which returned when her vision was clouded, for her petition stated that "owing to the unsafe condition of that portion of Market street at the junction of Oxford street, on the first day of February last, she slipped and fell, causing serious personal injuries, from which she has little prospect of recovering," and it asked for pecuniary recompense for these injuries.

Here was one of the sharp reversals that marked this unsettled period of transition. In her autobiography Mrs. Eddy wrote that it was not until "the latter part" of 1866 that she gained the "scientific certainty" of the truth of her discovery.[29] Appropriately enough she was granted leave by the city of Lynn on December 26 to withdraw the petition she had presented six months before when everything seemed to have turned against her.[30]

At that earlier period she had gone for temporary refuge to her Quaker friends, Thomas and Hannah Phillips, on Buffum Street. Thomas Phillips, a shoe manufacturer who had both the peaceful Quaker temperament and the Quaker flair for success, in his desire to help her was probably responsible for her petition to the city. Although they thought her ideas beyond them, both the elder Phillipses loved and admired Mrs. Patterson. To their skeptical married daughter, Susan Oliver, Thomas remarked: "Mary is a wonderful woman, Susie. You will find it out some day. I may not live to see it, but you will." Later Susan Oliver became a Christian Scientist, and in 1907 she recalled to Sibyl Wilbur her father's prophecy.[31]

The practice of silent prayer before meals at the Phillipses greatly impressed Mrs. Patterson, and it was to become the characteristic form of prayer in her own Church. She in turn gave her friends a practical illustration of the power of prayer when overnight she healed a painful felon on the finger of young Dorr Phillips, Susie's brother.[32]

For even as she walked through some very deep valleys, the upper heights were springing into light. We catch a sudden glimpse of this in an incident recounted by a Mrs. James Norton of Lynn. On one summer day in 1866 Mrs. Norton took her seven-year-old son George to Lynn Beach and left him there while she hitched the horse and went for water. The child had club feet and had never walked. When she returned she was stunned to find him walking hand in hand with a stranger. The mother and the strange woman looked in each other's eyes, then both of them wept and joined in thanks to God. The woman was of course Mrs. Patterson. The boy, who was completely healed, afterwards became a mechanical engineer and lived a happy and useful life.[33]

Much of the history of this period we can only guess at. Even the sequence of events is obscure. Apparently Patterson, soon after the eviction by the Russells, put in an appearance again, and husband and wife then moved into the boardinghouse of Mrs. George D.

Clark on Summer Street for part of July and August.[34] There, toward the end of August, he finally deserted her.

When she obtained a divorce seven years later, young George Clark, son of the boardinghouse keeper, accompanied her to court as a witness. Mrs. Patterson brought a charge of desertion. According to Clark's later affidavit,[35] when the judge asked why Patterson had deserted her she replied, "To escape arrest." "Arrest for what?" he inquired, and the answer was, "On account of his adultery." Clark then records that the judge without further ado ordered the clerk to write a bill of divorcement.

Mrs. Eddy's own fuller explanation is that her husband eloped with the wife of a prominent Lynn businessman, that shortly afterwards the deluded woman returned and came to ask her forgiveness and her intercession with the outraged businessman, and that Patterson then presented himself, all ready to be accepted back once more. He returned, according to Susan Oliver,[36] while Mrs. Patterson was again at the Phillipses, and Thomas Phillips so far forgot his Quaker nonviolence when he saw him standing in the door as to raise his cane and threaten him with it. But Mrs. Patterson restrained him and then took the decisive step herself. She told her once-loved Daniel with quiet firmness that they had come to the final parting of the ways.

Patterson paid a visit to Sanbornton Bridge in an effort to justify himself to his wife's family, and it may have been Abigail Tilton who persuaded him to make his wife an annual allowance of two hundred dollars. This he paid in small installments, but after a year or two these payments stopped.

The rest of his life was a sad and lonely one, spent for the most part in drifting around New England and ending in 1896 after a period of hermitage in Saco, Maine. But a poignant note comes out of those years. In 1900 one R. D. Rounsevel, owner of a hotel or boardinghouse in Littleton, New Hampshire, declared in an affidavit:

> *About the year 1872 Dr. Patterson, a dentist, boarded with me in Littleton, N. H. During his stay at different times I had conversation with him about his wife, from whom he was separated. He spoke of her as being a pure, estimable and Christian woman, and the cause of the separation being wholly on his part, that if he had done as he ought he might have had a pleasant and happy home as one could wish for. At that time I had no knowledge of who his wife was. Later I learned that Mary Baker G. Eddy, the discoverer and founder of Christian Science, was the above mentioned woman.*[37]

Rounsevel's wife added a comment which reveals all the pathos of a weak nature realizing too late what it has thrown away. In speaking of his wife, she said, Patterson would use the old expression that he "worshipped the ground she trod upon."[38]

Mrs. Patterson, for her part, was now stripped of everything that seemed to make life dear. She was forty-five years old, at the exact midpoint of her life. Fired with a vision that challenged the entrenched convictions of society, she had nothing outwardly to help her. Separated from her family, deprived of her son, estranged from her husband, she had nowhere to go but forward.

Her loneliness found expression in a melancholy little poem entitled "I'm Sitting Alone" which was published at this time.[39] Nowhere did there seem to be any place for her. After leaving the Clark boardinghouse she stopped with first one friend, then another, each stay ending with her being "evicted," if the malicious gossip of Julia Russell Walcott is to be believed. With her personal troubles and with the vision in her crying out for expression, she may well have been a burdensome guest to people whose horizon ended at the new Temperance Hall.[40] But sometime during the autumn she found an appreciative welcome in the more congenial home of the Ellises in Swampscott.

Fred Ellis was the village schoolmaster, a pleasant, cultivated young man, and his mother was a kindly soul whose heart went out in sympathy to Mrs. Patterson. Mother and son remained good friends to her through the trials of those early years, and in 1901 Fred Ellis wrote her:

> How many times I have thought of writing a line to try whether you still remember your old friends, Mrs. Ellis and her son, with any such interest as has ever gathered about my recollection of you and of our acquaintance, to me so delightful, in those far away days at Swampscott. . . .
>
> I have kept the even tenor of my way, teaching school with a persistence that would be monotony but for the stimulus and cheer that come through association with children. I have my own four and my thousand and more in school, to keep me feeling young. . . . .
>
> And you, you, what can I say! Words fail when I think of the marvellous work thou hast wrought!
>
> It may be presumption in me to address you. I do so, not in the light of the magnificence of your achievement, but out of my cherished remembrance of those precious evenings in the little sitting-room at Swampscott, when the words of Jesus, of Truth, were so illumined by your inspired interpretation.

*All that may have passed from your memory, but not from
mine.*

*Accept my heartfelt wishes for your further success, and for
your peace of mind under the irritating assaults of malicious
enemies.*[41]

In her reply Mrs. Eddy spoke of the death of "your dear mother
. . . a noble woman, wise, tender, true," and added, in words which
were not complacent simply because they came out of the depths of
total conviction, "Yes in your sweet little sitting room in Swampscott
words were said that will go down the centuries and echo through all
time." Then she added the human touch that so often endeared her
to friends and followers: "Do you forget your Christmas present to
me—that basket of kindlings all split by your hand and left at my
door? I do not."[42]

She would spend all day at the Ellises writing in her room. At the
end of the day, Fred Ellis reported, "she would read the pages to
Mother and me, inviting, almost demanding, our criticisms and suggestions."[43] And here at last we draw near to the real history of Mrs.
Patterson in this period of her life. For if one thing is sure, it is this:
the outward circumstances of her life, trivial and harassing as they
might be at times, faded into insignificance beside the tremendous
questions she was confronting, hour after hour and day after day,
alone in her room. There, with what she later described as "fierce
heart-beats,"[44] she explored the vast new universe that was opening
up to her gaze.

2

The manuscript on which she was probably working at that
time was composed of rough notes for the first volume of a projected
work of enormous scope, to be called "The Bible in its Spiritual
Meaning." Volume One was entitled "Genesis."[45]

The science and theology of the midcentury had locked horns
over the question of genesis, of beginnings. Darwin's *Origin of
Species* had, on the one hand, roused fundamentalist religion to
furious defense of a literal interpretation of the two creation accounts
in Genesis and had, on the other hand, inspired liberal religion to
apply evolutionary analysis to the Bible.

In the famous *Essays and Reviews*, published in England in 1860,
Benjamin Jowett and other prominent churchmen had reflected the
new Darwinian pattern of thought in their treatment of religion as
evolving from primitive origins to a purer monotheism and thence to
the Christianity of the New Testament, and the book had roused a
hurricane of controversy.

The sciences, too, were concerned with genesis in more respects than the origin of species. Darwin himself had drawn heavily on the extraordinary discoveries of Agassiz in embryology, discoveries illustrating that metamorphosis of the individual before birth which pointed to the evolution of the species.[46] In 1864 Pasteur demonstrated to a brilliant Parisian assembly that there is no such thing as spontaneous generation, that all life comes from germs. And on an icy February night in 1865 Gregor Mendel read to a provincial gathering in Germany the paper which, after long neglect, was to germinate in the modern science of genetics.

As a starting point for her own radical metaphysics, Mrs. Patterson went back to the beginning of all things. "In the beginning God." Quimby had started with animal matter; she would start with God, Spirit.

At the beginning of her manuscript she still related her discovery to Quimby's activities, as she was to do for several more years, but she now referred to the Quimby period as "the twilight of discovery." This she explicitly identified with the "evening" preceding the "morning" of the first day of creation in the Genesis account. As she explained this account, it had nothing to do with the creation of a material universe but described the step-by-step appearing, through revelation, of spiritual reality in all its pre-existent perfection. Ideas might stir murkily in human thought before the moment of revelation, but only when the light of Truth dawned could they begin to be understood in their inherent divine logic.

Later in *Science and Health* she would define "evening" in part as "mistiness of mortal thought," and "morning" as "revelation and progress."[47] Quimby had defined mind itself as a mist or vapor, and the metaphor is not inappropriate to his hazy amalgam of idealism and materialism. But the logic of Mrs. Patterson's new-found conviction of Spirit's allness compelled her to look for authority in another direction. Using the editorial "we" that was to mark her writings for some years to come, she now announced unequivocally, "Our only text book for the science of man is the Bible."[48]

Many years later she wrote that despite the stimulus of the Quimby period she had lacked "the one thing needed" until the experience of "the accident and injury called fatal, [when] the Bible healed me; and from Quimbyism to the Bible was like turning from Leviticus to St. John." Then, her account continued, she dropped forever the belief that the human mind healed disease and gained the great discovery "that God is the only healer and healing Principle, and that Principle is divine not human."[49]

The birth of a radically new idea is something that requires more than cursory examination.

Loren Eiseley, in *Darwin's Century,* has said that all the most diverse and seemingly unrelated phenomena of that period can be seen in perspective to be revolving "in a moment of heterogeneity before they crystallize into a new pattern with Darwinism at the center."[50] The tendency to pull religious phenomena into this pattern has proved irresistible. There is no spontaneous generation of ideas, it is said. Every religious development must be explained as evolution—or, utilizing an analogy from later genetic theory, as mutation—from an unbroken line of natural ancestors.

The compulsion on intellectual historians has therefore been strong to interpret Christian Science as an evolutionary development from Quimbyism, which in turn can be traced back to Mesmer. The trouble is that Mrs. Patterson's notes on Genesis can be fitted into this theory only by a most unscientific manipulation of the facts. For the germ of a new idea, alien to everything in Quimby, is already present in these notes: the concept of man as a perfect spiritual idea, made in the image and likeness of a God who is wholly good and wholly Spirit.

Christian Science in its completed form would present God not as acting through history to create man but as acting on history to reveal man. Rejecting the relativities of history as in any true sense determinative, Mrs. Eddy would write, "No advancing modes of human mind made Jesus; rather was it their subjugation, and the pure heart that sees God."[51] In the virgin birth she found the perfect symbol of a creation that was really revelation, the archetypal illustration of reality breaking through appearance in defiance of material modes of generation. As she saw it, the "seed" that produced Jesus was Mary's faint glimpse of Spirit as the only creator, the source of all true being. And it was this seed, she held, rather than his human heredity and environment, that decisively shaped the events of his later life.

The point is significant for the historian of Christian Science because it suggests that an understanding of that which is unique to Mrs. Eddy's thinking may be of first importance in understanding the final shape her system took. In one sense every original idea is of virgin birth, an element of pure novelty whose importance may be gauged by the degree to which it transforms its environment, including the mind to which it first appears.

Only the germ of Christian Science was present in Mrs. Patterson's early writings on Genesis. She herself later wrote of them in the preface to *Science and Health* (p. ix): "These efforts show her [the author's] comparative ignorance of the stupendous Life-problem up to that time, and the degrees by which she came at length to its solution; but she values them as a parent may treasure the memorials of a child's growth, and she would not have them changed."

A single example will illustrate the gradual development of her thought, as made clear by the innumerable revisions she was constantly making in her Genesis manuscript. An early version declares:

> *In the science of the bible we learn that God is a Principle, Wisdom, and the opposite of matter, error. . . . That in the beginning this principle created truth and as truth could not be without an opposite error, Truth & Error were the heavens and earth which were created.*

But this actually ran contrary to the conviction that was at the heart of her experience in February, and the logic of that conviction compelled revision. The next version read:

> *The eternal intelligence was a Principle, Love (fem.) & Wisdom (masc.). . . . Love was a solution of intelligence before the ideas were formed by Wisdom, and [this solution is] compared to water, the emblem of purity. Earth, being but the idea or shadow of the Principle creating it, was dark and void, i.e., the idea had no intelligence of its own and was without the identity Wisdom gave to it.*

Although this uses Swedenborgian terms, also found to some extent in Quimby, and is still far removed from the simplicity of her final interpretation, it moves a little further toward Christian Science.[52]

The constant changes in the manuscript make it difficult to read, though there are flashes of eloquence and poetry as the author moves through what in one place she calls "the dancing forms of thought in illusory shadows and the light of the principle unchanging." But, above all, the revisions show her determination to surrender whatever is not in accord with the "principle unchanging" to which she was now committed. Her developing interpretation of Genesis was embryonic Christian Science, passing through the drastic metamorphosis common to embryos, but it was governed by a definite principle of growth.

That principle was summed up for her at the end of Genesis 1: "And God saw every thing that he had made, and, behold, it was very good." God, as the Principle of perfection, could create nothing imperfect. Yet in the second chapter of Genesis, as in daily experience, she was confronted with the tragic imperfection of human life. Here was the age-old problem of evil, with which she had wrestled in her own body for so many years. How could she relate it to her new vision of infinite good?

She found a clue in the fact that the first Genesis account began with light springing from God, the second with a mist going up from the earth. As long as she thought out from the perfection of God she was bound to arrive at perfection, but to start from material appearances was to become lost in confusion. The clear-cut distinction she would later make between the two Genesis accounts as presenting respectively the "true" man of God's creating and the "false" man of mortal conceiving is present only in the most rudimentary way in these early notes, for she did not abandon at once the natural human inclination to find a logical reconciliation of the two.

The earth, like man, she described as a "reflex shadow" of the creative Principle, Spirit. So long as man recognized himself only as the shadow of Spirit, which was substance, all was well; but when he thought of himself as substance or matter, there went up a mist or false belief which confused everything. But this in effect still made God, who had given man the capacity to err, responsible for the production of false belief. Gradually it became apparent that every attempt to *explain* error could only legitimize it.

Eventually this led her to the conclusion that healing had its own logic—healing which did not explain error but wiped it out as an illegitimate contradiction of revealed Truth. She was then ready to present the two Genesis accounts as inspired portrayals of two opposed and irreconcilable ways of thinking, the one wholly true, the other wholly false. The arrival of her thinking at that point lay beyond the notes on Genesis, but the seed of the conclusion was implicit in the healing experience she had had in February.

To understand, to make explicit the nature of the real as she had glimpsed it at the moment of healing—here was the inspiration of those long hours she spent in her bedroom at the Ellises' with a whole new world of ideas flooding into her mind and out from her pen. Even the changes, corrections, interlineations, crossings-out, and variant interpretations that characterize her manuscript convey the sense of an extraordinary movement of thought. She was groping for ways to express her rapidly unfolding ideas, her words stumbling and tumbling over each other in the constant process of vision and revision.

There was no fixity or consistency in her use of words at this time. She was searching for a basic vocabulary, but her terms like her concepts were in continuous flux. And so she tried out her writings on the Ellises and perhaps on a few others, for she had to learn how to communicate as well as to understand.

Among her closest friends were the Charles Winslows of Ocean

Street, Lynn. Mrs. Winslow was a sister of the Phillipses, and a nephew of hers, Charles Allen Taber, often met Mrs. Patterson at her house. In an affidavit[53] which he furnished in 1913 he gave an invaluable picture of the impression made by her and her writings on a sympathetic but objective observer at this time. Describing his early meetings with her but referring to her by the name which she resumed two years after parting with Patterson, he wrote:

I felt a growing interest and found that she possessed a power of attraction different from that of any person whom I had ever met before. . . . I said to Mrs. Winslow that Mrs. Glover suggested Lucretia Mott whom we had met and held in high esteem. Mrs. Glover seemed to fill the room with her presence and the ideas which she expressed compelled our attention. . . .

Mrs. Winslow, a broad minded and well educated member of the Society of Friends, and my wife a zealous church member, had both made a careful study of the Bible, but Mrs. Glover led us toward an understanding of the Bible which neither of us had ever reached. The central principle of her conversation seemed to be the power over, the control of our physical and mental faculties, through the study of, the belief in and the daily practice of the teachings of Christ as she understood them. We said that she was reading into the Bible more than we could find in the text, but we had to admit that her ideas had a good foundation on the Bible and in the writings of some of the greatest religious teachers of the world. She made a protest against the idea, then somewhat prevalent, that we should take but little thought as to our bodies and our earthly lives, and consider only the life to come.

After a few meetings Mrs. Glover offered to my wife a manuscript of many pages. . . . The manuscript was difficult to read, being interlined and full of changes, and I did not read much of it. My wife became interested in it and read it with care. During the evenings and one Sunday while the manuscript was in my house, a large portion was read to me, and my wife and I talked over the doctrines set forth in it, not all new, but often suggesting new ideas. . . . Sometimes the alterations in the manuscript suggested that the writer was trying to find better language, so as to express more fully ideas which her mind had grasped, but which she could not put satisfactorily into words. Her intellect and spiritual nature had evidently absorbed certain Christian principles, which were not set forth in the Bible or in the theology of any church known to her as fully as she desired, and which she was trying to put into language more acceptable to her. . . .

After we had read the manuscript and were talking the matter over we realized that perhaps Mrs. Glover had cognition of certain great principles in the life and teachings of Christ which were not well understood or properly set forth by religious teachers.

What soon became apparent was that she herself must become a teacher. She was not ready to promulgate her evolving ideas simply through writing.

3

After a brief though happy stay at the Ellises, Mrs. Patterson for unknown reasons moved back to the Clark boardinghouse on Summer Street, sometime in the late autumn of 1866.

George Clark, the son of the family, was a swaggering, cocksure, but amiable young fellow who had only a few months previously returned from a voyage at sea. As "Yankee Ned, the sailor author," he later had a book of adventure published—with a vast amount of editing by the publisher, one assumes. In 1888, under the same name, he wrote out his reminiscences of Mrs. Patterson.[54] For Christian Science itself he had mirthful contempt—the idea that matter was unreal seemed to him self-evidently ridiculous—but his attitude toward Mrs. Patterson was compounded of awe, patronizing incomprehension, and genuine liking.

His account started off:

In the beginning, yes! to that point of departure we must come, as this now stupendous fallacy, certainly had a beginning. . . . She. She alone. this woman, Mary Baker, Glover, Patterson, Eddy, is the author of the Christian Science idea. But the beginning, was a very humble part, only an idea, only a verse that she happened to read, in St. Luke, that, rivetted her attention. . . . Little indeed, did I ever imagine, that I, a dashing sailor lad, would ever see, Mrs. Eddy occupying her elegant mansion on Commonwealth avenue, in Boston, when only a few years previous, she was glad to be at our humble table, in that little old-fashioned home of my mother's, at No. 35 Summer st, in Lynn. . . . One afternoon, she called me into her apartment, and after I had become seated, she said, "I want to tell you Georgie, that I have had a revelation, or a revealing of a mystery, that will give health, instead of sickness, and

eternal life, to us, instead of death." What power, or method?
has revealed it to you, was my calm inquiry. "Why! here it is,
in St. Luke only a few verses, that points out a renewed life for
me. . . ." And she read it again and again. But it possessed to
me, no more importance, than any other part of the Gospel,
accorded to St. Luke.

The incident probably occurred during her stay there in August. Clark's memory as to whether the passage was actually from Luke or one of the other gospels is hardly to be relied on. Mrs. Patterson may have been referring back to her revelatory experience in February or, more likely, to some new flash of inspiration which caused her on an impulse to call the young man in. Unpromising metaphysician though he was, he may well have reminded her of her own young George, now adventuring in the Wild West. As Clark said much later, she seemed always to be "hungry for hearts."[55]

He himself was much more attracted to the spiritualism that was the chief interest of his mother and many of the boarders. Clark was convinced that Mrs. Patterson was a real sensitive and could be a great medium if she would only take up spiritualism, but he stated that she viewed the suggestion with abhorrence. Out of politeness she would sometimes yield to the importunities of the others and sit through a seance, but afterwards she would argue—agreeably enough—against the validity of their beliefs, *"claiming that her Science, was far superior to spirit teachings, and manifestations, in any form."*[56]

By this time spiritism was sweeping the country. The people who turned to it at least showed mental curiosity and a willingness to consider the unorthodox, and it is not surprising that Mrs. Patterson found some of her first willing listeners among them. She sat at the head of the table in the Clark menage, and the ideas she voiced sometimes caused sharp arguments among the shoe workers who made up most of the boarders. But they listened to her with the lively interest of Yankee workmen of their time and place.[57]

One young man who was deeply drawn to her was Hiram S. Crafts. Like thousands of others he came to Lynn, with his wife, to work in the shoe factories for part of each year, returning for the remaining months to his home in East Stoughton (now Avon) some eighteen miles the other side of Boston, there to carry on his own cobbling. When the time came for him and his wife to leave Lynn in November, he pleaded with Mrs. Patterson to come with them and teach him how to heal.

Here was the thing that Quimby had never been able to do— nor any other healer who relied on his own charismatic powers. To

Mrs. Patterson at this time it seemed a very difficult demand. Alfred Farlow, who in later years talked with her about this and many other matters relating to the historical development of Christian Science, has given an interesting account of her discovery of the *how* of mental treatment. Referring to her healing in February he writes:

> *At that time it was not clear to Mrs. Eddy by what process she had been instantaneously healed, but she knew that her thought had turned away from all else in contemplation of God, His omnipotence and everpresence, His infinite love and power. It eventually dawned upon her that this overwhelming consciousness of the divine presence had destroyed her fear and consciousness of disease exactly as the light dispels the darkness. She afterwards "noticed that when she had entertained similar thoughts in connection with the ills of her neighbors they too were benefited and it was in this manner that she discovered how to give a mental treatment."*[58]

But the problem still remained as to how she could convey this to others. She herself has written:

> *When contemplating the majesty and magnitude of this query, it looked as if centuries of spiritual growth were requisite to enable me to elucidate or to demonstrate what I had discovered: but an unlooked-for, imperative call for help impelled me to begin this stupendous work at once, and teach the first student in Christian Science.*[59]

She accordingly moved to the plain little Crafts house in East Stoughton, taking along the furniture she had saved from her domestic shipwreck, to furnish their parlor in return for her board. There she began systematically to teach Hiram Crafts by the end of 1866.

"At that date I was a Spiritualist," Crafts declared in an affidavit in 1901, "but her teachings changed my views on that subject and I gave up spiritualism. . . . She taught me from the Scriptures and from manuscripts that she wrote when she taught me."[60] However, she apparently did not use the notes on Genesis (and this accords with her practice in teaching through the next few years), for in 1902 he wrote, "We used nothing outside of the New Testament, and had no manuscripts of any kind until after I had been studying six months,"[61] rather inaccurately dating the six months from August, 1866, when he first met her.

The only manuscript she is known definitely to have written during her stay at the Crafts home is a verse-by-verse exegesis of Matthew, chapters 14 to 17. While it illustrates her later statement that "these compositions were crude,—the first steps of a child in the newly discovered world of Spirit,"[62] it contains a "spiritual interpretation" of the feeding of the four thousand in chapter 15 that might serve as a parable of her own situation.[63]

In this interpretation, which illustrates the Alexandrian elaboration of allegory that marked these first "crude" compositions, the seven loaves and a few small fishes are defined as "seven ideas and a few small swimmers after more"; and lifted to the plane of Wisdom, these are said to have their meaning multiplied in boundless measure. Crafts, like most of the "small swimmers" who followed her at first, was far more interested in the practical business of healing than in the metaphysical dimensions of the Christian gospel. And she herself stressed that healing was the test of the accuracy of what she was teaching. So the problem was to raise such small swimmers as Crafts to the plane of wisdom where they could entirely dispense with material means in their healing.

In 1902 Crafts wrote to Calvin Frye:

> *Mrs. Eddy never instructed me to rub the head, or body, or manipulate in any form. But when I was a Spiritualist, I used to use water and rub the head, limbs and body. So, sometimes when I was studying with her I would try it, but I did not say anything to her about it. Be wise as a Serpent, and harmless as a Dove.*[64]

She must have discovered as time went on that he was doing this and decided that she had best suffer it to be so now. About 1896 she wrote:

> *After I had discovered in 1866, the proof that God, the divine Principle of man's being, does all the healing, my next step was to learn from experiment and experience the scientific rule for applying Truth to man's physical need before the patient understood this Truth. Here I halted as to the use of either material means or mental for such a result and left the student to learn from experience. At length I saw the impractical attempt through material means. . . .*[65]

By April, 1867, Hiram Crafts had sufficiently progressed in his healing work to move from the hamlet of East Stoughton to nearby Taunton, a town of sixteen thousand, to set up there as a healer. Mrs. Patterson, as part of the Crafts household, moved with them into the new quarters overlooking the attractive church green, site of a now demolished 1647 meetinghouse. Significantly enough the city seal of Taunton bears the words *Dux Femina Facti.*

Mrs. Patterson had a large, pleasant room on the third floor, she announced in a letter to Martha Pilsbury.[66] A further statement in the same letter shows that despite her straitened circumstances she maintained a normal feminine concern for good appearance—indeed that flair for style which never left her. "I bought me a little black and white straw bonnet," she wrote, "just the style and paid but 1.25 for it, trimmed [it] with the green ribbon I had, and that is all it cost me, and many have admired it."

On May 13th an advertisement appeared in the Taunton papers:

T o T H E S I C K.

—

DR. H. S. CRAFTS,

Would say unhesitatingly, *I can cure you*, and have never failed to cure Consumption, Catarrh, Scrofula, Dyspepsia and Rheumatism, with many other forms of disease and weakness, in which I am especially successful. If you give me a fair trial and are not helped, I will refund your money.

The following certificate is from a lady in this city,

Mrs. Raymond:—

H. S. CRAFTS, Office 90, Main street:

In giving to the public a statement of my peculiar case, I am actuated by a motive to point out the way to others of relief from their sufferings. About 12 years since I had an internal abscess, that not only threatened to destroy my life at that time, but which has ever since continued to affect me in some form or another internally, making life well nigh a burden to bear. I have consulted many physicians, all of whom have failed to relieve me of this suffering, and in this condition, while growing worse year by year, about three weeks ago I applied to Dr. H. S. Crafts, who, to my own, and the utter astonishment of my friends, has, in this incredibly short time, without medicines or painful applications, cured me of this chronic malady. In conclusion, I can only quote the words of a patient who was healed by his method of cure: "I am convinced he is a skillful Physician, whose cures are not the result of accident." I reside in Taunton, at Weir street Railroad Crossing.

ABIGAIL RAYMOND.

Taunton, May 13, 1867.

—my14-d'T&S&wlm

There is nothing here to suggest the emergence of a new form of Christianity. The newspapers of that day were full of such advertisements, with testimonials of every sort of quack cure. Yet behind this crudely worded appeal to the public lay Mrs. Patterson's conviction that the Christian disciple could best become a "fisher of men" by healing the sick. It was through his success in healing that he would draw men to the truth.

In her letter to Martha Pilsbury she had written, "The Doct. here is just beginning at great expense in a new place . . . but all that come to him sick he cures." She herself stood behind him, teaching him, helping him, taking especially difficult cases herself. Two written testimonials from James Ingham and Alanson Wentworth bear witness to healings she had brought about in Stoughton.[67]

Toward the end of July she was summoned by Martha to Sanbornton Bridge. Tanbark and straw were once more spread on the road before Mark Baker's old house, for inside it Martha's daughter, Ellen Pilsbury, lay dying of enteritis, given up by three doctors, according to her cousin, George W. Baker. George's mother, Martha Rand Baker, later wrote an account of what happened:

> *In a few moments after [Mrs. Glover] entered the room and stood by her bedside, [Ellen] recognized her aunt, and said, "I am glad to see you aunty." In about ten minutes more, Mrs. Glover told her to "rise from her bed and walk." She rose and walked seven times across her room, then sat down in a chair. For two weeks before this, we had not entered her room without stepping lightly. Her bowels were so tender, she felt the jar, and it increased her sufferings. She could only be moved on a sheet from bed to bed. When she walked across the room at Mrs. Glover's bidding, she told her to stamp her foot strongly upon the floor, and she did so without suffering from it. The next day she was dressed, and went down to the table; and the fourth day went a journey of about a hundred miles in the cars.*[68]

Describing the healing to a friend years later, Mrs. Baker added: "Such a change came over the household. We all felt . . . 'the angel of the Lord appeared and glory shone round.'"[69] However, Abigail Tilton, who was away at the time, did not share in the rejoicing. In a letter to Martha Pilsbury a few days later she wrote in regard to the sister she had once loved so dearly:

> *I am weary with her unjust distracted conduct, and wish she would let me and mine rest from her interruptions. . . . I have my private opinion that in the end no real good will result*

*from all the stir she has made about Ellen, but hope I am
mistaken and great benefit will result from her efforts yet.*[70]

From this time on, her bitterness was to increase to the point
of total estrangement. It is true that Mrs. Patterson had cost her a
good deal of worry and trouble over the years, but what seemed to
outrage her was the emerging spiritual authority of the youngest
sister. That anyone who had needed her help so often should dare to
speak like an oracle of God must have seemed a threat to the very
foundation of her own carefully built security and pride of position.

Another cause of sadness to Mrs. Patterson on this trip was that
her brother George Sullivan Baker, now blind and ill, evidently
refused her ministrations, despite the healing of Ellen. He was a disappointed man, his marriage with Martha Rand had not been a
happy one, and three months later he would be dead. He may have
preferred it that way.

A few days after Ellen's healing Mrs. Patterson returned to
Taunton. Although she would revisit Tilton several times in the
future, this was effectively her farewell to her family. Their slightly
uncomfortable gratitude for what she had done for Ellen did not
extend to their accepting her as the bearer of a new gospel. In the
first flood of wonderment at being well again, the girl herself willingly
accompanied her aunt back to Taunton, but that was soon enough
to be reversed.

The family presumably paid Ellen's expenses, but Mrs. Patterson's
financial state was at its lowest. In a kindly letter a day or two after
her return Mrs. Ellis of Swampscott sent her a gift of two dollars
and offered to buy some of the crockery she had left with the Newhalls
if it would help her. She also issued an invitation to her to come and
stop with them for a while and have a rest, but Mrs. Patterson was
unable to accept because she lacked the train fare.[71]

Moreover, everything was going wrong in the Crafts household.
Here, as at Tilton, provincial conservatism and the demands of a new
prophetic force were in conflict. From the outset Mrs. Crafts, an un-
educated and commonplace young woman, had viewed with unease
the potential threat to the small certainties of her life. Like her
husband, she had been a spiritualist; but unlike her husband, she was
unwilling to give up the neighborly gossip of table-rapping spirits.
Nor can she have been very happy about the financially precarious
career on which Crafts had embarked; she belonged to the workaday
world that believes a cobbler should stick to his last.

Ellen's arrival seems to have precipitated a crisis. The young
lady, a typical member of the Baker "aristocracy" of Sanbornton

Bridge, doubtless felt a certain dismay at the household. Her aunt wished her to have continued treatments from Crafts in order to establish her health on a firm basis and then worried about the influence he was exerting over her. Mrs. Patterson wrote Martha Pilsbury one of those "distracted" letters of which Abigail Tilton had complained,[72] and Ellen shortly afterwards returned to Sanbornton, repudiating once and for all her aunt, her healing, and the whole episode.

At that point the Taunton venture was abandoned. Crafts and his wife returned to East Stoughton sometime in August, and Mrs. Patterson went to the Winslows in Lynn. It seemed a hapless ending to a brave beginning; yet it taught the teacher that while people were glad enough to be healed, the actual impartation of the basis of her healing was bound to stir up opposition.

Her own explanation of the situation is hinted at in a passage in *Science and Health* (p. 28): "If the Master had not taken a student and taught the unseen verities of God, he would not have been crucified. The determination to hold Spirit in the grasp of matter is the persecutor of Truth and Love."

Crafts remained friendly and grateful to her throughout his life, though he returned to his shoemaking and showed only the most rudimentary grasp of her later teachings. A year after they parted she wrote him to inquire tentatively whether he would be willing to take up the work again, and he replied:

> *I should be willing to do all you ask if I was in different circumstances. You know how things stand with me, after all the trouble that we have had I feel the same interest in the developing of Truth and its principles. I know that I am not perfect and am willing to acknowledge that fact. But it would be impossible for me to come over there to help you at present. I should have no peace at home if I did. I have been through one hell and don't want to go through another. . . . Your letter was opened and read before I got it, if you send another have it delivered to me.*[73]

Several years after he died Sibyl Wilbur interviewed Mrs. Crafts, then a rather feeble old lady, who detailed her list of grievances against Mrs. Patterson, including the fact that the latter found fault with the way she ironed her cuffs. Her words are revealing:

> *She found fault with me about things and said I done 'em a puppus, and she carried herself above folks. . . . I wrote her to ask her to help us when Hiram died, and she didn't pay no*

attention to the letter. She has always lived for show and never for helping poor folks.[74]

Even more revealing is the letter asking for "help" which Mrs. Eddy never answered. It was written on February 2, 1907, at Brockton, Massachusetts, where Mrs. Crafts was then living with her brother:

Dear Mrs. Eddy:

> *Now Hiram has gone the people want me to tell them your history while you lived with us, the one that will pay me the most money if you will pay me the most I will keep still keep my mouth closed you can have your first choise I want you to be quick about it, not to delay for I don't want to be teased to death.*

With regards

Mary W. Crafts[75]

When she received no reply Mrs. Crafts—or rather, the brother with whom she then lived—did talk, and the talk was duly gathered up in an affidavit which spelled out her grievances and added the charge that Mrs. Patterson had tried to separate Hiram and Mary Crafts from each other.[76]

Nor was that the end of the Crafts episode. Sibyl Wilbur's description of Mrs. Patterson's first student as "a Yankee workman transcendentalized" was to be used decades later to support an elaborate charge that Christian Science is based on an obscure Hegelian document entrusted to Crafts by the great German-American scholar, Francis Lieber. (See Appendix D.) No one would have been more astonished than the simple East Stoughton cobbler to find himself portrayed as the intimate friend of Lieber and the noted Harvard professor Charles Follen. If he once touched greatness in his life, it was in quite another way.

In 1868 he had written Mrs. Patterson: "As to Doctoring again I do not think now that I shall ever do any more of it. If I was alone, perhaps it would be different. But as it is I must live out this miserable life in darkness and error."[77] He was the first of many students to feel that in his brief association with her he had experienced life at a height and intensity never to be known again.

4

The break with her family now complete, Mrs. Patterson stood entirely alone in the world. On August 13, 1867, she recorded the fact in a poem entitled "Alone."[78] The first three stanzas with their mournful refrain,

O weary heart, O tired sigh,
Alone to live! Alone to die!

spelled out her loss of husband and family, but the last two stanzas
looked up again:

Yet not alone, for oft I see
Bright forms that look in love on me,
To thee, thou lost ones, and my own—
I call, O, leave me not alone!
When answering tones this music pour—
Thy God is with thee ever more;
O better bliss, that knows no sigh,
O love divine, so full, so nigh.

And o'er the harp strings of the soul
Sweet sounds this trembling echo roll,
Thy love can live in Truth, and be
A joy, and immortality;
To bless mankind with word and deed—
Thy life a great and noble creed.
O glorious hope, my faith renew,
O mortal joys, adieu! adieu!

She told the Winslows that above all else she wanted a place
where she could be quiet and study and write. Being Quakers, they
thought of the little village of Amesbury, Massachusetts, tucked away
tranquilly where the Powwow River flows into the lower Merrimack.
There the Quaker Whittier lived, and life flowed along as quietly
as the great river.

The friends to whom the Winslows sent Mrs. Patterson could not
take her in, but she made her way to another house renowned for
its hospitality. It was a large, fifteen-room Georgian house at the foot
of Merrimac Street near the river, and it was owned by a retired sea
captain, Nathaniel Webster, who was now superintendent of cotton
mills in Manchester, New Hampshire. Captain Webster was away from
home except for every other Sunday, and his wife—a delightful old
spiritualist generally known as Mother Webster—kept the house filled
with fellow spiritualists, invalids, and unfortunates of one kind or
another. She herself was both a "drawing medium" and a "healing
medium," in the latter capacity prescribing remedies for many of her
waifs and strays.

When Mrs. Patterson announced that she had felt led to apply
there for lodging, Mother Webster put her own construction on the
words, threw up her hands, and said: "Glory to God! Come right in."

And there for the next ten months Mrs. Patterson was to live, through the golden days of autumn, the snows of winter, and the lilac-filled New England spring. She was given a large, sunny room with a fireplace, and Mrs. Webster's special "spiritual" desk at which to write, but she had to sit through some of her hostess's seances and a good deal of spiritualistic chit-chat as the price for her much-needed peace.

One young girl who was deeply attached to "Captain Nat. and Grandma Webster," as she called them, later recalled Mrs. Patterson as she was at that time—or Mrs. Glover, as she was now beginning to call herself again: "I have always remembered her eyes, just so full of love and tenderness. I often saw her and Mrs. Webster when they went to walk the first of the evening."[79] They would cross a little bridge over the Powwow, she wrote, and stand on the bank of the Merrimack, looking at the sunset together. Local gossip had it that Mrs. Glover would one day walk on the water.

Once again her writings are the best evidence of her actual footsteps of thought. The manuscript on Genesis was growing steadily now. Mrs. Webster referred to it rather disconcertingly as Mrs. Glover's "version of the Bible," as others were later to refer to it as "Mrs. Glover's Bible," but it was, more exactly, her metaphysical comment on the Bible, or at least on Genesis.

Her aspiration found expression in an "Invocation for 1868" which she sent to the *Lynn Reporter* at the beginning of the year:

> Father of every age!
> Of every rolling sphere!
> Help us to write a deathless page
> Of truth, this dawning year. . .[80]

Thirty years later, writing of this period, she described an interesting phenomenon. There seemed to be a curious coincidence between what she called the light of revelation and the light of day: "I could not write these notes after sunset. All thoughts in the line of Scriptural interpretation would leave me until the rising of the sun. Then the influx of divine interpretation would pour in upon my spiritual sense as gloriously as the sunlight on the material senses."[81]

But Mrs. Glover did not take the stenographic view of inspiration which makes the writer a mere unconscious medium of truth. She was *thinking* her way through the subject—it was in these notes on Genesis that she first announced that "the time for thinkers has come." At the end of the day she would sometimes tear up everything she had written when it seemed as though her developing thought had escaped the network of refractory words.

Meanwhile her sense of her own mission was growing. She wrote in her manuscript of the "science which has been revealed to me through the spiritual senses and which I have found [to be] truth in demonstration." The demonstration was all-important:

> A science new to man is yet old to truth; therefore while the discoverer or investigator of an eternal principle can see in the clear light of Science truth unveiled and no longer a miracle or mystery—to those who see it not a demonstration is required, so universal and unequivocal that none may deny.

She was also working on another manuscript which was to be used more directly in teaching others how to heal, but a discussion of this is best deferred to the next period of her life. At this point it is sufficient to note that when she tried to lead Mother Webster to a higher method of healing than reliance on spirit controls the good dame became exceedingly resistant and grew progressively disenchanted with her guest.

Finally, Mrs. Glover decided that the time had come to advertise for students, and on July 4, 1868, the following advertisement appeared in the *Banner of Light:*

> Any person desiring to learn how to heal the sick can receive of the undersigned instruction that will enable them to commence healing on a principle of science with a success far beyond any of the present modes. No medicine, electricity, physiology or hygiene required for unparalleled success in the most difficult cases. No pay required unless this skill is obtained. Address MRS. MARY B. GLOVER, Amesbury, Mass., Box 61.

Once again the advertisement speaks of a scientific curative method rather than of a new religious teaching. But the *Banner of Light* was a spiritualist paper, a not too unlikely though not too promising place to advertise in those days if one were looking for people willing to think unconventionally, but hardly the place to announce a spiritual philosophy that coolly rejected spiritualism. On the other hand, in an early version of her poem "Christ, my Refuge," published in a local paper in August, she felt it necessary to disavow any use of mediumship:

> I am no reed to shake at scorn,
>> Or from it flee,
> I am no medium but Truth's, to warn
>> The Pharisee. . . .[82]

Before either the advertisement or the poem appeared in print, a sudden change took place in Mrs. Glover's life. The Websters' grandchildren came from New York each summer to live in the big Amesbury house, preceded by their father, William R. Ellis, who, according to the later account by one of his daughters, would come up in advance "in order to clear my grandmother's house of broken-down Spiritualists and sick people."[83] Since Mrs. Glover's presence interfered with his vacation plans for the children, she was ordered to leave. When she was unable to find another place to go, he took the drastic step of turning her and her trunk out of the house on a dark and stormy night and locking the door after her.

With her went two other guests, either from sympathy with her or because they were similarly ejected. One of them, nineteen-year-old Richard Kennedy, was to play an important role in the drama of her life. The other, a Mrs. Richardson, guided her down the street to the home of Miss Sarah Bagley and then disappears from the story.

Miss Bagley was what used to be known as a New England gentlewoman in reduced circumstances. She might have been an additional spinster sister in *The House of the Seven Gables* or have come out of one of Mary Wilkins Freeman's stories. Supporting herself by her needle, she maintained an apple-pie order in her attractive little house, with its braided rugs and flowered quilts and gleaming copper and brass. Very willingly she took in Mrs. Glover and gave her a diminutive but spotless bedroom with a framed text on the wall: "He shall give His angels charge over thee."[84]

Soon Mrs. Glover had converted her hostess from a belief in spiritualism to acceptance of the new Science. Young Kennedy, who was working in a box factory, would join the two women in his free time for hours of eager study and discussion in what they called "the garden room." Late at night, as they pored over the Bible and her manuscripts in the lamplight, it would seem as though a world of unimaginable wonder were opening up to them.

Back on May 30, while she was still at the Webster house, Mrs. Glover had received a telegram summoning her to Manchester to help a friend of the Websters, Mrs. Mary M. Gale, who was critically ill with pneumonia. She had gone and healed her immediately, and Mrs. Gale's subsequent letters poured out her gratitude for the healing.[85] But while she was there, Mrs. Glover had noticed a small child in the house playing with a book, and when she picked up the book she read with delight the title *A Dictionary of the Bible,* edited by William Smith and published only the year before in Hartford, Connecticut.[86] Mrs. Gale ordered a copy for her and it arrived while she was at Miss Bagley's.

Up to this time she had had to carry on her writing without concordances or any of the normal aids to biblical study. Now she at least had one reference work to abet her, and her direct and indirect references to Smith's *Dictionary* even in the last edition of *Science and Health with Key to the Scriptures* show that she valued its aid. She was especially pleased to find the text of Genesis 6:3, "And the Lord said, My spirit shall not always strive with man, for that he also is flesh," rendered, "And Jehovah said, My spirit shall not forever rule [or be humbled] in men, seeing that they are [or, in their error they are] but flesh." Here was the very language of Science.

On at least one occasion Miss Bagley took her to visit Whittier. The poet had been exceptionally ill the preceding winter, writing a friend afterwards that even when near death he "was favored with a vivid sense of the goodness of God, and felt no anxiety nor fear." He was again showing signs of illness at the time Mrs. Glover visited him. Although the day seemed warm to the visitors, they found him in a closed room huddled over the fire, with a hectic flush and coughing continually.

He was much besieged by women visitors that summer—a neighbor, who was told of two ladies in the parlor waiting for him, exclaimed, "What! more of them!"[87]—and was in little mood for company. When Mrs. Glover remarked that the atmosphere outside seemed better than inside, he replied irritably, "If Jesus Christ was in Amesbury he would have to have brass-lined lungs to live here."[88]

But as she shared with him some of her ideas, so congenial to his own half-held faith in divine healing, his face changed and, in her own words, "the sunshine of his former character beamed through the cloud." When she rose to go he went to her with both hands extended and said, "I thank you, Mary, for your call; it has done me much good." A neighbor noted that following the visit he seemed completely recovered.[89]

In an 1868 poem entitled "The Meeting," Whittier wrote:

> Still struggles in the Age's breast
> With deepening agony of quest
> The old entreaty: "Art Thou He
> Or look we for the Christ to be?" . . .
> "Where, in my name, meet two or three,"
> Our Lord hath said, "I there will be." . . .
> But here, amidst the poor and blind,
> The bound and suffering of our kind,
> In works we do,—in prayers we pray,
> Life of our life, He lives to-day.

When *Science and Health* was published seven years later, Sarah Bagley took Whittier a copy of it.[90] He examined it, turning over the leaves slowly, then said, "Well, you will never be able to understand one-tenth part of it during your lifetime"—certainly an accurate commentary on both the book and Miss Bagley.

During the summer Mrs. Glover made several trips to Manchester to visit her former patient, Mrs. Gale, whom she was now attempting to instruct. On one of these occasions she wrote back to her Amesbury hostess:

> . . . of all rides I ever experienced was the one from Lawrence to Manchester. The cars were literally packed with passengers, much like a slave-ship, and amid sweat and groans we bore the passage—the [groans] were accompanied with sharp cries from the babies. Your Topsy could have behaved better.
>
> Mrs. Gale was apparently delighted to see me, gave me a highland welcome, and her parlor chamber to sleep in. At tea we had strawberries and the richest cream I have seen since "old days."[91]

But the summer was not an idyll of strawberries and cream. The disturbance with the Websters had clouded the atmosphere, bringing Mrs. Glover a return of old symptoms, and money worries were again pressing. Sarah Bagley was unable to keep her indefinitely on the little she was able to pay. Mrs. Gale lavishly promised her financial aid in renting a simple cottage where she could have the quiet she needed, but was shocked when Mrs. Glover took her promises too literally and was further disturbed by her spiritual mentor's frequent change of plan as circumstances altered.

At one point Mrs. Glover was determined to make her way out West to be with her son. But after a final distressing scene with Mrs. Gale over money matters, she made a sudden decision to accept instead an urgent invitation to return to Stoughton to stay with the Wentworths, whom she had met the year before when she was teaching Hiram Crafts. Sarah Bagley apparently did not even know where she had gone until an explanatory letter arrived, sent from Stoughton on September 10.

"O I am tired! tired!" the letter ended, "When will my rest come?" But four days later Mrs. Glover wrote: "God is with me, and I can wait on Him. I see more clearly than ever before I am to be lifted up higher for this."[92]

5

Alanson C. Wentworth of Stoughton ran a small farm and a part-time shoemaking shop. A Universalist and a lifelong Bible student, he "loved to argue about religion, and baited all the ministers that came into the neighborhood, especially the Methodist ones that [his daughter-in-law] Susie revered." The Bible "was always kept handy to him in its niche above the fireplace, before which he used to sit evenings," although he also enjoyed an occasional evening of cards, which further shocked the Methodist Susie.[93]

This young lady was married to his eldest son Horace, then twenty-six years old. The young couple lived elsewhere, but Horace sometimes helped his father in his cobbling business, although on the whole he preferred to let his wife earn a living for both of them. Horace was the sort of jovial ne'er-do-well who loves to play embarrassing practical jokes on respected citizens, thereby earning the appreciative guffaws of the boys at the corner.

Mrs. Sally Wentworth, Alanson's wife, was a practical New England housewife of even temper, devoted to her family, and supplementing their income by her own earnings as a "rubbing doctor"— something between a magnetic healer and a masseuse. She was said to have a natural instinct for helping the sick and was always to be found wherever there was illness.

The three Wentworth children living at home were Celia, twenty, a delicate, clinging girl, Charles, seventeen, a cheerful mild boy, and Lucy, thirteen, impressionable and impulsively affectionate. They formed a pleasant enough household in a simple village community where life fell naturally into a series of Rogers-group patterns. But with the advent of Mrs. Glover something entirely outside the usual patterns entered their lives.

It was Hiram Crafts who had first brought her over to visit them when she was living at East Stoughton. Lucy Wentworth later wrote, "When Hiram Crafts brought her to our fireside, we just felt as if an angel had come into our house."[94] Alanson Wentworth was immediately charmed by her interpretation of the Bible. Subsequently Mrs. Glover healed him of the sciatica which had crippled him for years and of his "inveterate" habit of smoking and chewing tobacco.[95] Celia's health greatly improved, and the whole family with the exception of the scoffing Horace and his straightlaced wife promptly fell in love with her.

Describing her as she was at that time, Lucy wrote:

> She was a lonely woman past her prime who at the time had seen much of life. In appearance she was very straight of figure, a little above the average in height, with shoulders rather broad for her small waist, small hands and feet, dark brown hair and gray eyes with a faraway look in them, that were very expressive, and under excitement seemed darker than they really were. . . .

Her wardrobe at this time consisted of a black and white plaid, also a few morning dresses. Her one best black dress was of very fine material, made after the fashion of that day and trimmed with narrow silk velvet ribbon. She kept her clothes very carefully. It made no difference what she wore, there always seemed to be a certain style about her.[95]

When she came to the Wentworths' in September, 1868, at their eager solicitation, they hoped that she would settle down and live with them indefinitely. That was not her own plan, although she was grateful for the haven.

"These golden Autumn days are very beautiful here," she wrote Sarah Bagley in October. "I have a large pleasant room with trees in front of my window and a horse to take me to ride. . . ." And in November she wrote that the Wentworths had been getting her out in a rather "laconic" style, giving several parties for her: "I attended one last eve and the evening previous—great style and much humor on both occasions." But she was "torn asunder almost by requests to heal the sick and somehow they keep me at it continually."[96] Once again her thoughts turned to the possibility of joining George Glover out West, but she finally abandoned the idea and settled down for what turned out to be an eighteen-month stay in Stoughton.

Now her life took on a new pattern. "Sarah," she wrote to her old Amesbury friend, "I never for a moment forget the pleasant hours we two have shared together, romping over *fences* or sewing, reading, &c side by side."[97] But the "romping" was now with young people, who furnished a sort of fresh-faced chorus to the serious business of those eighteen months.

For long hours every day she would be alone in her room, writing and searching. Then in the late afternoon she would put aside her pen and would sometimes go out for a little fresh air and exercise. Lucy, who adored her, later wrote:

She would often come to meet me on my way home from school and we would go for a short walk around the neighborhood. A favorite walk of hers was down across the fields to Aunt Lucy Porter's ancient house where my Cousin Kate lived who did the copying for her book. They were a hospitable family and made one feel very much at home. Mrs. Glover always said that the old house was full of cheer and was a rest to her after her busy day of writing and made her forget her troubles.[98]

A school friend of Lucy's wrote Mrs. Eddy in 1909:

Let us go back to the old days when we called you Mrs. Glover. There, now I can feel your arms about me as they used

to be in the Springtime long ago when we used to hunt the
anemone and you told me of the beautiful May flowers of your
native state. What a beautiful time that was! How we longed
for your coming in those days. And the evenings the children
spent with you in your chamber. How pleasant you always made
it for us. We knew we were always welcome.[99]

Several of the young people later recalled the evenings in Mrs. Glover's room. Lucy Wentworth is quoted as saying:

After she had worked for hours she always relaxed and
threw off her seriousness. Then she would admit us, my brother
Charles and me, and sometimes a school friend of Charles's.
The boys would romp in her room sometimes rather boister-
ously, but she never seemed to mind it.[100]

Charles Wentworth, who remembered her as cheerful and sprightly, wrote that "her sojourn with us was one of the brightest spots in my life." He added that she bought them a backgammon board and taught them to play backgammon; and learning that he loved stories, she subscribed to two fiction magazines, *Saturday Night* and *Chimney Corner,* "so we had all the reading we wanted."[101] The Wentworths were musical, and Mrs. Glover joined in their singing, her two favorite songs being "Speed Away" and "Star of the Twilight." And she entered heartily into the youngsters' games of checkers and euchre.

But her time with them was not all lighthearted relaxation. In the autograph album of one of the Wentworths' young friends she wrote, "Youth is a sculptor that chisels the model of manhood."[102] She took youth seriously. Celia clung to her for help,[103] and Lucy looked up to her as a model. Charles's school chum, William Scott, in 1907 recalled:

I was sixteen years old when Mrs. Eddy lived in Stoughton,
and I remember her very well. I recall that as often as two or
three nights out of every week for over two years, I used to
visit Mrs. Eddy with other young people of the town. Mrs.
Eddy was at that time living with Alanson Wentworth. We
were in the habit of visiting her to listen to her talks, for even
then she was regarded by those who knew her as a wonderful
woman. Some of the most pleasant recollections of my young
days center in that little room at the Wentworths.[104]

Her activities ranged further than Stoughton. During the past few years she had kept in occasional touch with the Good Templars, and in the fall of 1868 she lectured several times at a branch of that organization at or near the now famous Episcopal school for boys, St. Mark's, in Southboro.

Fifteen-year-old D. Lee Slataper was at that time a student at St. Mark's and his roommate was Oscar Whitcomb, a nephew of John B. Gough. On one occasion when Mrs. Glover came to lecture Oscar was at home sick with a fever. She asked Slataper about him, and he told her that at the doctor's orders he was giving the sick boy aconite. After the lecture she went back to their lodgings. The lad responded to her few words immediately, and next day when the doctor arrived he was back at his studies, perfectly well.

Slataper, who recounted the incident in a letter seventy years later,[105] added that twenty years after it happened he was drawn by curiosity to attend Mrs. Eddy's famous public address in Chicago (June 14, 1888) and recognized her at once as the Mrs. Glover he had known as a boy. Her eyes "still had that sympathetic look full of compassion and love, while her voice was full of assurance and conviction."

William Scott of Stoughton recounted an incident of healing which occurred in 1869.[106] His father John L. Scott was taken ill with intestinal trouble which caused him terrible agony. He was given various remedies, to no avail. Mrs. Wentworth, who was then practicing under Mrs. Glover's instructions, was sent for; but when she arrived she announced that Scott was in such a dangerous condition she didn't dare take the case. At her urging, young William hitched up the team and drove over for Mrs. Glover, who came at once and found the patient writhing in pain. She spoke to him with authority, and within an hour or two he was completely well.

The incident is revealing because it indicates a pattern that was to be followed for some years. Whenever Mrs. Glover's students found a case too difficult for them to heal they would turn to her, and in most cases she would take it over. Yet her effort was always to fit the student to heal the case himself. She repeatedly wrote of the danger of relying on her personality instead of on the divine Principle of her Science. The need for this was emphasized by the fact that she had not yet rid herself of the old Quimby tendency to take on the sufferings of those who clutched at her personally for healing.

The test of Science was whether it could be taught and practiced by others. Mrs. Wentworth was an eager student and seemed to get good results. She agreed to give Mrs. Glover board and lodging in return for the instruction she received, and since she made quite a respectable income from healing for the rest of her life, this was a small enough price to pay.

Like Hiram Crafts, she continued to employ some of her earlier methods along with the rudimentary metaphysical practice she was learning. Mrs. Glover had resigned herself to the fact that her early students were simply not ready to practice at her own spiritual level. It was a matter of letting the tares and wheat grow together until she could see more clearly how to separate them.[107]

The idealized figure of Quimby still played a frequent part in her conversation, and her reverence for the departed healer was one of the things that was loudly mocked by Horace Wentworth and his saucy cousin Kate Porter (later Mrs. Clapp) who did most of the copying of Mrs. Glover's growing mass of manuscript.[108] Horace was quite as opinionated as his father but without the latter's lively interest in the Bible, and his frank scorn of Mrs. Glover would often stir the other members of the family to indignant protest. Young Kate, who was bored to distraction by the manuscripts she copied, let her high spirits escape in mimicry of the author's mannerisms.

To an inquirer about her teachings, Mrs. Glover at this time wrote, "I am kept down by opposition and poverty, so that I cannot do what I otherwise could," but she added firmly: "We have enough beliefs, we want science and I have it for all. Do not believe this nor disbelieve it, 'come and see.' "[109] Nothing could keep her down for long.

Yet she was a lonely woman, as Lucy Wentworth said, with the inevitable loneliness of someone exploring new spiritual territory. In June she wrote an old friend in Rumney:

> I have not heard from you and the rest of the dear ones around you for a long time but even this silence and absence cannot blot out the memory of your family from my lonely heart. . . . Please write me all about yourselves and others that may be near you. Is Dr. Patterson in your vicinity now and how does he support himself? has he much business there? Does he ever call on you, and who does he board with?
>
> My eyes can almost look on you and the beautiful trees and streams and mountains that environ you. Is Ella a sweet little body at home yet, or is she married to—to—Oh! yes, I remember! Mr. Glove maker—what's the name? French, I believe. And your little boy is a young man now. Oh! what changes.
>
> I have just sent a work to the press for publication enti-tled—Science of Soul—I mean you shall read it sometime. I have written this and notes on the entire book of Genesis within the last year and this, besides laboring for clothes and other

expenses with teaching. I am worn almost out, have lost my love of life completely and want to go where the weary have a rest and the heavy laden lay down their burdens.[110]

The great news here was the completion of her manuscript. Three days later she wrote Sarah Bagley:

My volume is finished, Sarah, and ready for the press & the outcry that will follow it: first the ridicule, then the argument, and lastly the adoption by the public, but it may be long ere the public get it. . . . I only wish I were able to launch into the fullness of Christ, embrace the whole world in my love.[111]

She might be tired and discouraged at times, but when she was caught up into the universe of thought from which she drew her daily strength it was a different matter. Of her subjective life at this time she would write later:

For three years after my discovery, I sought the solution of this problem of Mind-healing, searched the Scriptures and read little else, kept aloof from society, and devoted time and energies to discovering a positive rule. The search was sweet, calm, and buoyant with hope, not selfish nor depressing. I knew the Principle of all harmonious Mind-action to be God, and that cures were produced in primitive Christian healing by holy, uplifting faith; but I must know the Science of this healing, and I won my way to absolute conclusions through divine revelation, reason, and demonstration.[112]

This was the inner history recorded in her manuscripts.

6

Mrs. Glover paid Kate Porter seven dollars to copy the manuscript she expected to have published. There is no evidence as to just what it was.

It was almost certainly not the "notes on the entire book of Genesis" which she mentioned in the letter to her friend in Rumney. These notes were to be Volume One of her projected book "The Bible in its Spiritual Meaning," but they were never offered to a publisher or even shared with her students. They represent Mrs. Glover's private sharpening of a tool of spiritual research. She soon decided that it was undesirable to continue this way through the whole Bible, but out of the experience and understanding gained by working on the Genesis notes she eventually forged the *Key to the Scriptures* which was added to later editions of *Science and Health*.

"The Science of Soul," to which she referred in her letter, was most probably a variant version of the short work generally known as "The Science of Man," supplemented perhaps with other manuscript material to make it bulky enough for a "volume." While no extant copies of "The Science of Soul" are known, there are numerous manuscript copies and versions of "The Science of Man," variously titled, several of them being in Mrs. Wentworth's handwriting.

The genesis of this key work, from which Mrs. Glover was to teach her earliest classes, has been befogged by misunderstanding. It has been confused by many biographers with a totally different manuscript entitled "Questions and Answers" written in whole or in part by Phineas Quimby. To clarify the matter one must go back to the days when Mrs. Glover, then Mrs. Patterson, was reading Quimby's manuscripts, writing her own gloss on them, leaving some of her own writings with him, and in general trying to reconcile her Christianity with his evolving system of suggestion.

Out of that period emerges a brief work composed of fifteen questions and answers, a work whose beginnings are shrouded in a rather unusual degree of mystery. The several copies of it now in the possession of the Quimby family in various handwritings are dated either February or June, 1862—in either case several months before Mrs. Patterson met Quimby—although in a letter to Georgine Milmine on March 13, 1906, George Quimby wrote of having "the original" in his possession "with the date '62 or '63 on it."[113]

There is no mention of this work in any of the lectures, articles, books, or known letters of the Quimby champions of the eighties and nineties—namely, Julius, Annetta, and Horatio Dresser, and George Quimby—until after a copy of it in Sarah Crosby's handwriting came into the possession of the editor of the *Christian Science Sentinel* and passages from it were printed in the *Sentinel* of February 16, 1899, to show how it differed from Mrs. Eddy's teaching. Horatio Dresser then replied in an article in *The Arena* in May, 1899, "The extracts quoted from Dr. Quimby in the Sentinel are from one of his earlier articles, and do not adequately represent him."

However, twenty-two years later when "Questions and Answers" had become the cornerstone of the Quimby charges against Christian Science, Dresser wrote, "Copies of this manuscript were kept on hand to loan to new patients, and some of the patients made their own copies."[114] But the only "new patient" actually known to have had, or have made, a copy of it, apart from Mrs. Patterson, was her one-time friend Sarah Crosby.[115] Until and unless a good deal more is unearthed about the origin and history of "Questions and Answers," there must remain some doubt whether it is an expression of Quimby's thinking before or after he met Mrs. Patterson.

His unquestionable stamp is on much of it, as when he writes: "God is the great magnet or mesmerizer. He speaks man, or the idea, into existence and attaches his senses to the idea and we to ourselves are just that and only that which we think we are. So is a mesmerized subject, they to themselves are matter."[116] Yet unusually idealistic elements are found in it also, as Horatio Dresser recognizes when he points out that in his other manuscripts Quimby "calls matter much more than a 'shadow' or 'idea.' "[117] The disparate elements in this work create more than the usual confusion to be found in Quimby's writings, as Dresser again recognized in his comments on it.[118] Some of the difficulties disappear if one assumes that part of the thinking in it emanates from a source other than Quimby.

At any rate, this is the document Mrs. Glover carried around with her for several years and always referred to as "Dr. Quimby's manuscript," whether or not she had any part in its composition or revision. She allowed a few of her early students to read it but did not teach from it.[119] On the evidence of her own writings at this period, the confusion of thought in "Questions and Answers" must have become increasingly disturbing to her. At some point she added a brief preface to it, in an effort to clarify it in the light of her new convictions, and she made further revisions in the text itself.[120]

This was the manuscript of which she wrote in an early edition of *Science and Health,* "The only manuscript that we ever held of his [Quimby's], longer than to correct it, was one of perhaps a dozen pages, most of which we had composed."[121] It is the manuscript that Mrs. Wentworth copied under the general title "Extracts from Dr. P. P. Quimby's Writings." Then followed the more specific title, apparently added by Mrs. Glover, "The Science of Man, or the principle which controls all phenomena." The preface, signed Mary M. Glover, was followed by the fifteen questions and answers, identified as "P. P. Quimbys Mss." A later copy, also in Mrs. Wentworth's handwriting, ran the preface and the rest of the material together, with slight changes and without any attribution to either author.

What has not been generally understood is that *The Science of Man* which Mrs. Glover later wrote, used as a classbook, copyrighted, published, and eventually incorporated into *Science and Health* as the chapter called "Recapitulation," was an entirely different work from this early hybrid product of the first stages of her transition from Quimbyism to Christian Science. She allowed Mrs. Wentworth to copy the earlier manuscript, but her own energies during the Wentworth period were devoted to the perfecting of the new work in which her deepening convictions found expression.

The first question in the Quimby "Questions and Answers" was:

"You must have a feeling of repugnance towards certain patients. How do you overcome it and how can I do the same?" The first question in *The Science of Man* is: "What is God?" The whole distance between Quimby's psychology and Mrs. Glover's metaphysics seems to be suggested in those two openings.

Fortunately we are able to follow fairly well the metamorphosis through which Mrs. Glover's work passed, for copies of it in its various stages exist in Mrs. Wentworth's handwriting.[122]

The earliest of these is entitled "Rudiments. The Science of Man. by Mary M. Glover. For the learner." This is composed of thirty-five questions and answers, entirely different from the fifteen in the Quimby "Questions and Answers." A slightly variant version is entitled simply "The Science of Man," but includes in the same manuscript another new essay "The Soul's Inquiries of Man." Mrs. Glover's growing awareness of the uniqueness of her discovery is apparent in a passage in this second "Science of Man":

> *Unless the principle is understood you cannot act in it and as it has never been taught in science by any written or published MSS from any known individual but me I claim that it cannot have been understood, except by Elijah, Jesus, his disciples and Paul, and their writings do not teach it unless you understand their scientific meaning, and not the interpretations which belief hath given them.*

Other versions followed, each one showing some advance over the earlier ones in clarity and consistency. What appears to be the best of them in Sally Wentworth's handwriting is very close in content to the classbook Mrs. Glover used with her first classes in 1870. It is entitled "The Science of Man by which the sick are healed, or Questions and Answers in Moral Science," and a single question and answer from it illustrates the sort of demand she was increasingly to make on her students:

> *Ques. How can I succeed in doing this [i.e., in casting out error with truth] so that my demonstration in healing shall be wonderful and immediate?*
>
> *Ans. By being like Jesus, by asking yourself am I honest, am I just, am I merciful, and am I pure? and being able to respond with your demonstration, to let your life and what you can do for the sick answer this, and not your lips.*

Where Quimby's system of healing had been a mental technique, with physical accompaniments, Mrs. Glover's was a religious discipline, moral as well as metaphysical; but she was still not ready to call it Christian Science, and Moral Science it remained for several more years. In its embryonic state, her system had not yet freed itself entirely from a Quimbyism which was basically incompatible with the deeper fundamentals of Christianity.

Under the lingering Quimby influence, she still permitted physical manipulation if the student could not rise to the purely spiritual method, although she tried to have him "spiritualize" even the manipulations. In an early version of "The Science of Man" she wrote:

> [*The practical application of the art is*] *first to leave your own belief or body when you will be in the principle & thus be able to speak to another this principle, which immediately controls the body. If this wisdom be not yet fully attained, the next method is by rubbing the head, while you at the same time take yourself utterly away from all thoughts of his complaints or their locality in matter. . . . What is matter? Nothing. . . . That which is called matter is a shadow of substance, but believing it substance makes it error, therefore matter is an error and belief.*

This passage illustrates how far Mrs. Glover still was from her later unequivocal position on such matters. Her explanation was that neither the students nor their patients could conceive of a healing practice that did not involve *doing* something materially. In later years she wrote:

> *Science is not obtained the moment wherein its Principle is discerned or discovered. The discoverer has to take footsteps therein before he can state scientifically a Science. . . .*
>
> *But in the beginning, to know how the students could mentally practice on the sick puzzled me. I had not by any* material *means or method demonstrated on the sick the power of divine Science and did not believe that my students at the start could reach my purely mental attitude of healing. I thought they must approach it from their standpoints and gain the results of Truth on themselves before they could practice through prayer and heal the sick.*
>
> *I learned from strict observation of metaphysical practice the impossibility of demonstrating Christian Science through any material method.*[123]

Related to the problem of cultivating her students' willingness to rely on spiritual power alone was the problem of conveying to them a system of spiritual values wholly apart from matter.

In the preface to the last edition of *Science and Health* (p. ix), in

the passage that speaks of her early crude essays in scriptural interpretation as "the first steps of a child in the newly discovered world
of Spirit," Mrs. Eddy goes on to speak of those other essays which
eventuated in *The Science of Man* as it was finally published:

> *She [the author] also began to jot down her thoughts on
> the main subject, but these jottings were only infantile lispings
> of Truth. A child drinks in the outward world through the
> eyes and rejoices in the draught. He is as sure of the world's
> existence as he is of his own; yet he cannot describe the world.
> He finds a few words, and with these he stammeringly attempts
> to convey his feeling. Later, the tongue voices the more definite
> thought, though still imperfectly.*

So through these years she stammeringly tried to describe the
new world she was daily discovering, and she "found a few words"
to convey her thoughts. Some of the words were ones that Quimby
had made familiar—truth and error, opinion and understanding,
principle and idea—though they were also commonplaces of the
schoolbooks she had known since girlhood and of the rationalistic
faith Albert Baker had shared with her. What is interesting to see
is the way her use of them was transformed by the new thing she
was trying to say through them.

At the heart of her message was the conviction that Life is
Spirit. Moses on the plain of Moab had declared: "See, I have set
before thee this day life and good, and death and evil; . . . therefore
choose life, that both thou and thy seed may live." To a wayward
and undisciplined people he brought this tremendous moral simpli-
fication, caught in two pairs of contrasting terms. With like simplicity
Mrs. Glover found her chosen terms ranging themselves in stark
antithesis. On one side were Spirit, Soul, Principle, Life, Truth,
Love—and all these words she was beginning to use as synonyms for
God, although she had not yet evolved her later system of capitalization to indicate that fact.[124] On the other side were all the words
that denied the infinitude and perfection of Spirit and Spirit's creation.

Just as the Mosaic contrast was no mere rhetorical figure but a
desperately serious confrontation of ultimate values, so Mrs. Glover's
paired opposites—truth and error, wisdom and ignorance, science
and belief, harmony and discord, soul and body, life and death,
reality and illusion, being and nothingness—were no mere semantic
exercise but a bold new way of shaping experience. They were tools
of thought through which the apparent dualism of human life could
be resolved in a point-by-point confrontation of the "unreal" by the

"real." To range one's thinking on the side of being was, she insisted, to have something *happen*. It was to have reality break through appearance, the Word become flesh.

Of words as words she always maintained a troubled suspicion. In *The Science of Man,* in answer to the question, "What is prayer?" she wrote in part, "Words can deceive, thoughts are more safe; until we have grown up to every word we utter, for every idle word we are judged by wisdom." Her emphasis then as later was on the need for demonstration rather than for profession, and by this she always meant demonstration in terms of practical living and particularly of healing.

In "The Soul's Enquiries of Man," written at that time, Soul's inquiries are practical Christian demands, as in the following typical passage:

> *Do you speak the truth and live the truth, up to your highest understanding of what is right, and think not to deceive? For nothing is hid from wisdom that shall not be revealed; and wisdom rewards and punishes; therefore at some time you will be rewarded according to a just judgment; then will the soul whisper to man, "If you suffer from error, your reward is in getting out of it; but if you suffer from truth, you will be rewarded with truth, and this will help you to rise above the world, and give you peace that the world knoweth not of. If when you are persecuted for truth you are so drawn into the atmosphere of your persecutors as to feel yourself their feelings of hate and malice, then are you in danger; but if when they curse, you can bless, then have you overcome your enemies and gained a great conquest over matter and error. . . ."*

After a number of such inquiries and instructions, this companion essay to *The Science of Man* concludes, "To live the above, will take you further into science than all else can do." Understanding was more than a matter of intellectual comprehension, and the whole development of Mrs. Glover's language at that time pointed in the direction of her later statement: "As Christian Scientists you seek to define God to your own consciousness by feeling and applying the nature and practical possibilities of divine Love."[125]

7

The Boston publisher whom Mrs. Glover consulted about her manuscript told her that he would need six hundred dollars cash in advance in order to bring it out. The terms were prohibitive, but she may have urged the Wentworths to raise the money by one means or another, and this may have contributed to a growing coolness on the part of the elder Wentworths. At any rate, no further steps were taken toward the manuscript's publication.

It is not easy to have a prophet as a member of a very ordinary household. The evidence shows that Mrs. Glover now lived for one thing only: the carrying out of the mission which she was sure God had given her. She was prepared not only to sacrifice for it but also to ask others to sacrifice, and not unnaturally her demands on her friends during these years sometimes seemed highly unreasonable to those of them who shared little or none of her vision of the future.

Young Richard Kennedy of Amesbury visited her at Stoughton several times, thus becoming acquainted with the Wentworths—and greatly taking the fancy of Lucy, who was fifteen years old by the time Mrs. Glover left there. In an interview in 1907 he said:

> The Wentworths were well enough in their way, as were the Crafts with whom Mrs. Eddy lived at an earlier period, and the Websters of Amesbury. It was an unfortunate fact that Mrs. Eddy with her small income was obliged to live with people very often at this time in her life who were without education and cultivation. It was never her custom to keep apart from the family. She invariably mingled with them and through them kept in touch with the world. She had a great work to do; she was possessed by her purpose and like Paul the apostle, and many another great teacher and leader, she reiterated to herself, "This one thing I do." Of course simple-minded people who take life as it comes from day to day find any one with so fixed an object in life a rebuke to the flow of their own animal spirits.[126]

Certainly this was true of Horace Wentworth, whose Grand Guignol account of Mrs. Glover's leaving Stoughton in a whirlwind of rage and vindictiveness in the early spring of 1870 has been denied in whole and in detail by other members of the family who were actually there at the time, as Horace was not.[127] From Mrs. Glover's correspondence with Sarah Bagley and "Dick" Kennedy, it becomes clear that she left in accord with her own established plans; and if some members of the Wentworth household were all but heartbroken at losing her and others sighed with relief, that is not altogether surprising.

Mrs. Glover herself showed a good deal of the patience needed by any spiritual leader in dealing with well-meaning little people who cling to him for help and guidance but who feel they can nevertheless lecture him on how to conduct his life. Back in the fall of 1868 Sarah Bagley had written her that a certain Mrs. B. considered that Mrs. Glover "needed discipline," but Miss Bagley's own diagnosis was that she needed "a more entire trust in God." Mrs. Glover may have looked at the words in amazement, but she wrote back with a mingled firmness and gentleness which pointed finally to Miss Bagley's own need to be willing to *work* instead of wish:

> *Now my dear, if you both could understand the spiritual or rather the scientific sense of the 9th Chap. of Luke you would see my life in its truer meaning. I am very grateful to you all for your kind care of me but my heavenly Father "feedeth me." Your desire, dear Sarah, to become purified of self, is a good one and a great one to attain; your prayer will never be answered, but your labor certainly will.*[128]

During her time at Stoughton she wrote Sarah Bagley a good many letters, exhorting, encouraging, scolding, sympathizing, teaching, confiding. On one occasion she would answer out of sad experience her correspondent's question whether she had no faith in any individual, "I have very little reason to have faith in any thing but wisdom, and my faith in [people] is just according to their wisdom, to the science they understand, & not according to what they think or believe of themselves."[129] But on another occasion she would write, throwing all caution to the winds: "I have just read Richard's letter in which he named your tenderness and your dear Mother's towards me in this unlooked-for-hour. . . . Was ever there a more glorious nature, a more noble soul than Richard Kennedy possesses?"[130]

During all this time she was giving Kennedy instruction, by letter and manuscript as well as through his occasional visits. For a while he instructed Miss Bagley—"Dickey," Mrs. Glover wrote her, "speaks in his high minded tone, willing to teach you"[131]—but the arrangement did not turn out to be satisfactory. He was a good pupil but not a good teacher, and Miss Bagley definitely wanted Mrs. Glover's instruction.

Kennedy's letters show an eager and apparently earnest young man: "In my future experience with the world, Mary, I do not expect to obtain applause and popularity. This could not be, for truth will have its opposite, and in this will be contention and strife."[132] But a more realistic hint of his future role lies concealed in another passage: "I have not seen Sarah of late as she is not situated so as to commence yet. I do not care to be in her influence until I am ready to rub her head."[133] He was already discovering his facility in manipulating people's thoughts when he manipulated their heads; soon enough he would find this more to his taste than rhetorical renunciations of popularity.

He had understandably decided that he did not want to stay in Amesbury but would like to venture out into a larger world to practice his newly acquired healing skill. This fitted in well with Mrs. Glover's conviction that the time was approaching for her to present her Science to a wider public. Together they considered the possibility of going into partnership in Boston or Lynn, he to do the healing part of the work, she the teaching.

On February 20, 1870, Kennedy signed an agreement: "In consideration of two years instruction in healing the sick I hereby agree to pay Mary M. B. Glover one thousand dollars in quarterly installments of fifty dollars commencing from this date."[134] But they were not quite ready to start. When Mrs. Glover left the Wentworths shortly afterwards, she went first for a six-week stay with Sarah Bagley at Amesbury, to give Kennedy a little more preparation for his public début and to fit Miss Bagley to carry on by herself after they had left.

This latter task was performed so well that for the rest of her life the good spinster supported herself very comfortably by her healing work. On April 23, 1870, she signed an agreement to pay Mrs. Glover 25 per cent of all the money she earned by healing, in return for the instruction she had received. Mrs. Glover later reduced the amount to 10 per cent, then still lower, and in 1876 the contract was canceled by mutual agreement.

Although Sarah Bagley stayed till the end of her days at what was still the pre-Christian Science stage of Mrs. Glover's teaching, she maintained a sort of ambivalent gratitude and querulous loyalty to her teacher. Samuel C. Beane, who officiated at her funeral in 1905, wrote: "Miss Bagley always spoke kindly and amiably of Mrs. Glover to me."[135] Another close friend, H. G. Hudson, wrote: "She bought and gave away to as many people fifty copies of Science and Health and other publications of Mrs. Eddy's. . . . She always quoted Science and Health in her practice which extended over twenty years [after its publication]."[136]

She was one of the many people who were to learn from Mary Baker Eddy at an early stage of the latter's development and then show none of her remarkable capacity for growth, thus to be left behind like fossilized specimens of a dead-end species. Something of this effect marks the reminiscence of a native of Amesbury whose Quaker grandparents used to have treatments from "Auntie Bagley":

She [Miss Bagley—or Mrs. Bagley, as he mistakenly refers to her] wore gray corkscrew curls on the side of her head—and to my child mind they looked like cast iron or steel turnings. One day Mrs. Bagley and "another lady" (who I afterwards learned was Mrs. Eddy) were at my Grandfather's house. I was taken with a stomach ache, and Mrs. Bagley tried to help me by holding me in her lap—but those "steel curls" frightened me. The other lady whom I just remember as a kind gentle lady then took me in her lap—and I felt very peaceful—I cannot remember the actual healing—but I am quite sure the pain left me.[137]

Miss Bagley, shaking her corkscrew curls, continued to "rub heads" as her lifelong friend Richard Kennedy did, but she always insisted that Mrs. Glover's teaching was quite different from Quimby's. The Quimby "Questions and Answers" she considered "not the same in line of thought," and she "declined to purchase it, regarding it as practically worthless."[138] Mrs. Glover was indeed the discoverer of Christian Science, Sarah Bagley maintained, but from her Amesbury world she looked with a slightly miffed amazement at the place Christian Science came to occupy in the world.

For when Mrs. Glover left for Lynn in May with Richard Kennedy, to teach and practice what at that time she called Moral Science, she was launching onto an ocean of events that would carry her an immeasurable distance from the quiet banks of the Merrimack. The validity of anything announced as a scientific discovery must be submitted to open trial with clashing theories, interpretations, and convictions in a pluralistic world. Mrs. Glover was ready at last to face that world.

Chapter
VII

Emergence
1870

In 1870 the American edition of a book by a French evangelical leader, E. de Pressensé, was published under the title *The Early Years of Christianity*. Some years later the book found its way into Mrs. Eddy's library, and was carefully read and marked by her. One of the scored passages refers to the skepticism made fashionable by Strauss and Renan:

> *We are persuaded that the best method of defense against the shallow skepticism which assaults us, and which dismisses, with a scornful smile, documents, the titles of which it has never examined, is to retrace the history of primitive Christianity, employing all the materials accumulated by the Christian science of our day; for it must be well understood among us that there is in truth such a thing as Christian science in the nineteenth century.*[1]

The history of primitive Christian Science, with its abundant documentation, affords an extraordinary opportunity to observe closely the genesis and evolution of a new religion. Moreover, an understanding of the nineteenth-century New England phenomenon can throw light even on the first-century New Testament narratives. Yet it was not as the bearer of a new religion but of a new therapy that Mrs. Glover presented herself in Lynn. Five more years of development were necessary before her discovery would stand before the world as Christian Science.

When she and Kennedy came to Lynn in May, 1870, they stayed first of all with friends, the Clarkson Olivers, but before long they had found more permanent quarters on the second floor of a house at the corner of South Common and Shepard Streets, opposite Lynn Common. The rooms were rented from a young woman, Miss Susie Magoun, who ran a private school for young children on the first floor.

Kennedy—affable, Irish, and just turned twenty-one—was soon a great success as a healer. Behind the scenes Mrs. Glover counseled, encouraged, directed; and gradually she drew around her the more promising students who thronged Kennedy's waiting room. On July 15 she wrote Sarah Bagley: "I have all calling on me for instruction. . . . Richard is literally overrun with patients. . . . We enjoy our *moments* of leisure more than can be named. On the evening of the fourth our rooms were filled with company to hear the concert given on the common by the brass band."[2]

While brass bands played and fireworks rocketed in little towns all over the United States to celebrate the Glorious Fourth, an increasingly industrialized America was plunging forward to more reckless tunes. The Gilded Age, about to be christened by Mark Twain and Charles Dudley Warner, was in full, inglorious swing. Even the optimistic Whitman was writing in *Democratic Vistas*:

> *I say that our New World democracy, however great a success in uplifting the masses out of their sloughs, in materialistic development, products, and in a certain highly-deceptive superficial popular intellectuality, is, so far, an almost complete failure in its social aspects, and in really grand religious, moral, literary, and esthetic results. . . . For I say at the core of democracy, finally, is the religious element. . . . The local considerations of sin, disease, deformity, ignorance, death, etc., and their measurements by the superficial mind, and ordinary legislation and theology, are to be met by science, boldly accepting, promulgating this faith, and planting the seeds of superber laws—of the explication of the physical universe through the spiritual—and clearing the way for a religion, sweet and unimpugnable alike to little child or great savan.*

Lynn itself was no longer the idyllic town where European visitors used to be told that shoe operatives were fit to be United States senators. The old artisan cobblers had given way to a postbellum factory system which was rapidly widening the gap between manufacturer and employee, while the floating population of part-time workers and the overcrowding of men and women in confined quarters led to deplorable moral conditions. Here was a labor situation that was soon to spring up in organized protest. Here too were the nervous restlessness and poor health that attended the new urbanization of America.

Orthodox medicine, by the standards of a century later, was in a very crude state. So far as results were concerned, there was often little to choose between it and the various patent-medicine cures to which millions of people turned. The line between orthodox and quack systems was often scarcely visible, and it was taken for granted by the general public that anyone who set himself up to heal should be endowed with the title of "doctor," as Quimby had been a decade earlier and as Kennedy now was.

This was the period when medical practice was popularly defined as "scientific guessing" and when one of the most respected physicians of the day, Oliver Wendell Holmes, told a class at the Harvard Medical School: "I firmly believe that if the whole *materia medica* could be sunk to the bottom of the sea, it would be all the better for mankind and all the worse for the fishes." In this state of chaotic *laissez faire,* the best and the worst existed side by side, and only time would be able to sort out the genuinely progressive from the venally fraudulent.

The Lynn papers advertised every sort of cure. "Mrs. S. E. Barry, Medical Clairvoyant, and healer of all diseases that are curable," nestled next to "African mineral water . . . sworn to cure . . . Neuralgia, paralysis, St. Vitus Dance." Because of the widespread interest in spiritualism, the *Banner of Light* from nearby Boston was much read in Lynn, and in a single issue one might find advertisements for a magneto-botanic physician, a trance healer, an electrophrenopathist, an electric physician, and medical treatment by the Nutritive Process.[3] One ardent Lynn spiritualist, Mrs. Lydia E. Pinkham, was soon to achieve a sensational success through the advertising image she was able to create for her homemade nostrum, the mystically virtuous Vegetable Compound.

Women played an increasingly important role in the ferment of the times. The census of 1870 showed fifty thousand more women than men in Massachusetts, and ten years later this figure had increased to seventy-five thousand. *Woman's Journal* was launched in Boston in January, 1870, by Lucy Stone, Julia Ward Howe, and other moderate feminists as a rival to Susan B. Anthony's more fiery periodical *The Revolution.* Lectures on woman suffrage, as well as on temperance, spiritualism, and evolution, filled the Lynn halls, as they filled halls throughout the country.

Science and religion shared the popular interest. As one writer on Lynn at this period points out: "Often a didactic sermon on Genesis would be printed by local papers side by side with a report of a Lyceum lecture on the geological formation of the earth."[4] The *Lynn Transcript* early in 1871 reported a sermon, "Sunrise of a Scientific Christianity," by a Congregational minister called Cook, but the phrase was derived from Mrs. Glover. Cook's courageous though unpopular exposure of moral conditions in the Lynn factories had drawn a letter of commendation from her in the same paper three weeks earlier, in the course of which she had written, "Purity is the baptism of scientific Christianity."[5]

Mrs. Glover herself had clipped out of the *Banner of Light* in December, 1869, the long reports of a series of lectures by Professor William Denton on the origin and antiquity of man—a popular exposition of new geological and biological discoveries, espousing Darwinism against the "Jewish Jehovah" and biblical fundamentalism.

Other items she cut from the same paper show why, for a time, she felt it necessary to keep an eye on that spiritualist organ. Words akin to her own but used in a context which gave them a meaning abhorrent to her were cropping up in it from time to time. One article in 1869, for instance, had declared, "How to drive away error with truth, is the highest practical teaching; and such teaching, in its own nature, is a direct emanation from the Divine Mind."

She appears not to have found it worth-while to scan the paper after 1869, but occasional phrases in it continued to show linguistic resemblances. An article early in 1871 addressed "God who art our father in wisdom and our mother in love," and "God, thou infinite and perfect principle of life," explaining that "He is not a personal God but . . . He exists as the great Mind of the Universe." If these phrases were not to be attributed to literary poltergeists,[6] then they must be the result of the *Zeitgeist,* but they in no wise endeared spiritualism to Mrs. Glover. In a copy of *The Radical* which Sarah Bagley sent her she marked her approval of an article attacking on scientific grounds the spiritualist habit of attributing everything to the agency of spirits, underlining especially one sentence: "This is the old spirit of theology, which, in this form, has only changed base."[7]

Theology, spiritualism, science, medicine, the exuberant materialism of a scandalous decade—all these Mrs. Glover now confronted. It was an atmosphere in which her Moral Science might well appear to be one more fly-by-night wonder, as Christianity itself had first appeared in ancient Rome to be merely another faddish mystery cult from the East.

On August 13 an advertisement appeared in the *Lynn Semi-Weekly Reporter:*

> MRS. GLOVER, *the well-known Scientist, will receive applications for one week from ladies and gentlemen who wish to learn how to* HEAL THE SICK *without medicine, and with a success unequaled by any known method of the present day, at* DR. KENNEDY'S OFFICE, *No. 71 South Common Street, Lynn, Mass.*

Two days later the following agreement was signed by two young men of Lynn:

We, the undersigned, do hereby agree in consideration of instruction and manuscripts received from Mrs. Mary Baker Glover, to pay one hundred dollars in advance and ten per cent. annually on the income that we receive from practising or teaching the science. We also agree to pay her one thousand dollars in case we do not practise or teach the above-mentioned science that she has taught us.

G. H. Tuttle, Charles S. Stanley.

Shortly after this, Mrs. Glover's first class began. It probably included, in addition to Tuttle and Stanley, Clarkson and Susan Oliver, a Mrs. J. R. Eastman, and perhaps Mrs. Addie Spofford, whose husband Daniel was later to play an important part in the history of Christian Science.[8] All signed agreements similar to the one quoted above. All joined because they wanted to learn how to *heal*—although Tuttle was a bluff young seaman who joined simply because his sister, Stanley's wife, asked him to as a result of the benefit she had received from Kennedy's treatment. When, after a few lessons, Tuttle himself cured a girl of dropsy, he was so startled that he dropped the whole thing forthwith.

The classes were held in the evenings and lasted for three weeks. Before entering the class each student received from Kennedy a treatment consisting of physical manipulation. After this anomalous prelude he was plunged into a spiritual atmosphere so breathtakingly different that he might have entered a new universe. This was, in fact, exactly what he was invited to do. Like Saul who went out looking for his father's asses, he was suddenly presented with a kingdom.

As a textbook for the course he was given a handwritten copy of Mrs. Glover's manuscript "The Science of Man, by which the sick are healed, embracing questions and answers in Moral Science." This he was expected to study assiduously and in part memorize. At the close of the class he was given "The Soul's Enquiries of Man" and a few other shorter papers. Daniel Spofford, who was not a member of the class, wrote fifty years later that after reading his wife's copies of the manuscripts several times he declared them to be "that for which the Christian Church had been looking for lo these eighteen centuries,"[9] and he determined to give his life to establishing their truth; but when he actually studied with Mrs. Glover five years later, he discovered that the mere manuscripts "were, compared to her expounding of them, as the printed page of a musical score compared to its interpretation by a master."[10]

Georgine Milmine recorded the testimony of early students of Mrs. Glover, given after decades of bitter estrangement from her:

[*They*] *still declare that what they got from her was beyond equivalent in gold or silver. They speak of a certain spiritual or emotional exaltation which she was able to impart in her classroom: a feeling so strong that it was like the birth of a new understanding and seemed to open to them a new heaven and a new earth.*[11]

Sibyl Wilbur, who talked to many of these same students, gives a vivid picture of the scene:

The students who were drawn together were workers; their hands were stained with the leather and tools of the day's occupation; their narrow lives had been cramped mentally and physically. . . . They could not come to Mrs. Glover in the daytime, for their days were full of toil. At night, then, these first classes met, and it was in the heat of August. In the barely furnished upper chamber a lamp was burning which added somewhat to the heat and threw weird shadows over the faces gathered round a plain deal table. Insects buzzed at the windows, and from the common over the way the hum of the careless and free, loosed from the shops into the park, invaded the quiet of the room. Yet that quiet was permeated by the voice of a teacher at whose words the hearts of those workmen burned within them.[12]

The extraordinary thing was that they were engaged in the study of metaphysics.

As a philosophical discipline, metaphysics shines with such great names as Plato and Aristotle, Aquinas and Averroës, Kant and Hegel, but in the later nineteenth century it was already beginning to fall into the discredit which fully overtook it half a century later. The age was distinguished by what one writer calls "antimetaphysical minds of the first order in every field of investigation."[13] About 1870 a loosely named Metaphysical Club was formed in Cambridge, not far from Lynn, by Charles Sanders Pierce, William James, Chauncey Wright, and the junior Oliver Wendell Holmes; here were the seeds of that pragmatic philosophy which accorded so well with the emphasis of the new age on *results*, on workability, on what Huxley called justification by verification; here was the insistence that if metaphysics was to survive it must come out of the academy into what James called "this real world of sweat and dirt."

Mrs. Glover's metaphysics did just that. Ontology became not just a study but a way of mastering experience. An academic study seventy years later would conclude that the philosophical uniqueness of Christian Science lay in the fact that for the first time in history a *practical* metaphysics had appeared.[14]

As in every subsequent class of Mrs. Eddy's, the instruction began with a direct confrontation of the question, "What is God?" People who had thought of Him as either a wrathful or a benign old gentleman in the sky were suddenly called upon to recognize Him as the Principle of being, the Soul of the universe. It is a measure of Mrs. Glover's success as a teacher that these terms blazed with meaning for her students.

The Science of Man began:

Ques. What is God?
Ans. Principle, wisdom, love, and truth.
Ques. What is this principle?
Ans. Life and intelligence.
Ques. What is life and intelligence?
Ans. Soul.
Ques. Then, what is God?
Ans. The Soul of man and the universe.
Ques. Is God man?
Ans. No, they are perfectly distinct and yet united. Soul or God is not man, nor is that which we call Soul in man; while they are ever united as substance and its shadow; Soul the substance, man its shadow.[15]

Here are theological and ontological terms with which the present-day student of Christian Science is familiar, along with the sense of God as the Being in whom all else subsists, but the characteristic Christian Science concept of man has not yet emerged out of the shadow.

It is not merely that the word "shadow" is used where later Mrs. Eddy would describe man as reflection, expression, manifestation. In *The Science of Man* as a whole the overwhelming reality of God seems to make the very idea "man" shadowy and insubstantial in comparison. God is set forth clearly as the Principle of man, but man as the idea of God is still in the process of formation, of emergence into light. Consequently the student at that time was told to identify himself with God in what was sometimes misconstrued as a pantheistic sense. Later she would make it clear that he must identify himself *as* man, or manifestation, in order to identify himself *with* God, his divine source, as Jesus Christ had spoken of himself always as the *son* of God, not as God the Father.

This development and clarification of her teaching would follow naturally from the foundation laid down in *The Science of Man,* but the foundation itself is clear: God is the Principle of all that really exists. And here she at once ran into difficulty with traditional theology.

Again and again she insisted that God is not "personal." It is evident that to her the words "person" and "personal" implied a human or physical being, and in this she was supported by the regnant definitions of Noah Webster. But "Principle" as she used it obviously did not mean an inanimate, impersonal *thing*. In her system Principle was Love, Life, Spirit, Soul, the conscious, willing, governing "I" of the universe. It was cause, source, origin, as Webster defined it. The opening words of Genesis *In the beginning* had been *in principio* in the Vulgate and ἐν ἀρχῇ in the Septuagint, and in the double meaning of the Latin and Greek terms there is some analogy with Mrs. Eddy's concept of the divine Principle as the beginning of all things.

When Paul Tillich later defined God as the ground of all being, with the German word *Grund* rumbling behind the English expression, he used the word in a somewhat similar way—and indeed one of the accepted definitions of Principle is ground or foundation. For that reason Tillich's defense of his ontological concept of Deity against the criticisms of his fellow theologians throws light on Mrs. Eddy's situation vis-à-vis orthodoxy. Protestantism, he wrote, too often fears that to speak of God as the ground of being or as "being itself" makes impossible a personal relation between God and man:

> *This fear would be justified if the assertion that God is being itself were not only the first, as it must be, but also the last statement about God. But there are many more statements, such as God is life and love and spirit, all of which are derived from revelatory experiences and all of which can be expressed ontologically. The personal character of God is no exception. It makes the person-to-person encounter between God and man possible, but it excludes the assertion that God is a person.*[16]

Mrs. Eddy had excluded the assertion in a passage in *Science and Health* (p. 116) written many years before:

> *As the words* person *and* personal *are commonly and ignorantly employed, they often lead, when applied to Deity, to confused and erroneous conceptions of divinity and its distinction from humanity. If the term personality, as applied to God, means infinite personality, then God is infinite Person,—in the sense of infinite personality, but not in the lower sense.*

On occasion she wrote of God as Person, but usually she preferred the word that conveyed the sense of His working through invariable, universal law.[17] As the years went on she would increasingly couple Principle with Love and would use the term Father-Mother to express the solicitude of the creator for His creation, but in her earliest classes she presented the subject with an abstract radicalism that was more than some of her students could take.

In her very first class there was a sharp reaction from the belligerently fundamentalist Charles Stanley, who had not counted on being confronted with a new theology. Stanley, a Baptist, nearly disrupted the class by his arguments and objections. He had no intention of giving up his anthropomorphic God and devil and his hard-shelled orthodoxy. He was there for a plain dollars-and-cents reason, to learn how to heal; and while Kennedy's manipulations made sense to him Mrs. Glover's metaphysics did not.

She, on the other hand, took the view that the members of the class were there to learn, not to teach; so toward the end of the second week she turned Stanley out of the class. He complained and accused but felt he had learned enough to set up as a "doctor"—which he did with fair success for some years, later becoming a homeopathic physician.

In *The Science of Man* Mrs. Glover warned her students that meekness as well as other moral graces was necessary for continued advancement in Science:

> *If you are seeking money in your practice more than a growth of your own, more than to be perfectly pure, and honest, and just, and meek, and loving, then are you asking of sense instead of Soul for happiness, and your patients will not recover as well; they will gain at first up to you, and then you are not sufficiently beyond them and near the Soul to carry them further away from sense by following you.*

Quimby had said that a man's character was of small importance in his practice and teaching of science: ". . . it is not absolutely necessary that he should be a good or a bad man."[18] Calvinist orthodoxy, too, had rejected as Arminian heresy the idea that moral virtue could have anything to do with salvation. But Mrs. Glover thought differently. *Moral* Science was a necessary preliminary to *Christian* Science.

2

Her next class was held in November. One of the members, Samuel Putnam Bancroft, has left an invaluable account of the period in his book *Mrs. Eddy As I Knew Her in 1870.*[19]

He stresses her devoted service to her students. In addition to the twelve lessons over a three-week period which constituted the

course, she gave them private instruction between lessons when necessary and treatment when requested. She "was always ready to respond
to the call of these students," Bancroft wrote, and they were never
really graduated:

> Every meeting with her was a lesson; every letter received
> from her. This continued for years. I have never known of any
> of her loyal students to complain of not receiving full value
> for money paid, or asking to have it refunded. For my own part,
> I will say that from my limited practice in healing I received
> many times the amount I paid her, besides enjoying over fifty
> years of almost perfect health.

This point is important, for Mrs. Glover had now advanced the
price of her course to the astonishing sum of three hundred dollars.
This was almost one-third of the average annual income of a Lynn
shoe worker. She herself wrote later that she was greatly troubled
at asking so large a fee but was led to do so by "a strange providence";
and the interesting fact is that even some of her "disloyal" students
felt as Daniel Spofford did when he wrote at the end of his life, "I
will say, and always have said, that her teachings in spiritual science
were beyond any money consideration."[20]

At the same time she reduced or even waived the fee altogether
for many of her students, as her small account books show.[21] Miss
Dorcas Rawson, a shoe worker and "Holiness Methodist," paid the
full three hundred dollars when she entered the November class;
but her sister Mrs. Miranda Rice, unable to obtain the money from
her well-to-do husband, was admitted free. Young George Barry,
whom Mrs. Glover was to heal of tuberculosis, could pay only half
but she receipted him in full; later he insisted on giving her the
rest. George Allen, a young man who subsequently became a prominent businessman in Lynn, paid the full amount. But all of them felt,
in Georgine Milmine's phrase, that what they got "was beyond equivalent in gold or silver."

Bancroft has left an interesting description of Mrs. Glover's
appearance at this time:

> Her features were regular and finely moulded. The most
> noticeable were the eyes, large and deep-set, dark blue and
> piercing, sad, very sad, at times, yet kind and tender. Her figure
> was a trifle above the average height, and she carried herself
> very erect. . . . When in conversation, the animation she dis-
> played added much to her attractiveness. It was the animation
> of conviction, not of excitement or agitation.

She had, Bancroft wrote, "the ability to make her listeners forget
the speaker in what she was saying." She was often discovering "untrod-

den paths of wisdom," and she "never failed to share with her students such additional wisdom as God revealed to her." She showed them "the loving-kindness of a mother, or the faithful devotion of a sister."

Something of the atmosphere of the little group comes across in these comments and in Mrs. Glover's own notes to her students. To Bancroft she wrote in December:

> *I was sorry you did not get my word sent you to meet with the class Sat. eve. at Mr. Oliver's. You first proposed it and I acted upon your suggestion. . . . I have a little Bible that I purchased for you about a week since and will be happy to send it to you by Dr. Kennedy at your next meeting. . . . You see I do not forget you and you must not forget yourself.*

She wrote Sarah Bagley on Christmas Day about the weekly alumni meetings at Clark Oliver's, where the students met "to talk science and benefit by arguing and discussing it" and where she looked in on them occasionally "to cheer their labors."[22] On Christmas Eve they had had a surprise party and presented her with a landscape painted by Clark Oliver and an elegant silver pitcher from the class, with Kennedy acting as spokesman. For the moment her cup of happiness was full.

She herself was in the habit of giving little gifts impulsively to those around her. To young Susie Felt who lived near-by and loved her with all the ardent idealism of a fifteen-year-old she gave a ring, a book, a photograph; to George Barry a copy of Whittier's *Snow Bound,* Tennyson's *Poems,* and a history of the Civil War. But mostly she gave Bibles. In the little Bible she presented to "Putney" Bancroft for writing the best interpretation of the first chapter of Genesis she wrote on the flyleaf, "With all thy getting, get understanding." And in the small Bible bound in purple velvet that she later gave to George Allen she wrote a verse admonishing him to keep it for the giver's sake but read it for his own.

These are small details, but, as she wrote in the autograph album of her nephew George Baker when he visited her at the end of 1870 after completing his studies at the New Hampshire Conference Seminary:

> If an avalanche roll from its Alp, ye tremble at the will of Providence;
> Is not that will concerned when the sere leaves fall from the poplar?
> A thing is great or little only to a mortal's thinking.[23]

So far as Mrs. Glover was concerned Lynn was a battlefield as momentous as any in the Franco-Prussian War. "I have the front ranks of the battlefield as yet," she wrote Sarah Bagley in January during the terrible siege of Paris. "When I am gone some of you will step forward and bear the blows in your turn; as it is you all have enough to suffer."[24]

Her generalship was at last coming to the fore, and she rallied her little ranks to face the coming onslaughts. She urged Putney Bancroft to take up the healing work full time; but when he replied, like the man in the parable, that he could not because he was about to take a wife, she wrote him with a certain iron realism, "I have no objection to your decision because I know experience is the best teacher." To Bancroft's half-apologetic statement that love had triumphed over wisdom her rejoinder was that it would be more correct to say that sense had temporarily overruled soul; then she added somberly, "I fear you will inherit this truth through the discipline of affliction."[25] Nevertheless she gave her blessing to the marriage, and after the wedding she wrote Sarah Bagley cheerfully that one of her students "has recently been married here in Lynn to a beautiful and worthy young lady."[26]

To some of the people around her she seemed austere, and to some autocratic, for her life was entirely dominated by the one purpose to which all else must be sacrificed. Miss Susie Magoun, who ran the nursery school downstairs, was highly critical of her, contrasting her intense single-mindedness with Kennedy's sociability. At times Mrs. Glover would administer sharp rebukes to her students. "I think you ought to be ashamed of your language to your teacher," she wrote Sarah Bagley on one occasion, "but then perhaps it does not appear to you as it would to others."[27] In another letter she told Miss Bagley of a widow who had recently studied with her and was doing wonderful cures, who accepted her instructions and carried out her directions, but who did not constantly consult her. Pointedly she related this student's success to the fact that "she loves me and leans on me in all confidence that I am right."[28] The future leader of a world movement is already perceptible in such remarks.

Commenting on her manuscripts as "pretty strong meat for babes in science," Bancroft wrote, "It is no wonder some of us failed to digest this food." Occasionally, he added, a student would try to stagger her with a difficult question: "These questions were received with kindness and answered with wisdom." But they were also answered with authority. Then she would reach out to them as she did to Bancroft when she wrote him: "Come, dear Putney, and tell me if you have aught against me. I have thought from what you once said that you regarded me as an adopted sort of mother."

If she made strong demands on her followers, she made even stronger ones on herself. Miss Magoun's future sister-in-law, who lived on the third floor of the same house and who liked Mrs. Glover as much as Miss Magoun disliked her, tells of Mrs. Glover's falling downstairs one morning and of Kennedy's carrying her upstairs, unconscious and bleeding.[29] The young girl was sent to get Bancroft, who came immediately and treated his teacher. In a few hours she was up and dressed, came down to supper as usual, and went on with her work without any fuss or complaint. Bancroft, referring to the entire twelve years during which he knew her, wrote, "I never saw her shed a tear when suffering almost mortal anguish."

At that time she was still influenced by the old Quimby belief in taking on the sufferings of those who clung to her, especially of her students' patients. Shortly after beginning her labors in Lynn she wrote her old friend Mrs. Mary Ellis of Swampscott:

> *Never did the life that seems appear so small to me as this year, and never the life that is so vast, so glorious. . . . My own health is greatly affected by the many sick ones that surround me but if I can aid them out of the dark places my feet have trod I am happier even though I suffer physically.*[30]

On such occasions she would sometimes ask help from her students. Four years later Bancroft, temporarily living in Cambridge, wrote in his diary:

> *I received a letter today from George Barry, giving me an account of a strange experience which my teacher passed through on Friday last, and which he was present to witness. It seems he called upon her with Mr. Hitchings, and, on rapping, heard a voice, hardly above a whisper, say "Come in." On entering, she arose to meet them, but fell back, lost consciousness, and, to their belief, was gathering herself on the other side. George went after Mrs. Rice, who came, and immediately a change took place. George had called on her mentally to come back, but Mrs. Rice called loudly, as for someone afar off, and the answer came, faintly at first, but stronger and stronger, till she was able to sit up and have the Bible and manuscripts read to her, and, finally, recovered.*[31]

In her copy of *The Early Years of Christianity* by Pressensé she marked with double emphasis the sentence, "He who is resolved to suffer and to die for God cannot be vanquished," but she also marked on the next page the words: "Moral resistance . . . knows no chances, no risks. It is linked to an immortal principle, and destined to certain triumph."

Bancroft wrote that Mrs. Glover was "absolutely fearless" in the face of sickness, and her healings during that period indicate as much.

The authority with which she could act is illustrated by her handling of the birth of a child to her student Miranda Rice. Called to Mrs. Rice's home in the middle of the night, she healed her immediately of her labor pains, told her to dispose herself comfortably on the bed, and said, "Now let the child be born," whereupon the birth at once took place. Mrs. Rice was at the same time healed of prolapsus of years' standing.[32]

Mrs. L. C. Edgecomb of Lynn gave written testimony of the healing of her year-and-a-half-old son, who had wasted away almost to a skeleton with a chronic bowel disease.[33] He could eat only gruel and had passed nothing but blood and mucus for many months. Mrs. Glover came up to the child's crib, took him in her arms, and held him quietly, then kissed him and put him back. In less than an hour he was out of his crib, playing, eating normally, and perfectly healed.

A score of hypotheses have been advanced to explain such healings as this. Mrs. Eddy's own explanation is to be found in *Science and Health* (p. 365): "If the Scientist reaches his patient through divine Love, the healing work will be accomplished at one visit, and the disease will vanish into its native nothingness like dew before the morning sunshine." Whatever the explanation accepted, many such cures by her were recorded by those who experienced, saw, or heard about them.[34] Other cases required longer treatment.[35]

Mrs. Glover had already learned from her experience with Ellen Pilsbury that the exuberant joy stirred in an individual by a sudden healing could sometimes change to a very different emotion if the individual felt his basic convictions too deeply challenged by what had happened. On occasion this could result in a later denial of the healing or, she warned, in an arrest of the recuperative process already begun.

This may be the explanation of the case of John C. Clarke, a young shoemaker who lived in the basement of the Reverend Philemon Russell's house where the Pattersons had stayed for a time in 1866. A striking healing of this young man is described in *Science and Health* (pp. 192f.), and the incident probably occurred in the early seventies. Mrs. Eddy's account implies that Clarke himself was unwilling to recognize the spiritual power by which he had been healed. Decades later he was quoted by hostile critics as saying: "*I didn't know she cured me. Have always had this same trouble and have it yet.*"[36] But his daughter-in-law Mrs. Grace M. Clarke wrote toward the end of her life:

> *My mother-in-law told me that at the time . . . Mrs. Glover, healed her husband, he had lain in bed eight months suffering from hip-disease which was caused by a fall upon a wooden spike*

in boyhood. . . . *Mr. Clarke returned to his work after the healing and worked every day thereafter.* . . . *As his daughter-in-law, I never knew Mr. Clarke to be in bed with any sickness after his healing and he lived to be over eighty years of age.*[37]

Mrs. Glover was soon to learn that her worst obstacles were neither the skepticism that rejected all spiritual power as superstition nor the dogmatism that pronounced her the tool of Satan. A man's foes are they of his own household, and her greatest challenge lay in her immediate circle.

Young Richard Kennedy was proving an immense success. An unidentified correspondent wrote to Sarah Bagley in March, 1871:

I find Dr. K. very pleasant, social and kind among those whom he has benefitted he is held in high esteem as far as I have been able to learn. . . . *The Dr's rooms are crowded daily, the interest continually increasing, so that he scarcely finds a moment's release from early morning till late in the evening.*[38]

Kennedy had nothing to do with the teaching of Moral Science, and as time went on and his self-confidence grew he began to grow restive under Mrs. Glover's close direction of his work. Moreover, she was beginning to insist that he should put less stress on physical manipulation as its incongruity with her own emphasis on moral regeneration became more evident.

From the outset she had tried to have him spiritualize this part of his practice. When he rubbed Sarah Bagley's head she had told him to think in terms of rubbing out the spiritualistic elements still present in that lady's thinking[39]; when he rubbed Charles Stanley's head she had told him to rub out in thought the dogmatism that made Stanley so intractable a student.[40] But the chief effect of Kennedy's rubbing seemed to be to encourage in his patients a high degree of personal dependence on him, as had been the case with Quimby and his patients, and the feeling of power was evidently not unpleasing to the young man.[41]

On June 1, 1871, Mrs. Glover recorded that she had received from Kennedy as her percentage on his practice through their one year in Lynn a total of $1,744. About this time Susie Magoun gave up her school in the house on Common Street, married one John M. Dame, and moved away, leaving Mrs. Glover and Kennedy to sublet from another tenant.

Though there were already faint stirrings of trouble between them, the two appeared to be on good terms when Mrs. Glover wrote a student, Frances Spinney, early in the summer: "I had a letter from the lady I visit in Portland this morning. . . . She seems full just now but says I can have a room any time. . . . Yesterday morning Richard took a fit to go to Portland but he will go to a Hotel or perhaps to the Islands."[42]

The casualness of her mention of Portland, so closely associated with Quimby, hints at the way she was steadily moving away from that episode of her life. Interestingly enough, however, she appears to have changed her mind about going there and to have gone instead to Tilton, as Sanbornton Bridge had now been renamed. From Tilton she wrote Miss Spinney on July 11, "They were glad to see me on my arrival, but really all is so changed since I were here that I feel as if I never wanted to come again."[43] Her new purpose made return to the outgrown past difficult.

On the other hand Kennedy's trip to Portland might serve as a symbol of his conscious turning back to the power of suggestion on which Quimby had wrought his cures a decade earlier. It is just possible that while there he got in touch with one of the Misses Ware[44] or made inquiry in other quarters about the Quimby methods, for when Mrs. Glover finally forbade all further use of manipulation, Kennedy cited Quimby's habitual use of this practice as a justification for his own continued employment of it.[45]

But the events which led to that decisive step had a drama and a significance of their own.

3

Some three months before Kennedy's Portland trip Mrs. Glover had received nine written questions from Wallace W. Wright, the twenty-five-year-old son of a Universalist minister of Amesbury. The young man was considering the possibility of joining her next class. The questions for the most part had been proposed by his father.

The first one asked, "Upon what principle is your science founded?" and Mrs. Glover wrote firmly in reply, "On God the principle of man." The sixth is of special interest: "Has this theory ever been advertised or practiced before you introduced it, or by any other individual?" In the manuscript Mrs. Wentworth had copied two or three years earlier[46] Mrs. Glover had written with assured conviction that no one except her had ever taught the Principle on which Science was founded and that only Jesus, the prophets, and the apostles had hitherto understood that Principle; yet in reply to Wright's question she wrote:

> *Never* advertised *and practiced only by one individual who healed me, Dr. Quimby of Portland, Me., an old gentleman who*

had made it a research for twenty five years, starting from the stand-point of magnetism thence going forward and leaving that behind. I discovered the art in a moment's time, and he acknowledged it to me; he died shortly after and since then, eight years, I have been founding and demonstrating the science.[47]

On the very eve of an experience that would finally clear up this confusion, Mrs. Glover for the last time publicly associated her teachings with Quimby's practice. The events that followed do more than any theoretical analysis to unravel the misunderstandings and resolve the contradictions in this situation.

Meanwhile, it is interesting to note Mrs. Glover's answer to the last question, "What do you claim for it in cases of sprains, broken limbs, cuts, bruises &c when a surgeons services are generally required?" In reply she wrote:

I have demonstrated upon myself in an injury occasioned by a fall, that it did for me what surgeons could not do. Dr. Cushing of this city pronounced my injury incurable and that I could not survive three days because of it, when on the third day I rose from my bed and to the utter confusion of all I commenced my usual avocations and not withstanding displacements etc. I regained the natural position and functions of the body.

. . . please preserve this, and if you become my student call me to account for the truth of what I have written.

In April Wright went through Mrs. Glover's third class. Although he paid the full amount, he remarked at the end to a classmate— George Allen's sister, Mrs. Ellen A. Locke—that the last lesson alone was worth the price of the whole course. Shortly afterwards he moved to Knoxville, Tennessee, where another of Mrs. Glover's students, Mrs. Addie Spofford, was already practicing Moral Science and her husband Daniel was engaged in the shoe trade.

Wright also began healing by the new method and at first was very successful. But he soon quarreled with Mrs. Spofford, rebelled against the discipline imposed on him by his healing work, found his doubts of the whole enterprise growing, and correspondingly lost his power to heal. In a rage he wrote Mrs. Glover and demanded five hundred dollars from her, his full tuition back and an extra two hundred to compensate him for his wasted time and wounded feelings. In the same mood he included in the letter insinuations about Mrs. Spofford's relations with Kennedy.

In her reply Mrs. Glover told him she wanted to hear no such gossip and refused his demand for money:

> *The happiness of life is in doing right, and in holding the consciousness of this and of having filled our short page of existence with worthy examples and worthy lessons for our fellow man. To be happy and useful is in your power, and the science I have taught you enables you to be this, and to do great good to the world if you practice this science as laid down in your MSS. Time alone can perfect us in all great undertakings, and . . . you cannot be perfect nor I cannot be perfect until we have passed through the furnace and are purified. You are now in a chemical.*[48]

This last word was one she had borrowed from Quimby, putting her own construction on it. For her it signified a temporary worsening of symptoms and stirring up of resistance in an individual or situation as the action of truth was felt. As "chemicalization," it survives in the vocabulary of Christian Science today. Certainly some sort of emotional ferment is evident in Wright's next letter to her.

What he has written about Mrs. Spofford and Kennedy is truth, not gossip, he insists. Mrs. Glover's students are generally unhappy. Deliver him from her example! He spurns her "base insinuations" against him:

> *The chemical you say I am in has been with me most of the time since I took this up, as I am "floored" in arguments with myself, and cannot sustain the positions your MSS. take. And my conversations with Mrs. S. are far from satisfactory, as the weight of my argument crushes any she is able to bring forward on the side of Science.*[49]

Shortly afterwards Mrs. Spofford came back to Lynn for a brief visit, and on her return to Knoxville at the beginning of October she wrote Mrs. Glover:

> *I wanted you to know that W. Wright was on his way to Mass.*
>
> *When I reached home, I found my practice was much run down. I shall have hard work to bring it up again, but I don't regret my journey, for I gained so much spiritually while with you.*
>
> *I did not talk with Wallace Wright for I saw it would do no good. He puts a false construction on everything I say. He said this, "I don't question the morality or Christianity of this Science,*

but I do doubt its application in healing the sick." You see that he is as full of conceit as ever. . . .

Be with us, dear Mrs. Glover and help us; for I am strangely drawn to this field of labor.[50]

The dissatisfied Wright stormed back to Lynn a month or two later, and toward the end of the year Mrs. Glover wrote Sarah Bagley:

Wright is all wrong at present. He gave the strongest protests of admiration for this Science when he was about to leave for the South and is come back and is going over his ground ranting about it with all his little capacity. When they told me he said he should ruin this Science here and at the South I told them to tell him to take a bucket and go for the Atlantic ocean and work to empty it.[51]

Wright procured a bucket and began dipping. His first step was to write a long letter which was published on January 13, 1872, in the *Lynn Transcript* under the title "Moral Science, alias Mesmerism." Telling of his experience in Knoxville and of his growing doubts that Moral Science was what it purported to be, he stated his conclusion that it was simply the science of mesmerism.

A week later Mrs. Glover replied in the same paper:

Mr. Wright says his principal reason for writing on the subject was to prevent others from being led into it. Here he is honest. 'Tis but a few weeks since he called on me and threatened that, if I did not refund his tuition fee and pay him two hundred dollars extra, he would prevent my ever having another class in this city.

She went on to quote from his first letter to her a sentence which read, "While I do not question the right of it, it teaches a deprivation of social enjoyment if we would attain the *highest* round in the ladder of Science," and she asked:

Was not this the "side" referred to in his newspaper article, in which he said, "Had I been shown both sides nothing could have induced me to take it up"?

Christianity as he calls it at one time, and mesmerism at another, cannot be the "two sides," for these are separated by barriers that neither a geometrical figure nor a malicious falsehood would ever unite.

Here for the first time she faced the issue of Christianity versus mesmerism that was to loom so large through the coming years; but before the next step was taken, she received a letter from Daniel Spofford which threw a little more light on the situation. Spofford, who was identified in the printed letterhead as "Dealer in Boots and Shoes, Market Square, Knoxville, Tenn.," wrote:

> *I have for a long time had a desire to write to you on matters relating to science; it seems as though I too should be in the good work; although I am in business at present such may not always be the case. Financially I suppose science would be a better success than most anything else, but setting that aside I would prefer to feel that I was doing some good and striving to advance the Truth. I find it is very hard for Mrs. Spofford to attend to her outside patients; frequently having to go a long distance in the evening through mud or rain to attend some one and often is quite weary but* never *sick. What I wish is that I might be sufficiently taught to at least attend to all of the outside patients wherever we may be situated. . . . Mrs. Spofford is having wonderful success and has recently completed* cures *that had been given up by the MDs. . . . I think she meets with success in nineteen cases out of twenty and has improved rapidly in the last two or three months, and when W W Wright says* We meet with but little success *he* lied *for he should have said* I *and told the reasons, which were primarily that he was practicing mesmerism or trying to which he acknowledges by his own statement; another was that he had the love of Mammon in front, and of God, behind.*[52]

A week later Wright's second letter appeared in the *Transcript*. Mrs. Glover in her earlier reply had quoted his words to her when he returned to Lynn—"My simple purpose now is revenge, and I will have it"—and Wright now explained that he had been provoked to say those "hasty" words by her language and tone when she refused to give him the five hundred dollars for which he asked. With these dubious credentials for the integrity of his purpose, Wright returned to his charge that what she taught was mesmerism:

> *[I do not] question the moral or Christian teachings which, as I before remarked, are used as a cloak to cover the real substance of this so-called science. . . . To live as this so-called science teaches would sever the affection between parents, and children, brothers and sisters, and forbid all mingling with society or friends. Why? Because it tells us that man is a delusion; that man, the noblest work of God, the result of His creative genius, the flowers in the fields, the mighty forests, the*

hidden wonders of the world, are all delusions, and the work of imagination.

The next week Mrs. Glover replied in the *Transcript* with what is really the first published statement of her early teaching:

Moral Science belongs to God, and is the expression or revelation of love, wisdom, and truth. It reaches the understanding, first through inspiration, and secondly, by explanation. Those who receive it must obey its requirements if they would understand it. . . . The idea that expresses moral science is physical, and we see this idea traced out in one continuous page of nature's bright and glorious character. Every blade of grass, tree and flower, declare, "How manifold are thy works, O Lord! in wisdom hast thou made them all."

The entire creation of God symbolizes nothing else but wisdom, love and truth. All that He hath made is harmonious, joy-giving and eternal. He also hath made man in His "image and likeness," and this must be a perfect man. . . . Moral Science is to put down sin and suffering through the understanding that God created them not, nor made he man to be the servant to his body. . . . All forms of suffering and disease, and even the winds and waves, obeyed the man, Jesus, through his God-being. . . . To be able to control our bodies by the soul, i.e. through God, is to be able not to let our bodies control us through the senses. . . . If ties of sense weaken, as the stronger and more enduring ties of soul strengthen, what matter? Love is not thus lost, but nearer, far, as we approach God, who is love. . . . All that is truth and its idea . . . is immortal . . . but mortality is not imagination, nor to be sneered at; rather is it to be understood so that it may be destroyed, even as Jesus gave the example, by bringing to light immortality. . . .

So far as I understand it, mesmerism is neither truth nor its idea, i.e. it is neither moral nor physical science, but simply an ism, originating in belief, by which one belief drives away another one, and the last may be even worse than the first. This, therefore, originates with man and not with God. Mesmer was the author of it, and never, to my knowledge, did he claim it was Moral Science; and I, who know no more of the practice of mesmerism than does a kitten, and think much less of it than did the originator, would be loath to steal his thunder, or to attempt to teach what I did not understand. Whereas I do claim to understand the Moral and Physical Science that I teach.[53]

In a letter to Mrs. Mary Ellis a few days later, Mrs. Glover described the newspaper controversy as another excitement for Lynn, to take the place of the Reverend Mr. Cook's philippics against immorality the winter before, and then she burst out, "O, Mrs. Ellis, God is my helper and I shall yet praise Him who is the health of my countenance and my God."[54] Certainly it seemed that the wrath of man was praising Him, for all copies of the weekly *Transcript* containing her article were sold out by the next day, so keen was the interest.

The next week Wright returned to the fray, treating the Lynn public to liberal quotations from Mrs. Glover's manuscripts, which he had earlier promised not to make public in any way. After ridiculing these passages he challenged their author to raise the dead, walk on the water, live twenty-four hours without air, and perform various other feats to prove her claims to inspiration—evidently, forgetful that it was Satan who challenged the Founder of Christianity to cast himself down from the pinnacle of the temple in order to prove that he was the son of God.

Even as a request for controlled experiments to prove the scientific validity of the new teachings, Wright's challenge left something to be desired. Mrs. Glover pointed out reasonably enough in a passage written two or three years later that her teachings at this period would have to be accepted "on the inductive method." The proof of even a part involved the whole Principle and made possible a presumptive acceptance of the whole:

> *Admitting the entire grounds of the science of being, it quickly follows our poor demonstration looks us in the face; but to this we reply, enough has been understood and proved, to reveal it science, and to prove, measurably, the blessing it brings. When speaking of this subject to others, instead of admitting the proofs we have already given of its Truth, we are often met with demands for more proof; therefore, we recommend you to read carefully what we have written, understand for yourselves, and establish your own evidence through demonstration....*[55]

But this was a later answer. Back in February, 1872, Mrs. Glover did not see fit to reply to Wright's challenge. Instead, a letter in the *Transcript* signed by George Barry, George Allen, Amos Ingalls, Dorcas Rawson, and Miranda Rice accused him of misusing the passages he had quoted from their teacher's manuscripts. Looking back on their progress, they wrote, they could see great gain, with much more ahead and "immensity looming up in the future." Unimpressed, Wright in a final letter published on February 24 announced that because of her silence in the face of his challenge "Mrs. Glover and her science are virtually dead and buried"—a judgment which, in Georgine Milmine's phrase, suggests that he did not possess the gift of prophecy.

Many years later, at a time when she was under fire, Mrs. Eddy wrote, "I do not regard this attack upon me as a trial, for when these things cease to bless they will cease to occur," and in *Science and Health* she would write. "Trials are proofs of God's care."[56] The blessing in Wright's attack was that it brought her face to face with the problem of mesmerism. This was the real challenge in his articles, not the jejune demand that she walk on the Atlantic.

In the course of the controversy Wright had made some telling criticisms of the physical manipulations which certainly belonged to animal magnetism rather than to Moral Science. Could Mrs. Glover cure a horse of scratches by rubbing its head? he asked. Mrs. Glover might have replied that she never taught that rubbing heads could cure anyone or anything; nevertheless the reasons she had given for permitting her students to continue this practice were still vulnerable to his criticism. He referred to her statement that mesmerism was one belief driving out another belief and then quoted from her manuscript the explanation that since belief was supposed to be located in the brain and people generally believed that the healer got nearer the patient through physical contact, the student might lay his hands where the belief was, to rub it out, even while turning his thoughts away from the body to argue down the belief. Was not this one belief driving out another? he asked. Was not this in fact mesmerism?

The very question was an evident shock to Mrs. Glover, but a salutary one. It brought to the surface the problem she had been struggling with in Kennedy for almost a year. While this has been interpreted as the problem of two very different temperaments working together, it was more basically a struggle over ultimate values. Friction had grown as the popular young healer resisted the demands which, as Mrs. Glover saw it, were inherent in the Science she taught. In a notation made many years later she listed three states in his attitude during that time: "1st Good resolves. 2nd Continual asking forgiveness. 3rd Hardness of heart, resolve to take own course."[57]

Dimly she was beginning to consider the possibility that the human mind undisciplined by religion might run wild with a sense of its own power. Christianity had always taught that the essence of religion was, "Not my will, but thine, be done." In her own terminology, spiritual sense, the expression of Soul, or God, could be used only for good, but "personal sense" was all there was to evil; it was, like the carnal mind of which Paul wrote, "enmity against God." Its resistance to the demands of spiritual sense might seem innocent or trivial enough in the first place; but if yielded to, might it not thwart further spiritual growth?

She might not wish to hear Wright's gossip about Kennedy's domination of Mrs. Spofford, but time was to show that in this at least he spoke the truth. Eventually Kennedy would turn Mrs. Spofford wholly against her teacher and would also estrange her from her husband. Forty years later some of his first patients were bound to him as closely as ever, still relying wholly on his manipulations for the alleviation of their ailments, still helpless to help themselves.

Genial young man that he was, Kennedy, despite the evidence of his early letters, would end by denying blandly that he had ever understood Mrs. Glover's teachings in the least or connected them with Christianity. He could hardly have hurt her more deeply than when he declared under oath a few years later that all he had ever learned from her was to rub people's heads. The poet Blake has written that "if a man is the enemy of my spiritual life while he pretends to be the friend of my corporeal, he is a real enemy," and reluctantly Mrs. Glover came to the conclusion that behind Kennedy's surface inoffensiveness was the carnal mind's enmity against God.

The matter came to a head as the result of Wright's public attacks. When that young man had first gone to Knoxville and was doing good healing work there in partnership with Mrs. Spofford, Mrs. Glover had noted a look of "indescribable envy" on Kennedy's face when she commented to him that she had expected just such good results from Wright. According to her later account, Kennedy replied, "I hope he will do well, but I am afraid you will be sorry you ever took [him] for a student of metaphysics."[58] After Wright had returned to Lynn and announced that his simple purpose was now revenge, Kennedy denounced his conduct but seemed to Mrs. Glover to show a secret satisfaction in it. On one occasion she surprised the two of them conferring together in what seemed a suspicious manner, and her later conclusion was that Wright was in part an unconscious tool of Kennedy, even though the two disliked each other.

The details of the situation are today wrapped in obscurity, but out of all this "chemicalization" one clear result emerged. Physical manipulation was abolished once and for all by Mrs. Glover. The students were told to erase from their manuscript copies of "The Science of Man" the one brief reference to it in that manuscript, and manipulation thereafter became the recognized badge of mesmerism.

At this point Kennedy rebelled, though an open break did not take place immediately. Two weeks after Wright's last article Mrs. Glover's extremely junior "partner" tore up his contract with her and announced that he no longer intended to pay her any percentage on his practice. Nonetheless, she continued to work with him for three months as best she could, trying to win him over from what she now felt was the disastrous error of his ways, especially his determination to stick to his manipulations and to what she saw as his control of his patients' thinking.

About this time she wrote Bancroft:

> . . . I am a fish out of water, when I am dragged away from wisdom and love into the grosser abyss of folly and hate, then I am not a fish at home. Truth is, I am so tired by the malice of my students, that up to this time, or a little prior to it, I have done nothing but love and praise, that I am losing my happiness and consequently my health in the dark labyrinth into which I gaze and stand upon the brink, thinking momently, will my students plunge therein? . . .
>
> Oh, how I have worked, pondered and constantly imparted my discoveries to this wicked boy that I shall not name and all for what! God grant me patience. Mrs. Susie Oliver told me once Richard said he thought I had suffered so much from bad students if he did not well it would kill me, but it won't. I most fear it will ruin my sweet disposition!
>
> I may as well jest over the absurd striplings that turn to rend me, to threaten me with disgrace and imprisonment for giving to them a discovery that money cannot pay for, but a little good breeding might have helped at least to reward the toil, and scorn, and obscurity, by which it was won for them.

To Sarah Bagley she wrote, "This hour is the one that must come before the sifting from the tares could take place that is necessary to purge my number of pupils and give me to know who are worthy to be my followers and who are not."[59]

Later in the spring she moved out to Peabody, a short distance from Lynn, to stay for some weeks with Peter Sim and his wife, Sim having been a member of the class she held that spring. Although she moved there for quietness so that she could write, she still went to Lynn almost every other day to try to heal the situation.

From Peabody she wrote Miss Bagley again on April 18. Speaking more openly of the "ruin" which some of her students—or rather, the "evil" in them—had been plotting against her, she declared:

> I have felt it and knew it, but instead of stopping their influence in the community and putting them on their own

*resources when they must have gone down, for nearly all my
time I have done little else than try to change this vile nature
in them and to sustain them and the cause. God will meet this
hour for me, and a doom is coming when the tares will be
separated from the wheat before the world, even as they are
before me today.*[60]

To her it seemed a time of great clarification as well as of trial.
Darkness was being separated from light, mesmerism from Science.
Finally, on May 11, the partnership with Kennedy was completely
dissolved, and he departed from the house on South Common Street
where they had listened to the band concerts so happily two years
before.

Almost unnoticed, the shade of Quimby went with him. Three
years later Mrs. Glover would write in the first edition of *Science
and Health:*

*In defence of mesmerism is urged, that Dr. Quimby manip-
ulated the sick. He never studied this science, but reached his
own high standpoint and grew to it through his own, and not
another's progress. He was a good man, a law to himself; when
we knew him he was growing out of mesmerism; contrasted with
a student that falls into it by forsaking the good rules of science
for a mal-practice that has the power and opportunity to do
evil.*[61]

The estimate of Quimby is a generous one; she had still not
plumbed the depths of the distinction between their two systems, a
distinction that went far beyond the use of physical manipulation.
But the essential point was clear; from the standpoint of Science all
mesmerism was malpractice, whether it was used with intent to do
good or to do harm. The magnetism which had held Quimby back
from reaching Science and the magnetism which had drawn Kennedy
away from Science were one and the same thing.

4

In the year 1872 a book was published which throws a strong
though indirect light on these events. Entitled *Mental Medicine,* it
was written by Warren F. Evans, the Swedenborgian minister who
visited Quimby in 1863 and who found the Portland healer's theory
and method in close agreement with his own.

Such later Quimby champions as Horatio W. Dresser and Charles
S. Braden have described Evans as a disciple of Quimby, although
this is not supported by anything in Evans' own writings. Even so,

it is essential to remember Dresser's unqualified statement that Evans simply wrote what Quimby meant to say and what he would have said if he had had the education and skill to do so.[62]

Apparently Sarah Bagley in 1871 had heard of Evans' activities or had run across his first book on healing—*The Mental Cure*, published in 1869—for Mrs. Glover had written her in that year: "I was interested in your account of that half scientist, a former patient of Dr. Quimby; why Sarah, they are getting inklings of this even in the practice of the M.D.'s."[63] *The Mental Cure* is discussed in Appendix C of this book. *Mental Medicine* in 1872 shows Evans firmly entrenched in his position.

The book is a virtual hymn of praise to what the author again and again calls "the magnetism of the hands," though he also adds that "the magnetism of the eye, through which the mind acts or goes forth, is of equal efficiency with that of the hand" (p. 49). Quimby of course had used both, though his theory made no mention of them. Meanwhile Evans has been reading James Braid of Manchester and William Gregory of Edinburgh and is able to give a more sophisticated account of the way in which suggestion operates in his own and Quimby's method of cure.

He was attracted by Gregory's idea of a "conscious impressible state"—a hypnoidal state in which the subject was not thrown into the hypnotic trance but retained full possession of his senses. Evans himself defined this as a state "in which the will of the operator and the simplest suggestion from him become the highest law of his patient's being" (p. 43). One's success in curing a patient depends on one's skill "in managing and controlling his mind" (p. 51). Even a "simple suggestion, made in the silent depths of your own consciousness" (p. 45) can change the movements of the stomach, the liver, or the kidneys of a patient.

From her observation of Kennedy, Mrs. Glover was to add that this sort of suggestion could also change the patient's attitude toward his friends, toward her, toward Science itself. All such control of one mind by another is characterized by her as a dangerous counterfeit of Science. Where was God in all this? she asked. Where was the subordination of the human will to the divine? She had formerly assumed that because the so-called mesmeric sleep was not involved in Quimby's method, or in Kennedy's practice, neither had any connection with mesmerism or animal magnetism; but if those terms were used as a generic description for mental suggestion or one mind controlling another, then Quimby and Kennedy in their different ways might both be described as mesmerists.

In his earlier book Evans had said of the force of suggestion, with its frequent accompaniment of physical manipulation, "Here is a power that can be turned to good account or perverted to evil" (p. 273). In *Mental Medicine,* on the other hand, he argued that this sort of suggestion could be exercised effectively only by those who used it with the highest motives. Not all advocates of animal magnetism would have agreed with this. One such advocate, writing in 1874, warned that the dangers of mesmerism came from the fact that it deprived "the subject of his own free will, of his autonomy, that the latter is solely at the mercy of the operator."[64]

Mrs. Glover, after further investigation, came to agree that this was so as long as the subject was unaware that he was being controlled by suggestion. In the lexicon of Christian Science animal magnetism would become synonymous with the operations of the carnal or mortal mind, however well-intended its use. Truth—mathematical truth, for instance—might be taught, learned, *known,* but it could hardly be "suggested."

Like Quimby, Evans had of course maintained from the outset that his magnetic-mental method of cure was the method used by Jesus, and in *Mental Medicine* he defined magnetism as "the science of the spiritual world" (p. 131). He linked Jesus with that pagan wonder-worker Apollonius of Tyana and asserted that the wonders of both are explicable by "the known laws of magnetism" (p. 208). It is then (p. 210) that he makes the sole reference to Quimby to be found in any of his eight books:

> *Disease being in its root a wrong belief . . . change that belief, and we cure the disease. . . . The late Dr. Quimby, of Portland, one of the most successful healers of this or any age, embraced this view of the nature of disease, and by a long succession of most remarkable cures, effected by psychopathic remedies, at the same time proved the truth of the theory and the efficiency of that mode of treatment. Had he lived in a remote age or country, the wonderful facts which occurred in his practice would have now been deemed either mythical or miraculous. He seemed to reproduce the wonders of the Gospel history. But all this was only an exhibition of the force of suggestion, or the action of the law of faith, over a patient in the impressible condition.*

Since Evans himself defined the impressible condition as a magnetized state not involving sleep, he was in effect describing Quimby as a magnetic doctor at the very moment that Mrs. Glover, through her experiences with Wright and Kennedy, was making the same discovery—but with a very different response.[65] The magnetism which

Evans regarded with approval Mrs. Glover vigorously repudiated. To her it was the mental and moral opposite of the healing power of Christ.

She never went back on her high estimate of Quimby as a man, nor did she deny that he was an "advanced" thinker. The same thing might be said of Evans, for that matter. But in her final judgment, both were hopelessly entangled in animal magnetism. After 1872 she drew the line of demarcation with increasing sharpness. In the last edition of *Science and Health* she would write (p. 460):

> *When the Science of Mind was a fresh revelation to the author, she had to impart, while teaching its grand facts, the hue of spiritual ideas from her own spiritual condition, and she had to do this orally through the meagre channel afforded by language and by her manuscript circulated among the students. As former beliefs were gradually expelled from her thought, the teaching became clearer, until finally the shadow of old errors was no longer cast upon divine Science.*

One shadow that persisted for several years was over the word "mind." Although she had never used the word in the semiphysical sense Quimby gave to it, she had not yet made the sharp distinction between "mortal mind" and "divine Mind" which enabled her to capitalize and elevate the word to serve in its higher sense as one of the seven synonyms for God: Mind, Spirit, Soul, Principle, Life, Truth, Love. By 1872 she was using all the other six terms but was still referring to God as Wisdom and Intelligence rather than as Mind.[66]

Wisdom and intelligence are generally thought of as qualities of mind, or mind in action, not mind as source or cause. A person might use some degree of wisdom and intelligence in pursuing his own ends, but Christianity had always taught that God cannot be *used.* As Mrs. Glover came to see it, Quimby had made a god of his own "wisdom" and used it for his own purposes, benevolent though they were; and as Evans explained that earthly wisdom and as Kennedy practiced it, she could see no reason why it might not be used for evil as well as for good. But when wisdom and intelligence were understood as qualities of true Mind, the Mind of Christ, then they became divine instruments of good rather than personal tools of power, and, as she saw it, mental suggestion yielded to the spiritual Science of Mind.

These were profound distinctions that she was searching out, and her thought was deeply stirred. Toward the end of 1872 she wrote Sarah Bagley: "I have never since my first perceptions of

God in science gained the understanding I have this year past and been able to so sift the tares from the wheat."[67]

5

In the middle of the newspaper controversy with Wright Mrs. Glover had one day opened her Bible to Isaiah 30:8, and had read the words: "Now go, write it before them in a table, and note it in a book, that it may be for the time to come for ever and ever."[68]

According to her later notation this was in February, 1872. Her letter to the *Transcript* on the third of that month probably signified an intention rather than an actual start on the book: "I am preparing a work on Moral and Physical Science, that I shall submit to the public as soon as it is completed."

Her chief purpose in moving out to the Sims' house in Peabody a little later was to get ahead with the writing of the book. Before the final break with Kennedy on May 11 she had completed sixty pages. This was the beginning of *Science and Health*.

The uproar that accompanied Kennedy's departure put an end to further work on the book for several months. An appalling letter at this time from Wright to Mrs. Glover began:

> It is evident to me that you desire Dr. Kennedy to leave the city, and I think, also, it would be for your interest to accomplish this end. . . . He thinks that I am your greatest enemy, and favor, if any, his side. Let him continue to think so; it will do me no harm. For my part, I [would] rather a person would come out boldly and fearlessly, as you and I did, facing each other, than to sneak like a snake in the grass, spitting his poison venom into them he would slay. I have said I owe Dr. Kennedy on an old score, and the interview I had with him last evening has increased that debt, so that I am now determined, if it be your object also, as two heads are better than one, to drive him from Lynn. . . .[69]

Here was "chemicalization" with a vengeance!

The fact of their communicating must be kept secret, Wright added, "as a friend in the enemy's camp is an advantage not to be overlooked." Mrs. Glover, who saw Kennedy's overt or covert influence behind the letter, replied evenly that she hoped Wright would always do right; but as to getting Kennedy out of Lynn, she recommended that he leave that to God: "If defrauded, and set at naught, God will one day justify his children."[70]

Further consultations between Wright and Kennedy were reported to her; rumors flew back and forth; suspicions grew. From this atmosphere of petty intrigue and accusation Mrs. Glover fled once more to Tilton. From there on May 27 she wrote her eminently sane young friend Fred Ellis: "O, Mr. Ellis, do talk with me about God, about wisdom, love and Truth. I am almost lost in this hour I am so bitterly tried by such accumulating falsehoods."[71]

Her loyal students rallied to her with a passionate longing to help her. George Allen wrote her that if he met either Wright or Kennedy he would be tempted to lift them to the other side of the street: "They . . . may come out with another plot but they must beware or next time something stronger than letters will be had to condemn them."[72] And in his next letter to her he burst out indignantly, "It seems to me all wrong, *wrong*, WRONG, that you must so suffer and be brought low."[73]

In the course of time the squalid intrigues of those whom she called "absurd striplings" would sink into insignificance, but the issue involved would remain the same even when the battle was on a global scale. It was, as Mrs. Glover saw it, the ancient struggle of self-will against the will of God, and even in its banal provincial setting it was given a new dimension by the liberated power of mind.

The great religious leaders have never looked on the clash of good and evil as a matter for detached philosophical debate. Renan, a few years earlier, had written with his usual ironic sympathy of the archetypal figure who gave his life for the world:

> *Jesus . . . was not able to receive opposition with the coolness of the philosopher, who, understanding the reason of the various opinions which divide the world, finds it quite natural that all should not agree with him. One of the principal defects of the Jewish race is its harshness in controversy, and the abusive tone which it almost always infuses into it. . . . Jesus, who was exempt from almost all the defects of his race, and whose leading quality was precisely an infinite delicacy, was led in spite of himself to make use of the general style in polemics. Like John the Baptist, he employed very harsh terms against his adversaries. Of an exquisite gentleness with the simple, he was irritated at incredulity, however little aggressive. . . . A critical philosopher would have said to his disciples: Respect the opinion of others; and believe that no one is so completely right that his adversary is completely wrong. But the action of Jesus had nothing in common with the disinterested speculation of the philosopher. To know that we have touched the ideal for a moment, and have been deterred by the wickedness of a few, is a thought insup-*

portable to an ardent soul. What must it have been for the founder of a new world?[74]

For the moment Mrs. Glover turned to the old world of Tilton, but there was little rest and solace for her there. Abigail Tilton was now the great lady of the town, wealthy, conscientious as ever, but with a heart made bitter and empty by the death of her only son Albert in 1870, to be followed a few years later by that of her only daughter. Martha Pilsbury was in Kansas with her daughter Ellen and the latter's husband. George Sullivan Baker had died in 1867, Samuel Dow Baker in 1869. There was little intimacy now between Mrs. Glover and George's widow, Martha Rand Baker; and while Samuel's widow deeply loved and admired her unorthodox sister-in-law till the end of her days, she did not live in Tilton nor could they have met often during the Lynn years.

After only a short stay among the disappearing landmarks Mrs. Glover moved on to Derry, New Hampshire, for a visit of a week or two with her kindly stepmother Elizabeth Patterson Baker, who was living there with a niece. The cool feeling between the two had long been healed, and in writing to her family Mrs. Glover would send love to her "dear mother."[75] Then back she came to Lynn, probably at the end of June.

A great musical festival in Boston that month celebrated the world peace following the Franco-Prussian War, but Mrs. Glover still had battles to fight, and the delight of listening to Strauss conduct his own waltzes was not for her. In a book entitled *Scenes and Incidents in the Life of the Apostle Paul* by Albert Barnes which her stepmother had given her she marked a passage that struck a solemn note:

> *In every case of persecution, whether in science or religion, the* CAUSES *are to be sought in something peculiar in the views advanced, as bearing on received opinions and on the state of the world; but there are general principles involved, which demand only a slight modification to enable us to understand why* Christianity *has been, from the beginning, compelled to make its way through scenes of suffering.*[76]

On arriving in Lynn, Mrs. Glover was presented by her loyal students with a huge, handsome, family-style Bible "as a token of their appreciation of her valuable services to them, and as a fitting emblem of her moral worth and goodness." This was accompanied by Cruden's *Complete Concordance to the Holy Scriptures,* an invaluable adjunct to her study.

At this time also she was giving increasing thought to the apostolic age, especially to the work of Paul. In her copy of *The Early Years of Christianity* by Pressensé, she marked a passage which evidently spoke to her heart:

> *Every great truth which is to win a triumphant way must become incarnate in some one man, and derive from a living, fervent heart that passion and power which constrain and subdue. So long as it remains in the cold region of mere ideas it exercises no mighty influence over mankind. . . . This man was St. Paul, and* never had noble truth a nobler organ.

The germ of Paul's conversion and transformation, wrote Pressensé, lay in his "moral nature," and the exponent of Moral Science marked that with interest, as she also did a later statement: "He then . . . received his calling . . . but *he had not then any conception of its greatness or of its cost.*" Again, in Henry Ward Beecher's *The Life of Jesus, the Christ,* Part One, published in 1872, she marked a passage which echoed her own conviction that the age of science could both receive light from and bring insight to the age of faith:

> *But far more important it is to observe the habits of thought, the whole mental attitude of the Apostolic age, and the change which has since come upon the world. Truths remain the same; but every age has its own style of thought. Although this difference is not so great as is the difference between one language and another, it is yet so great as to require restatement or, as it were translation. . . . If merely reading the text as it was originally delivered were enough, why should there be preachers? It is the business of preachers to re-adapt truth, from age to age, to men's ever-renewing wants. . . . Has the world no lore of love, no stores of faith, no experience of joy unfolded from the original germs, which shall fit it to go back to the truths of the New Testament with a far larger understanding of their contents than they had who wrote them?*

After reading and marking Beecher's book carefully up to page 53 she evidently decided that it was little to her purpose and merely skimmed it from that point on. From her reading at this period she drew confirmation, encouragement, useful illustrations, but nothing that modified or changed her own direct insights into the Bible.[77] Every age has its own "style of thought," Beecher wrote, and her necessity was to write a book which would define that style for today as she saw and felt it in the depths of her being.

She was not able to resume work immediately on returning to

Lynn. George Barry's diary for the summer and fall shows that he spent a great deal of time house hunting for her, but it seemed impossible to find exactly the right place. The months were marked by extraordinarily frequent and severe electric storms which matched her own unsettled condition. In August she moved into pleasant rooms at a Mrs. Chadwell's on Shepard Street, but Mrs. Chadwell was talkative and there were constant "demands from the sick" and "calls to see about," so that writing was almost impossible.

On September 9 Richard Kennedy wrote Sarah Bagley an item of news which showed his continuing interest in Mrs. Glover's doings:

> *Last Friday night Mrs. G. had a gathering of her students, she has something new on foot this time, or at least she is going to make a new movement, and this is the movement. She intends throwing out great inducements to all those who gather about her in this hour of her peril. She is the centre around which all the orbits must revolve and when one sees fit to step out from her circle they loose their equipoise and are known no more among men.*[78]

With brash and callow sarcasm he went on to say: "How fearfull to think of don't you almost shake with fear and awe at her terrible sublimity. But after all I ought not to speak of her she is not worth notice." As an historical judgment this last remark ranks with Wright's prophecy that Mrs. Glover and her Science were dead and buried, but for the next two or three years each of the young men might well have assumed that her movement had been effectively stopped.

Between 1872 and 1875 she held no more classes. Moving from boardinghouse to boardinghouse, she was absorbed in the writing that now took most of her time. For a while at the end of 1872 she lived with Dorcas Rawson and her mother, where everything was "so quiet pleasant scientific and comfortable" that she had "a better opportunity to write than ever before."[79] In January she wrote, "I am very happy this winter in the performance of my labors."[80] But this Elysian state did not last, and she moved back to the Clark boardinghouse where she had stayed in 1866. For six months she lived with Putney Bancroft and his wife, for six months with the George Allens. There were shorter stays in other places, for always there seemed to be difficulties that drove her on and always the need was for greater quiet in which to write her book.

Single-minded, she moved through an age of roaring sensationalism. The election of 1872 returned Grant and his sordid administration to power. Then came the Credit Mobilier scandal, the Great Bonanza following the discovery of silver in Nevada, and the disastrous stock market crash of 1873 which plunged Lynn into five years of terrible economic hardship. Critics have assailed Mrs. Glover for not leaping to the defense of the hard-pressed Lynn workingman in the labor struggles of that period, as Lydia Pinkham did; but she was striking out, as she saw it, for rights that would free men from the far more basic tyranny of matter.

Walt Whitman, looking at the tawdry scene, was writing with stalwart faith in his "Song of the Universal":

> Forth from their masks, no matter what,
> From the huge festering trunk, from craft and guile and tears,
> Health to emerge and joy, joy universal.
>
> Out of the bulk, the morbid and the shallow,
> Out of the bad majority, the varied countless frauds of men and states,
> Electric, antiseptic yet, cleaving, suffusing all,
> Only the good is universal.

This was the American hope, but *how* was health to emerge? If experience taught anything, it was that evil could not be counted on to generate good. The origin of good must lie somewhere beyond the craft and guile of the temporal scene. Mrs. Glover, looking for it, gazed into a timeless and flawless universe.

To be sure, there were hints and flecks of her own flawed times in the book she was writing, but they were not of its essence and would disappear for the most part from later editions. When Charles Sumner died in March, 1874, her antislavery ardor was rekindled, and she wrote into her manuscript, "Charles Sumner was a great man, because of his unswerving adherence to right; he had, more than others, the true idea, and less than others, the beliefs of man." The accents of Reconstruction sound in her references to "the martyrdom of John Brown" and "the crimes of Jefferson Davis." But in the perspective of years she would relate her discovery to the age in less ephemeral terms:

> *The voice of God in behalf of the African slave was still echoing in our land, when the voice of the herald of this new crusade sounded the keynote of universal freedom, asking a fuller acknowledgment of the rights of man as a Son of God, demanding that the fetters of sin, sickness, and death be stricken from the human mind and that its freedom be won, not through human warfare, not with bayonet and blood, but through Christ's divine Science.*[81]

Though not particularly interested in woman's suffrage at that time, she invited her friend Mrs. Ellis to attend with her a lecture on the subject by Mrs. Mary Livermore, and she entered into her manuscript her own protest against the disabilities fastened on women by law. It was during this period that she finally divorced Patterson. She was inseverably wedded to an idea, and even her marriage four years later to Asa Gilbert Eddy was first of all a means of carrying on more effectively the great task to which that idea committed her.

Back in 1871 George Glover, then twenty-seven years old, had moved from Minnesota to Dakota Territory, and a year later he became a Deputy United States Marshal. Two years after that, gold was discovered in the Black Hills, and before long the lure drew Glover into the wild, disordered society of Deadwood. An unpolished but essentially upright young man, unfortunately burdened with a slatternly wife, he seemed to drift further away from his mother's life with every step. Although they were later reunited for brief periods and felt the strong ties of duty and affection throughout their lives, they both realized at last that their feet were definitively set in different paths.

So far as he could, young George Barry of Lynn took the other George's place. He felt that through the Science he had learned from Mrs. Glover he had been literally reborn. No task was too arduous to show his love for her: he ran errands, performed chores, hunted rooms, attended to her finances, and above all copied and recopied her growing manuscript. He was the first of her students to ask if he could call her "Mother," the term which Civil War soldiers had used for their nurses and which had come to be associated with woman's ministry of healing. She in turn made a will leaving him everything she had, in recognition of his services.

Many of Mrs. Eddy's later students were to think of her as a mother; and her loneliness, on which so many have commented, found comfort in the term. Yet beyond all attachments of sentiment was the deeper relation of motherhood she bore to what she saw as the true child of promise: her book. Later she would write in that book, "When a new spiritual idea is borne to earth, the prophetic Scripture of Isaiah is renewedly fulfilled: 'Unto us a child is born, . . . and his name shall be called Wonderful.' "[82]

The Christ-idea, as she saw it, was the impersonal Truth which had been lived and demonstrated by the personal Jesus but was at hand for every man, woman, and child to embody in his own thinking and living. Something of this is expressed in a book *Absolute Religion* by the Congregationalist Thomas C. Upham, published in 1873, a year after Upham's death:

> *The time is hastening, when the true Christ-spirit will become incarnated in multitudes who will walk the earth; each*

a John, a Mary, each bearing his own name, and filling his own place, but each a member of that holy family of which Jesus Christ the Son of Mary and the Son of God is the Elder Brother. When the impersonal Christ is born into the world in the fullness of his nature, the rights and sacredness of woman who is the virgin mother will be understood and acknowledged. The woman's position has already been given. Without woman, without the aid of the sympathies which are connatural to her affectionate nature, he could not and cannot be born into the world. Born of woman once he is born of woman forever.[83]

There is nothing to show that Mrs. Glover knew of Upham's book. All her concern was now given to her own.

6

There is a tradition that on fine and not too windy days Mrs. Glover would frequently walk down to the Lynn beach with a bundle of manuscript under her arm. Making her way to a cluster of rocks which pointed out to the Atlantic, she would settle herself to write for hours on end, with nothing between her and the coast of Portugal but the rolling breakers and the gull-flashing air.

"Mortal existence is an enigma," she would write later. "Every day is a mystery."[84] The ocean that stretched before her might have stood as a symbol of the mystery. Here was the flux and formlessness from which all mortal things proceed and to which they all return —the great unplumbed, unconscious elements of the human mind. Out of this watery womb, said the biologists, planetary life had crawled. Here was the ultimate enigma.

During the troubled events of 1872 Mrs. Glover had had a dream —a "vision," she called it—which she afterwards related to a student. He recorded her words as follows:

I was pitched out of a boat into the sea and went down. While going down a clear consciousness came to me that I could have no human aid and must go to the bottom. When I reached the bottom (out of the depths He called me) the view was terrific. Green slime covered it and the most horrible reptiles hissed around me, but immediately a ray of light came down through the water and there burst in upon me the most gorgeous sunlight, "and there was no more sea."[85]

This suggested, in imagery half biblical, half biological, the mystery of evil. But the strange night vision only echoed the conviction of her waking hours: in the presence of God evil simply could not exist. "Science dispels mystery," she would write later, "and explains extraordinary phenomena; but Science never removes phenomena from the domain of reason into the realm of mysticism."[86]

At first she planned to call her book *The Science of Life,* and the title brought her to a direct confrontation of the new biology that was sweeping the world. Everywhere religion either shrank in horror from an evolutionary theory that looked to the blind stirring of primeval slime for the origin of man, or tried desperately to see in this blundering and ruthless process the work of a loving God.

Mrs. Glover took a different view. She readily granted that Darwin, whose *Descent of Man* had been published in 1871, might have given a reasonable explanation of the evolution of mortal man, but this, in her view, was not the man God had made in His own image and likeness. Although the words "evolve" and "evolution" occurred in her book again and again, together with such related words as seed, germ, species, generation, progenitors, propagate, and germinate, they were used metaphorically to describe the gradual appearing in human experience of the image, the true idea, of God.

"Life is not evolved, but evolves phenomena," she wrote, and in a later edition of her book she would say even more explicitly: "Spiritual evolution alone is worthy of the exercise of divine power."[87] It was the vision of Life as Spirit that had come to her in 1866, and all that had evolved in her thinking since then sprang from that germinal conviction.

Pasteur had announced in 1864, "Life is a germ and a germ is Life," but this was the life that ended in disease and death. Five years later young Friedrich Miescher had discovered that curious nucleic acid which, as DNA, is today hailed as the veritable stuff of life; but the man revealed through Christ was certainly not the product or the victim of a genetic code. To this basic distinction Mrs. Glover came back again and again. In a thousand different ways she emphasized the need for bringing to light the "true" man in place of the caricature presented by the senses.

This did not make for easy reading. In the preface to her book (p. 5) she wrote that owing to her explanations' "constantly vibrating between the same points" there must necessarily be "an irksome repetition of words," and that beauty of language must give place "to close analysis, and unembellished thought." The book made strong demands on the reader's seriousness of purpose.

At the end of *Democratic Vistas* Whitman had recently set forth what he called a new theory of literary composition:

> *Books are to be called for, and supplied, on the assumption that the process of reading is not a half sleep, but, in highest*

sense, an exercise, a gymnast's struggle; that the reader is to do something for himself, must be on the alert, must himself or herself construct indeed the poem, argument, history, metaphysical essay—the text furnishing the hints, the clue, the start or framework. Not the book needs so much to be the complete thing, but the reader of the book does. That were to make a nation of supple and athletic minds, well-trained, intuitive. . . .

Mrs. Glover apparently expected few such readers to begin with, and she commented realistically that "little justice is done metaphysics by a utilitarian people where the race is to the swift" (p. 275).

It was impossible to race through her own prose, with its constant going over the same ground in order to force the reluctant mind to come to grips with her basic propositions. "Because science reverses the positions of personal sense," she wrote, "human reason acts slowly in accepting it, contesting every inch of ground it occupies, while error, self-complacent and applauded, sneers at the slow marches of Truth" (p. 327). Despite the intellectual demands of Science, the person with a certain inner simplicity might first respond to it: "The honest fishermen who had little to leave, were those who left all for Christ, Truth, until progress compelled the change, and the learned Paul stepped forth for Truth" (p. 297).

There was a certain sardonic quality in some of the writing, as when she commented (p. 264) that "hybrids are rapes upon nature," or observed (p. 63), "Surely the 'tree of knowledge' produced a pigmy race of 'gods.' " Much of it had a sort of common-sense vigor: "Truth is practical, not theoretical, and we shall never have more until we practice what we already have" (p. 60). "Malice pursues the reformer through every avenue of society, and the evil that persecutes, and the pride that refuses aid, binds the hands and feet of philanthropy, and then calls for stronger proofs of active limbs" (p. 234). At its best the writing had a simple directness:

But is there not a smoother and broader path to harmony or heaven; and cannot Christianity be coupled with worldly peace and prosperity? The very nature of it is peace and blessedness, but its joys and triumphs are not earthly, they are passing away from matter to Spirit. By this we do not mean death, nor a sudden ecstasy; but the gradual fading out of material things, of earthly desires, possessions and pleasures, and the coming in of purity, Truth and immortality. The demands of personal sense will grow less, the appetite become simple, pride, malice and all sin yield to meekness, mercy and Love, until finally the belief of Life in matter yields to the consciousness that Life is Spirit, and Spirit, God (p. 146).

In contrast with a passage such as this, some of the writing seems to be a rush and tumble of words, as though the writer's thoughts were flooding ahead of her pen. Sentences are chaotic, punctuation erratic, quotations inexact, meanings obscure. Despite the fact that the entire manuscript was rewritten and rearranged three times during 1873–74, each time being copied out afresh by George Barry, grammatical and literary niceties were notably missing from portions of it. One reason was that the author's thinking was advancing by leaps and bounds even as she wrote; everything must be sacrificed to her developing ideas. The book was a textbook for living and was implicated in living.[88]

A letter which Mrs. Glover received from George Barry while she was writing her book illustrates the necessity that faced her.[89] Barry was on vacation in Maine. He wrote of stopping first with an old coast pilot, an honest, plain-spoken man, who later took him across the Sheepscott River to Westport, with the wind tipping the craft on her side and showering them with spray. "Your boy looked like an old salt," he wrote her, "with his Sou' Wester and heavy overcoat on."

Now he was stopping with a tough old farmer, "a fearful looking object" with "black hair and thick coarse black beard," a perfect replica of "the engravings of the giants which Jack the Giant Killer slew." Ignorant, profane, and sometimes roaring drunk though the man might be, Barry told Mrs. Glover that he enjoyed being there, and added a little primly, "One can learn even from such an illiterate specimen."

Here was a figure who might stand as a symbol of the particularity and contrariety of human life, its ornery, crotchety, idiosyncratic variety. Here was George Glover's Deadwood and, *mutatis mutandis*, London, Tiflis, Shanghai. Any author who hoped for universality must face toward this world, not flinch away from it, and Barry's letter showed his confidence that Mrs. Glover, immersed in authorship, still maintained her relish for the salt and savor of human life. Her book might announce the divine origin of man, but she intended it to speak to the human condition.

Within a century it would have to meet the test of speaking in Russian and Portuguese and Dutch, to congregations in Bombay and Warsaw and Buenos Aires, to student organizations in Oxford and Witwatersrand and the Braunschweige Technische Hochschule, to children in Dallas and Winnipeg, Stockholm and Jakarta, to business-men and housewives and farmers and actresses and deep-sea divers and research chemists.[90]

The book included a minimum of the vividly local and temporal. A scientific textbook, as Mrs. Glover intended it to be, must necessarily generalize, using a basic, technical vocabulary which covers the largest possible number of concrete instances. At the same time any work of Christian inspiration draws lifeblood from the enormous, rich, historical concreteness of the Bible. The Christ had been lived once in a particular corner of history by a particular person, and in order fully to transform human life, Science must be fully Christian.

The term "Moral Science" began to disappear from her vocabulary, and in the final draft of her book before it went to the printer the term "Christian Science" appeared in several places. At first she wrote it "Christian science," but in the last words of the last chapter, a chapter entitled "Healing the Sick," it took its present form:

> *Some of our present readers may wish to tone down the radical points in this work, others to cast them overboard, yet science will reproduce itself, and as mind changes base from matter to Spirit, there will be severe chemicalization. Truth cannot be lost; if not admitted to-day in its fullness, the error that shuts it out will occasion such discord in sickness, sin, etc., that future years will point it out, and restore at length the fair proportions and radical claims of Christian Science.*

The first or second draft of the book had been offered to a publisher in the fall of 1873 and had been rejected. After months of rewriting and recopying it was offered a second time in the spring of 1874 and was again rejected. Further rewriting followed.

Still entitled *The Science of Life* and still unpublished, it was copyrighted on July 7, of that year.[91] A week later Mrs. Glover found a printer, W. F. Brown of Boston, who was willing to bring it out if she would pay all costs.[92] On September 5 the manuscript was put into his hands. It was not destined to appear in print until more than a year later. Bogged in unfamiliarity, the printer undertook to make various small changes to improve the book, thereby altering Mrs. Glover's meaning fatally at times. This fact, together with innumerable carelessnesses in the printing, made proofreading a horror for her; at the same time her own developing thought made her want to revise as well as correct the proofs, and that did not make the printer's task any easier.

At some point the work stopped altogether for several months for unknown reasons, but Mrs. Glover later came to see the delay as providential, for it gave her a chance to incorporate in the book certain developing insights she considered crucial.

At another point she discovered that a book entitled *The Science of Life* was already in print and that she must change her title. For several weeks she waited, and then the title came: *Science and Health.*

It was an unlikely name for a textbook of metaphysics, but then there had never before been a metaphysic that *healed*. Several months later Dorcas Rawson brought her a copy of the Wyclif Bible in which the phrase in Luke 1:77 rendered "knowledge of salvation" in the King James Version is given as "science and health."[93] The twentieth century would emphasize the etymological relation between such words as heal, hale, whole, and holy, and it seems evident that for Mrs. Glover the word health meant spiritual wholeness.

The title, like everything else in Mrs. Glover's book, was *sui generis*. She herself later wrote of her works as "hopelessly original."[94] When Putney Bancroft in after years heard people question whether *Science and Health* had indeed originated with her, he would reply impatiently, "I heard her talk it before it was ever written," and in 1920 he wrote, "I do not claim Mrs. Glover was without faults, but Plagiarism was not one of them."[95] She seldom quoted, he added, except from the Bible, and the first edition of *Science and Health* bears him out.

Looking back on this period, Mrs. Eddy would write: "I had no time to borrow from Authors. Such a flood tide of truth was lifted upon me at times it was overwhelming and I have drawn quick breath as my pen flew on, feeling as it were submerged in the transfiguration of spiritual ideas."[96] Once she was convinced that she must write the book, nothing else counted. As Bancroft feelingly summed it up:

> When convinced of the necessity of promulgating that which had been made known to her, in book form, Mrs. Eddy secluded herself for over three years for that purpose, depriving herself of all but the bare necessities of life as she wrote. I have known her when nearly crushed with sorrow, but she wrote on. I have known her when friend after friend deserted her, but she wrote on. I have seen student after student bring ridicule and reproach upon her, but still she wrote on.

And now she was near the fruition of her labor.

7

At the beginning of 1875 Mrs. Glover was living in the boarding-house of the Amos Scribners on Broad Street, Lynn, but she engaged an agent to find her a house in Cambridge. It seemed to her that the intellectual atmosphere of that community would provide better soil for her teaching than Lynn.

At her urging, Putney Bancroft had opened an office in Cambridge and announced himself, with the extraordinary freedom of that day, as "S. P. Bancroft. Scientific Physician. Gives no Medicine." Circulars were sent to Harvard professors and prominent clergymen in the community, but none of them responded. Plans were made for Mrs. Glover to lecture there, but they fell through. The house agent, one Edward Hitchings of Lynn, failed to find her a Cambridge residence because, Bancroft explained, he wanted to marry Mrs. Glover and therefore was determined to keep her in Lynn.

By the end of January Bancroft abandoned his venture, discouraged by the poor response to his circulars. Mrs. Glover, who had sent him several patients and written him letters of encouragement and instruction during the two-month episode, learned from Richard Kennedy's landlord that Kennedy had been going frequently to Cambridgeport of late, and she concluded that he had been undermining Bancroft's work. She felt, too, that Putney should have located closer to Harvard.

Yet even if he had camped just outside the Harvard Yard, armed with formidable intellectual credentials, the atmosphere of the university under its new president, Charles W. Eliot, would hardly have been hospitable to a system which called in question the accepted philosophic assumptions of natural science. Lynn, provincial and self-absorbed, was destined to be Mrs. Glover's headquarters for seven more years, but they were not to be years of continued wandering.

One day in March, looking across the road from the Scribners', she saw a For Sale sign in the window of No. 8 Broad Street. By the end of the month she had bought the unpretentious little house for $5,650. It was necessary for her to rent most of it to tenants, retaining only the front parlor of the second floor for her personal use and a tiny bedroom on the third floor.[97] All the light and ventilation in this attic room came through a skylight in the sloping roof; but it was a quiet haven for her and on the wall she hung a framed text, "Thou shalt have no other gods before me," which opened on wider vistas than the skylight disclosed.

Now she could hold another class, and within a fortnight a little group of four was meeting regularly in her parlor. One of the four was Daniel Harrison Spofford, whose wife had studied with her in 1870. The Spoffords had returned to Lynn a short while before. Mrs. Spofford, now under the domination of Kennedy, had refused to share with her husband what she had learned from Mrs. Glover, but he had studied the latter's manuscripts and had grasped enough by himself to begin healing.[98] Hearing of this, Mrs. Glover had written him on February 1, "I tender you a cordial welcome to join my next class including instructions in healing without manipulation, 'without money and without price.' "[99]

Spofford was a gentle, idealistic person, then about thirty-three years old. He had had to work hard since boyhood but had educated himself and was gifted with a reflective and winning temperament. Something of this shows in the letter he wrote Mrs. Glover one night during the course:

> *Many, many times each day I ask myself, do we students realize what is held out for our possession. . . . Do we realize that we are moving to a position which while here, if we are faithful, brings us from the world probably nothing but trials and rebuffs? but that in ages to come these meetings in the upper chamber will have passed into history and that we will be blessed or cursed according to our fidelity in the preserving of Truth, until time shall be at an end. . . . O that I might be worthy; that I might have lived the life of righteousness to enable me to give to you, be it ever so little, of that living water which you must so desire to drink. . . .*[100]

It was this attitude that was to make Spofford Mrs. Glover's most outstanding student and most reliable helper until Asa Gilbert Eddy should come along a year later. Before long the advertisement of "Dr. Spofford, Scientific Physician," was appearing regularly in the *Lynn Transcript,* and several newspaper accounts of striking healings accomplished by him bore witness to his success. Now at least one student stood before the public as a full-time demonstrator of the new Science.

Toward the end of May Mrs. Glover gave a public lecture on "Christ Healing the Sick." It was reported by a Lynn paper as "well written and well delivered," but it was delivered only to "a select few."[101] Several days later at a meeting at 8 Broad Street Dorcas Rawson, George Barry, and Daniel Spofford were appointed a committee "to ascertain what a suitable hall could be rented for, and the amount which could be raised weekly toward sustaining Mrs. Glover as teacher and instructor for one year."[102]

A week later, on June 1, the committee reported, and the little group of students present drew up the following resolutions:

> *Whereas, in times not long past, the Science of Healing, new to the age, and far in advance of all other modes, was introduced into the city of Lynn by its discoverer, a certain lady, Mary Baker Glover,*
>
> *And, whereas, many friends spread the good tidings throughout the place, and bore aloft the standard of life and truth which had declared freedom to many manacled with the bonds of disease or error,*

And whereas, by the wilful and wicked disobedience of an individual who has no name in Love, Wisdom or Truth, the light was obscured by clouds of misinterpretation and mists of mystery, so that God's work was hidden from the world and derided in the streets,

Now, therefore, we students and advocates of this moral science called the Science of Life . . . have arranged with the said Mary Baker Glover, to preach to us or direct our meetings on the Sabbath of each week, and hereby covenant with one another, and by these presents do publish and proclaim that we have agreed and do each and all agree to pay weekly, for one year, beginning with the sixth day of June, A.D., 1875, to a treasurer chosen by at least seven students the amount set opposite our names, provided nevertheless the moneys paid by us shall be expended for no other purpose or purposes than the maintenance of said Mary Baker Glover as teacher or instructor, than the renting of a suitable hall and other incidental expenses, and our signatures shall be a full and sufficient guarantee of our faithful performance of this contract.

Signed	
Elizabeth M. Newhall	*$1.50*
Dan'l H. Spofford	*2.00*
George H. Allen	*2.00*
Dorcas B. Rawson	*1.00*
Asa T. N. Macdonald	*.50*
George W. Barry	*2.00*
S. P. Bancroft	*.50*
Miranda R. Rice	*.50*[103]

At the meeting a week later it was determined that they should be called Christian Scientists, that George Allen should be president of the group, George Barry secretary, and Daniel Spofford treasurer.

It was at this time that Mrs. Glover withdrew her membership from the Tilton Congregational Church to which she had belonged since the summer, thirty-seven years before, when she had wrestled spiritually with the Reverend Enoch Corser over the question of predestination. Gradually the ties of orthodoxy had loosened. After returning to Lynn in 1870 she had attended for several years the Unitarian Church of the Reverend Samuel B. Stewart but had not joined it. Now, as she took the first tentative step toward a church of her own, it was clear that she must sever the ecclesiastical links of the past.

The first Sunday meeting at Good Templars' Hall was held on

June 6, and other meetings followed on the four successive Sundays. Sometimes they were characterized in the paper as meetings, sometimes as services, and Mrs. Glover was variously described as preaching and as lecturing. The average attendance was about one hundred. After a few Sundays, "free thinkers" and spiritualists began to swell the numbers and to heckle Mrs. Glover in the question period which she permitted after her address. Putney Bancroft, who led the singing while his wife played the melodeon, later wrote: "On such occasions we were very proud of our teacher. . . . Calm and undisturbed, with not a particle of hysteria, she would answer question after question in a manner which, if it did not convince, never failed to satisfy the inquirer of her sincerity."

The last of these meetings, on July 4, was devoted to the subject of "Mesmerism and Moral Science Contrasted"—for the term "Christian Science" had not yet completely replaced the earlier designation. The following Saturday the *Transcript* carried a notice headed CHRISTIAN SCIENTISTS, announcing that services would be discontinued "during the warm season." Actually it was several years before public services were resumed and again advertised. The time had evidently not come to found a church.

On several occasions Mrs. Glover had said to students, "Some day I shall have a church of my own!" They thought, wrote Bancroft many years later, of a small Lynn church with a settled congregation; she thought in terms of a Church embracing the world. Yet it was not easy to envisage a Church founded on a Science, though Emerson had written in *The Conduct of Life:*

> There will be a new church founded on moral science, at first cold and naked, a babe in the manger again, the algebra and mathematics of ethical law, the church of men to come, without shawms, or psaltry, or sackbut; but it will have heaven and earth for its beams and rafters; science for symbol and illustration; it will fast enough gather beauty, music, picture, poetry. . . .

At that period Mrs. Glover still half hoped the traditional churches would accept Christian Science, but she also recognized their vested interest in the past. Her distrust of church organization as she had known it found expression in the first edition of *Science and Health:*

> The mistake the disciples of Jesus made to found religious organizations and church rites, if indeed they did this, was one the Master did not make. . . . No time was lost by our Master in organizations, rites, and ceremonies, or in proselyting for cer-

tain forms of belief: members of his church must answer to themselves, in the secret sanctuary of Soul, questions of the most solemn import.

Yet her references even at that time to a church of her own showed her equal distrust of a wholly individualistic approach to Science. Her greatest struggles in the thirty-five years ahead of her arose from what she increasingly came to see as the necessity of marrying church organization with individual demonstration.

More and more she recognized that only Christian discipline could relate her vision of absolute Science to the manifold needs of men. At first she seemed to hesitate between forming a scientific society and a church, and within the next few years she would actually form both the Christian Scientist Association and the Church of Christ, Scientist; but education and worship were finally to be fused in a unique way, symbolized by the "Lesson-Sermon" studied by individual Christian Scientists on weekdays and read at church services on Sunday. Thus *Science and Health* would come to be regarded as both a scientific and a denominational textbook, as a manual of healing and a key to the Scriptures, as reasoned argument and revealed truth.

First, however, it had to be published, and in the spring of 1875 came that delay of several months during which Mrs. Glover did not hear from the printers and during which she became convinced that she must add a further account of mesmerism as she had thus far observed it. At this time she associated it solely with physical manipulation as practiced by Kennedy and had not extended the term to cover the vast range of mental suggestion which she later denounced as mesmeric in nature.

The new section was inserted into the last chapter on "Healing the Sick." Interestingly enough, this chapter in manuscript had been lent by her to one Prescott, in whose house Kennedy lived. While in Prescott's possession it was stolen, and she was convinced that Kennedy was the culprit.[104]

Nevertheless, despite all delays and harassments, the months before the publication of *Science and Health* were happy ones. Bancroft later wrote:

> *I consider the summer of 1875 the most harmonious period of the twelve years from 1870 to 1882. . . . I never knew her so continuously happy in her work. Although she was writing, teaching and preaching, and occasionally treating some severe case beyond a student's ability to reach, her physical and mental vigor seemed to be augmented rather than depleted.*

In August she held another small class which included two students from Boston, one from Pennsylvania, Bancroft's brother, Henry, and a young woman named Florence Cheney. Mrs. Glover, convinced that Miss Cheney would make an excellent wife for George Barry, genially conspired to throw the two young people together and achieved the desired result. In a letter which mentioned Barry's accompanying her home from Mrs. Glover's the evening before, the young lady wrote:

> *I enjoyed one of the pleasant evenings that I must ever remember as among the happiest, and most profitable I have known. For truly, dear Mrs. Glover, you call out all the good in my nature; not alone, I think, by your teachings, but your very presence inspires one with a respect and love for the pure, the beautiful & true; making one more fully realize the blessed privilege of living a noble, unselfish life.*
>
> *Every day am I thankful for the good fortune that led me to you and for the interest you have shown in me, an entire stranger.*[105]

An example of Mrs. Glover's care for her students' work, as mentioned by Bancroft, occurs in the reminiscence of Mrs. Ethel B. West, who in 1875 was a small girl in Lynn.[106] Spofford boarded with her grandmother, with whom she also lived. One day she fell down a deep stairwell at school and was carried home "gravely injured." Spofford offered to heal her, and in a short time she was so improved that she thought it would be "smart" to show herself at school. The horror and alarm expressed there caused a relapse, and she was brought home again unconscious.

This time Spofford was unable to bring about any change and he went off to enlist Mrs. Glover's aid. No sooner was Mrs. Glover informed than the girl was instantly and completely healed. Although both she and her family remained strongly prejudiced against their benefactor because of what they heard about Christian Science at that time, the incident lay imbedded in the girl's memory, and thirty years later she became a Christian Scientist.

Numerous disquieting rumors about Mrs. Glover flew around Lynn in those days, and many a good citizen felt bitter hostility to what he supposed her to be. Others stared with blank curiosity at the sign that appeared outside 8 Broad Street, "Mary B. Glover's Christian Scientists' Home," with an open Bible pictured on one side, a cross and a crown on the other. Many shared the sentiment of Putney Bancroft's uncle, a deacon of the Congregational Church: "My boy, you will be ruined for life; it is the work of the devil."

Yet the days moved steadily toward the event that was to be the justification for all Mrs. Glover's struggles. In later years she would speak several times of the nine years of hard labor that brought her to the point represented by the first edition of *Science and Health,* and in one place she wrote:

> *From 1866 to 1875, I myself was learning Christian Science step by step—gradually developing the wonderful germ I had discovered as an honest investigator. It was practical evolution. I was reaching by experience and demonstration the scientific proof, and scientific statement, of what I had already discovered. My later teachings and writings show the steady growth of my spiritual ideal during those pregnant years.*[107]

Finally, on October 30, the book was published,[108] and Mrs. Glover's discovery for the first time stood out for the general public to see. Years later when Christian Science had become a worldwide movement, she spoke of the notable and noble men and women she could call as witnesses to it but added that she preferred to call attention instead to "my best witness, my babe! the new-born of Truth, *Science and Health with Key to the Scriptures*—that will forever testify of itself, and its mother."[109]

Then, as now, the book seemed a farrago of contradictions to many casual readers. Others felt like her nephew George W. Baker, who wrote on the flyleaf of a presentation copy that "not being quite up to the standard of goodness, and belief, he couldn't make head or tail of it, and so did not derive any advantage, physically, from an honest, desperate, and futile endeavor to read it through"—though various marked passages in the book show that he was struck by some of its concrete moral teachings.[110] Then there was the cousin who wrote her a letter full of patronizing masculine badinage, recalling her as the gay and beautiful young girl he had known years before but expostulating that she had now got into pretty deep waters.[111] And there was stony silence from her sisters.

Yet other readers caught a glimpse of something more. A reviewer in the *Boston Investigator* wrote:

> *We shall watch with keen interest the results of "Science and Health." The Work shows how the body can be cured and how a better state of Christianity can be introduced (which is certainly very desirable). It likewise has a hard thrust at Spiritualism, and taken altogether is a very rare book.*

The *Christian Advocate* of Buffalo went further:

> *This book is a metaphysical treatise showing how disease is caused and cured by mind. The book is certainly original and contains much that will do good. The reader will find this work*

not influenced by superstition or pride, but striking out boldly and alone. Full of Philanthropy, Self-Sacrifice and Love toward God and Man.

Most encouraging of all to Mrs. Glover was the letter she received early in the new year from the Concord philosopher, Amos Bronson Alcott. On January 17 Alcott wrote her:

The sacred truths which you announce, sustained by facts of the Immortal Life, give to your work the seal of inspiration—reaffirm in modern phrase the Christian revelations. In times like ours, so sunk in sensualism, I hail with joy any voice speaking an assured word for God and Immortality. And my joy is heightened the more when I find the blessed words are of woman's divinings.[112]

Here at last was recognition from the world beyond Lynn, the world where preoccupied hosts fought huge, ambiguous, shadowy battles. The time for thinkers had come, *Science and Health* announced. Well, let the thinkers come; this was the merest beginning. Alcott's seraphic ideals would dissolve into mist before the onslaught of events in the coming century, but *Science and Health* proclaimed a vision that measured itself against disaster, a faith that undertook to stand or fall by its grasp of the concrete—by its healing of the irremediable, its deliverance from the unendurable. One might almost say it *invited* the twentieth century.

Appendices
Notes
Index

1821	July 16	Mary Morse Baker born in Bow, rural township adjoining Concord, New Hampshire.
1834	Spring	Probably professes faith at "protracted meeting" (revival) at Old North Church, Concord.
		Albert Baker (brother) is graduated from Dartmouth College.
1835	January 27	Mary Ann Baker (grandmother) dies.
	Summer	George Sullivan Baker (brother) leaves Bow.
1836	January	Baker family moves to farm 22 miles northward and one mile from Sanbornton Bridge (renamed Tilton in 1869), N.H.
1838	July 26	Joins Congregational (Trinitarian) Church at Sanbornton Bridge.
1841	October 17	Albert Baker (born Feb. 5, 1810) dies.
1842		Attends Sanbornton Academy at Sanbornton Bridge. (Probably attended Woodman Sanbornton Academy and possibly Holmes Academy at Plymouth before then.)
1843	December 10	Marries George Washington Glover.
	December 25	Glovers leave Boston for Charleston, South Carolina.
1844	c. February 1	Glovers move to Wilmington, North Carolina.
	June 27	Husband dies. She returns to Sanbornton Bridge farm three weeks later.
	September 12	Son, George Washington Glover II, born.
1846		Runs experimental primary school.

1849	November 21	Mother, Abigail Ambrose Baker, dies. Shortly after, moves with father, Mark Baker, and son into new house in Sanbornton Bridge.
1850	December 5	Father remarries. She goes to live with sister, Abigail Tilton, and family.
1851	May	Son George goes to live with Mahala and Russell Cheney in North Groton, N.H.
1853	June 21	Marries Dr. Daniel Patterson and moves to Franklin, N.H.
1855	March	Pattersons move to North Groton.
1856	April	Son George, now nearing 12 years of age, taken to Minnesota by Cheneys. She hears from son in 1861 but does not see him again until 1879.
1860	March 19	Pattersons move to Rumney, N.H.
1862	March	Patterson captured by Confederate soldiers, escapes in autumn, returning just before Christmas.
	June	She goes to Dr. W. T. Vail's Hydropathic Institute at Hill, N.H., for treatment.
	October 10	Arrives in Portland, Maine, for treatment from Phineas P. Quimby, is greatly benefited for a time and spends rest of year there.
1863	January	Returns with Patterson to Sanbornton Bridge.
	July	Goes to Portland and is there, off and on, during next nine months.
1864	March	Goes to Warren, Maine, for two-month visit with Miss Mary Ann Jarvis and sister.
	June	Rejoins husband in Lynn, Massachusetts.
	Autumn	Visits Mrs. Sarah Crosby in Albion, Maine, for few months, then returns to Lynn with husband.
1865	October 6	Mark Baker dies at Sanbornton Bridge.
1866	January 16	Quimby dies at Belfast, Maine.
	February 1	She is seriously injured by fall on ice in Lynn.

	February 4	Healing occurs in home at 23 Paradise Road, Swampscott, adjoining Lynn.
	March	Pattersons move to house of Reverend Philemon R. Russell in Lynn, where Patterson temporarily deserts her.
	Summer	Briefly reunited, they move to Clark boardinghouse on Summer Street, Lynn, where Patterson finally leaves her. She meets Hiram and Mary Crafts, fellow boarders.
	Autumn	Moves several times, spending several weeks with the Ellises in Swampscott, and finally returns to Clark boardinghouse. Begins notes on Genesis.
	November	Moves to East Stoughton (now Avon), Mass., lives with the Crafts on Pond Street, and teaches Hiram Crafts.
1867	April	Moves with Crafts household to Taunton, Mass., at 8086 Main St.
	Summer	Visits Sanbornton Bridge. Heals niece, Ellen Pilsbury.
	Autumn	Moves to Amesbury, Mass., and stays at home of Websters. Meets Richard Kennedy.
1868	c. June	Moves to home of Sarah Bagley, 227 Main St., Amesbury.
	Summer	Meets John Greenleaf Whittier.
	September	Moves to home of Wentworths on Center St., Stoughton, Mass.
1869		Completes notes on Genesis and several versions of "The Science of Man" while at Wentworths.
1870	c. February	Returns to Miss Bagley's at Amesbury.
	May	Moves to Lynn, headquarters for next 12 years.
	June	Establishes teacher-practitioner partnership with Richard Kennedy in house at S. Common and Shepard Streets.

	August	Holds first class, using "The Science of Man" (copyrighted that year) as textbook.
	December	Holds second class, which includes George Allen, George Barry, S. P. Bancroft, Dorcas Rawson, and Miranda Rice.
1872	January	Wallace W. Wright attacks her teachings in *Lynn Transcript*.
	February	Controversy in *Transcript* continued. She begins writing *Science and Health*.
	May 11	Breaks with Kennedy.
	July	After visit to Tilton, returns to Lynn and begins two-year period of moving from house to house while writing *Science and Health*.
1873	November 4	Obtains divorce from Patterson in Salem, Mass., court.
1874	September 5	Manuscript delivered to printer.
1875	March	Buys house at 8 Broad St., Lynn. Afterwards writes additional section for last chapter of *Science and Health*.
	June 1	Eight students band together to support Sunday services led by her at Good Templars Hall. Discontinued after five weeks.
	June 13	Obtains letter of dismissal from Congregational Church, Tilton, after 37-year membership.
	October 30	*Science and Health* published in first edition of one thousand copies.
1876–1910		Devotes rest of life to founding of Christian Science.

The system of "New Thought" which emerged in the 1880's is often traced to Quimby as its chief fountainhead. This is probably correct if it is understood to mean Quimby as interpreted by Julius A. Dresser.

Dresser, a young man of some intellectual ability and religious feeling, became acquainted with Quimby in 1860 and a member of the Quimby coterie in the early months of 1862. He brought to the association an intellectual good order which Quimby lacked but an inability to learn how to heal.

As a ready writer entering upon a career as a newspaperman he might have been expected to write a good deal for the press about Quimby, as others already were doing. The interesting fact is that with one possible (and significant) exception he wrote nothing on the subject until 1883, after he had studied with Mrs. Eddy's student Edward J. Arens, and again in 1887, after he had studied with Mrs. Eddy herself.

Because of this, the one possible exception becomes of interest. A letter in the *Portland Advertiser* on March 22, 1862, entitled "Outline of New Principles in Healing Disease" is signed simply "D." It is the one writing of that period which brings a degree of order out of the Quimby chaos. It stresses the idealistic rather than the materialistic elements in Quimby's thought and, except for a reference to the fact that Quimby heals the sick "by a full knowledge of their feelings, which he takes upon himself," it ignores the crucial but intellectually equivocal role of clairvoyance in the Quimby charisma. It is an incipient attempt to make a coherent philosophy out of an empirical psychology and as such it has a claim to be considered the forerunner of the New Thought philosophy of mind over matter.

The significant parts of the lengthy letter follow:

> Dr. Quimby claims that he cures disease under the guidance of a principle, which being understood must set free the sick. Consequently his system so far as he carries it, is an intelligible one, and his opinions in regard to disease, entirely new and

original. Instead of treating the body as an intelligent organization, with independent life, he finds the life and intelligence in
the man, who occupies it. His process reverses their relation to
each other, making the visible form, the shadow, while the
everlasting substance is not seen in the natural world. His theory
separates them and brings to light the pure intelligence of man,
letting it work in the world of matter as master and not slave.
From this stand-point he advocates the cause of the sick against
the whole world, for everybody believes that the body is diseased
and the mind or real man is not affected. He says the voice of
the sick is not heard in the world; it is what the well say about
them that gets the public ear, while they, passive and helpless,
are completely controlled by the influences coming from the
knowledge of those whose duty it is to cure them. He also says
the well, know nothing of themselves about the sick, and consequently their judgment is uncharitable and fallible. It is his
duty to get the sick free from the charges made against them,
and this he does by a full knowledge of their feelings, which he
takes upon himself. These feelings which are the evidences
against them, he explains in a way that destroys what they prove
to the world. Statements made by him to the sick have a strange
sound, and need an explanation to render them intelligible; for
he often tells a person he has no disease when nothing is plainer
than that he has. Here comes in his peculiar belief, which to him
is knowledge. He does not trace disease to a hidden or mysterious source, or no source at all, neither does he pay any respect to it as though it came from God. He refers it directly to
man himself, under the dominion of errors invented by man,
and believed in as true and of independent origin, and to cure
it intelligently, and in the most beneficial way to mankind, is to
destroy the error on which it is based. Then he lifts disease
from its pretended basis of truth, and places it on its proper
basis of error, consequently in his reasoning, disease is not the
ruling power, and he does not admit it, except as a deception.
In demonstrating this position, he comes in contact with prejudices which are as strong as our existence, and in many cases
meets with opposition from the strong and bitter religious prejudices, which are so common in the community. He cannot admit a disease and then cure it any more than a court can pro-
nounce judgment on a criminal without trying the case. Dr.
Quimby gives the sick the same chance for their health as an
indicted supposed criminal has for his life, and if he, by analys-
ing his symptoms, can destroy the evidence of disease, then the

patient is cured. In this, he follows no track before trodden by men, and ventures into a field entirely unknown to the regular physicians, and hence he cannot be ranked with any association of practitioners. . . .

Then when it is asked by what power Dr. Quimby cures disease, it is answered, by the knowledge of the wisdom that gives man the control of his body, and the understanding of which produces health and happiness. Just according as man walks in the knowledge of this truth, he is wise and happy; but any deviation from it, admitting matter superior to man, creates an error, which really imprisons him.

Ages of education have condensed these errors into living facts, and now nothing is plainer to those who still are young, than the inevitable approach of many sorrows and trials. To free the burden of life of one of its greatest evils and prepare the way for greater works of the same plan, is the effect of the establishment of Dr. Quimby's system. In a brief communication like this, it is impossible to do justice to a subject like this. Time will prove that his cures are wrought under a *principle,* that *must* work out the redemption of mankind from disease; and his system will be found based on eternal principles, and as capable of being explained and understood, as the science of astronomy, or music.

The reason for not assigning this letter definitely to Julius Dresser is that when his widow published her book *The Philosophy of P. P. Quimby* in 1895 she attributed the letter to Emma Ware. This, however, cannot safely be taken as conclusive evidence that Julius Dresser did not write it, for the two ladies may have decided that the attribution to Miss Ware was called for under the circumstances then prevailing.

By 1895 the Quimby controversy was in full swing, and it was an embarrassment to the Quimby proponents that so much had to rest on the word of the two Dressers. In an 1887 lecture Julius Dresser had stated that he and his wife had owed their lives to Quimby for almost twenty-seven years and that "thousands of others could make a similar testimony," but of those "thousands" only Dresser had come forward publicly. His son Horatio, who was born the day after Quimby's death and who later became the outstanding champion of Quimbyism, frequently quotes in his writings "a Quimby patient" or "a former student of Dr. Quimby's," but upon investigation these ambiguous references usually seem to indicate his father or mother.

If Miss Ware did write the March, 1862, letter in the *Advertiser* signed "D," she would seem to have been the most intelligent and articulate of the little group, and she might consequently have been expected to play a larger role in the activity in the 1880's leading to the formation of New Thought. Yet on January 9, 1883, she wrote Edward J. Arens (A.):

> Now that his [Quimby's] voice is hushed and his presence vanished, my own confidence in the knowledge I desired from him & my want of success in making that knowledge practicable or even intelligible is such, that I do not feel as though I was the one to do any sort of justice to him. . . . You who can heal, must have a more powerful grasp upon truth than I who cannot change the human system. Dr. Quimby could act upon flesh & blood—could dissolve matter, could feel in himself the torments of the sick, he was clairvoyant, he understood the supernatural.

This does not sound much like the writer of the March 22, 1862, letter in the *Advertiser*. Like so much else connected with the Portland healer, that letter ends in a question mark.

APPENDIX C: **Warren Felt Evans**

Before 1872 Evans had published several books. Two early ones on Swedenborgianism entitled *The Celestial Dawn* and *The New Age and its Messenger* were written just before and just after his visit to Quimby. They were filled with familiar yet freshly felt Swedenborgian doctrines: "Heaven is a spiritual state . . . the conscious indwelling of God in the soul." "Though heaven is not a material world, but a spiritual realm, it is far more *real* than this earth. . . . The things of earth are only shadows projected from heavenly substances." "Nature is a transcript of the divine Mind."

Swedenborg's teaching, "the science of sciences," is said to show the exact correspondence between earthly things and heavenly truths as unfolded in the Bible. The divine Mind, however, is "deeply vailed" in the letter of the Scriptures. "It is only by the divine Comforter, that we can gain anything more than a mere surface knowledge of the Gospel." The Old Testament, writes Evans, was the age of the Father, the New Testament the age of the Son: "The next, which we doubt not has had its birth, will be the age of the Holy Spirit, when Christ will come as the Comforter, the Paraclete."

In these early books there is nothing about healing, but in 1869 appeared *The Mental Cure* dealing with the subject that now occupied Evans to the exclusion of all else. It started again with "the spiritual science of Swedenborg" and with a Swedenborgian use of such terms as "Life," "Love," "Truth," and "Mind" for God, but it quickly got down to the practical business of healing.

No mention is made of Quimby anywhere in the book. In fact Evans writes of himself: "The author had but little in works on mental or physiological science to guide him in his investigation, but was under the necessity of following the light of his own researches, experiments and intuitions." But Quimby's ideas are all there in different language, as Horatio Dresser noted. Man has a natural body and a spiritual body, the latter described as a "nerve-projected form" (p. 66). Evans, unlike Quimby, has no objection to the word "magnetism," and he writes, "Magnetic manipulations act upon this department of our being [the spiritual body], and go to the root of all diseased action" (p. 63). In clairvoyance, somnambulism, and the trance the subject "becomes invested . . . with the powers and perceptions of the spirit-life" (p. 63).

Throughout the book Evans extols the "superior value of the magnetic, or, more properly, the psychological method of treatment" (p. 215) in which "mind acts upon mind" (p. 71), though usually with the assistance of the hands, for the vital force is "poured forth from the palms of the hands more copiously than from any other part of the body" (p. 73). There are, he writes, "a variety of phenomena, passing under the names of Mesmerism, Psychology, Biology, Animal Magnetism, Pathetism, Hypnotism, and even Psychometry, that are reducible to one general principle,—the influence or action of mind upon mind, and the communication of spiritual life from one person to another, who is negatively receptive of it" (p. 252).

Like Quimby and other magnetic healers he gave absent treatments: "This spirito-magnetic influence can be transmitted independently of spatial distance. We have experimented with it at a distance of over a thousand miles, and once between New Hampshire and Louisiana" (p. 274). Manipulations upon the operator's person are said to affect the "spiritual" body of the subject miles away. Or another technique—and one which Quimby frequently used, according to his letters—is said to be possible: "Instead of applying his hands to himself, the operator may *in thought* apply them to the person he would affect, and where and in what way the diseased condition would require. This mental act affects the spiritual organism of the invalid, and through this the physical body" (p. 275).

It is interesting that for Evans, as for Quimby, there was no line between suggestion with religious overtones and the crudest beliefs inherited from Mesmer. Even as late as 1872 in *Mental Medicine* Evans had no doubt of the existence of a magnetic fluid diffused through space and flowing between the celestial bodies, the earth, and animated beings (p. 131). He did not doubt the effect of a magnet on the human body: "Even the magnetic sleep may be induced by it. As a therapeutic agent I have found it far more valuable than the electromagnetic battery" (p. 132). He advocated the use of magnetized water (p. 138). Like Quimby, who told young Charles Norton (see p. 157) that because of the earth's magnetic currents "light complexioned persons should face east while being treated, dark complexioned persons should face north," Evans found the patient's position important; preferably the recipient of treatment should sit with his back to the north pole. "This will increase his susceptibility to the psychic influence, and tend to invert the magnetic poles of the body.

The brain, which is normally positive, or the north pole of the body, will become negative, and its magnetism will flow downward to the feet" (p. 48).

This sort of fatuity, though interwoven with elements of rational psychology and Swedenborgian idealism, makes Evans' books, enormously popular in their own day, dead as doornails in ours. His importance today is purely historical: for the backward light he throws on Quimby and the forward light on New Thought—of which, together with Dresser, he may be considered one of the founders.

In 1936 a book entitled *Mrs. Eddy Purloins from Hegel* by Walter M. Haushalter was printed in Boston by A. A. Beauchamp and in London by the Rationalist Press. Recognizing the impossibility of explaining Mrs. Eddy's metaphysics by Quimby's psychology, the author proposed a different explanation. She had stolen her ideas, he announced, from a manuscript entitled "The Metaphysical Religion of Hegel" by Francis Lieber, the respected nineteenth-century German-American political scientist. The manuscript thus described was printed in the book in full.

In the April 3, 1937, issue of the *Christian Science Sentinel* the following "item of interest" was published:

> In 1930–1933, The Mother Church was invited to buy what was offered as proof that Mary Baker Eddy got some two hundred lines for "Science and Health with Key to the Scriptures" (which contains eighteen thousand lines) from an admirer of Hegel's philosophy. The alleged proof consisted of two handwritten papers: (1) a purported article or essay headed "The Metaphysical Religion of Hegel by Christian Herrmann"; (2) a purported letter dated April 21, 1866, addressed "Friend Hiram" and signed "Christian Herrmann." The letter purported to be from a man of German birth, hard pressed for money, who was returning to Germany after a long stay in the United States. "Friend Hiram" was said to be Mrs. Eddy's first pupil, Hiram S. Crafts.
>
> Not at all convinced by the papers in question, the Directors of The Mother Church declined to consider buying them.
>
> In 1936, there was published in Great Britain and in the United States a book by an author who participated in the foregoing attempts to sell. It included the following features, described as "newly discovered": (1) a purported article or essay headed "The Metaphysical Religion of Hegel by Francis Lieber—'Christian Herrmann' "; (2) a purported notation on the cover of the same paper, as follows: "N.B. This is Metaphysical

Basis of Healing and Science of Health. Same as 'Christ-power' and 'Truth-power' Mary Baker"; (3) a purported letter dated April 7, 1866, addressed "Mr. Hiram Crafts Secretary of Kantian Society Boston Lyceum. Friend Hiram" and signed "Francis Lieber 'Christian Herrmann.'" The book included what were represented as exact reproductions of the foregoing features in type and in handwriting. The author also asserted that the first and third of the foregoing features were written by "none other than the noted publicist and educator, Dr. Francis Lieber."

Francis Lieber (1800–1872) . . . was a professor in Columbia College (now Columbia University) in New York City. . . . In 1866, Hiram S. Crafts was a heel finisher in a shoe factory at Lynn, Massachusetts.

In 1930–1933, during the solicitations just described, none of the solicitors who spoke or wrote at that time made any assertion or claim corresponding to the purported notation by "Mary Baker" just quoted. Nor did any of them make any assertion or claim that the letter or manuscript then offered for sale was written by Francis Lieber. On the contrary, they spoke as if Christian Herrmann were an actual person.

After the book in question was published, The Christian Science Board of Directors, disbelieving that the documents in question were genuine and desiring opinions from disinterested experts, put specimens of Mrs. Eddy's handwriting and specimens of Francis Lieber's handwriting (of which there are plenty), with copies of the book in question, into the hands of Mr. Albert S. Osborn and Mr. Elbridge Walter Stein of New York City, who are two of the best-known authorities on handwriting and questioned documents in the United States. These experts were consulted separately, and each of them tested the documents in question separately, but both of them reported the same conclusions, and each of them reported his conclusions and his reasons for them in detail, at length, and in positive words. The gist of their findings was that neither the purported notation by Mary Baker nor the purported signature was in the handwriting of Mary Baker Eddy, and that neither the purported letter nor the purported manuscript reproduced in the book nor the purported signature of Francis Lieber was in his handwriting.

In 1955 a book entitled *Ordeal by Concordance* by Conrad Henry Moehlman was published by Longmans Green of New York and London. Dr. Moehlman, a church historian who was for many years James B. Colgate Professor of the History of Christianity at Colgate-Rochester Seminary, had been assigning the Lieber-Hegel document to one of his classes each year as a linguistic-historical problem, and each year the result was the same. The students came to the unanimous conclusion that it was a forgery plagiarized from *Science and Health* rather than the other way around. Dr. Moehlman's book documented his own reasons for reaching such a conclusion.

A single small example must serve here. According to the Haushalter claim, Lieber is supposed to have written in 1866 in the document in question: "The treatment by Hegel is on the lines of Baader and the Theodicy of Liebnitz. Evil is negation, the absence of Essence. The negation of evil is finite and not connected with God. . . ." But in Otto Pfleiderer's *The Philosophy of Religion on the Basis of its History,* published in London in 1887, one reads in Vol. 2, pp. 61 f., these words: "Krause's solution of the problem [of evil] is quite on the lines of Leibnitz's theodicy. Evil . . . is negation, in part a simple want of essence. . . . Evil as non-essential has its sphere only in the finite and . . . is not to be connected with God. . . . "

Obviously the learned Pfleiderer neither could nor needed to plagiarize from a highly inaccurate essay about Hegel which (a) either had been stowed away with an obscure New England shoemaker eleven years earlier, or (b) had not yet been composed. On the other hand, the difficulties disappear if a date between 1887 and 1930 is accepted for the composition of the essay—especially toward the latter end of the period, when a person engaged in such a fabrication might well feel he could borrow a few phrases from a forgotten 1887 history of philosophy without danger of detection. It is instructive to compare this real borrowing noted by Moehlman with the "plagiarism" implied by Haushalter when he points the reader from the "Lieber" passage quoted above to a sentence in the last edition of *Science and Health* (p. 470): "If God, or good, is real, then evil, the unlikeness of God, is unreal."

The Lieber-Hegel charge collapses so ignominiously under any sort of thorough examination—linguistic, documentary, historical, philosophical—that it is ironic to note that at the time it was made the august *Times Literary Supplement* of London hailed the Haushalter document as unassailably authentic. What may be valuable in the episode is its negative evidence. The fabricator of the essay shrewdly judged that if one were going to produce a "father" for Christian Science, Quimby was wholly inadequate. But the paper-thin "Hegel" he produced served the purpose no better.

Abbreviations Used in Notes

A.   Archives of The Mother Church.

C.   Congressional Library.

L.   Longyear Foundation.

Unpublished writings of Mary Baker Eddy:

A&M.   Articles and Manuscripts.   35 vols.

L&M.   Letters and Miscellany.   94 vols.

Published works of Mary Baker Eddy:

S&H.   (*Science and Health with Key to the Scriptures*)

Mis.   (*Miscellaneous Writings*)

Ret.   (*Retrospection and Introspection*)

Un.   (*Unity of God*)

No.   (*No and Yes*)

My.   (*The First Church of Christ, Scientist, and Miscellany*)

1. Quoted in *The Shaping of American Religion,* eds. James Ward Smith and A. Leland Jamison (Princeton: Princeton University Press, 1961), p. 233.

2. Record book of Union Church, April 18, 1822.

3. See p. 33.

4. Irving C. Tomlinson, *Twelve Years with Mary Baker Eddy.* (Boston: Christian Science Publishing Society, 1945), p. 16. Tomlinson, who heard the story from Mrs. Eddy, had been a Universalist minister himself. Another nephew, James Baker of Derby, Vermont, was a Universalist preacher. In a letter to Mark's third son on October 22, 1833, he wrote: "They tell you, you say, that I am a preacher of the Gospel that Satan preached to Eve. . . . I know, however, that I have a book called the bible which teaches me the contrary." Yet the theological difference does not seem to have kept him from being received very warmly by the Bakers, including Mark. In a letter to the same son on October 26, 1843, the heretical James wrote that the names of Mark and Abigail were no less "fresh in my mind than when a stranger they comforted me; for all their kindness I remember."

5. This is one point on which Mrs. Eddy and her most hostile biographer, Georgine Milmine, were agreed. See *Ret.,* p. 5, and Milmine, *Life of Mary Baker G. Eddy* (New York: Doubleday, Page & Co., 1909), pp. 5 ff.

6. A. Reminiscences of Mrs. Ellen G. Winkley re father, and Florence W. Saunders letter re Lyman Durgin. Milmine in the *McClure's* article of 1906–07 which form the basis of her *Life of Mary Baker G. Eddy* wrote (Vol. XXVIII, No. 3, p. 228), "Mark's neighbors, half-admiringly, half-affectionately, called him 'Squire Baker' and 'Uncle Baker.'" When the *Life* appeared two years later in book form, the words "half-admiringly, half-affectionately" had been carefully deleted, along with all other statements or phrases which might reflect any credit on the Baker family.

7. A. Winkley reminiscences. This same boy, as an old man, was indignant at the description of Mark Baker in *McClure's.*

8. *Lewiston* (Maine) *Evening Journal,* March 4, 1907.

9. This statement rests on the evidence of the Baker family letters in L.

10. Emerson's *Journal,* May 4, 1841.

11. See the book of that name by Perry Miller, Cambridge: Belknap Press of Harvard University Press, 1956. The present difficulty in understanding the Puritan mind and character is suggested by Miller's statement, p. 49: "In the vicinity of Boston one can encounter an aversion that amounts to settled hostility against any

account implying that the founders of New England were primarily occupied with religious ideas . . ."

12. Lucy Larcom, *A New England Girlhood* (Cambridge, 1889), p. 91.

13. A. Reminiscences of Clara Shannon, for physical description of Abigail Ambrose Baker. In a poem by Mary Baker Eddy (then Mrs. Patterson), written some years after her mother's death, occur the lines:

> O sweet that home where *Mother* smiled
> It paid a father's frown.

14. Obituary of Abigail Baker by Richard S. Rust, D.D., in *New Hampshire Patriot and State Gazette*, December 6, 1849. Even Milmine described her in *McClure's* as a "gentle, capable, conscientious New England housewife" who was "always a peaceful and inspiring influence"—though this mild little tribute was transmuted in the later *Life* into the dry comment that she was "pious and thrifty" and was remembered for her "patience and industry."

15. When Lyman Beecher, then a student in the Yale Divinity School, asked his fiancée Roxana in 1797 whether she was prepared to rejoice if God should damn her for His glory, she replied that to be damned meant to be desperately wicked and she couldn't see how it would contribute to God's glory for her to be desperately wicked. At that, Beecher exclaimed, "Oh, Roxana, what a fool I've been." See Lyman Beecher Stowe, *Saints, Sinners and Beechers* (Indianapolis: Bobbs-Merrill, 1934), p. 31. Mark Baker was not so easily persuaded.

16. A. *A&M* 1–10032. "Shade and Sunshine."

17. Almost sixty years later, however, when reading proof for a new edition of his poems, Whittier wrote with slightly ironic deprecation, "I hope I am correcting a little of the bad grammar and rhythmical blunders which have so long annoyed my friends who have graduated at Harvard instead of a district country school."

18. *Society in America*, Vol. 2 (New York, 1837). The later quotations from Harriet Martineau are from the same volume.

19. This is one of the innumerable details brought to light in recent years by the exhaustive researches of Jewel Spangler Smaus into the Baker family background. I am greatly indebted to Mrs. Smaus for her incomparable knowledge of relevant material in the Bow and Tilton areas.

20. *The Minister's Wooing* (Leipzig, 1859), pp. 64 ff.

21. Clifford P. Smith, *Historical Sketches* (Boston: Christian Science Publishing Society, 1941), p. 11, and Smaus researches.

22. A. *A&M* 27–11025.

23. L. Letter to George S. Baker, September 2, 1848. The book referred to is *The Doctrine of the Will* by Henry P. Tappan (New York, 1840). This is a closely reasoned examination of will, causality, freedom, contingency, reason, etc. The author takes issue with Jonathan Edwards on many points.

24. L. Letter of April 9, 1844.

25. A. *A&M* 27–11058. Examples she gave are: "Count that day lost whose setting sun finds no good done." "A word that's flown is in your hearer's power and not your own."

26. A. *L&M* 46–9579.

27. From her earliest to her latest years Mrs. Eddy was accustomed to mark and make marginal comments in her books, many of which are now in A. or in the library of her Chestnut Hill home. The list of books given by Ernest Sutherland Bates and John V. Dittemore in their *Mary Baker Eddy* (New York: Knopf, 1932) is extraordinarily incomplete.

28. L. Albert Baker papers.

29. Around 1870 John Baker, son of Mark's nephew Aaron, moved the main part of the Mark Baker house to his own farm where he used it chiefly for storing apples and allowed it to fall into complete disrepair (A. Reminiscences of Mrs. John Baker). A photograph of it in this bleak state was run in *McClure's* in an obvious attempt to discredit the etching done by John Baker's son Rufus on the basis of his parents' and Mrs. Eddy's memories of how it had looked sixty or seventy years earlier. The standard size for the main part of the house would have been about 35 feet by 27 feet. Rufus Baker's picture is probably essentially accurate. A more idealized painting was done later by E. L. Henry. It is interesting to compare Holmes's lyrical description of the salt-box genre in *Elsie Venner* with Milmine's reference to the Baker house as "a small, square box building of rudimentary architecture" (*McClure's*) and "of wood, unpainted, and extremely small and plain" (*Life*, pp. 10 f.).

30. See pp. 44, 45 *et passim*. Many biographers, following Milmine, have projected back into the Bow days accounts which were gathered from critical sources in Tilton (Sanbornton Bridge) and which belong to the period after 1835. For instance, Bates-Dittemore have an old neighbor from Bow remembering Mark Baker driving in haste "for Dr. Nathaniel Ladd" and shouting. "Mary is dying." But Dr. Ladd lived in Tilton, and was known to the Bakers only after 1835. The Baker physician while the family lived at Bow was Dr. Peter Renton of Concord. (See bills paid to Dr. Renton in L.)

31. See, however, Tomlinson, *Twelve Years*, p. 13.

32. A. Reminiscences of Clara Shannon.

33. A. Letter of Fred N. Ladd, November 21, 1906. Also Ladd Reminiscences.

34. Henry Thoreau, paddling up the Concord and Merrimack Rivers on a famous canoe trip, is an example of this sort of thinking. Keenly observant of the natural life around him, he still felt that nature was somehow a part of *him*. Later he wrote:

> The seasons and all their changes are in me. I see not a dead eel or floating snake, or a gull, but it rounds my life and is like a line or accent in its poem. Almost I believe the Concord would not rise and overflow its banks again, were I not here. . . . Those sparrows, too, are thoughts I have. They come and go; they flit by quickly on their migrations, uttering only a faint *chip*, I know not whither or why exactly.

This is a half-serious statement of the philosophical idealism that Jonathan Edwards in his "Notes on the Mind" shared with Berkeley. Carlyle at this time was fetching up draughts of such idealism from the bottomless wells of German philosophy and was writing in his essay on Novalis, "To a Transcendentalist, Matter has an existence, but only as a Phenomenon: were *we* not there, neither would it be there; it is a mere Relation . . . having itself *no* intrinsic qualities; being, in the common sense of that word, Nothing." See also my book *Christian Science: Its*

Encounter with American Culture (New York: Holt, 1958), chapter on "The Prophetic Spirit."

35. In Teilhard de Chardin's theory of a noosphere or envelope of thought emerging from and redirecting the evolution of planetary life—or at least in as much of his theory as is acceptable to a humanist like Julian Huxley—one finds biology itself absorbing such heterodox speculations.

36. Quoted in A. Hunter Dupree, *Asa Gray* (Cambridge, Belknap Press of Harvard University Press, 1959). The author of this excellent biography contrasts Gray, the friend and champion of Darwin, with Thoreau, to whom Gray was only a disembodied *Manual of Botany*. Cf. Emerson's statement in *Nature* (1836): "I cannot greatly honor minuteness in details, so long as there is no hint to explain the relation between things and thoughts; no ray upon the *metaphysics* of conchology, of botany, of the arts, to show the relations of the forms of flowers, shells, animals, architecture, to the mind, and build science upon ideas."

37. A. *A&M* 11001A. Mary Baker, like practically every other American of her generation, was a devoted reader of Scott. Steamboats plying the Ohio and Mississippi were called the "Lady of the Lake" and the "Marmion," as they were later called the "Corsair" and the "Mazeppa" when the vogue of Byron superseded that of Scott as poet. However, as the author of the Waverly novels, Scott maintained his popularity unabated. Mary Baker responded to the influence of both Scott and Byron, a dual influence which dominated American popular taste until it was succeeded by that of Mrs. Hemans.

38. Published in Concord, 1895. Vol. I, p. 59.

39. A. Thomas was not the first Baker to come to America, though he was the first direct ancestor of the Bow Bakers to come. He was preceded by an uncle, John Baker, a few years before.

40. Hugh A. Studdert Kennedy, *Mrs. Eddy* (San Francisco: Farallon Press, 1947), pp. 5 f.

41. Although in recent years the history of science has become a recognized discipline, science itself is concerned always with the validity of a theory rather than its history. Toward the end of her life Mrs. Eddy wrote, "I do not find my authority for Christian Science in history, but in revelation" (*My.*, p. 318).

42. Quoted from Paine, *The Rights of Man,* in Mary Burt Messer, *The Science of Society* (New York: Philosophical Library, 1959). Miss Messer discusses the significance of the Paine statement from the standpoint of Christian Science.

43. L. Baker papers.

44. *Moby Dick* (Garden City: Garden City Publishing Co., 1937), pp. 166 f.

45. See the biographies of Emma Willard, Elizabeth Cady Stanton, and Susan B. Anthony by Alma Lutz. Miss Lutz is one of several Christian Scientists who have made contributions to the literature of feminism.

46. *Ret.*, p. 13.

47. A. *A&M* 4–10134.

48. Rev. W. Gale, quoted in *A Brief History of the First Congregational Church in Pembroke, N. H.,* by Rev. Isaac Wiley, Bristol, 1876.

49. L. B. Stowe, *Saints, Sinners and Beechers*, pp. 45 f.

50. *Oldtown Folks* (Boston, 1896), p. 26. The idea of nature as Calvinist is further developed by the same author in *The Minister's Wooing*, where a distraught character exclaims: "I have thought, in desperate moments, of giving up the Bible itself. But what do I gain? Do I not see the same difficulty in nature? I see everywhere a Being whose main ends seem to be beneficent, but whose good purposes are worked out at terrible expense of suffering, and apparently by the total sacrifice of myriads of sensitive creatures. I see unflinching order, general good-will, but no sympathy, no mercy. Storms, earthquakes, volcanoes, sickness, death, go on without regarding us. . . . The Doctor's dreadful system is, I confess, much like the laws of nature. . . ."

51. Mrs. Eddy herself attributed her long years of invalidism primarily to the "misinterpretation" of the Bible with which she had struggled. See *Mis.*, p. 169.

52. See, e.g., *Ret.*, p. 13.

53. *Ibid.*

54. L. Letter of February 6, 1844. Too much significance should not be read into this phrase in view of Mrs. Baker's letter to her son George on August 7, 1849, in which she says, "I hope I shant be left to worship your Picture I *Love* it though not Supremely."

55. Tomlinson, *Twelve Years*, p. 17.

56. *S&H*, p. 1. Cf. the answer to the question, "What is prayer?" in the Westminster Shorter Catechism: "Prayer is an offering up of our desires unto God, for things agreeable to his will, in the name of Christ, with confession of our sins, and thankful acknowledgement of his mercies."

57. *Ibid.*, p. 13. The whole chapter entitled "Prayer" in which this passage occurs is the best possible introduction to Mrs. Eddy's religious thinking. See also the discussion of prayer in Bronson Alcott's *Conversations with Children on the Gospels* (1836), especially the comments of six-year-old Josiah Quincy: "It is wrong . . . to speak prayer and not pray. We . . . must feel the words we say, and we must do what belongs to the words. . . . We must ask God for help, and at the same time try to do the thing we are to be helped about."

58. *A New England Girlhood*, pp. 54 f.

59. Tomlinson, *Twelve Years*, p. 17.

60. A. *L&M* 89–13271.

61. *Message for 1901*, p. 32.

62. *Message for 1902*, p. 2.

63. It appears in its revised form in Mrs. Eddy's *Poems*, p. 32. The original version is in Mary Baker's girlhood notebook.

64. Mrs. Eddy wrote (*My.*, p. 311), that her early religious experience seemed to culminate when she was twelve. The intense religious excitement connected with a revival frequently brought on emotional crises in sensitive children. Not infrequently children of twelve or even younger would "profess their faith" at the "protracted meetings" of a revival period, even though they might not be admitted to church membership. See note 62, chap. 2.

65. L. Baker papers.

66. This characterization, which contradicts the picture of her as either a sickly little hysteric or a saintly little paragon, is based on the primary evidence available from the period, including her girlhood letters.

67. A. Tomlinson notes.

68. *L&M* 27–11025. *Ret.,* p. 10.

69. A. Jewel Spangler Smaus material.

70. A. *A&M* 6–10219.

71. See, e.g., p. 63 f.

72. In a copy of Sherwin Cody's *Word-Study* (1903) which she acquired during her eighties, Mrs. Eddy marked a single passage:

> We must begin our study at just the opposite end from the Latin or Greek; but our teachers of language have balked at a complete reversal of method, the power of custom and time has been too strong, and in the matter of grammar we are still the slaves of the ancient world. As for spelling, the irregularities of our language seem to have driven us to one sole method, memorizing: and to memorize every word in a language is an appalling task.

73. The only known copies, in Albert Baker's own handwriting, are among his papers in the Baker collection in L. These were in the possession of George Sullivan Baker's widow and son during all the years Mrs. Eddy was writing on Christian Science, which were also years of estrangement from her family.

74. In one of his college papers he commented on the well-known influence of "company, habit, situation, and even natural scenery" on the mind in early youth, then went on to say that this was strikingly illustrated among women. While it was logical to assume that by nature women's minds were not inferior to men's, their status and education put before them one object only: to please. From this followed "that indecision and dependence of mind; that credulousness, and affected sensibility, and fondness, which characterize their manners." Again: "The object of their pursuit, and indeed the entire business of their lives, is to please. And what is their character? Frivolous, to say the least. . . . We by no means impute it to their fault, but to the necessity of their situation"—i.e., to the fact that they had not been educated to see things in their proper relations.

75. It is of course possible that Mary Baker inadvertently misdated the poem and that actually it refers to her grandmother, whom she may well have regarded as a "friend."

76. This child was, however, to pass away as a young woman without any offspring of her own. Interestingly enough, Mary Baker was the only one of the six Baker children who would have living descendants a century later.

77. These family letters, now in L., were preserved by George Sullivan Baker's son and constitute the chief source of information about the Baker family from 1835 on. They did not come to light until after the Milmine *Life* was published in 1909.

78. Milmine, *Life,* p. 108, n. Milmine adds that in her old age Abbie, then Mrs. Tilton, stated that her love for Mary was "all gone now," but this change in sentiment did not occur until the 1860's.

79. All the Baker girls taught school at one time or another.

80. L. Her early letters to George were printed in full in "The Girlhood of Mary Baker Eddy" by Isaac F. Marcosson, *Munsey's Magazine,* Vol. XLV, No. 1 (April, 1911).

81. The farm was sold to one Josiah Rogers for six thousand dollars, a good sum in those days. Later Aaron Baker, the heretical Universalist cousin, bought it back.

82. A. Letter of Mary Virginia Gault, November 24, 1930.

Notes: *Chapter Two*

1. L. January 20, 1836.

2. L. April 24, 1836.

3. The youngest Baker joined in the plea, although it is evident she did not feel the real social humiliation of her older sisters.

4. A. Tomlinson notes—Mrs. Eddy's account, December 29, 1901.

5. L. August 5, 1836.

6. L. August 23, 1836. An additional comment is of interest: "The girls are better off here than anywhere else at present."

7. Milmine in *McClure's,* Vol. XXVIII, No. 3 (January, 1907), p. 233.

8. L. In Joseph Baker letter to George Baker, April 28, 1832.

9. C. Letter to P. P. Quimby, April 10, 1864.

10. L. May, 1, 1836.

11. A. Letter of S. B. G. Corser, July 17, 1902.

12. See also her comment in *Society in America:* "All American ladies are more or less literary: and some are so to excellent purpose: to the saving of their minds from vacuity. Readers are plentiful: thinkers are rare."

13. A. Reminiscence of Harriet Chamberlain Smith.

14. L. March 27, 1837.

15. L. May 2, 1836.

16. See p. 54 and notes 77, 78.

17. *Mis.,* p. 283.

18. A. Reminiscenses of members of Dunmore family, etc.

19. A. *L&M* 21-2678.

20. L. April 17, 1837.

21. A. April 9, 1876.

22. Milmine *Life* and Ray Perkins reminiscences in A., quoting Thomas M. Towns and Joseph C. Wyatt. These two acquaintances of Mary Baker in her youth and young womanhood stated that her popularity aroused the resentment of one Hannah Sanborn who, as an old lady, was the source of many of the more sensational charges against Mrs. Eddy which were accepted as gospel by Milmine and the biographers who followed her. Wyatt reported that he had seen Miss Sanborn as a girl "turn away in disgust" as the young man she wanted walked home with Mary Baker instead of her. Perkins, reporting Towns and Wyatt, inadvertently

refers to her as "Miss Dearborn," the confusion probably arising from the fact that her father's name was Dearborn Sanborn. See M. T. Runnels *History of Sanbornton, N.H.*, Vol. II (Boston, 1881), p. 667.

23. The phrases quoted are from *McClure's;* these and the other details in the description are agreed on by critics and friends alike.

24. A. Reminiscences of Sarah Clement Kimball.

25. L. February 6, 1844.

26. L. Letter of Mahala Sanborn, May 6, 1844.

27. L. Letter of Luther Pilsbury, May 17, 1848.

28. A. Reminiscences of Edwin J. Thompson.

29. L. Samuel P. Bancroft letter to Mary Beecher Longyear.

30. A. Sarah Clement Kimball reminiscences.

31. A. George W. Baker letter to Mary Baker Billings, April 22, 1924.

32. L. February 6, 1844.

33. L. December 30, 1836, and April 17, 1837.

34. A. *L&M* 21–2679. There is some question of the authenticity of this letter. See note 64, below.

35. Interview with Allan McLane Hamilton in *New York Times,* August 25, 1907.

36. A. *A&M* 1–10020.

37. A. Letter of John H. Bartlett, June 17, 1847.

38. A. See, e.g., passage she copied from the *Literary Gazette* into autograph album of her teacher, Sarah Jane Bodwell.

39. L. January, 1837.

40. L. April 17, 1837.

41. L. July 18, 1837.

42. L. October 15, 1837.

43. A. *L&M* 21–2678.

44. L. December 10, 1836.

45. L. April 17, 1837.

46. L. October 13, 1837.

47. L. January 29, 1840.

48. L. December 24, 1840.

49. A. February 16, 1840.

50. See p. 53 f.

51. A. Florence W. Saunders letter re Lyman Durgin.

52. A. Notebooks. "Charleston" written above poem.

53. George Saintsbury once described it as "an enormous soliloquy addressed by an actor of superhuman lung-power to an audience of still more superhuman endurance."

54. The single year of 1836 saw the publication of Emerson's *Nature*, Bronson Alcott's *Conversations with Children on the Gospels,* George Ripley's *Discourses on the Philosophy of Religion,* Orestes Brownson's *New Views of Christianity, Society, and the Church,* Convers Francis's *Christianity as a Purely Internal Principle,* and W. H. Furness's *Remarks on the Four Gospels.* Yet all of these together did not create the excitement generated among Americans by the publication in the same year of *Pickwick Papers.* A Dickensian romp in a stagecoach had a clear advantage over transcendental cajolements to hitch one's wagon to a star.

55. John W. Nevin, quoted in Richard Hofstadter, *Anti-Intellectualism in American Life* (New York: Knopf, 1963), p. 83.

56. L. March 27, 1837. In a letter to an old college friend on July 10, 1838, Albert wrote: "Dickey tells me he thinks of turning his attention to the study of Law. I am glad it is so. He is too clean a fellow for a theologian, asking pardon of the mitre." Mrs. Eddy's own reference to her desire to join the Methodist Church is in A. *L&M* 37–4919.

57. A. August 12, 1838.

58. *An Account of the Seventy-Fifth Anniversary of the Congregational Church of Northfield and Tilton,* Concord, 1897, p. 25.

59. A. Letter from S. B. G. Corser, August 4, 1902.

60. A. Henry Robinson interview with Mrs. Eddy, 1902

61. This phrase may be objectionable in so far as Calvin's God was the God of Augustine and of other thinkers in the Augustinian tradition—and because New England Puritanism departed in important respects from pure Calvinism. Nevertheless the peculiar logical rigor of Calvinism did set it off from other developments of Augustinian theology, and this characteristic remained an essential feature of Edwardsian and post-Edwardsian thought.

62. *Ret.,* pp. 14–15. It is possible that this incident belongs to a different experience. If she gave a "confession of faith" at a "protracted meeting" in a revival when she was twelve (see note 64, chap. one), she may very well have been questioned at that time at the "anxious seat." The two experiences may have merged in her memory, which would account for the confusion about whether she was twelve or seventeen at the time. She adds in her account that many of the church members wept at her answer, and congregational weeping was a very common occurrence in revival meetings roused to a high emotional pitch by the questioning of those at the anxious seat. See Reverend Calvin Colton, *History and Character of American Revivals of Religion* (London, 1832), p. 91, and Orville Dewey, *Letters of an English Traveler on Revival of Religion in America* (Boston, 1828), p. 109.

63. L. September, 1836.

64. A. *L&M* 21–2680. This is one of three letters from "Mary" to Augusta, dated respectively January 6, 1839, April 6, 1839, and April 9, 1840, from Meredith Bridge, N.H. They have always been assumed to be from Mary Baker and are quoted from extensively by Bates-Dittemore. The copybook hand closely resembles Mary Baker's, but a handwriting expert consulted refuses to give a positive opinion as to whether it is hers. The internal evidence casts considerable doubt on the matter. The letters seem to imply that the writer is living with her mother in Meredith Bridge rather than merely visiting there, and they speak of Sanbornton

Bridge as "your" village. The friendship with Augusta seems to rest solely on a school friendship at Holmes Academy in Plymouth (see note 77, below). Until a conclusive identification is made the three letters should be used cautiously.

65. *Mis.*, p. 203.

66. This is in accord with her teaching that true spirituality unmasks sin but does not ignore or cover it up.

67. This Shaker settlement furnished the locale for Hawthorne's story "A Canterbury Tale."

68. Mrs. Baker wrote Mary (L. May 6, 1844), "Your pocket handkerchief pedler called here & had much chat. . . ."

69. See p. 42. Also reminiscences of Addie Towns Arnold in A. This Christian Scientist and student of Mrs. Eddy wrote: "She undoubtedly knew the Shakers. . . . They came to Tilton regularly all the time I lived there peddling things they had made. Everyone in Tilton knew them and was more or less acquainted with their doctrines and practices."

70. The official *Life and Gospel Experience of Mother Ann Lee,* Canterbury, n.d., states: "As *Father,* God is the infinite Fountain of intelligence, and the Source of all power—'the Almighty, great and terrible in majesty' . . . But, as *Mother,* 'God is Love' and tenderness." See *Brief Account of Shakers and Shakerism,* Canterbury, n.d., for statement of four principles. Among the many denominational hymnals which Mrs. Eddy collected in her later years is a *Shaker Hymnal,* copyright 1908 by the Canterbury Shakers, and inscribed: "To Rev. Mary Baker G. Eddy with sincere love and best wishes of Shaker friends."

71. See my book *Christian Science,* p. 91. Also "The Motherhood of God," *The Christian Science Journal,* Vol. 80, No. 12 (December, 1962).

72. Entered by Mary Baker in her notebook August 18, 1843.

73. Smith, *Historical Sketches,* p. 42.

74. L. February 6, 1844.

75. The craving for education among many girls of limited means is illustrated by the Lowell mill girls, of whom Lucy Larcom wrote in *A New England Girlhood:*

> Many of them were supporting themselves at schools like Bradford Academy or Ipswich Seminary half the year, by working in the mills the other half. Mount Holyoke Seminary broke upon the thoughts of many of them as a vision of hope . . . and Mary Lyon's name was honored nowhere more than among the Lowell mill-girls. Meanwhile they were improving themselves and preparing for their future in every possible way, by purchasing and reading standard books, by attending lectures and evening classes of their own getting up, and by meeting each other for reading and conversation.

76. *Ret.,* p. 10, and *My.,* p. 304. Milmine's charge that Mary Baker's education ended when she reached long division in the district school has been repeated by two generations of critical biographers despite the easily accessible documentary evidence to the contrary. The Milmine statement rested on the assertion of the same old lady who was the source of so many other remarkably inaccurate charges (see note 22, above). The Milmine description of Sanbornton Academy is equally unsupported by the facts. The *Patriot* on August 7, 1841, ran an advertisement for Sanborn's High School (as it was called briefly in one of the verbal

changes which so confuse the picture): "Instruction will be given in the Latin and Greek languages, and such other departments of science as have been pursued in other Literary Institutions under his instruction. . . . Whole number of scholars the past year 286."

77. The evidence for her attending Holmes Academy rests on the three letters dubiously attributed to Mary Baker (see note 64, above). The academy catalogue for the terms in question does not show her as a student, although this is not conclusive as she may have been there for only part of the term or terms. Bates-Dittemore accept her attendance as a proved fact, but I strongly doubt it.

78. The catalogues for the Woodman Sanbornton Academy for certain crucial years are missing. In any case their evidence might not be conclusive, for some students attended for special instruction without being listed. The researches of Jewel Spangler Smaus have brought to light the fact that Sarah Bodwell, who taught the district school in the summer of 1836 when Mary Baker attended it, also taught later at the Woodman Sanbornton Academy, and it is in this latter capacity that Mrs. Eddy seems to have referred to Miss Bodwell as her teacher.

79.The *Patriot* on September 16 and December 2, 1841, made mention of Martha as an especially able preceptress at the academy.

80. Article by Julia Sargent's daughter in *Lake County* (Minnesota) *News,* reprinted in *Concord Patriot* of February 21, 1907. Mrs. Eddy's sister-in-law, Martha Rand Baker, added (A. Perkins reminiscences) that whenever Sanborn left the room for a few minutes he would ask Mary Baker to take charge of the class during his absence.

81. Mary Baker used her notebook for both original poems and poems copied from other authors. Usually it is perfectly clear which was which, but in a few cases there is a little doubt. These particular lines come from her long poem "Shade and Sunshine," part of which may conceivably be a pastiche of admired passages from other poets.

82. See, e.g., *S&H* 117:24 and 173:26.

83. *My.,* p. 304.

84. *Ibid.*

85. See also passage quoted from Whately on p. 134 f.

86. A. *A&M* 6–10219. Her acquaintance with Locke's distinction between primary and secondary qualities—and her rejection of the distinction—is evidenced in a statement in *S&H,* p. 512: "From the infinite elements of the one Mind emanate all form, color, quality, and quantity, and these are mental, both primarily and secondarily."

87. See *Les Deux Chemins* (Brussels, n.d.) and *Le Pouvoir de l'Esprit* (Neuchâtel, 1937) by a contemporary French mathematician, W. Rivier, for an interesting attempt to carry Berkeley's reasoning beyond the mental nature of matter to the mental nature of the space-time of relativity physics, with a side glance at Mrs. Eddy.

88. Later governor of Iowa and United States senator from Iowa.

89. L. October 28, 1838.

90. L. April 5, 1838.

91. The view of conservative Whiggery was expressed in a Boston paper in 1834: "A farmer never looks as well as when he has a hand upon the plough . . . with

his huge paw upon the statutes what can he do? It is as proper for a blacksmith to attempt to repair watches, as a farmer, in general, to legislate."

92. Russel B. Nye writes in *William Lloyd Garrison and the Humanitarian Reformers* (Boston: Little, Brown & Co., 1955), p. 76: "Political journalism since the turn of the century had been marked by bad taste, vilification, and abuse. A vocabulary of epithets was standard journalistic practice." That Albert's own response to abuse was at least pointed is evident from a letter of Franklin Pierce to him, January 16, 1841: "That *General* must have found his position to be a very awkward one. You pounced upon him all round without mercy and I must confess that I have rarely noticed a more easy, off-hand facility for saying very provoking things that it were difficult to gainsay and mighty hard to bear."

93. In an article entitled "Reformers" (*Mis.*, pp. 237 f.), Mrs. Eddy mentions that as a child she had heard the awful story that William Lloyd Garrison "helped 'niggers' kill the white folks" and contrasts that with her mature admiration for the man. Mark may have met Garrison personally, though it is unlikely that the latter literally visited the Baker homestead. Mark's antipathy to the abolitionists persisted down to the Civil War.

94. See *My.*, p. 276.

95. L. November 23, 1837. Earlier he had written George, 'I would not live in such a continual fever as you are in, for all Connecticut, onions and everything."

96. L. January 29, 1840. The *Boston Morning Post* described the February 3 speech before the Bay State Association as "one of the most sound and eloquent political discourses—distinguished alike for the elegance of its style and its logical correctness." Franklin Pierce wrote Baker congratulating him on the praise his speech had evoked.

97. He was sick for about three months with a kidney affection—not cancer, as Milmine claimed. Died October 17, 1841.

98. October 21, 1841. Another part of this tribute, making mention of his intense interest in metaphysics, is reprinted in *Ret.*, p. 7, but is inadvertently attributed to Isaac Hill through a confusion of the *New Hampshire Patriot* with *Hill's Patriot*.

99. L. March 21, 1842.

100. Many of the poems cited in these chapters have slight, if any, poetic merit, but they throw valuable biographical light on their author.

101. L. February 16, 1840.

102. It might be hard to support this generalization by letter and verse, but I record honestly the strong impression conveyed to me by her early writings as a whole.

103. L. April 5, 1838.

104. A. Letter from Smith's granddaughter, Mary Brent Whiteside, July 28, 1933. Also letter from grandson, Hoke McAshan, June 2, 1930.

105. See editorial in *Atlanta Journal*, September 14, 1908: "His was a scholarship such as the South has rarely ever seen, combined with a gentleness and courtesy, the fine flavor of a high gentility and a native vigor of intellect which could not fail to place him among the notable figures of the South," etc.

106. See Smith, *Historical Sketches*, p. 31.

107. A poem entitled "The Mourner" by M.M.B. in *Godey's Lady's Book* in 1843 has been conjecturally assigned to Mary Baker by Bates-Dittemore, but a reprinted version of it in a later anthology shows it to have been by another writer with the same initials. However, Mary did later contribute to *Godey's*. See text, p. 108.

108. A. *L&M* 21–2682. Dated February 24, 1843. Although James Smith bored her with his piety on this occasion, she later came to value his earnestness and integrity, and in her autograph album she wrote under his contribution that he was "one of the *best friends* I ever had." However, she apparently rejected him as a suitor. See Lyman Powell, *Mary Baker Eddy: A Life Size Portrait* (Boston: Christian Science Publishing Society, 1950), p. 285, note 26.

109. L. This undated letter has hitherto been attributed to the year 1839 when Mary visited her brother Samuel in Boston, and it has been assumed to refer to Haverhill, Massachusetts, rather than Haverhill, New Hampshire. But a careful consideration of the internal evidence makes the present placement inevitable.

110. A. From the journal kept by Mary Baker during her White Mountain trip.

111. See particularly the sections of *The English Mail-Coach* (1849) entitled "The Vision of Sudden Death" and "Dream-Fugue."

112. *The Sickness unto Death*, tr. Walter Lowrie (Princeton: Princeton University Press, 1941), pp. 37 f.

113. See p. 76 and note 5, chap. 3.

114. A Copied by her into her notebook with a notation of the date and circumstances.

115. A. Notebook. "Written on leaving N. England at the Grave of Albert Baker, Esqr."

116. He was the same age as Albert Baker and closely resembled George Sullivan Baker in appearance.

117. Mrs. Eddy in later years referred to him as "Colonel" Glover, and Bates-Dittemore suggest that in those easy antebellum days in the South he may well have been referred to as colonel. Dickens announced that every other man he met on his American tour seemed to be called colonel. George Sullivan Baker was appointed to the staff of the governor of New Hampshire with the rank of colonel on June 12, 1844.

118. His letters to "Frend Baker" have generally been assumed to have been written to Samuel Baker, but examination of the originals at L. shows clearly that they were addressed to George Baker. The spelling is Glover's own. The prosperity is borne out by the Charleston Register of Means Conveyance between 1839 and 1842, which shows that he possessed real estate of considerable value, two transfers being made to him and thirteen by him to others during these years. Milmine's description of him as a "bricklayer" is no more correct than her description of his parents as neighbors of the Bakers at Bow.

119. L. May 19, 1841.

120. A. "Phrenological Character and Talents of Mr. George W. Glover as given January 21, 1841" by William P. Hebard, Charleston.

121. Mrs. Glover was later to express regret that he had no appreciation of poetry (Daniel Patterson letter of May, 1853, in A., quoted in part, on p. 112). His portrait, however, does give a hint of sensitiveness not evident in his letters.

122. This is the paradox of which Thomas Mann has given a classic statement in *Tonio Kröger*.

123. A. May 24, 1844. In view of Glover's business in Haiti (see p. 71) it may be that the friend was a Haitian.

124. Mrs. Glover described the scene later in a note made in her scrapbook opposite a clipping of the Sigourney poem.

125. Mrs. Eddy stated that for some years after her marriage to Glover she carried around the blueprints of their house in Charleston, but this could have referred to blueprints of a house that he planned to build for her there.

126. He might also have had slaves whom he used in his construction work. However, the size of his payroll in 1841 suggests that at that time, at least, he was having to hire other men's slaves for this work.

127. A. This information comes from the indefatigable researches of Elizabeth Earl Jones into every detail of Mrs. Glover's life in the South.

128. L. Letters of Mark and Abigail Baker and of Martha Pilsbury, February 6, 1844.

129. Mrs. Glover wrote a poem entitled "Odd Fellowship" while in Wilmington, and later she contributed extensively to Oddfellow publications.

130. A. Interview with Harriet Brown Huntington by a Boston newspaperman, H. W. Sears, c. 1901, and reprinted as part of a longer article in the *Greensboro* (N.C.) *News* in 1906.

131. A. Copied into her notebook, June 1, 1844.

132. There she was undoubtedly shown the house where Flora MacDonald lived when she came from Scotland with her memories of Bonnie Prince Charlie, a romantic Jacobite story to stir even a romantic daughter of the Covenanters.

133. A. "Mrs. Eddy in North Carolina" by Elizabeth Earl Jones, p. 59, quoting account given by Miss Rebecca Hodges of Fayetteville to Sue Harper Mims, in 1909.

134. A. Jones notes, p. 26.

135. An exhaustive search of the Charleston and Wilmington papers has not brought any such articles to light. Southern newspapers were definitely not publishing antislavery views in those days.

136. *Wilmington Chronicle*, June 12, 1844.

137. The story accepted by Bates-Dittemore and other biographers is that the supplies were stolen from the wharf by one of the gangs of pirates or robbers who operated on a dramatically large scale up and down the coast. In her later years Mrs. Eddy could not remember whether the material was lost by theft or fire. The *Wilmington Chronicle* for April 24, 1844, reports a large loss of lumber and building materials by a fire on the wharf; it states that the material was not insured and adds, "A considerable part of the loss falls upon persons abroad, on whose account naval stores had been purchased." This would fit in with the Haiti cathedral project; so it is possible that Glover's loss may have come from fire rather than theft.

138. The contemporary accounts all describe the disease as "bilious fever." Mrs. Eddy's explanation was that the authorities wished to cover up the fact that the dreaded yellow fever had appeared. The daughter of Dr. Repiton, chaplain of St.

John's Lodge, supported the claim that Glover had died from yellow fever (A. Letter of Mrs. Robert W. Lamb to J. V. Dittemore, June 9, 1920), as did Harriet Brown Huntington (see footnote 130, also A. Jones notes, p. 15). An item in the *Wilmington Chronicle*, September 25, 1844, began, "We are assured that reports of unusual sickness in Wilmington are in circulation," and sought to reassure the public. If a few isolated cases of yellow fever appeared, it is conceivable that the authorities might have wanted to keep the matter quiet until it became clear whether the disease was likely to reach epidemic proportions.

An obituary, written by the Reverend Albert Case and published in the *Freemasons' Monthly Magazine* iv, 7, (January, 1845), p. 221, describes the deathbed scene in these words: "Conscious that the time of departure was at hand, he calmly arranged his business—prepared for the removal of *her* he loved, to the home of her youth, and consoled her with the thought that they 'would meet again in heaven'—said he—'I have a precious hope in the merits of my Saviour'. . . . He departed in hope and peace."

139. The "governor" whom Mrs. Eddy described as attending the funeral may have been former Governor Dudley of North Carolina, who lived in Wilmington and has been identified as a friend of the Glovers during their stay.

140. This poem was not published until December, 1845, in *The I. O. O. F. Covenant,* but its placement in her notebooks seems to indicate that the author wrote it not very long after Glover's death.

Notes: *Chapter Three*

1. It is inconceivable that he would have been described as "indigent" at the time of death if he had possessed a large number of slaves. Carl Sandburg quotes an unnamed Kentuckian as saying to Lincoln: "You might have any amount of land, money in your pocket, or bank stock, and while traveling around, nobody would be any wiser; but if you had a darky trudging at your heels, everybody would see him and know you owned a slave. It is the most glittering property in the world. If a young man goes courting, the only inquiry is how many negroes he or she owns." Quoted in *Abraham Lincoln: The Prairie Years*, II (New York: Harcourt, Brace, 1926), p. 23.

2. It was impossible to free slaves in South Carolina except by special action of the legislature. In North Carolina they could be freed legally but there is no record of any such action by Mrs. Glover. However, it was possible for her simply to let them go free, as owners did from time to time, although this sometimes led to later legal complications.

3. L. February 6, 1844.

4. L. February 6 and May 6, 1844.

5. In her earlier letter Mrs. Baker also referred to the "twilight meeting": ".·. . the hour appointed by you and me is precious." In Mrs. Glover's poem "The Emigrant's Farewell," which is a revision of her earlier poem writen "when expecting to leave for the West Indies" and which was published in *The I. O. O. F. Covenant* in May, 1846, occur the lines:

Mother at eventide, alone
Commune with me afar.

6. The exact date of publication is not known. The Sondley Library in Asheville, N. C., contains incomplete issues and items from this periodical, and the poem referred to is included among these, but without an indication of the date of issue. No complete file of the magazine is known to exist today.

7. George Sullivan Baker wrote a letter of elaborate thanks, in the flowery rhetoric of the time, which was published in the *Wilmington Chronicle*, August 24, 1844.

8. L. Letter of Repiton's daughter, Mrs. Robert W. Lamb, June 9, 1920.

9. A. Notebook: "Written on leaving N. Carolina July 19th 1844."

10. The data on her trip are taken from her "Journal of the Journey from Wilmington, South [sic] Carolina" in her Notebook.

11. IV, 7, (January 1845) p. 221. Magazine published in Boston, edited by Reverend Albert Case, who invited Mrs. Glover to make further literary contributions.

12. A. Notebook. See also the lines:

> The while my soul in sackcloth sighs,
> O beauteous dust, to gaze on thee!

13. A. Clara Shannon reminiscences.

14. It has usually been said that this was a spinal injury; but see p. 95, for Dr. Ladd's diagnosis which may have led to this assumption.

15. L. May, 1844.

16. In a letter of December 26, 1847, Mrs. Baker wrote her son George that "Mary has had her Child baptised called his name George Sullivan agreeable to her own desire." She must have changed her mind later, for he was known as George Washington Glover throughout the rest of his life.

17. The evidence for this is abundant and occurs in all periods of her life.

18. *Ret.*, p. 90.

19. A. Clara Shannon reminiscences.

20. A. *Ibid.*

21. Published 1835. This is one of the didactic novels of the period, comparable to those of the popular Maria Edgeworth and unutterably dreary to a modern taste.

22. See p. 117.

23. *S&H*, p. 236.

24. A. Notebook: "Written on the 9th of May on parting with my babe."

25. Quoted in *The Nineteenth-Century World*, eds. Guy S. Métraux and François Crouzet (New York: Mentor, 1963), p. 39.

26. A. *L&M* 78–11150. March 5, 1848.

27. G. L. Plimpton, reported in Ray Perkins material in A.

28. Elizabeth Peabody is generally credited with introducing the kindergarten on the Froebel model to the United States in the 1860's.

29. A. Sarah Clement Kimball reminiscences.

30. A. Thomas F. Page letter, April 25, 1898.

31. A. Roland Hall Sharp memorandum, August 20, 1935, quoting Fred A. Smart of Tilton School. Another development was a change in the seminary's title to New Hampshire Conference Seminary and Female College.

32. A. Rust letter to Mrs. R. F. Marshall.

33. A. Statement dictated by Martha Rand Baker to Ray Perkins. This is confirmed by letter of Rust's son, Charles H. Rust, January 24, 1907. Mrs. Baker added: "Dr. Rust always thought a great deal of [Mrs. Glover]."

34. A. *L&M* 78–11150. March 5, 1848.

35. A. Irving C. Tomlinson notes.

36. Mrs. Glover's friend John H. Bartlett was among the founders of this society in 1846–47, and she may well have played a part in its formation. The 1847 catalogue states: "[The young ladies] from week to week assemble for the purpose of improving their faculty of reasoning, extemporaneous discussions, power of composition, etc., etc. A more powerful display of female talent is seldom witnessed than is occasionally brought forth at the public exhibitions of this society."

37. One statement in this article is of interest: "'Fontenelle has humorously remarked:—'woman has a cell less in the brain, and a fibre more in the heart, than man!' Now we contend not for the truth of the former part of this statement, whereas the latter we *admit*." Cf. Tomlinson, *Twelve Years*, p. 133.

38. Modern psychology would regard the very state of her body, of her nerves, as a state of protest.

39. Perry Miller, ed., *Margaret Fuller: American Rebel* (New York: Doubleday-Anchor, 1963). In one way or another most of the Transcendentalists tended to look on sickness as the Puritans looked on original sin.

40. *S&H*, p. 34. She also wrote a poem "Woman's Rights" which was published in 1853 and is found in changed form in her *Poems*, p. 21.

41. July 17, 1845.

42. *Christian Science*, New York, 1907, p. 106. It is interesting that in her copy of Tupper's *Proverbial Philosophy* Mrs. Glover marked the line: "Masculine sentiments, vigorously holden, well become a man."

43. A. Notebook. No title.

44. From the military point of view it would be more correct to say that it unfolded General Winfield Scott, but Scott did not ride into the Presidency on his exploits.

45. January 20, February 10, March 16, and July 6, 1848. The last of these appeared well after the war had ended.

46. Another poem entitled "Lines on the Masonic Meeting of Generals Quitman and Shields, U.S.A. at a Festival of the Fraternity in Charleston, S. Carolina," and published in the *Freemasons' Monthly Magazine*, March, 1848, contains an interesting phrase in regard to war:

> Invincible valor their Masonry teacheth,
> Whose bosoms were bared for our country's defence;
> 'Twill humanize war where its influence reacheth,
> And Discord to *Harmony* yield its offence.

47. Journal entry quoted in *Francis Parkman* by Howard Doughty (New York: Macmillan, 1962), pp. 69 f.

48. Gerard Manley Hopkins, *Poems* (New York: Oxford, 1948), p. 105.

49. February 7, 1850.

50. Poems by her ardently supporting Pierce appeared in the *Patriot*, July 28 and October 20, 1852. The second one ends:

> Is there no bard imbued with hallowed fire
> To wake the chords of Ossian's magic lyre,
> Whose numbers, breathing all his flame divine,
> This Patriot's name to ages would consign?

This makes clear that the often-repeated story of a quarrel between Mrs. Glover and Mrs. Tilton over Pierce's election cannot be true in its traditional form. They may well have differed sharply over some of the issues in the election, but they were united in their support of Pierce.

51. The Baker view was that expressed by Hawthorne in his campaign biography of Pierce: "Pierce fully recognized, by his votes and by his voice, the rights pledged to the South by the Constitution. This, at the period when he so declared himself, was comparatively an easy thing to do. But when it became more difficult, when the first imperceptible movement of agitation had grown to be almost a convulsion, his course was still the same. Nor did he ever shun the obloquy that sometimes threatened to pursue the northern man who dared to love that great and sacred reality—his whole, united, native country—better than the mistiness of a philanthropic theory."

52. A. *L&M* 62-8901. January 1, 1853.

53. See especially *S&H* 225:23–28.

54. A valuable modern assessment of this book is to be found in the work of a Christian Science writer, Henrietta Buckmaster, *Let My People Go* (New York: Harper, 1941).

55. L. January 22, 1848. The written date on this letter looks more like 1846 than 1848, but internal evidence supports the later date.

56. The letter mentions that she has been able to "fix the bosoms" of his shirts for him—"the first I ever did for anyone." From other references in the Baker letters, it is clear that she participated in domestic tasks when her health permitted, but she was evidently spared much of the routine and drudgery of farm life. See statement of Abigail Baker on p. 95.

57. A. *L&M* 78-11150.

58. L. March 20 [1848].

59. A. Sarah Clement Kimball reminiscences. These also contain a description of the Reverend Corban Curtice, the Congregational minister who had replaced Enoch Corser in 1843: "He met with two accidents, injuring first one and then another of his legs. After that, when he would go up into the pulpit he would fling out one and then the other in such a funny fashion that we children enjoyed watching him. He sat on a high chair through his lengthy sermons and when he had sent everyone to hell he would weep sadly out of the wrong corner of his eyes."

60. In 1902, after having lived for many years in Ohio, he returned east for the summer and paid a two-hour visit to Mrs. Eddy at her home in Concord.

61. A. *L&M* 78-11150. March 5, 1848.

62. The name of John H. Bartlett in this letter (first printed in *Munsey's* in 1911) has usually been read and transcribed as John M. Burt, but the context makes it probable (even if the handwriting does not) that the reference is to Bartlett.

63. L. September 2, 1848.

64. A. June 17, 1847.

65. There are several autobiographical themes woven into the story, but without significance. It may be dismissed as a product of the ill health of the period and of the author.

66. A choice example from this anthology is the following stanza by a now mercifully forgotten female poet:

"I love to love," said a darling pet,
Whose soul looked out through her eyes of jet,
And she settled down like a fondled dove,
And lisped, "Dear Mama, how I love to *love!*"

67. L. September 2, 1848.

68. Mark Baker had been making some successful investments in railroad stocks and was in a state of comparative prosperity.

69. A. Mrs. Martha Smith (mother of Hildreth Smith) to Mrs. Glover (then Patterson), September 18, 1858.

70. A. *L&M* 73–10468. November 22, 1849. Two months earlier she had written to a friend who had recently lost her mother (L. letter to Priscilla Wheeler, September 28, 1849):

Rejoice, my dear Friend, that *Her* joy is unspeakable and full of *glory*. I know, a chord that hath been so harshly thrilled in our affections, and stilled forever! can yield but melancholy music, the echo of harp strings broken long ago! Yet to your well disciplined mind I need not speak of the importance to your self, not to dwell with aching memory on the past— "for it comes not back again." The virtues of the parent stem dwell in the fruit and blossom, and the Mother still *lives* in her daughter—and with what pleasure (I had almost [said] pride) you may perpetuate the living remembrance. I *pray* that you have found consolation in all these, and many more weighty considerations. . . .

71. See, *e.g.*, the stanza:

I bless thee, Mother, precious guide,
For my most sacred share
In all the secrets of thy heart,
Thy sorrow and thy prayer;
Supporting faith be mine below
Life's parting words to greet;
Thy mantling virtues o'er me throw
Till child and Mother meet!

72. L. Baker papers.

73. L. December 26, 1847, and August 7, 1849.

74. Such a legend is the Milmine statement that Dr. Ladd diagnosed Mrs. Glover's trouble as "hysteria mingled with bad temper." This charge was made in a letter to Miss Milmine by a second cousin of Mrs. Eddy's, Mrs. M. C. Whittier, who was fourteen years old at the time of Mrs. Baker's death and in her seventies when she

volunteered this information. In the same letter she went on to say of Mrs. Eddy: "Even good sensible people about everything else, to be carried away with *this* woman, will prove one of the rounds of 'witch craft'—and if the managers of public affairs were on duty as in Salem 100 years ago, I'm sure she'd have the *same* treatment and *her* life taken upon the gallows." This amiable old lady seems rather flimsy authority for a statement which runs contrary to the first-hand evidence regarding Ladd's view of Mrs. Glover. It was doubtless her use of such "authorities" as this that caused Milmine later to write Dr. Lyman P. Powell that not in every instance were the witnesses she used "the kind of sources we would have chosen." (Powell, *Mary Baker Eddy*, p. 6).

75. A. Note in diary of Asa Gilbert Eddy as to what Ladd told Mrs. Glover. Her own references in the intervening years bear out the fact that this was her understanding of her disease until she discovered Christian Science.

76. L. January 22, 1848.

77. L. November, 1850.
78. *Ibid.*

79. This passage refutes the often-repeated statement, stemming from Milmine, that Mark Baker accused his daughter of not being willing to "own" her child.

80. L. Letter to Priscilla Wheeler, December 2, 1850.

81. L. April 22 [1851].

82. A. This is the poem which in *Ret.* she called "Mother's Darling."

83. L. August 10, 1851.

84. L. January 4, 1852.

85. This is the contraption which Milmine, Dakin, and others have described with some disingenuousness as a "cradle." Mrs. Eddy (*My.*, p. 315) ironically thanked the "enterprising historians" of *McClure's* for their testimony to the power of Christian Science "which they admit has snatched me from the *cradle* and the grave."

86. Mrs. Eddy (*My.*, p. 313) stated she was ignorant of the "various stories" told about this and added, "I only know that my father and mother did everything they could think of to help me when I was ill."

87. For more detailed discussion of her relation to these systems, see pp. 116, 135 ff., and 168.

88. *Ret.*, p. 24.

89. Vol. 5, No. 3 (June, 1887).

90. *Ret.* p. 31.

91. *Poems*, p. 64.

92. Herman Melville, *Moby Dick*, chap. seven. Cf. the conversation between Pierre and Isabel in *Pierre*, chap. 19: "It is the law." "What?" "That a nothing should torment a nothing, for I am a nothing. It is all a dream—we dream that we dreamed we dream."

93. Actually the article is stylistically superior to much of her writing at that time. The influence of eighteenth-century models seems apparent.

94. A. Notebook. Also *Poems*, p. 64.

95. H. A. L. Fisher, *Our New Religion* (New York: Jonathan Cape and Harrison Smith, 1930), pp. 41, 60.

96. Published in *The Covenant*, July, 1847.

97. Published in *New Hampshire Patriot and State Gazette*, June 1, 1848.

98. Published in *The Covenant*, October, 1846.

99. A. Sarah Clement Kimball reminiscences.

100. A sonnet on the theme "They that seek me early shall find me" in her notebook expresses this very beautifully. If written by Mrs. Glover herself it is one of the finest poems she ever wrote, but the authorship is not quite clear.

101. L. Letter to Priscilla Wheeler, December 2, 1850.

102. L. Letter to George S. Baker, January 22, 1848.

103. L. Letter to George S. Baker, September 2, 1848.

104. L. B. Stowe, *Saints, Sinners and Beechers*, p. 99.

105. Tupper's biographer, Derek Hudson, in *Martin Tupper* (London: Constable, 1949), pp. 47 f. suggests *Proverbial Philosophy* as a "source" for *Science and Health* on the basis of one or two vague references to "mind" and "error," but any real resemblance between the two collapses under critical examination.

106. See Loren Eiseley, *Darwin's Century* (New York: Doubleday, 1958), for a sympathetic account of the impact of this book.

107. L. Baker collection.

108. Cf. Harriet Beecher Stowe's comment in *Uncle Tom's Cabin* regarding a very different sort of captive:

> Though parted from all his soul held dear, and though often yearning for what lay beyond, still was he never positively and consciously miserable; for, so well is the harp of human feeling strung, that nothing but a crash that breaks every string can wholly mar its harmony; and, on looking back to seasons which in review appear to us as those of deprivation and trial, we can remember that each hour, as it glided, brought its diversions and alleviations, so that, though not happy wholly, we were not, either, wholly miserable.

109. Her reminiscences in A. contain the following passage: "I, although not being a Christian Scientist, was positively enraged at the articles in McClure's Magazine. . . . They were so absolutely untrue. There was a mean, underlying current in them, and I should think the author, whoever he or she is, would have them on his or her conscience. . . . Mrs. Eddy was so entirely unlike the run of New England country people that they could not understand her."

110. Mrs. Kimball (Sarah Clement) added: "Mrs. Tilton was inclined to be the dressy member of the family. She was peculiar in her dress. She would wear white when no one else thought of doing so." Mary was "always neatly but simply dressed."

111. As a plaintiff in the Next Friends' Suit, 1907.

112. A. Clara Shannon reminiscences.

113. The popularity of such "keepsake" volumes was enormous—gift books, literary annuals, collections of edifying trifles. Between 1846 and 1852 an average

of sixty such anthologies was published each year in the United States. The success of *Gems For You* is shown by the fact that a second edition appeared in 1855.

114. Actually two: Ernest Sutherland Bates and John V. Dittemore. But as collaborators on a biography Bates-Dittemore may be considered a single critic. They write in the Milmine-Dakin tradition but with a sophistication which permits an occasional compliment to Mrs. Eddy despite their generally cynical portrait.

115. A. *L&M* 62–8903. March 29, 1853.

116. A. March 31, 1853.

117. A. April 11, 1853.

118. A. *L&M* 62–8900. April 29, 1853.

119. A. *L&M* 62–8899. May 2, 1853.

120. A. Sarah Clement Kimball reminiscences.

121. In a determined effort to prove a lifelong "morphine habit," Milmine quoted Mrs. Hannah Philbrick who, along with Mrs. Mary Whittier, was the source of all the most sensational charges against Mrs. Glover during the Sanbornton years. The animus of these two ladies and the proved unreliability of several of their more remarkable charges invite a certain skepticism. In this case, such evidence as is available points to exactly the opposite conclusion from the Philbrick charge. See p. 195 and note 6, chap. 6.

122. A. *L&M* 62–8899. May 2, 1853.

123. Undated but evidently May, 1853.

Notes: *Chapter Four*

1. A. Lucy Clark Bancker letter to Mrs. Eddy, March 22, 1890. Also affidavit of Katharine H. Bancker, March 13, 1930.

2. Bates-Dittemore in *Mary Baker Eddy*, p. 41, consider this fact sufficient to discredit the extravagant stories told by Milmine on the subject. Relevant material in A. includes affidavit by Mrs. William (Caroline A.) Rowell and reminiscences of Addie Towns Arnold and Sarah Clement Kimball. On one occasion Clarke's mesmeric experiments resulted in the forming of an expedition to Lynn, Massachusetts, to unearth some of Captain Kidd's treasure, which Clarke's subject described as being buried there. The Bakers' hired man, John Varney, participated in the luckless adventure, and this appears to be the flimsy basis on which the whole story has been transferred to Mrs. Patterson herself.

3. A. Albert E. Miller letter, May 5, 1907.

4. A. *A&P* 31–11244. Glover's daughter, Mrs. Billings, stated after his death that as he grew up he wanted to go to school but Cheney insisted that he work on the farm instead.

5. A. Elmira (Myra) Smith Wilson reminiscences, confirmed by affidavit on January 11, 1907. The date of the Cheneys' departure to the West is made unquestionably clear by a letter from Mrs. Mark Baker to George Baker in L. dated June 6, 1856. This refutes the curious hypothesis of Bates-Dittemore that the Cheneys left before the Pattersons moved to North Groton.

6. See p. 144.

7. *Ret.*, p. 21.

8. L. April 27, 1856.

9. A. This scrapbook, to which she paid particular attention during the bleak middle years, should not be confused with the two notebooks in which she copied her own and others' poems, chiefly during her earlier years.

10. L. June 6, 1857. It is not clear what the tragedy to "Sam" was, unless the reference was not to her brother Samuel but to his son of the same name. The young man was lost at sea about this time.

11. This appears in her published *Poems* under the title "Constancy."

12. A. It is not clear from his handwriting whether the last number is a seven or a nine. The reference to Fremont would have been appropriate in either year. Samuel Baker remarried on November 2, 1858, and his reformation may have taken place either as a prerequisite to or as a result of his marriage. His wife was a former missionary who doubtless found his attendance at Theodore Parker's services reprehensible. The reason for the disagreement between George Sullivan and Martha Rand Baker is unknown, but they did part for a time, and this fact permanently cooled Mrs. Patterson's erstwhile friendship for Martha.

13. A. Affidavit of Mrs. William Rowell and other statements quoted by Sibyl Wilbur in article in *Human Life*, Vol. IV, No. 5 (February, 1907).

14. A. Turner reminiscences. Myra Wilson in her affidavit confirmed this: "I think she was much misunderstood, everybody around us was rugged and strong and did not seem to have patience with her, implying at times that her inability to eat certain things was a notion, I well remember of being influenced myself of this insinuation and so one day without her knowledge prepared her food with a very little butter—one of the things she could not eat—and after her meal she remarked 'From the way I feel I should think I had eaten something with butter in it if I did not know differently,' however, I never deceived her after this as I knew she did suffer from it."

15. *Plymouth* (N.H.) *Record*, July 23, 1904.

16. A. Bailey reminiscences.

17. A. Mrs. Chard's reminiscences probably refer to the Rumney period (1860–1862) immediately following the Groton years, though she herself was living in North Groton when her early memories were recorded.

18. L. Barlow notes. A. Kidder reminiscences.

19. Miller, ed., *Margaret Fuller: American Rebel*, p. 220. Mrs. Gaskell's charming picture of English village life in *Cranford* appeared in this decade. Miss Fuller granted that in some long-established rural societies the inherited wisdom and loyalty of the past might exempt the inhabitants from her strictures.

20. This is something different from the attitude of the romantic *femme incomprise,* of the village Madame de Staël or the George Sand *manquée.*

21. Mrs. Sylvester Swett quoted in Sibyl Wilbur, *The Life of Mary Baker Eddy* (Boston: Christian Science Publishing Society, 1933), p. 59.

22. A. Myra Smith Wilson reminiscences.

23. A. F. B. Eastman affidavit.

24. A. Elizabeth Earl Jones notes.

25. One catches a glimpse here of the Mrs. Eddy of later years who, when she was passing through deep waters, would rally herself for her daily ride through Concord at any cost.

26. The years 1859–60 and perhaps earlier.

27. A. Mrs. Sylvester Swett reminiscences.

28. Browning's "Childe Roland to the Dark Tower Came" might stand as the strenuous moral comment of the age on a wilderness which T. S. Eliot's century would see as a universal wasteland.

29. A. Eastman affidavit. This actually took place during 1860 or 1861 in Rumney, but it throws light equally on the Groton years.

30. This is true of all those brought up in the Puritan tradition who took their spiritual heritage seriously.

31. Judging from her later teaching, this chapter had a deep personal import for Mrs. Eddy.

32. *S&H*, p. 574. *No*, p. 34.

33. Something of what is symbolized may be suggested in the famous chapter on whiteness in *Moby Dick* and the chapter on snow in Thomas Mann's *Magic Mountain*.

34. *Mis.*, p. 87. Early in life she marked a passage in Pope's "Essay on Man" (in the Lindley Murray *Reader*) to which she returned again and again in later years:

> All are but parts of one stupendous whole,
> Whose body Nature is, and God the soul;
> That, chang'd through all, and yet in all the same;
> Great in the earth, as in th' etherial frame;
> Warms in the sun, refreshes in the breeze,
> Glows in the stars, and blossoms in the trees,
> Lives through all life, extends through all extent,
> Spreads undivided, operates unspent.

In these lines Pope's deism lapsed clearly into pantheism, but the interpretation Mrs. Eddy gave to them in her writings was far from pantheistic. God was never in physical appearances, however beautiful. The nature in which He manifested Himself was wholly spiritual, always outside matter. This left material appearances as merely imperfect symbols of spiritual realities.

35. Cf. Thoreau's treatment of the wild and savage in the chapter on "Higher Laws" in *Walden* and Melville's suggestive passage on the demonic in *Moby Dick:*

> Tell me, why this strong young colt, foaled in some peaceful valley of Vermont, far removed from all beasts of prey—why is it that upon the sunniest day, if you but shake a fresh buffalo robe behind him, so that he cannot even see it, but only smells its wild animal muskiness—why will he start, snort, and with bursting eyes paw the ground in phrensies of affright? There is no remembrance in him of any goring of wild creatures in his green northern home, so that the strange muskiness he smells cannot recall to him anything associated with the experience of former perils; for what knows he, this New England colt, of the black bisons of distant Oregon?

No: but here thou beholdest even in a dumb brute, the instinct of the knowledge of the demonism in the world. Though thousands of miles from Oregon, still when he smells that savage musk, the rending, goring bison herds are as present as to the deserted wild foal of the prairies, which this instant they may be trampling into dust.

36. Wilbur, *Life*, pp. 59 f. Oliver Wendell Holmes made some pertinent observations on women's nervous diseases in the chapter entitled "The Sunbeam and the Shadow" in *Elsie Venner*. See also William James's discussion of inspiration and neurosis in chapter one of *The Varieties of Religious Experience*.

37. Agassiz's great *Essay on Classification* was published in 1857, but most of Mrs. Eddy's allusions to him appear to refer to his later *Methods of Study in Natural Science*.

38. Kierkegaard, *Purify Your Heart* (London: C. W. Daniel, 1937). The title is more usually translated *Purity of Heart*.

39. *S&H*, pp. 172, 191.

40. Wilbur, *Life*, p. 62, based on Mrs. Kidder's own statements. Several people who knew Mrs. Glover intimately during the years of her widowhood in Sanbornton have denied that she had any interest in spiritualism, while Milmine on the other hand gives the usual number of sensational stories to prove that she was a full-fledged believer. The truth appears to lie somewhere in between. Mrs. Glover went into the new craze only enough to find out that she couldn't believe in it. Milmine was unable to collect any gossip in Franklin or North Groton which would support the charge that Mrs. Patterson was then interested in spiritualism.

41. A. Reminiscences of Clara Shannon, Adam Dickey, and others.

42. Alfred Farlow, Mrs. Eddy's first Committee on Publication, assiduously followed up each report of this sort which appeared in the press, only to have it melt away into misunderstood hearsay and irresponsible invention, frequently followed by embarrassed retraction.

43. See p. 56. Also *My.*, p. 30.

44. Dr. Maxwell Finland in a Shattuck lecture, quoted in the *Saturday Review*, May 24, 1962. See also Emerson's statement in his *Journal* for 1837:

The . . . complaint . . . is made against the Boston Medical College . . . that those who there receive their education, want faith, and so are not as successful as practitioners from the country schools who believe in the power of medicine

45. Warren F. Evans, *Soul and Body* (Boston, 1876), p. 33.

46. J. J. Garth Wilkinson, *The Human Body and Its Relation to Man* (Philadelphia, 1851).

47. Page 156. See also pp. 152–153.

48. Norman Beasley, *Mary Baker Eddy* (New York: Duell, Sloan and Pearce, 1963), p. 347. Quoted from Mrs. Eddy's interview with the Masters in the Next Friends' Suit, 1907.

49. *Ibid.* In her verbal account to the Masters Mrs. Eddy appears to have mixed the two cases as described in *S&H*—not surprisingly, perhaps, considering the trying circumstances.

50. *Ret.*, p. 33.

51. A. Myra Smith Wilson reminiscences.

52. Herman Melville, *The Confidence-Man* (New York: Grove Press 1955), p. 132. Even Thoreau, when the November mood of his later years chilled his vital forces, could write in his Journal: "Is not disease the rule of existence? There is not a lily pad floating on the river but has been riddled by insects. Almost every shrub and tree has its gall, oftentimes esteemed its chief ornament and hardly to be distinguished from the fruit. If misery loves company, misery has company enough. Now, at midsummer, find me a perfect leaf or fruit."

53. For a physical healing see p. 23. Her letters and poems give evidence of the latter kind of healing. Referring to God as "too *good* to be unkind," she wrote Martha Rand in 1848: "On Him you may rely, and find a Father and a friend. This is my only consolation, *unworthy* as I am—and 'tis the greatest I can recommend to those I love" (L. Baker collection).

54. A. Tomlinson diary. Again this appears to have taken place at Rumney rather than North Groton, but in the same general period of her life.

55. A. *A&M* 71–10106.

56. On Florence Nightingale's birthday, May 12, 1857, Elizabeth and Emily Blackwell opened their epoch-making hospital in New York. Women's traditional relation with the healing ministry was entering a new phase of authority.

57. The air at this time was alive with the question of whether miracles were possible in a world governed by law. More and more writers were suggesting that a miracle may be the expression of a law not yet understood.

58. Sarah Josepha Hale, *Three Hours, or the Vigil of Love, and other poems*, Philadelphia, 1848.

59. See, for instance, *Transactions of the Medical Society of New Jersey*, 1866, poem entitled "Christian Science" read by the president of the society, Abraham Coles, at the annual meeting on January 23, 1866. It was written by Coles himself.

60. L. First-hand evidence on the Groton and Rumney years is scant, but most of it was gathered through the initiative and energy of Mary Beecher Longyear. Today L. owns both the Groton and Rumney houses where Mrs. Patterson lived.

61. Page 58. She also made clear, however, that home is a state of mind rather than a physical place.

62. In her scrapbook is a newspaper clipping of a poem which she related stanza by stanza to specific years of her life. Opposite a stanza describing "the storm of sorrow" which extinguished once and for all the glory of life she wrote "1856." This was the year young George Glover was taken away to Minnesota. The date "1859" was written opposite an almost equally dolorous stanza which, however, went on to say:

> Let the present have its torture
> > And the past its store of ill,
> To the Future—to the future
> > We will look with gladness still.

The resilience of the lines matched the resilience of the verses which she soon began writing again.

63. A. Alfred Farlow, "Facts and Incidents Relating to Mrs. Eddy," p. 194.

64. L. Mrs. Longyear's notes on conversations with old Rumney inhabitants.

65. A. *L&M* 62–8898.

66. A. *L&M* 21–2683. Dated August 17, 1861.

67. However, in the poem to Major Anderson she had already written:

Yet would I yield a husband, child, to fight
Or die the unyielding guardians of right,
Than that the life blood circling through their veins
Should warm a heart to forge new human chains.

68. A. Letter of David Hall quoted in *LaCrosse* (Wisconsin) *Leader Press,* January 4, 1911.

69. A. At this early stage of his imprisonment Patterson did not sound uncheerful.

70. L. May 12, 1862. "O! how dark are the mysteries of *His* hand when it is laid so heavily upon us!" the writer exclaimed somberly.

71. A. Mrs. Patterson expressed her own affectionate anxiety at this time in a poem entitled "To a Bird Flying Southward" which recalled some of her earlier feelings for North Carolina.

72. A. Unmounted. December 2, 1861.

73. L. Tenney reminiscences. Cf. *Theory and Practice of the Movement Cure* by Charles Fayette Taylor published in 1861:

The special influence of the mind and will upon the general bodily nutrition is daily manifested and acknowledged by every physician. . . . Hope to the sick man brings life and health; despair to the well man brings disease and death. . . . Bad news impairs the appetite. . . . Melancholy destroys the action of the bowels, causing constipation. . . . Now, all this indicates that there may be a *Medical Psychology.*

74. C. Quimby material. Letter of October 14, 1861.

75. C. *Ibid.* Letter of May 29, 1862.

76. C. *Ibid.* Letter of August, 1862.

77. A. Letters of Mrs. Mary A. Baker to Mrs. Eddy. Also Mrs. Baker's letter to Irving C. Tomlinson, August 20, 1901.

78. Letter of Mrs. Baker to Calvin A. Frye, February 14, 1902.

79. They might conceivably have left from Tilton, taken a boat down the Merrimack to Portsmouth and thence by sea to Portland, but this seems unlikely.

80. Longfellow, "My Lost Youth."

81. *Belfast Republican Journal,* March 26, 1923, on nineteenth birthday of Mrs. Augusta J. Frederick.

82. A. Letter of George A. Quimby to Daniel H. Spofford, December 13, 1878.

Notes: *Chapter Five*

1. *The History and Philosophy of Animal Magnetism,* by a Practical Magnetizer. Quoted by William Lyman Johnson in Quimby compilation (A.).

2. Quimby letter in *Portland Daily Advertiser,* February 17, 1862.

3. Horatio W. Dresser, ed., *The Quimby Manuscripts* (New York: Thomas Y. Crowell Co., 1921), p. 72.

4. *Ibid.*, p. 75.

5. Quoted from Quimby manuscripts in Annetta G. Dresser, *The Philosophy of P. P. Quimby* (Boston: George H. Ellis, 1895), p. 87. Cf. Joseph Smith in *Doctrine and Covenants:* "There is no such thing as immaterial matter. All spirit is matter, but it is more fine or pure, and can only be discerned by purer eyes; We cannot see it, but when our bodies are purified, we shall see that it is all matter."

6. John Bovee Dods, *The Philosophy of Electrical Psychology* (New York: Fowler and Wells, 1850). A review of the book, followed by a column and a half of illustrative material, appeared in the *Belfast Republican* on June 14, 1850.

7. In her book *The Philosophy of P. P. Quimby*, Annetta G. Dresser quoted Quimby's *Advertiser* letter of 1862 as follows: "The subject I had left me, and was employed by ——, who used him in examining diseases in the mesmeric sleep." The printed letter in the *Advertiser* (see note 2 above) has the name of John Bovee Dods where Mrs. Dresser left a blank. The reason for her reluctance to draw attention to Dods is suggested by the parallel passages between the two. For instance, on p. 150 of his book Dods writes, "Man is an epitome of the universe, and all the elements in exact proportion are most skillfully combined in his system." On p. 77 of the Dresser book Quimby is said to have described man as "an epitome of creation, 'with all the elements of the material world.' " In the first edition of *S&H* Mrs. Eddy also wrote that "man epitomizes the universe" but went on to say that she had "made the discovery through spiritual sense, that the body of Soul embraces the universe, and that man is the full idea of Life, Substance and Intelligence" (p. 229). Her meaning is made clearer in the last edition of *S&H* where she speaks of man (p. 502) as "including" the universe and writes (p. 475): "Man is idea, the image of Love; he is not physique. He is the compound idea of God, including all right ideas."

8. Dods, *Electrical Psychology*, pp. 82 f. This sort of statement was by no means unique to Dods. Cf. Andrew Jackson Davis commenting on homeopathy in the first volume of *The Great Harmonia* 4th ed. (Boston: Sanborn, Carter & Bazin, 1855), pp. 248 f.

> "Hahnemann reveals and demonstrates most conclusively the relations, connections and sympathies, existing between the magnetism of medicines and the magnetism of the organization; he recommends the practitioner to *dilute, shake, manipulate, magnetize, and spiritualize,* his medicines for the purpose of potentializing and widening the circumference of their influence upon the system; he plainly teaches it is by this process that medicines become penetrative, operative, and remedial; and yet there are but few of his disciples that know or believe anything concerning the magnificent and world-revolutionizing developments of Human Magnetism or spiritual philosophy. Homeopathists comprehend something of the mode by which the magnetism or spirit of the medicine acts upon the magnetism or spirit of the human system; but that *spirit can act upon spirit,* and develop powers and capabilities in the human soul of which the world has had no previous knowledge, is too inconsistent, they generally think, with all nature, to be for one moment admitted. And yet they profess to believe that the 'Homeopathic healing art develops for its purpose the *immaterial'* (dynamic) *virtues of medicinal substances,* even in those substances, which, 'in a

natural or crude state, betrayed not the *least medical power* upon the human system.' "

9. This runs counter to the Dresser contention several decades later, but the Dressers offered no evidence from the Belfast years to support their position.

10. A. This is one of many affidavits and written statements gathered mostly by Alfred Farlow between 1899 and 1908.

11. A. Farlow collection.

12. Among these are the accounts of Annie G. Morrill of Manchester, New Hampshire; Helen M. Austin, Haverhill, Massachusetts; Emma A. Thompson, Minneapolis, Minnesota; Amos Weston, Boston, Massachusetts; Martha J. Hinds, Port Townsend, Washington; Sarah M. Day, Everett, Massachusetts; Lydia P. French, Durham, New Hampshire; Angelina Paine, Portland, Maine; Sarah T. Fifield, Boston Highlands, Massachusetts; George Watson, Reading, Pennsylvania; E. J. Morrison, New York, New York; and Elizabeth Ulmer, Minneapolis, Minnesota.

13. Letter of F. L. Town in *Portland Advertiser,* March 6, 1862.

14. A. This occurs in one of the three letters doubtfully attributed to Mary Baker (see note 64, chapter 2).

15. November 24, 1857.

16. A. Norton in later years became a Christian Scientist, but his account maintains an admirable objectivity. While he scouted the idea that there was any significant relation between Quimby's theories and Christian Science, he retained his admiration for the character and intellectual adventurousness of the little "doctor."

17. These notes were the basis of the Norton account in A.

18. Quoted in Randall Stewart, ed., *The American Notebooks by Nathaniel Hawthorne* (New Haven: Yale University Press, 1932), p. lxxv.

19. *The Quimby Manuscripts,* pp. 144 f. While "The Truth is the Cure" might suggest the biblical words, "Ye shall know the truth, and the truth shall make you free," the explanation or "truth" which Quimby gave to his patients was often on a markedly unbiblical level, as when he wrote a patient in 1861 (*ibid.,* p. 114):

> You know I told you about your stooping over: this stooping is caused by excitement affecting the head. This contracts the stomach, causes an irritation, sending the heat to the head. This heat excites the glands about the nose, it runs down the throat and this is all there is about it. It will affect you sometimes when you are a little excited, and you will take it for a cold.
>
> Remember how I explained to you about standing straight. Just put your hands on your hips, than bend forward and back.
>
> This relaxes the muscles around the waist at the pit of the stomach. This takes away the pressure from the nerves of the stomach and allays the irritation. Now follow this and I will work upon your stomach two or three times in three or four days.

20. Annetta Dresser, *Philosophy of P. P. Quimby,* p. 49. Also Julius Dresser, *The True History of Mental Science* (Boston: Alfred Mudge & Son, 1887), p. 18: "He even had no fixed name for his theory or practice." In a letter to Edward J. Arens (February 23, 1883) George Quimby wrote, "He called it his 'Theory' of healing the sick" (A.).

21. *The Physician,* volume one of Davis's four-volume work *The Great Harmonia,* appeared in 1850 when Quimby's thinking was in an early formative stage. On p. 116 Davis writes: "Remember that diseased organs or parts are simply *evidences* that the spiritual equilibrium has been constitutionally or generally disturbed. Consequently, this spiritual disturbance *is the disease,* and *not* the multifarious and momentarily changing symptoms which are locally experienced. Hence to restore scrofulous, tuberculous, or cancerous matter to its proper position in the animal economy, the original spiritual harmony must be re-established. And here the question may be asked—'How can you re-establish this original harmony?' I answer, the spiritual principle must be addressed by, or reached through, the same mediums which it employs, as instrumentalities, in operating upon and governing the organism. I have shown these mediums to be electricity and magnetism."

22. Andrew Jackson Davis, *The Principles of Nature,* 13th ed. (New York: Charles Partridge. 1866), p. 326. The two following quotations are from pp. 47 and 50 of the same book.

23. Davis and Poe were both especially concerned with the beginning and the end of things, with genesis and apocalypse. See Perry Miller, *Errand Into the Wilderness,* chapter on "The End of the World."

24. One finds such historians as H. A. L. Fisher and Charles S. Braden at opposite extremes on this matter.

25. A. Letter to Eugene Wood, October, 1901.

26. George A. Quimby letter of June 20, 1907, quoted in John Whitehead, *The Illusion of Christian Science.* Also H. Dresser in *Handbook of the New Thought* states that Quimby had some familiarity with Swedenborg's views through conversations with a New Church minister in Portland.

27. *The Quimby Manuscripts,* p. 71.

28. A. Emily Pierce letters.

29. George Bush, *Mesmer and Swedenborg* (New York: John Allen, 1847).

30. Volume one, p. 291.

31. See, e.g., vol. 2, of *The Great Harmonia,* pp. 380, 389, 391. The idea is developed further in *The Penetralia* (Boston: Bela Marsh, 1857), pp. 106, 118:

> "Jesus" is the Greek for the Hebrew word "Joshua;" and the term "Savior" is the English rendering. The word "Christ" was annexed to distinguish him from many others bearing the first name. "Messiah" is the Hebrew for the Greek word "Christ;" and the term "Anointed" is the English translation. . . . Jesus was a local man; the "Christ?" that means a principle. . . . The Christ-principle, then, is universal. It shone through several natures before Jesus, shone through him when he existed, and still shines through every good word and work.

32. Little attention so far has been paid to the crucial importance of clairvoyance to Quimby. In part this may be because most investigators have followed the lead of the Dressers, who could not fit this relic of mesmerism into their metaphysical interpretation of Quimby.

33. *The Quimby Manuscripts,* p. 189.

34. *Ibid.,* p. 409. On p. 342 Jesus' healing of the centurion's servant is cited as a clear example of clairvoyance.

35. What Quimby means by a "spiritual" identity is disclosed in such a passage as the following from *The Quimby Manuscripts* (p. 213) in commenting on a patient:

> Her body had an identity apart from the earthly body, and this sick (spiritual) body is the one that tells the trouble. This body seemed to be holding up the natural body, till it was so weak it could barely sit up. This spiritual body is what flows from, or comes from the natural body, and contains all the feelings complained of. It speaks through the natural body, and like the heat from a fire has its bounds, is inclosed by walls or partitions as much as a prison. But the confinement is in our belief, its odor is its identity; its knowledge is in its odor; its misery arises from false ideas, and its ideas are in itself, connected with its natural body. This is all matter, and has an identity. The trouble, like sound, has no locality of itself, but can be directed to any place. Now as this intelligence is around the body, it locates its trouble in the natural body, calls it "pain" or by some other name. Now the sick person is in this prison, with the body, which body feels as though it contained life. But the life is in the spiritual body, which being ignorant of itself places its own identity in the flesh and blood.

36. *The Quimby Manuscripts*, p. 172.

37. February 13, 1862. Cf. William James' statement in 1864: "A doctor does more by the moral effect of his presence on the patient and family than anything else"—Gardner Murphy and Robert O. Ballou, eds., *William James on Psychical Research* (New York: Viking, 1960) p. 7.

38. *The Quimby Manuscripts*, p. 263.

39. A. Affidavits and reminiscences of Helen M. Austin, Amos Weston and mother, Sarah M. Day, Frank H. Weller, Agnes M. Jenks, Martha J. Hinds. Among other similar statements is a letter from one Gorham D. Gilman to Georgine Milmine, December 18, 1906, intended to furnish her with further ammunition against Mrs. Eddy. Telling of his visit to Quimby in Portland and of Quimby's rubbing his sister's head, he reported that when asked about his method Quimby replied: "I do not know much more about it than you. There is nothing occult about it that I know of. I simply know that I have this power given to me. I do not understand what it means; do not know what it is, or where it comes from. I simply know of its possession. I make no claims of originality or any supernatural gift." Gilman then continues: "He seemed a simple, straightforward man desirous of doing good and relieving suffering. My point is that Dr. Quimby distinctly disavowed any 'revelation' or supernatural power. Saying 'I do not know,' while Mrs. Eddy, a pupil, claims to know it all."

40. Footnote by Horatio Dresser in his revised (1899) edition of his father's printed lecture *The True History of Mental Science*.

41. A. Mrs. Thompson's account in *The Christian Science Journal* of November, 1886, was authenticated by her father, mother, and aunt. The more detailed account quoted on p. 165 was given as an affidavit in 1907.

42. Only a minimal portion of them is in his own handwriting. See discussion on pp. 181 ff. of the possibility that some material by a writer or writers other than himself may have been mixed with his own writings and attributed to him by the copyist.

43. *The Quimby Manuscripts*, pp. 112 f.

44. A. *A&M* 16–10408.

45. Letter to *Portland Courier*, November 7, 1862.

46. A. *A&M* 16–10409.

47. Second letter to *Portland Courier*, November, 1862.

48. C. Letter of March 10, 1863.

49. Letter to *Boston Post*, March 7, 1883.

50. This letter proves neither as much nor as little as polemicists have claimed. It shows without question that she believed she had received both the cure and the explanation for which she had been searching, but it shows that she felt there was a "principle" which still eluded her grasp. At that time she had no doubt that Quimby could impart it to her. Later she came to feel (A. *A&M* 67–9659) that only in his reiterated injunction not to place intelligence in matter did he approach Science but that this negative insight was useless without a revelation of the true nature of Mind, Spirit, or God, for otherwise intelligence was simply shifted from matter to what she came to call "mortal mind."

51. Cf. *S&H*, p. 275: "The starting-point of divine Science is that God, Spirit, is All-in-all, and that there is no other might nor Mind,—that God is Love, and therefore He is divine Principle. To grasp the reality and order of being in its Science, you must begin by reckoning God as the divine Principle of all that really is."

52. A. Hinds correspondence and affidavit.

53. See, e.g., *S&H*, p. 467.

54. *Unity*, p. 18.

55. *The Quimby Manuscripts*, p. 436.

56. A. Mrs. Hunter (then Mrs. Hinds) wrote Alfred Farlow in 1907, "I have great respect for Dr. Quimby and could not say a word against him." But she also stated on various occasions that he was generally known as a magnetic healer. She had read and copied some of his manuscripts and kept them for several years afterwards, though without any particular interest in them.

57. *Mis.*, p. 379.

58. C. Letter of March 8, 1863.

59. C. Letter of January 12, 1863.

60. C. Letters of January 12 and 31, 1863.

61. C. Letter of September 14, 1863.

62. L. November 14 [1863?].

63. A. *A&M* 16–10408.

64. *Mis.*, p. 378.

65. A. *A&M* 16–10408 and 16–10409. *Mis.*, p. 379.

66. A. *A&M* 16–10407.

67. A. *A&M* 16–10409.

68. A. Letter of Mary A. Baker to Irving C. Tomlinson, August 20, 1901.

69. Dresser's diary for the late months of 1861 and early months of 1862 has been deposited recently in the library of Boston University. It does not show

whether he had already started his newspaper career by October, 1862, but he may very well have done so. Although Dresser had been healed by Quimby in the summer of 1860, it was not until early in 1862 that he came to Portland from Waterville, Maine, in order to learn more of Quimby's theory. What the diary does show clearly is the inaccuracy of Horatio Dresser's statement in *The Quimby Manuscripts* (p. 5) that Julius Dresser "spent his time" after June, 1860, in "conversing with new patients" and explaining Quimby's theory and methods to inquirers.

70. According to George Quimby, they did this with meticulous care, never changing the original wording in any respect, though they did correct the spelling.

71. A. Letter to Edward J. Arens, October 2, 1882.

72. A. Hinds reminiscences.

73. Milmine, *Life.*, p. 58.

74. A. Letter from George Quimby to Daniel H. Spofford, December 13, 1878.

75. *New Hampshire Patriot,* November 26, 1862, and *Portland Advertiser,* December 19, 1862.

76. A. John Patterson's letter of Demember 28, 1899, to Mrs. Eddy.

77. A. "To Whom It May Concern," signed by Governor N. S. Berry, October 23, 1862.

78. C. The rest of Mrs. Patterson's letters to Quimby show that her ailments started to return almost immediately after she wrote this hopeful letter.

79. C. Letter of January 31, 1863.

80. C. Letter of March 10, 1863.

81. *Portland Daily Press,* October 21, 1863.

82. *Ibid.*

83. These are journalistic verses, the general level of which is suggested by two lines from a poem published in the *Daily Press* on November 16, 1863:

The present, if grievous, is quickly away,
Our trials are bubbles exploding to-day.

84. L. November 14 [1863?].

85. A. According to his daughter, Mrs. Billings, he re-enlisted on January 15, 1864. Mrs. Billings states that he corresponded with his mother fairly regularly at this time and adds, "Father also carried a photo of his mother throughout the entire war."

86. *Portland Daily Press,* December 31, 1863. The published version differs slightly from the one in her notebook.

87. October 27, 1863.

88. In an essay entitled "Der Szientismus" (*Gesammelte Aufsätze,* III, pp. 460–479), the church historian Karl Holl noted with some surprise that the Christian doctrine of redemption through suffering continued to play a part in Mrs. Eddy's thinking after her discovery of Christian Science and that it was possible to find a logical connection between this doctrine and her basic metaphysical position. Her use of the word "Wisdom" in the quoted passage on Paul relates her to the

Christian tradition rather than to the gnostic self-sufficiency implied in Quimby's use of the word.

89. A. Unidentified newspaper clipping.

90. Andrew Jackson Davis, *The Great Harmonia,* Vol. 2 (Boston: Benjamin B. Mussey & Co., 1851), p. 289.

91. See note 20, above.

92. Davis, *The Great Harmonia,* Vol. 2, pp. 312 f.

93. *The Quimby Manuscripts,* pp. 393 f.

94. A. Abigail Dyer Thompson reminiscences.

95. *My.,* p. 307.

96. *The Quimby Manuscripts,* p. 198.

97. Ernest Renan, *Life of Jesus* (New York: Modern Library, 1927), pp. 149 f.

98. A. Crosby letter to Horace T. Wentworth, November 14, 1903.

99. *The Philosophy of P. P. Quimby,* p. 49.

100. *The Quimby Manuscripts,* p. 438.

101. Letter to *Boston Post,* March 9, 1883.

102. A. *A&M* 16–10408.

103. Letter to *Courier,* November 7, 1862.

104. Published with the same title by Alfred Mudge & Son, Boston, 1887. In the March, 1888, issue of the *New England Magazine,* George Quimby wrote that after his father moved to Portland at the end of 1859 the Misses Ware became his patients and that later they "suggested to him the propriety of putting into writing the body of his thoughts." George Quimby adds, "From that time he began to write out his ideas, which practice he continued until his death." This statement would seem to cast doubt on dates earlier than 1860 or 1861 attributed to Quimby's written explanations of his theory.

105. June, 1888. Swartz, who allied himself with the Quimby forces at this time, went on to say a little defensively, "All literary people know that manuscripts proper consist of the views written by an individual, or his views penned by another for him, provided that he corrects, approves, and appropriates the same."

106. This was Mrs. Eddy's own assumption in the 1880's when George Quimby was categorically refusing to allow even friendly outsiders to examine the manuscripts. In a letter dated November 11, 1901 (quoted in William Lyman Johnson compilation in A.) George Quimby wrote: "She heard many of his essays read; wrote many herself which she submitted to him for inspection and correction. But she never left any of hers with him and never had any of his to look at." Since the younger Quimby had by that time destroyed most of the originals it is unlikely that investigation today can settle the matter definitely.

107. Fisher, *Our New Religion,* p. 25.

108. Horatio Dresser on page 17 of *The Quimby Manuscripts* describes the later articles as "not so clear" as the early ones. However, in *Health and the Inner Life* (p. 12) he had written in 1906 that the "later writings, never seen by Mrs. Patterson-Eddy, are much clearer on the crucial points." Dresser's frequent reversals of

judgment on such matters as this compound the confusion of the manuscripts themselves.

109. A. *A&M* 6–10242.

110. C. March 31, April 5, April 10, April 24, May 24, May [?], 1864.

111. This "penalty doctrine," as it has been called, was to haunt her for a number of years. In the third edition of *S&H* (1882) she wrote (p. 38): "In years past we suffered greatly for the sick when healing them, but even that is all over now, and we cannot suffer for them."

112. See *S&H*, pp. 184 f. The reference to her "metaphysical treatment" seems to indicate that in retrospect she considered this a genuinely spiritual healing in line with her later development after 1866. Seen in this light, her 1866 experience becomes only the most decisive of several steps taking her toward the point of development represented by the first edition of *S&H* in 1875. In that edition she gave 1864 as the year of discovery and continued to do so for several years afterward until she had sorted out her ideas more thoroughly. See *S&H*, pp. viii:28–32 and 460:24–32.

113. C. Letter of July 8.

114. A. Crosby letter to A. A. Beauchamp, December 11, 1909: "I had a most unselfish love for her and deep sympathy with her, when in her poverty she came to me,—no money—scarcely comfortable clothing—most unhappy in her domestic relations."

115. C. Letter of April 5, 1864.

116. A. Letter of July 21, 1903.

117. A. Letter of May 16, 1907.

118. A. One of the letters further admonished her: "Be ye calm in reliance on self, amid all the changes of natural yearnings, of too keen a sense of earth joys, of too great a struggle between the material and spiritual." Not surprisingly, it went on to recommend that she turn her attention to P. P. Quimby.

119. Albert Baker, with his warnings against religious fanaticism and self-delusion, may well have symbolized to Mrs. Patterson the path of spiritual rationality. Some such conscious or unconscious identification may have resulted in his choice for the ill-conceived experiment with Mrs. Crosby.

120. A. Crosby letter to Lyman Powell, May 16, 1907.

121. A. In a letter to Georgine Milmine describing the occasion, Mrs. Crosby asserted that she did not think the "S" who signed the newspaper account was Dr. Sheldon—he was too dignified!—but elsewhere in the letter she slipped up and remarked that the newspaper notice showed that Mrs. Patterson had given "Dr. Sheldon" (i.e., the writer of the article) the impression that she had lived in the south some thirty years.

122. A. The alternation between lavish sentimentality and sharp-tongued asperity in Mrs. Crosby's letters in later years suggests that she may not have been a wholly reliable friend—or witness.

123. A. Farlow, "Facts and Incidents," quoting a Miss Moulton of Lynn. Also letter of Mrs. H. A. Kelly to Mrs. Eddy, September 15, 1906.

124. A. Edwin J. Thompson Reminiscences. At the time the *McClure's* articles were appearing, Thompson in a letter to J. H. Thompson (January 28, 1907)

protested what he considered to be their unfairness and added: "I did not understand her at that time, any more do I at present, but that does not matter. I like to see fair play, especially if there is a woman in the case, and if anyone does right, or what their conscience tells them is right, let them be treated right by their fellow human beings."

125. February 3, 1866.

126. Mrs. Patterson's only known reference to this event is in a poem written some months later when she wrote of the "midnight day" when Justice grasped the sword

> And on her altar our loved Lincoln's own
> Great willing heart did lay.

127. C. Letters from Daniel Patterson to Quimby, April 24, 1865, and from Mrs. Patterson to Quimby, July 29, 1865.

128. Several published statements in earlier years had said or implied that his system was as exact as any science, but none had actually called it a science.

129. See p.

130. A. Letter of October 2, 1882.

131. H. Dresser, *A Message to the Well* (New York: Putnam, 1910), p. 88.

132. A. J. Swartz in *Mental Science Magazine* (March, 1888), p. 135.

133. H. Dresser, *Health and the Inner Life* (New York: Putnam, 1906), p. 119.

134. See Appendix D. Also pp. 268 ff.

135. L. Letter of September 7, 1865, from Mrs. Patterson to Martha Pilsbury.

136. C. From this point on, she and Glover seem to have corresponded only intermittently until he finally came to see her in 1879.

137. Her financial and domestic straits at this time, as well as her own and Quimby's failing health, mark this as one of the lowest points in her experience.

138. A. Affidavit of Jane T. Clark (quoted also in part in Smith, *Historical Sketches*, p. 50). Mrs. Clark writes that after treating her husband "Mr. Quimby would go out to his barn, or garden, and work off the pain and disease from his own body, claiming that the treatment drew the disease from the patient into himself. After a few days Mr. Quimby told us that he was having a new experience in that he had found it impossible to rid himself of the discomfort and pain taken from Mr. Clark."

139. The poem was not actually published in the *Lynn Reporter* until February 14.

Notes: *Chapter Six*

1. Affidavit of Alvin M. Cushing, quoted in Milmine, *Life*, p. 84.

2. A. Edwin J. Thompson reminiscences.

3. Cushing affidavit.

4. A. Cushing letter to Lyman P. Powell, June 14, 1907.

5. *Ibid.*

6. Cushing affidavit. Cushing pointed out that the one-eighth of a grain of morphine was given "not as a curative remedy, but as an expedient to lessen the pain of removing," and its effect was so immediate that, he added, "Probably one-sixteenth of a grain would have put her sound asleep." Bates-Dittemore make the disingenuous comment (p. 112 n.), "This seems conclusive evidence that she had not as yet yielded far to the habit." Medically it would seem to be conclusive evidence that there was no habit.

7. L. George Newhall reminiscences. Quoted in Smith, *Historical Sketches,* pp. 55 f. Also Florence M. Lampard reminiscences in A.

8. This, at least, was how he described the diagnosis to Sibyl Wilbur in 1907. See Wilbur, *Life,* p. 124.

9. A. Cushing letter to Powell.

10. Wilbur, *Life,* p. 124. However, Cushing told Miss Wilbur that he "afterwards prescribed a more highly attenuated remedy." In his affidavit he did not indicate what remedy or remedies he prescribed.

11. A. Adah E. Cook reminiscences. Cushing's difficulty in remembering is understandable in view of the following passage from Powell, *Mary Baker Eddy,* p. 110: "It was in the summer of 1907 that the author had a long talk as well as correspondence with Dr. Cushing, who was spending his last years in Springfield, near the author's Northampton home. Across the twoscore years he recalled with pride the days when he was a popular doctor and a man of social consequence in Lynn. His eyes brightened in describing the 'spanking' team which he often drove on sunny afternoons along the Lynn speedway. He observed that one day he had prescribed for as many as fifty-nine patients."

12. A typical statement is that in A. *A&M* 27–11057: "When I met with an accident in 1866 I at first took Dr. Cushing's medicine and it did me no good then I quit taking it."

13. A. Henry Robinson reminiscences. Cushing affidavit states he did not even call on the Sunday but did return on the Monday when, according to Mrs. Eddy's account, she sent for him to show him she was well.

Cushing also stated that he was called again to treat Mrs. Patterson for a cold on August 10, 1866, and for several days thereafter, and that these visits were recorded in his medical day book. After this statement was published in the *Springfield* (Mass.) *Union* on October 17, 1900, Alfred Farlow visited Cushing and was shown the entries in the day book but found that the charges were made against Patterson without indication as to whether Patterson himself or his wife had been treated (A. note on Farlow's reply to the *Union*).

When Cushing later repeated the same statement in an article in the *Homeopathic Envoy* Farlow wrote that journal: "Dr. Cushing declares that he allowed me to read his record of these matters. . . . What he showed me was not a record of any proceedings whatever; simply a few entries on his book against the name Patterson. There is nothing to prove what his charges were for." Quoted in *Human Life,* Vol. IV, No. 8 (May, 1907), p. 8.

Among the Farlow papers in A. is a list of three items from Cushing's log-book:

"May 13 Dr. Samuel [sic] Patterson $1.00
"Aug. 12 Patterson   1.00
"Aug. 13 Patterson   1.00
"These items all occur under the date of 1866."

This would seem to be somewhat less than conclusive evidence for August visits to Mrs. Patterson. That Cushing himself was not entirely objective is suggested by his statement in a letter to Miss Milmine on February 14, 1907 (A.): "You are certainly showing the old lady up all right. . . . My sons and others are very much stirred up that my name should appear in such a sacreligious [sic] affair as Christian Science."

14. A. Abbie Whittier Griffin affidavit.

15. A. Arietta Brown Mann affidavit. Quoted in Smith, *Historical Sketches*, pp. 57 f.

16. A. Henry Robinson reminiscences.

17. A. *A&M* 27–11029: "The shadows of the dark valley gathered around me but I could barely see enough to trace a scriptural passage which I regret to say I cannot recall but it changed the scene." In several early editions of *S&H* she wrote of turning to Mark 3 but in her article "One Cause and Effect" (*Mis.*, p. 24) she tells of opening up to Matthew 9:2, and this is the passage which stands as her final recollection of the incident.

18. Interview with Lilian Whiting in the *Ohio Leader*, reprinted in *The Christian Science Journal*, Vol. III, No. 5 (August, 1885), p. 87.

19. *Mis.*, p. 24. See also *S&H*, p. 108.

20. This was told to me by M. Adelaide Still, Mrs. Eddy's maid from 1907–1910 and for some years Mrs. Sargent's close friend and companion.

21. A. Henry Robinson reminiscences.

22. *Message for 1901*, p. 32, *Message for 1902*, p. 2, *Mis.*, p. 21.

23. Letter in *Boston Post*, March 7, 1883.

24. *Ibid.*

25. A. The reference to "two days" probably means two days after she recovered consciousness on Friday morning, which would be correct. Later she usually referred to the healing as the third day after the *accident*, which was also correct.

26. A. Letter of March 2. 1866.

27. Written March 19, published April 4. The Newhalls' nephew, George Gilbert, in a 1935 interview in L. stated that after Mrs. Patterson's fall "Mrs. Newhall was much concerned for fear that Mrs. Patterson would be an invalid and that they would be unable to rent their house for the summer as they usually did. Then, one day about a week after the fall, she looked out of the window and saw Mrs. Patterson walking across the lawn." The recollection of this old gentleman sixty-nine years after the event may not be correct in every detail, but it does link Mrs. Patterson's recovery with the renting or selling of the Newhall house.

28. Bates-Dittemore mildly note (p. 110) that Mrs. Walcott "cannot be regarded as an impartial witness."

29. *Ret.*, p. 24.

30. A. The Court Records of Essex County, Massachusetts, show that on February 1, 1867, David [sic] Patterson and his wife, Mary M. Patterson, brought suit against the city of Lynn for damages sustained by Mrs. Patterson through a fall on Market Street. Possibly it was Patterson who this time took the initiative. Separated from his wife and confronted with the difficulty of giving her even a modest an-

nual sum to keep her going, he at least joined forces with her in this renewed attempt to obtain financial compensation for the accident. The suit was settled at the March Term, 1868, by an entry of "Neither Party."

31. Wilbur, *Life*, p. 140.

32. *Ibid.*

33. A. Elizabeth Harding account. Miss Harding's interest in Christian Science was first aroused when her mother was told of the incident by Mrs. Norton years later. Her mother also signed the account. Cf. the following testimony by one Neal Heely Hayes of Boston published in Judge Clifford P. Smith's *Christian Science: Its Legal Status* (Boston: Christian Science Publishing Society, 1914), p. 83:

> From the time of my birth my feet were imperfect; I did not walk until I was three years old. After I was otherwise full grown my feet were less than half the size they should have been, their structure was abnormal, and I had no use of my toes. This condition continued until I was thirty-five years old, three years after I began to read Christian Science literature. During these three years I received much physical as well as moral benefit from Christian Science, but no change took place with respect to my feet. Indeed I did not expect them ever to be different.
>
> Something occurred, however, to correct my thought about myself. A friend of ours whose feet were somewhat like mine, went to a hospital for an operation. The "dissection of thoughts" which this incident aroused, and the earnest study of Christian Science which ensued, brought about a complete change in my feet. Five weeks after this more active mental work began, and within the course of twenty-four hours, the size and shape of my feet became in every way normal. Even the nails, which had been defective, became natural. I was obliged to get new shoes the next day, and the difference in my walk was noticeable at once to all who knew me.

34. Her movements at this time cannot be followed with precision. A fragment from an unidentified diary for July, 1866, in A. (possibly Susan Oliver's) reads:

Monday 16th
Mrs. Patterson came tonight—we have quite a house full.
Tues. 17th
Mrs. Paterson went to Rumney.

35. A. Dated January 1, 1907.

36. A. Farlow, "Facts and Incidents."

37. A. Dated February 3, 1900.

38. A. Farlow, "Facts and Incidents."

39. *Lynn Reporter*, September 12, 1866.

40. The *Lynn Reporter* of August 4, 1866, describing the dedication of the hall, noted that a "dedicatory hymn, written by Mrs. Mary M. Patterson, was sung by the audience with fine effect." Mrs. Patterson did not at once divorce herself from her former interests and activities.

41. A. Letter of November 16, 1901. About 1955 after giving an address to an interfaith group in Braintree, Massachusetts, I was approached by a charming old lady who informed me that she was Fred Ellis's daughter and had often heard her father speak with affection of Mrs. Eddy.

42. A. *L&M* 43–5670. January 21, 1903.

43. A. Letter to M. Louise Baum, May 3, 1914.

44. *Christ and Christmas*, p. 17.

45. A. No attempt has been made to sort into strict order the variant versions of various portions of this manuscript.

46. The genesis of Darwinism itself is suggestive in connection with the subject of this book. Loren Eiseley writes in *Darwin's Century* (New York: Doubleday, 1958), p. 187:

> Although Darwin was in the habit of repudiating violently any intimation that he had profited from Lamarck, we have already seen that he was acquainted at an early age with English versions of the latter's work and in 1845 there is a reference in an unpublished letter to Lyell re. "my volumes of Lamarck." His rather cavalier rejection of his distinguished forerunner is tinged with an acerbity whose cause at this late date is difficult to discover. Darwin, although he added a meager and needlessly obscure historical introduction to later editions of the *Origin*, was essentially indifferent to his precursors.

Since Lamarck, however, failed to glimpse the principle of natural selection, he lacked the insight which was at the heart of Darwin's contribution to biology, whereas the thing which Darwin did take from him—belief in the inheritance of acquired characteristics—is now discredited. There may be an intuitive rightness in Darwin's description of Lamarck's as a book "from which . . . I gained nothing."

47. *S&H*, pp. 586, 591.

48. Cf. *S&H*, p. 110: "In following these leadings of scientific revelation, the Bible was my only textbook."

49. A. *A&M* 16–10409. Cf. *A&M* 4–10125. "While considering deeply these grave subjects my heart grew sore with hope deferred and I sought God diligently and with the Bible in my hand, searching its precious pages, I found Him . . . and the scales fell from my eyes and from seeing men as trees walking I saw trees talking, all nature declaring God is wisdom, God is Love." The final part of the sentence may refer to a passage in her November 7, 1862, letter in the *Portland Courier*.

50. Eiseley, *Darwin's Century*, p. 57.

51. *Mis.*, pp. 360 f.

52. Swedenborgian terms were very much in the air. In the *Bibliotheca Sacra* for October, 1928, Hermann S. Ficke attempted to establish Mrs. Eddy's direct indebtedness to a *Dictionary of Correspondences* drawn from Swedenborg's writings (Boston, 1847). This tends to break down under close examination. For instance, Ficke puts the definition of "Ark" from the Glossary of *Science and Health with Key to the Scriptures* against the definition from the *Dictionary of Correspondences* as follows:

Swedenborg	MRS. EDDY
ARK. By the Ark going forward were represented combats and temptations.	ARK. . . . The ark indicates temptation overcome and followed by exaltation.

But when one turns to the full definition in the two books one finds the following in the *Dictionary of Correspondences:*

ARK, the, rep. heaven, in the supreme sense the Lord, consequently the divine good. A.C.4926. A. s. the inmost heaven. A.C.9485. The translation of the a. (2 Sam. vi. 1-17) s. the progression of the church among men, from its ultimates to its inmost principles. Ap. Ex.700. By the a. going forward, were rep. combats and temptations. A.C.85. By the a. resting, is s. regeneration. A.C.850, 851. By reason of the decalogue therein contained, the a. was the most holy thing of the church. D.L.W. 53, 61. Its going forth s. liberty. A.C.903. In Gen. viii, it s. the man of the ancient church who was to be regenerated. A.C.896. A. of Jehovah (Num. x. 31–36) s. the Lord as to divine truth. Ap. Ex.700. The a. (in 2 Sam. vi. 6, 7) rep. the Lord, consequently all that is holy and celestial. A.C.878. Noah's a. (Gen. viii. 18) s. the state of the man of the most ancient church, before regeneration. A.C.876.

The definition in *S&H* (p. 581) reads as follows:

ARK. Safety; the idea, or reflection, of Truth, proved to be as immortal as its Principle; the understanding of Spirit, destroying belief in matter.

God and man coexistent and eternal; Science showing that the spiritual realities of all things are created by Him and exist forever. The ark indicates temptation overcome and followed by exaltation.

It is always a tricky matter to posit a direct cause-and-effect relationship on superficial verbal correspondences. In this case it seems safe to say only that Swedenborg and Mrs. Eddy were both interested in the "spiritual" rather than the literal interpretation of Scripture.

53. A. January 14, 1913.

54. A.

Christian Science
is it not
A gigantic illusion
by Geo. Ed. Clark,
"Yankee Ned" the sailor author.

55. Wilbur, *Life,* p. 147.

56. This testimony both refutes and explains the muddled statement of Mrs. Richard Haseltine which Milmine, Dakin, and others have used to support the charge that Mrs. Patterson was a medium. In a sermon given *circa* 1879 (A. *A&M* 22–10628) Mrs. Eddy told of a spiritualist's copying a paragraph from her notes on Genesis and captioning it a "wonderful communication from the spirit world," while declaring that she was controlled by the spirit of Jesus Christ. This incident also makes more intelligible Mrs. Haseltine's curious statement.

57. This was the age in which the maids on Brattle Street, Cambridge, studied Greek on their Thursday afternoons off.

58. A. Farlow, "Historical Facts concerning Mary Baker Eddy and Christian Science."

59. *Mis.,* p. 380.

60. A. December 19, 1901.

61. A. Letter to Calvin Frye, February 23, 1902.

62. *S&H,* p. viii.

63. A. Mrs. Eddy retrieved this manuscript from Crafts in February, 1902, paying him $4.50 for the expenses he incurred in having it photostated and in swearing

out an affidavit. (This involved two or three trips from his home in Hebron, New Hampshire, to the neighboring town of Bristol.) This is apparently the basis for the Milmine charge that Mrs. Eddy paid his expenses to deliver a mysterious manuscript into her hands at her home in Pleasant View, Concord. The correspondence between them shows that he did not come to Concord, while the manuscript itself is eminently devoid of mystery.

64. A. February 23, 1902.

65. A. *A&M* 16-10407.

66. A. *L&M* 78-11153. April 28, 1867.

67. A. The Ingham testimony was published on p. 338 of the first edition of *S&H*. The Wentworth testimony is included in Farlow, "Facts and Incidents," but is mistakenly attributed to the year 1873.

68. A. This was published in the third edition of *S&H* but was mistakenly attributed to Elizabeth P. Baker, Mrs. Eddy's stepmother. The account was confirmed by George W. Baker in a letter to Mary B. G. Billings, April 22, 1924.

69. A. Addie Towns Arnold reminiscences.

70. L. August 4, 1867.

71. A. *L&M* 78-11154.

72. *Ibid.*

73. A. November 27, 1868.

74. *Human Life,* Vol. IV, No. 8 (May, 1907), p. 16.

75. A. This was written at the time that reporters for *McClure's* were scouring the countryside for additional ammunition for the Milmine *Life.*

76. Among the Farlow papers in A. is a statement by Charles Wentworth that he did not believe this charge, for it would have been impossible to keep such a domestic situation out of the neighborhood gossip of so small a community.

77. A. November 27, 1868.

78. A. Published in *Ladies' Home Journal,* June, 1911.

79. A. Annah E. Davis reminiscences.

80. Published January 4, 1868, but signed "Mary Baker Glover. Swampscott, Mass. Jan. 1st." Apparently she visited the Ellises during the holiday season.

81. *My.,* p. 114.

82. L. Clipping dated August 2, 1868, found in Bagley papers. The same poem had been published on February 15, 1868, in the *Lynn Reporter* as "Poetry" by Mary M. Patterson.

83. Mary Ellis Bartlett affidavit quoted in Milmine, *Life,* pp. 115 ff.

84. Mary Beecher Longyear, *The Story of a House* (Brookline: Longyear Foundation, 1947), p. 3. The Bagley house, together with several others where Mrs. Eddy once lived, is maintained by L. today.

85. A. On August 8, 1868, she wrote, "I feel dear Mrs. Glover that I owe you all I am able to do for you and then my debt would never be discharged."

86. A. *L&M* 66-9567.

87. Samuel Thomas Pickard, *Life and Letters of John Greenleaf Whittier* (Boston: Houghton Mifflin, 1894), vol. 2, p. 535.

88. A. *A&M* 27–11063.

89. When a cousin of Whittier's, Mrs. Gertrude Behr, investigated this incident years later she found a neighbor who recalled it clearly. See Peel, *Christian Science*, p. 53 n.

90. A. *A&M* 27–11063. In telling this story Mrs. Eddy referred to Sarah Bagley as Whittier's cousin. Actually Miss Bagley's sister was married to a Whittier cousin.

91. A. *L&M* 31–3916. July 5, 1868.

92. A. *L&M* 55–7797 and 55–7800.

93. Letter from Doris H. Blake, Wentworth's granddaughter, to Kenneth Hufford, quoted in Hufford's *Mary Baker Eddy and the Stoughton Years* (Brookline: Longyear Foundation, 1963), p. 18. Also Marion W. Harrington reminiscences in A.

94. L. Letter of Lucy Wentworth Holmes, November 12, 1936. Quoted in Hufford, *The Stoughton Years*, p. 4.

95. L. Letter of Lucy Wentworth Holmes, February 10, 1922.

96. A. *L&M* 59–8305 and 59–8307. About this time she paid a brief visit to the Winslows in Lynn, and it was then she brought about the healing of Mrs. Winslow which has usually been attributed to 1866. Referring to this visit, she wrote: "When I went there Mrs. Winslow was very lame and sick, had not walked up stairs naturally for years and given up trying to go out at all. I stopped two days and when I came away she walked to the Depot with me almost a mile. They were one and all urgent for me to stay, but I am not of their opinion. I don't want society." *L&M* 59–8306.

97. A. *L&M* 59–8306.

98. L. Letter of February 10, 1922.

99. A. Letter of Florence Scott Lothrop, April 24, 1909.

100. Wilbur, *Life*, p. 177.

101. A. Charles O. Wentworth reminiscences.

102. A. Album of Frank Porter.

103. Although Celia's health improved during Mrs. Glover's stay, she had a relapse after her departure and passed away in 1871.

104. A. Farlow, "Facts and Incidents."

105. A. June 17, 1938. Also letter of July 20, 1938.

106. A. H. L. Cobb letter of January 10, 1907.

107. The fact that Quimby had manipulated his patients also served to excuse the practice so long as the Quimby influence on her lasted.

108. Horace Wentworth letter in *Stoughton Sentinel*, October 17, 1903.

109. A. January 17, 1869 (?).

110. A. *L&M* 62–8866.

111. A. *L&M* 55–7798.

112. *S&H*, p. 109.

113. A. It was unlikely to have been the original, since the three copies now in the Quimby manuscript collection are all in other hands.

114. *The Quimby Manuscripts*, p. 165.

115. Quimby is reputed to have had "thousands" of patients during the Portland years.

116. C. The wording of this passage varies slightly but nonessentially in different copies of the article.

117. *The Quimby Manuscripts*, p. 176 n.

118. *Ibid.*, p. 105.

119. The testimony on this is unanimous. Only Horace Wentworth (who was not a student) claimed otherwise. George Quimby wrote Miss Milmine in his March 13, 1906, letter: "Why don't you find out *certainly* whether Mrs. Eddy *did teach* from that *article?* . . . I've only the Stoughton mans word for it." On the other hand, Mrs. Glover did let her first two or three students read and study "Questions and Answers" for themselves, according to her correspondence with Sarah Bagley, and this may lie behind Horace Wentworth's claim.

120. When an anonymous writer (probably Miss Milmine) wrote an article in the *New York Times* on July 10, 1904, drawing parallels between "Quimby's" words in the newly discovered Wentworth "Questions and Answers" and Mrs. Eddy's words in *S&H*, he or she very curiously attributed to Quimby statements from Mrs. Glover's preface. As a result some of the parallels are actually between words written by Mrs. Eddy at different periods of her life. Of course, this may be true even when the statements are taken from the body rather than the preface of "Questions and Answers."

121. *S&H* (6th ed.), p. 4.

122. A. At least five versions in Mrs. Wentworth's handwriting are known.

123. A. *A&M* 16–10407.

124. She did not use Mind as a synonym for God at that period. See p. 271.

125. *Message for 1901*, p. 1.

126. Wilbur, *Life*, p. 178.

127. See Hufford, *The Stoughton Years*, pp. 32 ff.

128. A. *L&M* 59–8307.

129. A. *L&M* 59–8308.

130. A. *L&M* 59–8304.

131. A. *L&M* 59–8300.

132. A. September 12, 1869.

133. A. Undated, probably summer, 1869.

134. A. This was later the basis of a lawsuit in 1878.

135. A. Letter of August 28, 1905.

136. A. Letter of August 28, 1905.

137. A. Stephen Babcock reminiscence.

138. A. Samuel C. Beane letter.

Notes: *Chapter Seven*

1. E. de Pressensé, *The Early Years of Christianity* (New York: Carlton and Lanehan, 1870), p. 5. The words "Christian science," as Pressensé uses them, obviously have an entirely different meaning from that given them by Mrs. Eddy.

2. A. *L&M* 31–3919.

3. I am indebted for many of these details to an unpublished Harvard honors thesis: Langley Carleton Keyes, "Mrs. Eddy's Science; a study of the historical setting and development of the Christian Science movement in Lynn, Massachusetts," Harvard, 1960. Mr. Keyes has tried, however, to force Christian Science into the spectrum of "spiritualist" (i.e., spiritist) thought.

4. *Ibid.*

5. *Lynn Semi-Weekly Reporter*, February 1, 1871.

6. Mrs. Eddy on several occasions referred back to some person or persons as having surreptitiously copied passages from her earliest manuscripts and put them into circulation.

7. July, 1869. This same issue contained an article by A. Bronson Alcott entitled "Personal Theism," which includes the sentence: "And are not all men [God], as far as they resemble him, as they are born out of their senses,—that is, born again into the Spirit and mind of God."

8. Mrs. Spofford may have been in the second class in December. The evidence on this point is not clear. An agreement similar to Tuttle's and Stanley's was signed by both Spoffords on August 17, 1870, but Daniel did not have class with her until five years later.

9. L. Spofford letter to Mary Beecher Longyear, June 17, 1921.

10. Milmine, *Life*, p. 158.

11. *Ibid.*, p. 156.

12. Wilbur, *Life*, pp. 189 f.

13. Philip P. Wiener, *Evolution and the Founders of Pragmatism* (Cambridge: Harvard University Press, 1949), p. 106. Wiener cites as examples: Maxwell, Tyndall, Mendelaev, Pasteur, Lister, Claude Bernard, Koch, Helmholtz, Hertz, Kirchhoff, Mach, Stallo, Gibbs, and Darwin.

14. Doctoral dissertation by Henry W. Steiger, "A Philosophical Investigation of the Doctrine of Christian Science," Department of Philosophy, Boston University, 1946.

15. A. This is the version which Mrs. Glover apparently used for her first class.

16. From article in *Reinhold Niebuhr, His Religious, Social, and Political Thought*, eds. Charles W. Kegley and Robert W. Bretall (New York: Macmillan, 1956), p. 41. See also Perry Miller, *The New England Mind: The Seventeenth Century* (New York: Macmillan, 1939), p. 9, re. the Puritan's theology:

> "God" was a word to stand for the majesty and perfection which gleam through the fabric of the world; He was Being, hardly apprehensible to

man, yet whose existence man must posit, not so much as *a* being but as *The* Being, the beginning of things and the sustainer, the principle of universal harmony and the guide.

17. *No* 20:8–13.

18. *The Quimby Manuscripts*, p. 348.

19. Published by Longyear Foundation in 1923. All subsequent quotations from Bancroft are from this book unless otherwise indicated.

20. L. Spofford letter of June 27, 1921.

21. A. In the class of four which included Daniel Spofford, in April, 1875, Spofford paid nothing, two members paid one hundred dollars each, and the remaining member paid two hundred dollars.

22. A. *L&M* 31–3920.

23. A. The lines appear to be from Tupper.

24. A. *L&M* 59–8299.

25. Mrs. Glover's letters to Bancroft are printed in full in his book.

26. A. *L&M* 31–3923.

27. A. *L&M* 59–8311.

28. A. *L&M* 31–3922. She may have referred to Mrs. Helen M. Blood, who studied with her in April, 1871.

29. A. Statement of Mrs. Carrie G. Colby in Farlow, "Facts and Incidents." Mrs. Colby's dates (recalled many years later) are obviously awry, but her personal comments are interesting: "Saw Mrs. Eddy every day; sat at the same table with her. She was very pleasant. I saw nothing about her that was wrong; you can hear all sorts of stories. . . . McClure's claim their history is unbiased. It is not unbiased history because they gathered their information from prejudiced people. They have been to Dr. Kennedy. They have been to Mrs. Dame [the former Susie Magoun]. Mrs. Dame has nothing special against Mrs. Eddy. Simply was not favorable; thinks it is bad, and does not want any of her family to believe in it. When we were looking at Mrs. Eddy's picture, to me the picture looked pleasant and sweet, but to Mrs. Dame it looked different."

30. A. *L&M* 43–5665. Letter of July 23, 1870.

31. This entry would seem to point to the fact that such an attack was a great rarity rather than the frequent occurrence which some biographers have assumed it to be. Bancroft writes as though this was the first time in his four years' close association with Mrs. Glover that such a "strange experience" had occurred.

32. Her testimony was printed in *S&H* (16th ed.), pp. 179 f. See also Peel, *Christian Science*, pp. 77 f.

33. *S&H* (1st ed.), p. 353.

34. Published accounts are to be found in Smith, *Historical Sketches*, pp. 69–87; Tomlinson, *Twelve Years*, pp. 46–65; and *A Century of Christian Science Healing*, Christian Science Publishing Society, 1966, pp. 6–10.

35. In her sworn testimony in the Barry case in 1878, Mrs. Eddy stated that she had treated George Barry once a week for a year.

36. Bates-Dittemore, *Mary Baker Eddy*, p. 115. I have been unable to find the original source for this story.

37. A. Grace M. Clarke reminiscence. In most accounts the name is spelled Clark.

38. L. Letter of March 19, 1871.

39. A. Kennedy letter to Mrs. Glover in summer [?] of 1869.

40. A. Choate notes on Kennedy testimony in 1878 against Stanley and Tuttle. Kennedy, thoroughly hostile to Mrs. Eddy by 1878, dryly testified that her instructions were to rub out belief in a "personal God," which probably had reference to Stanley's rather primitive and anthropomorphic theology.

41. See p. 285 regarding his continued hold on his earliest patients. Mrs. Colby (see note 29 above) remarked of one of these, Frances Spinney: "She is kind of sour against Mrs. Eddy; gives everything to Dr. Kennedy. . . . I felt sure that this Miss Spinney was going to give Mrs. Eddy credit for her healing, but Dr. Kennedy did the treating, and he was Mrs. Eddy's student. He comes to Miss Spinney's now [1907] and visits her."

42. A. *L&M* 31–3928.

43. A. *L&M* 31–3929.

44. In a letter to a student in Portland in 1880 Mrs. Eddy makes an obscure reference to such a possibility. *L&M* 32–4080.

45. The passage in *S&H* (1st ed.) quoted on p. 268, gives a revealing hint of the argument Kennedy advanced to justify his use of manipulation.

46. See p. 233.

47. New York Public Library.

48. A. *L&M* 63–9012. August 16, 1871.

49. A. Letter of August 24, 1871.

50. A. Letter of October 2, 1871.

51. A. *L&M* 31–3923. Probably December 20, 1871.

52. A. Letter of January 20, 1872.

53. February 3, 1872. This article is reprinted as Appendix 2 in Norman Beasley, *The Cross and the Crown* (New York: Duell, Sloan and Pearce, 1952), pp. 569 ff.

54. A. *L&M* 43–5663.

55. *S&H* (1st ed.), p. 403.

56. *My.*, p. 143. *S&H*, p. 66.

57. A. *L&M* 99–9853. It needs to be remembered that Kennedy was still in his early twenties. It is hardly surprising that he found the role of martyr and hero, on which he had embarked so eagerly a few years earlier, less than appealing as time went on. Also he was doing extremely well financially, and this increased his sense of independence. By June 1, 1871, Mrs. Glover had received from him as her share of his first year's practice a total of $1744. On March 11, 1872, he refused to pay her anything further. A Declaration and Answer made part of Plaintiff's exceptions in the case of Glover vs. Kennedy (January 6, 1879) states "that defendant paid to plaintiff as her share of the profits of this partnership the sum of $2200 to $2300."

58. *S&H* (3rd ed.), II, p. 10.

59. A. *L&M* 59–8311.

60. A. *L&M* 59–8302. In another letter of uncertain date (31–3926) there is evidence of the influence which Kennedy continued to exercise over Miss Bagley, an influence which grew with the years. Mrs. Glover wrote her: "I have endeavored to teach you what I knew would be such a great blessing . . . and then Sarah, came the 'cup' for me to drink, that you should deny me and say 'all you ever had learned you had gained from Richard,' but the hour is now past, it has been drank, and I can now forgive it. . . . I sometimes think of you among the others and perhaps you sometimes think of me but more frequently I *go* to you to bless and instruct you."

61. Pp. 373 f. She further stated that Quimby passed away "years before ever there was a student of this science, and never, to our knowledge, informed any one of his method of healing."

62. See p. 190.

63. A. *L&M* 55–7801.

64. Countess C. de St. Dominique, *Animal Magnetism (Mesmerism) and Artificial Somnambulism* (London, 1874), p. 209. The author continues (p. 213), "Immorality, ignorance, vanity, carelessness on the part of the magnetizer, give rise to the inconveniences which have continually been pointed out in these pages, and which are detrimental alike to the lucidity and to the health of the subject."

65. Quimby himself felt that his theories separated him from magnetism as he understood it. Evans, on the other hand, saw an essential continuity between Quimby's earlier and later practice.

66. She began to use the term in the second edition of *S&H* which was published in 1878.

67. A. *L&M* 55–7802. December 12, 1872.

68. A. Note by Mrs. Eddy in Bible (AA9).

69. *S&H* (3rd ed.), p. 12.

70. *Ibid.*

71. A. *L&M* 43–5664.

72. A. Letter of May 24, 1872.

73. A. Letter of May 30, 1872.

74. Renan, *Life of Jesus,* pp. 297 ff.

75. A. On April 6, 1875, two months before her death, Mrs. Baker wrote Mrs. Glover an affectionate note addressed to "My own Dear Daughter" and ending, "My love to yourself and all who are kind to you."

76. Albert Barnes, *Scenes and Incidents in the Life of the Apostle Paul* (Philadelphia: Zeigler, McCurdy & Co., 1869).

77. This statement is based on a careful reading of the books she read and marked during this period. John S. C. Abbott's *History of Christianity*, published in Boston in 1872, was not read by her at that time. An 1877 edition of this book, with an 1881 calendar sheet in it as a marker, was part of her later library and was the apparent source of some of her allusions to Christian history and tradi-

tion, e.g., her references to Polycarp, Justin Martyr, Luther, and Melancthon. But her interest, in these cases, was evidently in finding examples to illustrate or embellish a point she was making rather than in the author's conventional Christian theme.

78. L. In his letters to Miss Bagley at this time Kennedy attempts to give spiritual comfort and counsel, but he is evidently straining on tiptoe to imitate Mrs. Glover's manner. However skilful a rubber of heads, he was evidently not cut out to be a religious teacher. Actually, very little is known about his character. On the basis of Miss Milmine's description, many writers have tended to stress his "sociability," but in an 1873 letter to Miss Bagley he writes: "I am not as fond of going about as the general class of people. I have neither found but few acquaintances."

79. A. *L&M* 55–7802. Letter of December 13, 1872, to Sarah Bagley.

80. A. *L&M* 31–3925. Letter to Sarah Bagley.

81. *S&H*, p. 226.

82. *S&H*, p. 109.

83. Thomas C. Upham, *Absolute Religion* (New York: G. P. Putnam's Sons, 1873), pp. 251 f. See also p. 49: "God is both Fatherhood and Motherhood. And from the eternal Fatherhood and Motherhood, furnishing, in their co-existent and co-operative duality, the only conceivable basis of such a result, all things proceed." Also p. 73: "Generically, or considered in the whole of its extent, the trinal out-birth, otherwise called the Son of God, without which the eternal Fatherhood and Motherhood could have neither name nor power nor meaning, is the whole of creation from its lowest to its highest form."

84. *S&H*, p. 70.

85. A. *A&M* 20–10494.

86. *S&H*, p. 80.

87. *S&H*, p. 135.

88. Bancroft wrote to Mary Beecher Longyear (L) on August 29, 1920, that 1872 to 1875 were Mrs. Glover's "most trying years." She moved from house to house, driven on by the friction that almost inevitably seemed to arise in small-minded households after she had been there a while. The students alternately clung to her and turned on her. One student sued her in the Lynn Police Court to recover the $150 she had paid in advance for tuition. (Mrs. Glover failed to appear and judgment was rendered for the plaintiff.) Mrs. Glover herself filed suit for divorce from Daniel Patterson on October 6, 1873, and a decree was granted seven weeks later. On Thanksgiving Day of one of these years she wrote Bancroft:

> They tell me this day is set apart for festivities and rejoicing; but I have no evidence of this except the proclamation and gathering together of those who love one another. I am alone today, and shall probably not see a single student. Family ties are broken never to be reunited in this world with me. But what of those who have learned with me the Truth of Moral Science; where do they find their joys; where do they seek friendship and happiness? Shall I see one of them today? . . .
>
> Now, dear student, do you understand me? Do you think I want an invitation to dine out today? Oh no, you cannot so misconstrue the mean-

ing; but I wish you all were awake in this hour of crucifixion, awake to the sense of the hour before you and the oil you need in your lamps at that coming of the Bridegroom.

George Allen told Georgine Milmine that the six months in 1873 when Mrs. Glover stayed with him and his wife were the worst he ever lived through, but her subsequent six-month stay with the Bancrofts was a happy one which had to be terminated only because of insufficient privacy to carry on her informal teaching and counseling.

89. A. Letter of October 19, 1873.

90. Cf. *A Century of Christian Science Healing*, Chapter 2, Section 3.

91. A. Mrs. Eddy's notebook.

92. A. *Ibid.* and L. Barry diary. The manuscript was not sent to the printer until September 5.

93. In most copies of the Wyclif Bible the phrase used is "science of health," but in others it is "science and health." See Thomas L. Leishman, *Why I Am a Christian Scientist* (New York: Thomas Nelson & Sons, 1958), p. 205.

94. *Mis.*, p. 371. *Ret.*, p. 35.

95. L. Letter to Mrs. Longyear, September 12, 1920.

96. A. *A&M* 26–10934.

97. Her classroom was apparently on the first floor, though Spofford's reference to the "meetings in the upper chamber" (see p. 286) suggests that she may have used the second-floor parlor on occasion.

98. A. Spofford letter to Mrs. Glover, April 26, 1875, and Mrs. Glover's reply (*L&M* 55–7807), April 28, 1875.

99. A. *L&M* 55–7804. February 1, 1875.

100. A. Letter of April 26, 1875.

101. *Lynn Semi-Weekly Reporter*, May 26, 1875.

102. A. Spofford memo book.

103. A. It was probably at this meeting that Mrs. Glover announced the changed title of her book: *Science and Health*. The following day she wrote to Washington to have the book copyrighted under its new title.

104. A. *L&M* 55–7807.

105. A. Letter of July 27, 1875.

106. A. Ethel B. West reminiscence.

107. A. *A&M* 16–10402.

108. By this date seven hundred dollars had been paid to the printers—five hundred on February 9, 1875, and two hundred on August 14—by Barry and (apparently) Edward Hitchings. Another student, Elizabeth Newhall, also advanced a sum to pay for the printing costs, she and Barry between them contributing a total of fifteen hundred dollars. On November 12 Spofford, probably acting as agent, paid five hundred more. The book bore the imprint "Christian Scientist Publishing Company."

109. A. *A&M* 16–10402.

110. A. Mrs. Glover also sent a copy of the book to her old friend, Richard S. Rust, now corresponding secretary of the Freedman's Aid Society of the Methodist Episcopal Church in Cincinnati, and received a friendly but vague reply from him.

111. A. Letter of D. Russell Ambrose, December, 1876.

112. See Peel, *Christian Science,* chapter two.

Index

Mary Baker Eddy (*cont.*)
72, 76–78; motherhood, 78–81, 84, 97, 98, 118, 126, 253, 278, 279, 291; relations with children, 81, 82, 104, 107, 108, 116, 122, 123, 187, 225–227, 240, 253, 256; lack of direction, 83, 84, 89–91, 117, 123, 124, 140, 141; prophetic glimpses, 84, 86–88, 116, 124, 127, 133, 139, 169, 180; mother's death, 94, 134; loss of son, 97–99, 107, 112, 116–119, 123, 144, 177, 184, 190, 278; deteriorating health, 78, 95, 98, 99, 116, 119, 120, 130, 145, 171, 326; search for health, 99, 111, 137, 138, 141, 145, 146, 160, 188; religious questionings, 100–106, 130, 132, 138, 139; second marriage, 109–112, 120, 121, 140–142, 145, 174, 175, 177, 184, 185, 187, 190, 239; North Groton life, 116, 117, 121–125, 129, 135; attitude to spiritualism, 133, 134, 168, 184, 186, 187, 211, 212, 220–222, 246, 333; interest in homeopathy, 111, 135, 136, 172; loss of home, 139, 140; renewed activity, 144, 145; appeal to Quimby, 146, 147, 159, 160, 171, 172; recovery, 167–169, 171, 175; Christian theism, 169–172, 177, 183, 271; relapse, 171, 172, 175, 185; Portland activities, 173, 174–178, 181; study and writing, 171, 180–182; visit to Miss Jarvis, 183–185; visit to Mrs. Crosby, 181, 185–187; farewell to Quimby, 188, 190, 192, 198, 199, 205, 268, 271; fall and healing, 195–201, 205, 259, 345; early healings, 201, 215, 222, 223, 228, 240, 255–257, 290; end of marriage, 200–203; break with family, 191, 203, 215–217, 218, 274, 291, 314; friendship with Ellises, 203, 204, 208, 273, 277; notes on Genesis, 205–210, 220, 229, 230; stay at Clarks, 210, 211; stay with Crafts, 211–218, 225; stay in Amesbury, 219–224; life in Stoughton, 224–230, 236, 237; early manuscripts, 221, 225–236, 249, 251; Kennedy partnership, 222, 237–240, 243, 244, 246, 247, 253, 257, 258, 355; first classes, 247–249, 251–253, 259, 267, 285, 286, 290; theology, 206–208, 235, 249–251, 271; leadership, 254, 273, 288, 289; struggles, 255, 273, 289, 354, 357; Wright controversy, 258–265, 272, 273; Kennedy break, 265–268, 272, 273, 276; evolving thought, 280; writing the book, 272, 275–277, 279–284, 289; teaching and preaching, 285–288, 290; publishing of book,

283, 289, 291; *Ret.*, x, 29, 100, 118; poems quoted, 7, 14, 25, 43, 46, 51, 55, 67, 72, 77, 78, 80, 85, 87, 98, 102, 103, 109, 142–144, 192, 219–221, 323–326, 335, 344
Eden, 13, 17, 47, 129, 130
Edgecomb, Mrs. L.C., 256
Edgeworth, Maria, 324
education, 10, 29, 54, 80, 117, 123, 289, 318
Edwards, Jonathan, 10, 11, 21, 310, 311, 317
Einstein, Albert, 13
Eisley, Loren, 206, 348
electricity and electric, 147, 153, 155, 159, 161, 167, 172, 221
electromagnetism, 151, 168, 302
Elements of Christian Science, 139
Elements of Logic, 56, 134
Eliot, Charles W., 285
Eliot, T.S., 134, 332
Ellis, Fred, 203, 204, 208, 210, 273, 347
Ellis, Mary, 203, 204, 208, 210, 216, 255, 264, 277
Ellis, William R., 222
Emerson, Mary Moody, 47
Emerson, Ralph Waldo, 5, 47, 123, 125, 126, 129, 288, 312, 317, 333
"Emma Clinton, or A Tale of the Frontiers," 93
English Reader, 28, 40, 70
Enlightenment, 7, 11, 28, 56, 151
Enterprise, Minn., 118, 190
environment, 16, 40, 89, 206
Episcopal Church, 70, 72, 228
errand into the wilderness, 5, 115, 338
Essay on Classification, 333
Essay on Liberty, 125
Essays and Reviews, 204
Eureka, 161
Evans, Warren Felt, 189, 190, 268, 269, 271, 301–303
Eve, 47, 129, 168, 311
evil, problem of, 12, 53, 105, 106, 207, 265, 271, 279, 307
evolution, 107, 131, 206, 243, 280, 291

Faraday, Michael, 100, 151
Farlow, Alfred A., 212, 333, 340, 345
fate, 89, 93, 104
Fear and Trembling, 65
Felt, Susie, 253
Female Poets of America, 93
Few Days in Athens, A, 126
Ficke, Hermann S., 348
Fisher, H.A.L., 182, 338
Fletcher, Richard, 58

Men and Women, 125
Mendel, Gregor, 205
Mental Cure, The, 269, 301
Mental Medicine, 268–270, 302
Mental Science Magazine, 182
Meredith, George, 130
Mesmer and Swedenborg, 163
Mesmer, Franz A., 151, 206, 263
mesmerism. See animal magnetism
Messer, Mary Burt, 312
Metaphysical Club, 248
metaphysics, 28, 58, 162, 179, 213, 233, 234, 248, 284, 305, 312, 320, 341
Methodism and Methodist, 48, 50, 64, 81, 189, 225
Methods of Study in Natural Science, 333
Metternich, 13
Mexico and Mexican, 13, 84, 85
Miescher, Friedrich, 280
Mill, John Stuart, 125
Miller, Charles K., 154
Miller, Perry, 309, 353
Millet, Carrie, 196
Milmine, Georgine, 247, 252, 265, 309–311, 315, 318, 321, 327, 328, 330, 333, 339, 349, 350, 352, 357, 358
Milton, John, 28, 47, 126
Moby Dick, 106, 332
Moehlman, Conrad Henry, 306, 307
Monroe, James, 13
Moral Science, 233, 234, 240, 246, 251, 257, 259, 261, 263, 265, 275, 283, 288
morality, 10, 40, 233, 235, 244, 245, 251, 255, 257, 262, 275
Morehead, John, 71
Morgan, Emma. See Thompson, Emma A.
Mormons, 115
morphine, 111, 195, 345
Morrill, Alpheus, 99, 111
Moses, 235
Moses, George, 115
Mott, Lucretia, 83, 209
Mount Holyoke Female Seminary, 54, 116, 318
Mrs. Eddy As I Knew Her in 1870, 251
Mrs. Eddy Purloins from Hegel, 305
Murray, Lindley, 27, 40, 70

Napoleon, 13
Nashua Gazette, 140
nature, 14–16, 22, 26, 46, 55, 107, 129–132, 137, 138, 142, 161, 263, 301, 312, 313, 332
New England, 5, 6, 12, 67, 72, 79, 115; education, 7, 8, 27, 28, 54, 80, 81; intellect, 7, 8, 15, 39, 48; theology, 7, 9, 22, 353

Newhall, Armenius, 200, 216
Newhall, Elizabeth M., 287, 358
Newhall, George, 196
New Hampshire, 3, 12, 15, 17, 19, 58–60, 88, 108, 121, 123, 130, 144, 174, 176
New Hampshire Conference Seminary, 10, 81, 253, 325
New Hampshire Patriot and State Gazette, 58, 60–62, 64, 85, 87, 94, 108, 152, 320
New Manual of Homeopathic Practice, 135
New Testament, 6, 53, 103, 138, 139, 171, 204, 212, 243, 275
New Thought, 166, 170, 297, 300, 303
Newton, Isaac, 56, 101
Nietzsche, F.W., 106
Night Thoughts, 46, 47, 100
Nightingale, Florence, 138
North Groton, N.H., 97, 116, 117, 121, 122, 128, 139, 141
Norton, Charles A. Quincy, 156–158, 337
Norton, Mrs. James, 201, 347

Oberlin College, 54, 139
Oddfellows, 70, 83
Old North Church, 24, 26, 88
Old Testament, 143, 171
Oliver, Clarkson, 243, 247, 253
Oliver, Susan, 201, 202, 247, 267, 347
ontology, 248–250
Ordeal by Concordance, 305
Origin of Species, 131, 204
Osborn, Albert S., 306
Ossian, 116

Page, Thomas F., 82
Paine, Thomas, 18, 312
Paracelsus, 151
Paradise Lost, 47
Parker, Theodore, 120, 331
Parkman, Francis, 86
Pasteur, Louis, 205, 280
Patterson, Daniel, 109–112, 115–117, 119, 120, 122, 125, 135, 139–142, 145, 146, 159, 174, 175, 177, 185, 187, 191, 195, 200–202, 229, 278, 345, 357
Patterson, James, 145, 176
Patterson, John, 174
Patterson, Mary M. See Eddy, Mary Baker
Paul, 162, 177, 233, 237, 266, 275, 281, 341
Peabody, Elizabeth, 324
Pembroke, N.H., 4, 6, 17, 21, 26
Pestalozzi, 27, 81

Pfleiderer, Otto, 307
Philbrick, Hannah. *See* Sanborn, Hannah
Phillips, Dorr, 201
Phillips, Hannah, 188, 201, 209
Phillips, Thomas, 188, 201, 202, 209
Philosophical Magazine, 100
Philosophy of Electrical Psychology, 153
Philosophy of P.P. Quimby, 299, 336
phrenology, 68, 95
Pickwick Papers, 317
Pierce, Benjamin, 19, 30, 59
Pierce, Charles Sanders, 248
Pierce, Franklin, 9, 19, 30, 42, 58, 59, 88, 108, 145, 320, 326
Pilsbury, Amos, 31
Pilsbury, Ellen, 81, 90, 96, 215–217, 256, 274
Pilsbury, Luther, 31, 41, 63, 90, 96
Pilsbury, Martha Baker, 31, 32, 34, 37, 38, 44, 45, 54, 55, 61, 63, 64, 81, 82, 90, 92, 96, 98, 108, 117, 119, 139, 190, 214, 215, 217, 274
Pilsbury, Mary Neal, 96, 108, 119
Pinkham, Lydia E., 245, 277
Plato, 55, 248
Plymouth Record, 122
Poe, Edgar Allan, 77, 93, 126, 159, 161
Pope, Alexander, 14, 28, 126, 332
Porter, Kate, 226, 229, 230
Portland, Me., 146, 147, 158, 162, 173–176, 178, 183, 185, 188, 257, 258
Portland Daily Advertiser, 164, 165, 174, 297, 300
Portland Daily Press, 175–177, 189
Portland Evening Courier, 167, 168, 172, 181
Pouvoir de l'Esprit, 319
Powell, Lyman P., 186, 328, 345
Poyen, Charles, 151, 158
Practical Instruction in Animal Magnetism, 151
pragmatism, 57, 248
prayer, 23, 24, 52, 102, 170, 197, 236, 315
predestination, 23, 50
Pressensé, E. de, 243, 255, 275
Principles of Geology, 16
Principles of Nature, 160
Progress of Animal Magnetism in New England, 151
Protestant and Protestantism, 7, 25, 250
Proverbial Philosophy, 92, 105, 325, 329
psychoanalysis, 95

psychology, 162, 169, 171, 179, 233, 297, 302, 303, 305, 335
psychosomatic medicine, 95
psychotherapy, 152, 171
Puritans and Puritanism, 3, 5, 7, 10, 13, 18, 19, 26, 29, 47, 52, 72, 90, 309, 317, 325, 353
Purity of Heart, 132

Quakers, 188, 201, 202, 219, 239
"Questions and Answers," 231–233, 240, 352
Quimby, Augusta, 147
Quimby, George, 147, 162, 170, 173, 181, 182, 231, 342, 352
Quimby, Phineas Parkhurst, 146, 147, 167, 173, 184, 186, 211, 228, 229, 235, 245, 255, 260, 297–303, 305, 307, 336; history, 152–156, 158, 188–190; character, 155, 157, 171, 183, 251, 268, 271, 337; reputation, 155, 156, 164, 165, 173, 184, 270; theory, 152–154, 157, 158, 160, 162, 163, 166, 168–172, 177, 179–181, 189, 190, 199, 205, 268–270, 337; practice, 154–158, 162, 164, 165, 172, 175, 189, 199, 233, 234, 258, 259, 268, 269; manuscripts, 181–183, 231–233, 240, 342; influences on, 153, 154, 162, 163, 179, 182, 232, 338

Radical, The, 246
Rand, Martha. *See* Baker, Martha Rand
Rawson, Dorcas, 252, 264, 276, 284, 286, 287
Raymond, Abigail, 214
reason, 29, 55–58, 134, 135, 151, 230, 280, 281, 289
religion and religious, ix, 5, 10, 19, 22, 23, 26, 40, 44, 47–49, 51–53, 100, 103, 109, 124, 139, 160, 162, 170, 171, 179, 182, 233, 243–245, 265, 273, 280
Renan, Ernest, 180, 243, 273
Renton, Peter, 313
Repiton, A.P., 72, 76, 322
Republican and Argus, 94
revelation, 55–57, 105, 127, 134, 205, 206, 210, 220, 221, 230, 263, 289, 312, 339, 348
revivalism, 48, 313, 317
Revolution, The, 245
Revolutionary War, 19
Rice, Miranda, 252, 255, 256, 264, 287
Richardson, Mrs., 222
Rivier, W., 319
Rounsevel, R.D., 202
Rumney, N.H., 125, 141, 142, 146, 229
Russell, Philemon R., 200, 256

Rust, Richard S., 81, 82, 91, 92, 94, 359

Saco, Me., 145, 174, 176, 202
Saintsbury, George, 316
Samuel, 133
Sanborn, Dyer H., 54, 319
Sanborn, Hannah, 315, 330
Sanborn, Mahala, 78–80, 97, 116–118, 144
Sanbornton Academy, 54, 81, 92, 318
Sanbornton Bridge (Tilton), 33, 37–41, 47, 48, 50, 53, 59, 63, 82, 91, 106, 215, 216, 258, 274
Sand, George, 126, 331
Sargent, Julia, 55
Sargent, Laura, 197
Sartor Resartus, 126
Satan, 104, 105, 257, 264, 311
Saturday Night, 227
Scarlet Letter, The, 91, 106
Scenes and Incidents in the Life of the Apostle Paul, 274
Schiller, J.F., 126
science, ix, 16, 29, 54, 55–58, 101, 107, 137–139, 151–153, 169, 179, 189, 205, 221, 234, 240, 244–246, 262, 264, 270, 281, 282, 289, 291, 301, 314
Science and Health, x, 34, 41, 134, 136, 223, 239, 256, 284, 291, 292, 305, 329, 348, 358; composition and style, 272, 280–284, 289; quoted, ix, 80, 83, 140, 171, 172, 205, 206, 217, 232, 235, 250, 256, 265, 268, 271, 280, 281, 283, 288, 307, 319, 340, 343, 348, 349
Science of Life, 280, 283
Science of Man, 231–236, 247, 249, 251, 266
"Science of Soul," 229–231
Scott, John L., 228
Scott, Walter, 17, 312
Scott, William, 227, 228
Scott, Winfield, 325
Scribner, Amos, 284, 285
Seabury, Annetta. See Dresser, Annetta G.
Seasons, The, 92
second law of thermodynamics, 29, 130
Sedgwick, Catherine, 80
Septuagint, 250
Shakers, 53, 318
Shakespeare, 39, 47, 51, 61
Sheldon, Dr., 187, 343
Shelley, Percy Bysshe, 45
Sickness unto Death, 65
Sigourney, Lydia H., 69, 126
Sim, Peter, 267
Slataper, D. Lee, 228

slavery and slaves, 60, 70, 71, 75, 85, 88, 89, 108, 277, 322, 323
Sleeper, William, 90, 95
Smaus, Jewel Spangler, 310, 319
Smith, Hildreth, 63, 71
Smith, Hoke, 71
Smith, James, 64, 321
Smith, Joseph, 336
Smith, Myra (Elmira), 117, 125, 135, 136, 141, 331
Snow Bound, 253
"Soul's Enquiries of Man," 233, 236, 247
Spinney, Frances, 257, 258, 355
spiritualism, 132–134, 160, 162, 168, 184, 186, 211–213, 216, 219–222, 246, 288, 291, 333, 349, 353
Spock, Benjamin, 77
Spofford, Addie, 247, 259, 260, 262, 266, 285
Spofford, Daniel H., 247, 252, 259, 262, 285–287, 290, 354, 358
Staël, Madame de, 126, 331
Stanley, Charles S., 247, 251, 257
Stanton, Elizabeth Cady, 83, 118, 312
Stein, Elbridge W., 306
Stewart, Samuel B., 287
Still, M. Adelaide, 346
St. Mark's School, 228
Stone, Lucy, 245
Stoughton, Mass., 224, 226, 227, 237, 238
Stowe, Harriet Beecher, 8, 15, 22, 89, 106
Strauss, Johann, 243, 274
Suckling, John, 43
suggestion. See animal magnetism
Sumner, Charles, 143, 177, 277
Sunday-Book, The, 108
Swampscott, Mass., 191, 195, 200, 203
Swartz, A.J., 182, 189
Swasey, Augusta. See Holmes, Augusta
Swasey, Samuel, 63
Swedenborg and Swedenborgianism, 160, 162, 163, 189, 207, 268, 301, 303, 338, 348, 349

Taber, Charles Allen, 209
Talleyrand, 13
Tappan on the Will, 10
Taunton, Mass., 213, 214, 216, 217
Taylor, Zachary, 85
Teilhard de Chardin, Pierre, 314
temperance movement, 88
Tenney, John A., 145
Tennyson, 253
theology, 4, 7, 10, 20, 22, 50, 53, 56, 95, 105, 107, 170, 171 179, 210, 246, 249, 250, 317, 353, 355